Oil Money

A VOLUME IN THE SERIES

THE UNITED STATES IN THE WORLD

Series Editors: Benjamin A. Coates, Emily Conroy-Krutz,
Paul A. Kramer, and Judy Tzu-Chun Wu
Founding Series Editors: Mark Philip Bradley and Paul A. Kramer

A list of titles in this series is available at cornellpress.cornell.edu.

Oil Money

Middle East Petrodollars and the Transformation
of US Empire, 1967-1988

David M. Wight

Cornell University Press
Ithaca and London

First published 2021 by Cornell University Press

Printed in the United States of America

Library of Congress Cataloging-in-Publication Data

Names: Wight, David M., 1985– author.
Title: Oil money : Middle East petrodollars and the transformation of
    US empire, 1967–1988 / David M. Wight.
Identifiers: LCCN 2020042677 (print) | LCCN 2020042678 (ebook) |
    ISBN 9781501715723 (hardcover) | ISBN 9781501715747 (pdf) |
    ISBN 9781501715730 (epub)
Subjects: LCSH: Petroleum industry and trade—Political aspects. |
    United States—Foreign economic relations—Middle East—History—
    20th century. | Middle East—Foreign economic relations—
    United States—History—20th century.
Classification: LCC HD9560.6 .W54 2021 (print) | LCC HD9560.6
    (ebook) | DDC 337.7305609/045—dc23
LC record available at https://lccn.loc.gov/2020042677
LC ebook record available at https://lccn.loc.gov/2020042678

For Mom, Dad, Michelle, Layla, and Clara

Contents

Acknowledgments   viii

List of Abbreviations   x

Introduction   1

1. Oil, US Empire, and the Middle East   10
2. The Road to the Oil Shock   31
3. Pursuing Petrodollar Interdependence   60
4. The Triangle to the Nile   85
5. The Petrodollar Economy   108
6. Visions of Petrodollar Promise and Peril   136
7. Reform and Revolt   170
8. Revolution and Invasions   195
9. Recoveries and Crises   225
10. End of an Era   252

Conclusion   278

Notes   289

Bibliography   325

Index   339

Acknowledgments

This book would not have been possible without the support of numerous people and institutions; I am indebted to all of you.

This project originated at the Department of History of the University of California Irvine, continued within the postdoctoral programs at the Belfer Center for Science and International Affairs at the John F. Kennedy School of Government at Harvard University and the Dickey Center for International Understanding at Dartmouth College, and was completed at the Department of History at the University of North Carolina at Greensboro. The final product was only possible through not only the financial support of these institutions but also the intellectual engagement of their faculty and students. Additionally, this research received support from the Gerald R. Ford Foundation Research Travel Grant, the Kugelman Research Fellowship from the Center for Citizen Peacebuilding, and the Society for Historians of American Foreign Relations' Samuel Flagg Bemis Dissertation Fellowship and Dissertation Completion Fellowship.

Special mention must go to Emily Rosenberg, who provided unsurpassed inspiration and guidance for this project. The early faith and ongoing advice of Michael McGandy and Mark Bradley at Cornell University Press in the potential of this book also sustained my writing over the years. More scholars than I can name have exchanged ideas and provided feedback about chapters that has immeasurably improved the final product of my research. Special thanks goes to Noel Anderson, Mary Barton, Thomas Borstelmann, Suparna Chaudhry, Sean Fear, Udi Greenberg, Eric Hundman, Sabrina Karim, Mark LeVine,

Shanon Fitzpatrick, Fredrik Logevall, Erez Manela, Edward Miller, Jennifer Miller, Amy Offner, Anne Parsons, Robert Rakove, Daniel Sargent, Kristina Shull, Thomas Sizgorich, Jennifer Graham Staver, Thomas Storrs, Annessa Stagner Stulp, Stephen Walt, Odd Arne Westad, William Wohlforth, Salim Yaqub, Amina Yassine, Thomas Zeiler, and an anonymous reviewer.

Great thanks are also due to the many archivists that provided invaluable assistance to me during my research. The countless people who extended their welcome or a friendly conversation while I traveled for research have my heartfelt thanks as well. To all of my family and friends, thank you for your support and for providing much-needed breaks from the research and writing process. A special note of thanks to my family in Lebanon and the American Research Center in Egypt is due for their exceptional hospitality. To Mom and Dad, thank you for the immeasurable love, education, support, and opportunities you have provided me. To Layla and Clara, thank you for brightening the final years of writing with your smiles and wonder.

My greatest thanks are reserved for my wife, partner, and best friend, Michelle. You invested in and sacrificed more for this project than anyone. Your love and support made this book possible, and I am forever grateful.

Abbreviations

AIOC	Anglo-Iranian Oil Company
Aramco	Arabian-American Oil Company
AWACS	Airborne Warning and Control System
BIS	Bank for International Settlements
CIA	Central Intelligence Agency
FBI	Federal Bureau of Investigation
FLN	Front de Libération Nationale
FMS	Foreign Military Sales
FY	fiscal year
IEEPA	International Emergency Economic Powers Act
IMF	International Monetary Fund
IOP	Iranian Oil Participants
IPC	Iraq Petroleum Company
LDC	less developed country
MDC	more developed country
MENA	Middle East and North Africa
MNOC	multinational oil companies
NATO	North Atlantic Treaty Organization
NIEO	New International Economic Order
NSC	National Security Council
NSDD	National Security Directive Decision
NSDM	National Security Decision Memorandum
OEC	oil-exporting country

OECD	Organisation for Economic Co-operation and Development
OPEC	Organization of the Petroleum Exporting Countries
PLO	Palestine Liberation Organization
UAE	United Arab Emirates
USSR	Union of the Soviet Socialist Republics

Oil Money

Introduction

On November 5, 1974, a year into the "oil shock" of markedly higher petroleum prices that was bringing the oil-exporting countries (OECs) unprecedented profits, White House chief of staff Donald Rumsfeld sent a memo to US deputy national security advisor Brent Scowcroft. Rumsfeld began the memo by arguing that "financial, nuclear, and space capabilities represent a unique triad of symbols of power in today's world." While the United States' nuclear and space capabilities remained powerful, "America's financial preeminence has dwindled. . . . The financial power of the future is clearly the Arab Nations." Following this line of reasoning, Rumsfeld proposed that Washington offer to cooperate with a consortium of Arab nations to develop an Arab space program that would "make them virtually the equals of the U.S. and U.S.S.R. in this field within a decade" and "be jointly manned by American and Arab astronauts." Rumsfeld estimated the program would have a start-up cost of $7–$10 billion and an annual cost of $1 billion thereafter. Funding would come from the sparsely populated oil-rich Arab states, while the labor force would largely be drawn from more populous Arab states, both oil rich and oil poor. Rumsfeld admitted the endeavor would be expensive but maintained the cost would not be prohibitive, as the projected Arab balance-of-payments surplus would total at least $50 billion in 1974 alone, money that Rumsfeld claimed "the Arabs are now frantically seeking some use."[1]

Rumsfeld argued that a space program would appeal to Arab leaders as a means toward modernization. "While the Arabs do not wish to become Americanized or Europeanized or Christianized," Rumsfeld stated, "they do wish to become modernized—to have the intellectual as well as physical advantages of the modern western world." The space program would bring new industries and the education of "technicians, scientists, engineers, managers" to the Arab world, inculcating modern industrial, economic, social, and political systems. Rumsfeld also argued that a space program offered a positive alternative to the stalemated struggle against Israel for generating Arab pride. "The common people—the fellahin—are anxious to start another war, but that must be the last thing that rational Arab leaders want," Rumsfeld contended. "From their point of view, diversion of interest from Israel would in itself make the space effort promising." Rumsfeld mused: "Remember how proud the Egyptians were when they broke even in the Yom Kippur war? How much more proud they would be to be world leaders in space. How much more pleasant for our sheikh to fete a returning Arab astronaut rather than a returning Arab terrorist."[2]

For Rumsfeld, the primary benefit of the program for the United States would be stronger ties with a more stable Arab world. "We must not consider the Arab world as our enemies in the long term," Rumsfeld insisted. "The U.S. must live in a world in which the Arabs not only control petroleum which the U.S. needs for survival, but are among the world's major powers who [sic] must be dealt with on any subject. It is essential that we be friendly with the Arabs, and this will only be possible if we give them something they want and which they cannot easily obtain elsewhere." A joint space program would establish the United States as a valuable partner to Arab development and serve as leverage for obtaining Arab cooperation on issues like oil prices. Rumsfeld further argued that the modernization of Arab societies would reduce radicalism in the area, stating that "the mullah or mufti would be harder pressed to sway an electronic technician than a camel herder toward some reactionary political position." Rumsfeld also noted the potential benefits to the US economy, arguing that most contracts for the project would be awarded to US firms and that Arab spending could be used to subsidize the expense of the US space shuttle program. Finally, Rumsfeld concluded his pitch by invoking the Cold War. "If the Arabs were going to develop a space mission in cooperation with either the U.S. or the U.S.S.R., which would we rather it be?" he rhetorically asked.[3]

It does not appear that others in the US government seriously considered Rumsfeld's proposal. In some ways, it was one of the more outlandish ideas on how to utilize Arab wealth. But in key ways the memo exemplified mid-1970s' responses to the enormous sums of moneys being accumulated by the OECs of the Middle East, moneys popularly called "petrodollars" during the period to denote their acquisition from petroleum sales.

First, Rumsfeld's memo typified how the sheer number of Arab, and Iranian, petrodollars, accruing at a rate of nearly $200 million per day, inspired the interest and even awe of many Americans.[4] In the White House, as well as in Congress, federal agencies, and governors' offices, officials debated how petrodollars might impact their constituencies and reshape global economic and political orders. Businesses and banks, from multinationals to local establishments, calculated how petrodollars might transform their markets. News and entertainment media provided regular commentary on how petrodollars were transforming the world. This attention to petrodollars was by no means exclusive to the United States; across the globe, governments, corporations, and general publics concerned themselves with the repercussions of the ongoing Arab and Iranian windfall.

Rumsfeld's proposal also mirrored the hopes and assumptions of many other US policymakers and businesspeople regarding petrodollars. In their view the newfound wealth of the Arab world and Iran dramatically increased their power and importance; how the Arabs and Iranians expended their petrodollars would have momentous ramifications for global economic and political structures. The key, then, was to ensure Arab and Iranian leaders used their petrodollars in ways constructive to US goals, rather than in opposition. To achieve this, these Americans argued, the US government and US corporations should provide their advanced technology and services in exchange for Arab and Iranian monetary deposits and political cooperation. The Arabs and Iranians would thus pay for their own modernization under US tutelage—bringing investments and jobs to a US economy racked with both inflation and recession (in part caused by higher oil prices), and development and education to Middle East societies that aspired to Western standards of living. Modernization projects, be it a space program or something more down to earth, would also have salutary political effects on Arab and Iranian societies vis-à-vis the United States. They would reaffirm and extend US alliances with the governments of the Arab world and Iran within the context of the Cold War. They would produce moderate political beliefs among average Arabs and Iranians, defusing crises like the Arab-Israeli conflict. They would ensure that the United States and its allies would continue to have access to Middle East oil at a tolerable price. In short, by significantly integrating the Middle East and US economies via petrodollar flows, the increased power of the Arab nations and Iran from petrodollar wealth would be utilized to preserve and enhance US global power.

Wittingly or unwittingly, however, Rumsfeld did not recognize in his memo that there might be resistance to his or similar US modernization schemes, or that interdependence might produce unintended results. Arab and Iranian leaders, "rational" or otherwise, might use their petrodollar power to better challenge US prerogatives if they appeared to clash with their own perceived interests. Many newly trained Arab or Iranian electronic technicians might feel alienated by high levels of US influence in their society and government and resist it. And many Americans might oppose closer ties with the Arab world and Iran out of concern about foreign influence in US institutions.

This book argues that the surge in petrodollar profits of oil-rich states during the long 1970s facilitated a fundamental transformation in the relationship between the Middle East and North Africa (MENA), on the one hand, and the international empire that the United States had forged since World War II, on the other.[5] Early studies on the role of petrodollars in global affairs during the 1970s and 1980s were based primarily on public records, field research, economic data, and journalism.[6] In the past decade scholars utilizing newly declassified records have included the global impacts of petrodollars as aspects of their larger arguments, contributing to an emerging reevaluation of the international history of the 1970s and 1980s.[7] Methodologically, this book seeks to build on the varied insights of these works in three key ways. First, it utilizes a wealth of new sources, particularly from declassified governmental records and popular Arab, Iranian, and US media. Second, it takes the relationship between the United States and the MENA as a region, rather than select countries, as its scope and places petrodollars at the center of its analysis. Third, it provides the most comprehensive coverage of different types of impacts of petrodollars on relations between the MENA and the United States during the period, with analysis extending to a wide range of international and transnational actors, and to the economic, diplomatic, military, political, social, and cultural realms.

My research reveals how the petrodollar boom of the long 1970s spurred far-reaching changes in the operation of US empire in the MENA and the role of the MENA within US empire. In this book the words "empire" and "imperialism" are not used as ones of moral opprobrium, nor are they used in alignment with any of the historical actors that employed such terminology to describe the United States and its actions. Instead, they are used as terms of analysis. During the mid-twentieth century the United States possessed and wielded such disproportionate power over large parts of the world that few terms other than empire suffice. Furthermore, employing an imperial framework keeps in focus the role of power in shaping processes like globalization that are often falsely presented as apolitical and strictly technocratic. Paul Kramer has usefully characterized the United States in this period as constituting an "international empire," defined as "an imperial project in which order was produced through the coordination of multiple, 'legitimate' nation-states, the promotion, management, and disciplining of flows and connections between them, and disproportionate power within multilateral bodies."[8] Through international empire the United States used its power over other legally sovereign nation-states to advance its political and economic interests, particularly through their integration into the US security complex and global capitalist networks of trade and investment. Often countries' governments (or governments in waiting) cooperatively entered into this system of US empire to accrue the benefits of US commerce, aid, and military support, even as they sought to gradually increase their relative power and autonomy vis-à-vis the United States.

This book provides an important example of how the United States successfully maintained its international empire in the face of repeated challenges from partners and adversaries alike. The United States achieved this by accommodating the rising power and ambitions of its oil-rich MENA allies and utilizing their enhanced wealth for shared ends, thereby transitioning to a new system of cooperative empire. From the 1920s through the 1960s the United States implemented a system of cooperative international empire in the MENA wherein the oil-rich states of the region exported cheap petroleum that underpinned the economic growth of the United States and its allies (as well as the latter's political allegiance) and the US government and oil companies provided security and economic assistance to the MENA regimes. During the early 1970s this order was disrupted when the oil-exporting MENA countries secured significantly higher petroleum prices and petrodollar revenues, threatening US influence in both the MENA and the larger world, especially in the wake of the alliance-threatening 1973 Arab oil embargo against the United States. Corporate and governmental leaders in the United States and allied MENA countries avoided a permanent rift, however, by negotiating a transition to a new system of empire based on the "recycling of petrodollars." In this new formation the leaders of the United States and its MENA allies, especially monarchical Iran and Saudi Arabia, departed from cheap oil as the foundation of their relationship and instead repurposed their ties on the use of the MENA countries' newfound petrodollar wealth in joint projects mutually perceived as useful to shared interests; these included massive military buildups and unprecedented development projects in the MENA countries, foreign aid and lending projects in the larger Third World, and investment programs in the United States, all of which served to augment the geopolitical power of the US-led alliance and the global expansion of an increasingly deregulated capitalism. In this new order the United States still constituted the dominant power, but its oil-rich allies, particularly Iran and Saudi Arabia, had far greater influence and favorable treatment.

The transition to this new imperial order undergirded by petrodollar ties was part of a global trend during the long 1970s toward rapidly increasing international flows of investments, trade, travel, media, and communications, connections that powerfully bound together the economic fates and cultural imaginations of disparate peoples across much of the world. Today these processes are often collectively described as "globalization," but in the 1970s the scholars who increasingly noted such contemporary phenomena used the term "interdependence." The term could denote both a state of being and a strategy pursued or nurtured. State and nonstate leaders could choose a variety of courses in how or when to embrace or disengage from interdependence, but their choices were also constrained by material realities. Increased economic interdependence between countries generally generated greater economic gains, but it also meant those countries had to increasingly consider the concerns of their trading partners lest they spur an economically harmful reaction. "International economic intercourse both enlarges and confines the freedom of countries to act according to their own lights," the economist Richard Cooper wrote in 1968 in *The Economics of Interdependence*. "It enlarges their freedom by permitting a more economical use of limited resources; it confines their freedom by embedding each country in a matrix of constraints which it can influence only slightly, often only indirectly, and without certainty of effect. . . . [A country] can abandon unilaterally the tacit international code of good behavior only if it is prepared to accept the adverse reaction of other countries."[9]

Cooper focused on interdependence between the United States and its Western European and Japanese allies in the book, a natural choice given the unsurpassed size of these countries' economies and trade relations with each other at the time, but his ideas would also ring true for the petrodollar interdependence that rapidly developed between the MENA countries and the United States in the following years. Indeed, I argue the MENA should be understood as an important region in the rise of US-led interdependence/globalization during the 1970s, on par with those of the Americas, Western Europe, and East Asia. As the largest economy and the locus of an immense sum of new capital, respectively, the United States and the oil-rich MENA countries had powerful structural economic incentives to reach agreements on the uses of petrodollars. These incentives go a long way in explaining why leaders in the two regions often overcame disputes and persisted in reconstituting US empire along the lines of petrodollar interdependence.

At the same time, however, economic structures were not strictly determinative; diverse leaders and communities chose different priorities and courses of action that were informed by a variety of considerations and ideological outlooks. The leaders in the White House, many US corporations, and allied MENA governments all shared a belief that petrodollar interdependence between the MENA and the United States served their national and/or corporate economic and security interests. Yet even among allies powerful disagreements arose, leading MENA and US leaders to sometimes limit their pursuit of interdependence and to even threaten hostile action against each other. US and allied MENA leaders had to consciously work together to perpetuate the interdependent US-led imperial order in the face of clashing concerns.

Furthermore, I show that the US-led petrodollar order had a tendency to reinforce structures of conflict, economic disparity, and governmental unaccountability, especially since the US and allied governments utilized oil wealth to marginalize and violently repress the interests and political participation of oppositional groups, particularly MENA leftists and antimonarchical Islamists. These tendencies generated a high degree of hostility to US empire and interdependence within communities in both the MENA and the United States over fears that the other would undermine their own sovereignty, cultural and governmental traditions, economic interests, and human rights values. Governments such as those of Algeria, Iraq, and Libya often chose to align themselves in opposition to US empire; from a very different position Israel remained a US ally but fought to undermine Arab-US petrodollar ties. Some leaders and communities within the United States and the Arab and Iranian monarchies also challenged parts or all of the US-led petrodollar order as counter to their interests, and sometimes succeeded in undermining this order. In the most extreme case Iranian revolutionaries overthrew the shah, in large degree over anger at perceived injustices regarding interdependence with the United States, and established a new government that not only withdrew from the system of US empire but proved to be one of its most powerful challengers in the MENA. This book thus demonstrates how empire and interdependence, when not responsive to popular demands, can lead to challenges to them and even their overthrow.

For both the peoples of the MENA and the United States, the beginnings of our contemporary phase of globalization largely began in the context of the oil shocks and petrodollar economy of the 1970s. Empire, it has been observed, produces cultural narratives to justify itself, while also generating narratives of opposition.[10] The same is true of economic systems. In the struggle over competing visions of petrodollar orders, cultural debates played a prominent role. This work thus analyzes how Americans, Arabs, and Iranians deployed narratives about petrodollar ties to mobilize popular support for their economic and political visions. While the records of Arab and Iranian governments of the period remain largely (although not entirely) inaccessible to researchers, a rich array of Arab- and Iranian-language newspaper articles, treatises, and works of fiction are available and provide a vantage point into the concerns of both MENA governments and opposition movements.[11] Representations of each other, both positive and negative, profoundly shaped how Americans, Arabs, and Iranians first grappled with and sought to make sense of globalization and the rapid changes it brought.

From the early 1970s to the mid-1980s the petrodollar revenues of MENA oil exporters facilitated numerous transformations of US empire and the larger international order. The increased wealth of the MENA played an important role in increasing the balance of US international attentions to the region, distinct but interrelated with the issues of access to oil and Cold War rivalries. Within the MENA the petrodollar boom established unprecedented ties between the Arab world and the United States that would persist for decades, changing Saudi Arabia from a modest to a top-tier US ally and Egypt from a Soviet client to a US one, but also transforming Iran from a powerful US ally to a powerful opponent. As a region the MENA ceased to be a place where US empire dominated a product (oil), but instead came to dominate financial flows, with the United States using MENA petrodollars to maintain its own empire globally; commitments that had previously been delegated to the United States and its Western allies were increasingly financed by oil-rich MENA allies. MENA petrodollars became a critical source of lending and investment for US banks, businesses, and governments. The success of Arab and US leaders in ensuring that the reinvestment of these petrodollars largely occurred through private institutions rather than multilateral ones would facilitate the expansion of neoliberal globalization in much of the Second and Third Worlds. Oil wealth greatly increased the importance of arms exports to US global trade and influence. Petrodollars funded the rapid modernization of large swaths of the MENA, making the region a far more significant consumer of state-of-the-art US military, developmental, and commercial goods and services. Oil wealth increasingly funded aid to US allies around the world, including governments from the United Kingdom to South Korea and anti-leftist insurgencies from Afghanistan to Nicaragua. Finally, petrodollars greatly expanded the number of cooperative networks between the MENA and the United States, while also growing the ranks of those actively opposed to MENA-US interdependence; both sides produced a flurry of new cultural narratives to support or condemn US-led globalization and empire.

In response to the oil shocks of the 1970s, the United States successfully reconstituted and maintained its empire by utilizing MENA petrodollars. The United States bore the significant costs of higher petroleum prices, but it off-set these costs by collaborating with allied MENA states to utilize petrodollars for shared purposes. MENA states that cooperated with the United States increased their power in many ways; those that sought to resist US influence increasingly found themselves punished. Yet while many leaders found the US-led petrodollar order beneficial to their interests, the economic disruptions and authoritarian violence this system fostered also drove many Americans, Arabs, and Iranians to resist it, sowing conflict within the MENA and the United States and with each other. The consequences of these struggles would persist long after oil revenues plummeted in the mid-1980s, as would many of the structures established during the petrodollar era of the long 1970s.

Chapter 1

Oil, US Empire, and the Middle East

In March 1965 Abdullah al-Tariqi addressed the fifth Arab Petroleum Congress of the Arab League in Cairo. Tariqi had previously served as Saudi Arabia's oil minister, where he had tirelessly called for the renegotiation of oil concessions to the Western multinational petroleum companies on terms more favorable to Arab countries. Now speaking as a private citizen, Tariqi declared that "the present status of the oil industry in the Arab countries is a perfect example of the economic colonialism" of Western powers; indeed, it was "colonialism in its worst form." Western colonialism, he argued, was driven by a desire to control the natural resources of Africa, Asia, and Latin America and use them for the benefit of Western development at the expense of colonized peoples. While the West had largely been forced to abandon direct rule over its colonies in recent years, it had merely "substitute[d] its old form of domination by a new one. . . . Military occupation was thus replaced by alliances, of defense treaties, and economic agreements, and hence guaranteed the control over the resources of the countries colonized." As an example, Tariqi explained that the US oil consortium Arabian-American Oil Company (Aramco) had taken advantage of Saudi Arabia through agreements that kept Saudi oil revenues artificially low, minimized the investment of US capital in the country to impede Saudi industrialization, and excluded Saudis from high-level positions in order to prevent them from acquiring the skills needed to control their nation's most important industry. Given the colonial nature of US and European oil companies, Tariqi concluded that the "nationalization of oil production in the Arab countries is a necessity dictated by the national interests of these countries."[1]

Tariqi provided a critical summation of US international empire in the MENA since the 1920s. Constructed by both US multinational oil companies (MNOCs) and the US government, US empire in the MENA sought to ensure the cheap, plentiful flow of oil from the region to Western consumers. Initially, the United States primarily secured its influence over the MENA and its oil through the empires of its British and French allies, international empire in the second degree. Starting with Saudi Arabia, however, an increasing number of MENA countries became direct client states of the United States from the 1930s to the 1960s. Whether primarily clients of the United States or European powers, however, a similar logic of cooperative empire operated for oil-rich MENA countries, in which friendly elites received Western military support, aid, revenues, and expertise to assist state building projects and secure their regimes in exchange for their commitment to fight communism and supply cheap oil. The United States pursued a similar dynamic with the oil-poor MENA countries for related ends.

US and European empires in the MENA generated popular local resistance to client regimes and their Western backers, however. This resistance to the US-led order developed in part due to poor labor and human rights conditions, cultural and religious alienation toward encroaching foreign social systems (including capitalism), and nationalist aspirations. US support for Israel further inflamed Arab and Iranian opinion. Tied to all these issues was the tendency of Western client regimes to deny their populations genuine opportunities for political participation and use security forces, Western trained and supplied, to suppress dissent. Notably, Iran and most Arab polities in the aftermath of World War II were monarchies, and all of these monarchs served as Western clients. During the 1950s and 1960s some of these Arab monarchies were overthrown by leftist nationalist movements far less accommodating to the United States and more closely aligned with the Soviet Union. The most powerful of these was Egypt, which would increasingly challenge US allies like Saudi Arabia up to the 1967 Arab-Israeli War.

The leftist challenge reinforced for the United States and the MENA monarchies the sense of need for a political alliance wherein the former strengthened the latter with developmental and military assistance. At the same time, however, the monarchies regularly clashed with the MNOCs and Washington over the control of petroleum. The monarchies sought greater petrodollar revenues to develop their countries' economies, enlarge their regional geopolitical influence, and increase their autonomy from the West. While US actors accommodated such demands to a point, they ultimately worked in opposition to this goal, as cheap, US-controlled oil remained a primary objective.

This situation increasingly led oil-rich US allies in the MENA to collaborate with each other and additional oil-rich countries to challenge the US-dictated terms of the global petroleum economy. Growing US support for Israel would likewise increasingly push US-allied oil-rich Arab governments to join Arab countries more hostile to Washington in challenging the United States. In sum, cooperative US empire in the two decades after World War II provided benefits to both the United States and its MENA allies, but it also contained tensions that challenged its longevity.

In 1928 a consortium of US oil companies, including Gulf Oil and the predecessors of Exxon and Mobil, acquired from the European firms of British Petroleum, Shell, and Compagnie Française Pétrole a 23.75 percent share in their Iraq Petroleum Company (IPC). The European firms in part acceded to the agreement because of diplomatic pressure from Washington, which sought to secure US strategic and commercial access to foreign oil supplies via US MNOCs. The union created the first US presence in the Middle East oil industry. It also established the corporatist partnership that would largely structure US relations in the MENA until the 1970s, wherein the MNOCs secured US national security interests related to oil on behalf of Washington in exchange for the diplomatic and legal support of the US government.[2]

The deal marked the dawn of a new era in MENA-US relations. While the two regions had previous transnational ties such as trade, missionary work, and immigration, US corporations had largely eschewed direct investment in the region and Washington had considered the area of little strategic concern. By the 1920s the entire Arab world had fallen under the direct or indirect control of European powers, primarily France and the United Kingdom. This included Iraq, where the British imposed a new monarchy, the Hashemite dynasty, which remained subservient to London even after Iraq acquired de jure sovereignty in 1932. Iran, nominally sovereign under the monarchy of the new Pahlavi dynasty, was similarly dominated by the British. This enabled Europeans to control the earliest two oil industries in the MENA, with the British monopolizing Iran under the Anglo-Iranian Oil Company (AIOC) and the British, Dutch, and French sharing power in Iraq under the IPC. The inclusion of US companies in the IPC marked the beginning of the end of Europe's hegemony over the MENA's petroleum and political affairs. Increasingly, US corporations and the US government would dominate the MENA, driven by the desire to control the region's oil, eventually establishing an empire.

The United States employed multiple forms of empire in the course of its history. In the nineteenth century it established itself as a territorial empire, securing the length of the North American continent by subjugating the American Indians and defeating Mexico. In 1898 the United States established an empire of overseas colonies in the Caribbean and Pacific that included Puerto Rico and the Philippines. In the twentieth century, however, the United States increasingly adopted cooperative international empire over other sovereign but weaker states. Under this model, the United States promoted the formal sovereignty of other nations, but the US government and/or US corporations also leveraged their economic, technological, and military superiority as inducements to foreign governments to accept US oversight and management over key aspects of their domestic and foreign policies.[3] International empire offered distinct benefits to both the United States and cooperating states. Though forgoing direct control, the United States exerted powerful influence abroad while reducing military and administrative costs and domestic and international opposition. In cooperating with the United States, weaker countries obtained US aid, expertise, commerce, and/or military protection that could strengthen their economies and state institutions. In joining the IPC, which dominated Iraq's economic and political system, US oil companies extended US empire to the MENA for the first time.

Gulf Oil would follow up on its entry into the IPC in 1933 by striking a fifty-fifty joint venture with British Petroleum in the British protectorate of Kuwait. It would strike oil in February 1938, significantly expanding US influence over that country and MENA oil reserves generally. The first country in the oil-rich MENA to come under predominantly US influence would be Saudi Arabia. Declared a kingdom in 1932, Saudi Arabia had been established in the previous three decades through the conquests of Ibn Saud. The Saudi monarch secured the support of Wahhabi religious leaders, members of a conservative tradition within Sunni Islam, by granting them theocratic oversight of social customs. Ibn Saud also accepted a formal British protectorate over his domains in return for military aid in 1915; and even after obtaining British recognition of his government's full sovereignty in 1927, he remained dependent on British support, his country a de facto part of the United Kingdom's empire of special treaty states in the Middle East. In 1933, however, King Ibn Saud opted to grant an oil concession to a US company, the predecessor of Chevron, beginning a decades-long US monopoly over foreign influence in Saudi oil affairs. Another US company, Texas Oil (later Texaco), joined the venture three years later, and their joint subsidiary, soon to be named Aramco, struck oil at Dammam in March 1938, initiating the Saudi oil industry.

The critical role of petroleum to military success during World War II solidified the view of the US government that Middle East oil constituted a vital strategic interest. During the war, Washington provided lend-lease aid to Saudi Arabia to ensure the stability of Ibn Saud's rule, further supplanting British influence in the country. In Iran and Iraq, by contrast, the United States opted to uphold British preeminence. This support extended to London's decision to depose and exile the neutralist Iranian monarch Reza Shah Pahlavi in 1941 and replace him with his son, Mohammed Reza Shah Pahlavi, a bright but insecure young man. The United States would provide lend-lease aid to these countries as well, however, to help keep them in the allied camp. During the war US leaders also began to discuss Iran as an important barrier to a possible Soviet challenge to Western control over Arab oil.[4]

At the end of World War II, the Soviet Union and the United States emerged as the two remaining global superpowers. The war convinced most US foreign policymakers that the vital security and economic interests of the United States required the reconstruction of a regulated global capitalist economy, the prevention of any single power from dominating Eurasia, and a policy of nonappeasement toward hostile dictatorships. Conversely, the war imbued Soviet leaders with a renewed conviction to gradually spread communism across the globe and, more immediately, to establish the security of the Union of the Soviet Socialist Republics (USSR) by dominating neighboring polities. Pursuing competing ideological and strategic visions, the Soviet Union and the United States proved unable to transcend their differences, and by 1947 had entered into an adversarial contest for global supremacy, the Cold War, in which most of the world, including the MENA, bifurcated into Soviet and US spheres of influence.[5]

The administration of US president Harry Truman made Western access to Middle East oil a top priority in its Cold War strategy of restoring global capitalism and countering the Soviet Union. While the United States produced two-thirds of the world's oil and was a major petroleum exporter in 1945, it was becoming clear that the MENA held unparalleled reserves of oil, which meant that the region would play an important role in the development of the global energy market.[6] At the same time, Aramco sought to begin the large-scale export of Saudi oil to realize the profit-making potential of its investment. The US military and the State Department supported Aramco's goal, as they sought to expand oil production in the Eastern Hemisphere to ensure ample supplies of petroleum would be available to it there while also helping to conserve deposits of oil in the Western Hemisphere that constituted a more easily defended strategic reserve. In 1948 Aramco admitted Exxon and Mobil as partners, both to acquire additional capital for the infrastructure needed to reach European markets and to enlist their support in avoiding a costly price war with the IPC and the AIOC. The expansion of Aramco created an interlocking set of partnerships among Chevron, Exxon, Gulf Oil, Mobil, Texaco, British Petroleum, Compagnie Française Pétrole, and Shell through their joint ventures in Iraq, Kuwait, and Saudi Arabia. Collectively controlling the vast majority of exported oil in the world, the eight MNOCs joined forces to create a producer cartel that regulated oil output and pricing to avoid costly competition with each other. The MNOCs also steadily increased the export of Middle East oil, which facilitated the economic growth of the United States and the reconstruction of its major allies. As early as 1948 a US government study determined that the loss of Arab and Iranian oil production, estimated at 11 percent of the noncommunist world's total, would force the United States to either adopt strict domestic energy rationing or risk the failure of Western Europe's recovery under the Marshall Plan.[7]

Over the next two decades the Western economies built themselves up on cheap and plentiful oil. From 1949 to 1970 US oil consumption grew by 180 percent, Western European consumption by 1,350 percent, and Japanese consumption from a few thousand to 4.4 million barrels a day. The rapid growth in oil use played a key role in the phenomenal economic recovery of the Western countries after World War II. From 1948 to 1973 the combined GDP per capita of the more developed countries (MDCs) of Western Europe, North America, Japan, Australia, and New Zealand more than tripled.[8] Oil also constituted the largest internationally traded good in terms of value and volume. In the decades after World War II the vast majority of internationally traded oil (and exports generally) was sold in dollars, linking the value of oil and the dollar together, and the reason why most revenues were *petrodollars* as opposed to a different petro-currency (such as the distant second petro-pound).[9]

While the Truman administration looked to the MNOCs to export oil from the Middle East, it primarily looked to the British, and to a lesser degree the French, to respond to local political challenges and keep the Soviets shut out of the MENA. Whereas Moscow lacked any allied states in the region in 1945, the British and French retained formal or informal control over most MENA states. The British also fielded significant military forces in the region; in 1952 the British maintained over sixty-four thousand troops and a string of military air and naval bases from Libya to Iraq to South Yemen.[10] While the Truman administration did keep Saudi Arabia under the US aegis and began a military training program in Tehran, for the most part it was content to leave the defense of the Middle East to the British as a cost-saving division of labor.

Yet while the Truman administration looked to the British and French to defend the MENA, the Europeans were weakened by World War II and faced emboldened anti-imperialist movements in the region fighting for two inter-related goals: an end to formal and informal Western rule and an improvement in their standard of living. In Iran political factions challenging British political and economic influence in the country grew in strength. In March 1945, Egypt, Iraq, Jordan, Lebanon, Saudi Arabia, and Syria formed the Arab League, with the goal of achieving closer relations between Arab countries and advancing the cause of their independence and welfare. France and the United Kingdom in turn made selective tactical retreats from formal empire in the hope of main-taining informal influence. In 1945 Lebanon and Syria obtained independence from France, and Jordan and Libya gained independence from the United King-dom in 1946 and 1951, although the Jordanian and Libyan monarchies remained reliant on the British.

Up to the 1940s, many Arabs and Iranians had viewed the United States as a potential ally against European imperialism due to the lack of US territorial ambitions in the region and friendly transnational ties forged with Americans via missionaries, modernizers, and immigrants.[11] After World War II, how-ever, the behavior of US oil companies and Washington increasingly gener-ated elite and popular anti-US attitudes in the MENA.

For the Arab and Iranian leaders of oil-rich countries, the MNOCs were a mixed blessing. For MENA governments, the petrodollars furnished to them by the MNOCs in exchange for oil concessions constituted a vital revenue stream for state development. The Truman administration also looked to US oil cor-porations to serve as a primary modernizing force in the region, believing that the revenues, jobs, and infrastructure would strengthen host countries' eco-nomic and political resilience to communist subversion while avoiding local perceptions that the United States acted in an imperial fashion.[12] Yet while many US leaders genuinely sought the modernization of less developed coun-tries (LDCs) in the Global South, the United States also led the reconstruction of a global capitalist system wherein the LDCs continued to suffer from a dearth of capital and low prices for their primary exports, raw materials, while the MDCs of the Global North retained the bulk of global capital and high prices for their industrial product exports. In the aftermath of World War II, the lead-ers of Asia, Africa, and Latin America increasingly embraced the ideology of Third Worldism, which emphasized divisions between the Global North and the Global South over the East-West division of the Cold War and called for both the end of European political colonialism and a restructuring of the global economy, wherein the relative value of raw material exports would be increased to fund the industrialization of the Global South and bring its standard of living on par with the Global North.[13] In the oil-rich countries of the Third World, anticolonial elites, displeased with the MNOCs dominance over their most valuable resource and majority cut of revenues, increasingly articulated the idea of sovereign rights over natural resources as a justification for the renegotiation of oil concessions with or the nationalization of the MNOCs in their countries. The MNOCs strongly resisted these ideas, as they sought to minimize the amount of revenues shared with host countries, prevent local governments from having a say in decisions on pricing or production, and bar local nationals from holding management positions in order to maintain their control over the oil industry and maximize their profits. Over time, leaders of oil-rich MENA countries across the political spectrum grew increasingly frustrated with the MNOCs, as well as with Washington's support for them.[14]

The practices of US oil companies also created new, radicalized proletariats throughout the region. The US MNOCs introduced racial segregation to their camps in Iraq and Saudi Arabia and subjected Arab laborers to inadequate housing, lengthy and unsafe work conditions, and lower pay than Westerners. In 1945 the first labor strike against Aramco occurred when Arab employees protested poor working conditions and unequal pay. The company responded by violently suppressing the strike, but it would not be the last.[15] In Iraq labor protests in 1946 and 1948 against the IPC were similarly suppressed by the use of lethal violence and arrests by corporate and governmental forces.[16] Such mistreatment generated anti-US and anticorporate sentiment among Arab oil workers and their larger communities.

The escalating conflict between Arabs and Zionists also generated elite and popular Arab anger at the United States. In early 1947, London announced it would soon withdraw from its mandate over Palestine and leave the resolution of the Arab-Zionist conflict to the newly established United Nations. Most Arabs felt the creation of a Zionist state in Palestine would constitute a pernicious form of Western imperialism and unfairly deny the nationalist aspirations of Arab Palestinians. The Truman administration, out of both humanitarian concern for European Jewish survivors of the Holocaust and political concern for retaining American Jewish voters, worked vigorously to ensure that the UN approved a partition plan for Palestine that would include a Zionist state and promptly recognized the new state of Israel once it declared its independence in 1948. The Truman administration's support for Israel significantly soured popular Arab sentiment toward the United States and strained US relations with Arab countries, though none of the oil-rich monarchies risked a break with Washington while dependent on the MNOCs for revenues.[17] The member states of the

Arab League did declare war on the newly founded Israel to uphold Arab Palestinian claims, but the armies they fielded all met with defeat, and Israel expanded
its borders beyond those delineated in the UN partition plan. This military rout
increased popular Arab nationalist convictions, particularly within armed forces,
that the current Arab governments were inadequate and too dependent on the
Western powers.

With the outbreak of the Korean War in 1950, the Truman administration
increasingly feared communist overthrows of existing governments in Africa
and Asia, and that communists would exploit rising anti-Americanism in the
MENA to this end. The US government thus placed renewed emphasis on
ensuring the oil-rich monarchies received adequate funds to maintain their
stability and loyalty. In the Arab world the Truman administration looked to
the MNOCs as the conduit for this assistance. Arab leaders were increasingly
demanding a significantly greater share of revenue from the MNOCs, which
in the late 1940s paid the host countries only a fraction of the profits earned
from the sale of their oil. Pressed by Riyadh and Washington, Aramco agreed
to a fifty-fifty split of profits with Saudi Arabia in 1950 but also received from
the US government a legally questionable tax deduction on its operating income that effectively shifted the cost of the increased funding to Saudi Arabia
from Aramco to US taxpayers. The impact was immediate; in 1950 Aramco
paid $50 million in US income taxes and disbursed $66 million to Saudi Arabia, while in 1951 Aramco paid $6 million in US income taxes and disbursed
almost $110 million to Riyadh. With encouragement from Washington, the
MNOCs agreed to a fifty-fifty profit split with the Iraqi and Kuwaiti governments in 1951 as well.[18] The increase in petrodollar profits for the Arab states
facilitated the Truman administration's decision to only commit under $1 mil-
lion in economic assistance to Iraq and Saudi Arabia from 1950 to 1952.[19]

In Iran, however, the British, who continued to monopolize the Iranian
petroleum industry through the AIOC, refused to adopt a fifty-fifty profit-
sharing deal. From 1950 to 1952 the US government provided Iran with over
$83 million in economic and military assistance, but this was not enough to
head off rising Iranian anger over the position of the AIOC.[20] The initial weakness of the new shah, Mohammed Reza, had shifted power to the Iranian
parliament, creating a space for pluralistic, democratic politics that had been
absent under the authoritarian Reza Shah. In this new political environment,
a wide range of Iranian parliamentarians, including secular leftists and Islamists,
formed a coalition, the National Front, to challenge the power of the AIOC. The
National Front was led by the Iranian prime minister Mohammad Mosaddeq,

whose popularity and antimonarchical views made him an adversary of the shah. In 1951 Mosaddeq nationalized the AIOC after it refused to grant a fifty-fifty deal with Iran.

Horrified by the specter of their own host countries nationalizing their businesses, the MNOCs coordinated a near-global boycott of Iranian petroleum, causing Iran's oil exports to drop by 97 percent, pummeling the Iranian economy and straining the finances of the government in Tehran. The MNOCs benefited, and Mosaddeq suffered, from the fact that the global oil market was experiencing an extended period of surplus and the loss of Iran's output could be made up for by other countries, including Arab producers. Despite this, Mosaddeq remained politically popular as he persisted in defying the Western corporations. Considering Mosaddeq's nationalization of the AIOC a national security threat, the British government began to conspire to effect a coup against Mosaddeq. While opposed to the nationalization, the Truman administration counseled London to reach an accommodation with Mosaddeq. The new administration of US president Dwight Eisenhower, however, was far more concerned that the ongoing political impasse could create an opening for Iranian communists to seize power in Tehran. The Eisenhower administration thus approved a Central Intelligence Agency (CIA) plot to overthrow Mosaddeq in collaboration with the British, the shah, and his Iranian allies. In August 1953 the coup was successfully implemented, aided by the unrest generated by the economic damage of the oil boycott. The coup secured the shah's leadership of Iran and placed Mosaddeq under house arrest until his death in 1967.[21]

The coup also established Iran as part of the US empire. The shah embraced the United States as his top ally to overcome both British interference in and domestic opposition to his rule. For Washington, he ensured the flow of Iranian oil to the West, provided US intelligence with listening posts toward the USSR, and cracked down on communists. In return, the US government instituted a marked increase in aid to Iran and in 1954 oversaw the establishment of a more favorable oil agreement for Iran. Seeking to ensure US influence over Iranian oil matters and increase Iran's revenues, the US government pressured both a reluctant United Kingdom and hesitant US oil companies to establish a new consortium in Iran that ended the British oil monopoly in Iran. The new consortium, the Iranian Oil Participants (IOP), included all eight of the MNOCs of Aramco and the IPC, with the US companies collectively holding a 40 percent share. While Tehran theoretically retained the title to Iran's nationalized oil industry via the National Iranian Oil Company, in practice the MNOCs controlled it via the IOP, which reserved decision making over production levels and operations. The MNOCs did agree to a fifty-fifty deal, with the US companies receiving the same tax deduction as Aramco, significantly increasing Iran's oil revenues at the expense of US taxpayers. The increasingly authoritarian shah utilized these increased funds to centralize his hold on power, strangle Iran's nascent democracy, expand the military and intelligence services, pursue state-led capitalism and Westernization, and marginalize the influence of Shia religious leaders. Yet widespread knowledge of the US government's role in the 1953 coup and subsequent support for the shah alienated Iranian leftists and Islamists from Washington, who had previously held a positive or neutral view of the United States.[22]

The Iranian coup also reaffirmed the power of the MNOCs in the Middle East. They had demonstrated that they could bring the Iranian oil industry to a halt and lobby home governments to overthrow hostile governments. Mosaddeq served as a warning to other MENA leaders. The fifty-fifty deals, while bringing greater revenues to host governments, had not significantly cut into corporate profits due to the Western governments' tax credits. The deals had also preserved for the MNOCs the final decision over production rates and the price of oil, which host countries could only seek to influence through negotiations.

Yet if it appeared to Washington that Iran was settling into a favorable relationship, the Arab world looked to be drifting toward an anti-Western posture. In 1952, amid anti-British riots, Egyptian military officers overthrew the pliant monarchy in Cairo and declared a republic. Gamal Abdel Nasser, a charismatic colonel and leader of the coup, soon established himself as the popular authoritarian president of Egypt. Leading the culturally influential and most populous Arab country, Nasser powerfully championed pan-Arab nationalism, Third Worldism, secularism, and antimonarchism. In 1954 he secured an agreement from London for a phased withdrawal of British troops from Egypt, completed in June 1956. Also in 1954 Algerian nationalists led by the Front de Libération Nationale (FLN) began a bloody seven-year guerilla war against French rule. The FLN skillfully broadcasted its struggle in media across the world, inspiring violent revolutionary resistance to Western imperialism across the Third World.[23]

Ongoing resistance to Western power in Iraq and Saudi Arabia likewise appeared emboldened. In 1953, the Iraqi government declared martial law in Basra province after oil workers went on strike protesting poor wages and conditions. Egypt maintained a relentless propaganda campaign within Iraq attacking the monarchy for enslaving the Iraqi people to the Western powers through its military ties to the United Kingdom.[24] Saudi Arabia likewise experienced continued labor and political unrest. In 1953, thirteen thousand workers joined a strike against Aramco in multiple camps, demanding collective bargaining and political rights. The Saudi army had to be deployed to put down the strike, which paralyzed the oil industry for three weeks. Shortly thereafter, antimonarchical leaflets with a red hammer and sickle heading flooded the town of al-Khobar, imploring the people to kill the Saudi royals "because of their joint actions with foreign imperialists" and exploitation of laborers. "O workers!" the leaflet declared. "Get rid of the American pigs and seize the profitable (exploiting) oil company . . . unite because the Arab Peninsula is for the Arabs." A new wave of strikes roiled Saudi Arabia in 1955 and 1956, leading the Saudi government to adopt harsher tactics, including the deportation of suspect foreign workers, the outlawing of work stoppages, and the reported torturing to death of labor leaders.[25]

The Eisenhower administration feared that the rise of Arab nationalism could endanger Western access to cheap petroleum and fatally undercut US global designs that hinged on the capitalistic recovery of Western Europe. In part this was due to the tendency of Arab nationalists to call for the overthrow of oil-rich, Western-backed monarchies in the region. More broadly, Arab nationalists called for Arab oil resources to come under the shared political control of all Arab states, both oil rich and oil poor, initially under the auspices of an inter-Arab petroleum organization and ultimately under a unified Arab state. Such an outcome could result in radical oil-poor states cutting off the flow of cheap petroleum from Arab Gulf states. Finally, in 1953 the Soviet Union broke relations with Israel and soon thereafter began an overt campaign to win the allegiance of the Arab nationalists, voicing solidarity with Arab nationalists against Israel and Western colonialism.[26]

Seeking to prevent an Arab nationalist threat to Western access to Arab oil, the Eisenhower administration initially worked to bring Nasser into the system of US international empire. In 1955 Eisenhower significantly increased US economic assistance to Cairo, put forward a new Arab-Israeli peace initiative, and offered to include Egypt in a new anti-Soviet defensive alliance with other Middle East states and the United Kingdom. Continued US economic and diplomatic support to Israel, however, coupled with aggressive Israeli military actions on Egyptian soil, led Nasser to ignore the US peace initiative. Desiring an end to the British military presence in Egypt, Nasser likewise turned down membership in the US-backed alliance. When the Eisenhower administration went ahead and organized the Baghdad Pact, a defensive alliance between the United Kingdom, Iran, Iraq, Pakistan, and Turkey, with an informal advisory role for the United States, Nasser publicly denounced Iraqi prime minister Nuri al-Said as an "Anglo-American stooge" and waged a successful campaign to prevent any other Arab states from joining the pact. In 1954 Syria signed the first major purchase of Soviet arms, followed by Nasser the following year, both seeking to counter Israel's military strength.[27] France and the United Kingdom attempted to mollify Arab nationalists by granting Morocco, Sudan, and Tunisia independence in early 1956, but Nasser and the FLN continued to challenge their influence in the MENA.

Nasser's growing ties with the communist world led London and Washington in July 1956 to cancel a joint $200 million aid package to Egypt for construction of the Aswan Dam, a major part of Nasser's development program. In retaliation Nasser nationalized the British-owned Suez Canal Company, whose revenues he intended to use to fund the dam project. Outraged, the United Kingdom reached a secret plan with France and Israel to militarily invade Egypt in order to seize back the canal—the French supporting the plan due to Nasser's support for the FLN, and Israel due to its escalating border tensions with Egypt. The three countries did not disclose their plot to the United States, hoping to leave Eisenhower with a fait accompli.[28]

In late October the Anglo-French-Israeli militaries launched their assault and quickly routed Egyptian forces in the Sinai. Despite his antipathy toward Nasser, the duplicity of his allies outraged Eisenhower, and he feared that US influence in the Arab and Third worlds would be forever lost to the Soviets if he supported the invasion. Eisenhower's fears were augmented by Moscow's vocal support for Egypt, which even came to include a public threat to attack London and Paris with rockets, a threat he took seriously. Seeking to avert global catastrophe and the loss of US influence in the Arab and Third worlds, Eisenhower applied massive diplomatic and economic pressure on the United Kingdom, France, and Israel to accept an immediate cease-fire and then withdraw from Egyptian territory. This included the United States embargoing Western Hemisphere oil to France and the United Kingdom in conjunction with Arab cutoffs of oil, causing an energy crisis in Western Europe. Finding their situation untenable, the Europeans withdrew from Egypt in December, and Israel in March 1957. Eisenhower's actions did provide a boost to Arab esteem for the United States, but British and French influence in the MENA had been further diminished and the Soviet Union's military and diplomatic ties with Egypt grew further. Additionally, Nasser's successful stand against the Europeans and Israelis generated widespread popularity for him and his calls for pan-Arab nationalism across the Arab world, endangering the authority of other Arab governments, particularly those with close ties to the West.[29]

Fearing that the spread of Nasser's Pan-Arabism and Third Worldism would diminish US influence in the Arab world and leave it open to Soviet machinations, Eisenhower launched a major new security program for the MENA in January 1957. Dubbed the Eisenhower Doctrine, it committed the United States to significantly increase economic and military aid to Iran, Iraq, Jordan, Libya, Morocco, Saudi Arabia, Lebanon, and Tunisia, and if necessary, to militarily intervene to prevent the spread of communism in the Middle East. A publicly unstated but key objective of the doctrine was to marginalize Nasser's brand of Arab nationalism, manifested in part by a near total cutoff of US aid to Egypt. The Eisenhower administration attempted to build up the Saudi king Saud, who had succeeded his father, Ibn Saud, upon his death in 1953, as an "Islamic pope" who could counter Nasser's secular nationalism, but Saud proved ineffectual on the world stage. Arab popular opinion proved largely cold toward the Eisenhower Doctrine and enamored with Nasser's Pan-Arabism. In the spring of 1957 Jordan's King Hussein had to fend off an attempt at his overthrow by Nasserist Jordanian and Palestinian military officers. In February 1958, Syria merged with Egypt to form the United Arab Republic, with Nasser as its president. Arab nationalists were jubilant.[30]

Seeking to counter the threat that the United Arab Republic presented to their own rule, the Iraqi and Jordanian monarchies promptly declared their own merger, the Arab Union, a move the United States supported. In July, however, Iraqi military officers opposed to the monarchy's close ties to the United Kingdom and the United States led a successful coup in which they executed King Faisal II, several royal family members, and Prime Minister Nuri. Eisenhower eschewed any Western military effort to restore the Iraqi monarchy, believing with good evidence that there was little Iraqi support for such a campaign and that it would inflame global opinion. Under the new government, Iraq promptly dissolved the Arab Union with Jordan and withdrew from the Baghdad Pact. While the leadership of Iraq would change repeatedly during the 1960s via a succession of coups and deaths, each new government maintained cold relations with Washington. Iraq had followed Egypt in falling out of the US international empire.

Baghdad's withdrawal from the Anglo-American orbit did not rupture its relationship with the IPC, however, as Iraq remained reliant on the company to reach global markets. Whether politically aligned with the United States or not, MENA oil exporters faced the same issue of Western control over the sale of their resource. Furthermore, in the 1950s there was a surplus of readily available oil, and while global consumption grew at a rapid rate, global production grew even faster, depressing prices. For most of the decade the MNOCs partially appeased host governments in the Middle East by boosting production while keeping posted prices stable, gradually increasing the MENA countries' share of global oil production. In 1960, however, the MNOCs decreased the price of Middle East oil by roughly 10 percent in response to competition from cheap oil exports from the Soviet Union. This resulted in a sizable reduction of government revenues for host countries, a fact made all the more odious to MENA leaders because the MNOCs often did not consult with or forewarn them before announcing the cuts. Nasser hoped to capitalize on the popular outrage against the price cuts by organizing a pan-Arab oil cartel under his leadership, an outcome feared by the Eisenhower administration, but the Iraqi government, seeking to maintain its autonomy in Arab affairs, resisted this plan. Instead, Iraq pursued a still Middle East heavy but more international cooperative effort with Iran, Kuwait, Saudi Arabia, and Venezuela. Meeting in Baghdad in September 1960, ministers from the five states (including Tariqi) founded the Organization of the Petroleum Exporting Countries (OPEC) with the stated purpose of increasing their countries' oil prices. The oil-rich rather than pan-Arab nature of OPEC was a blow to Arab nationalist aspirations, but OPEC also constituted the first significant Third World effort to collectively challenge the power of the Western MNOCs. Learning from Mosaddeq's experience, the members of OPEC also pledged solidarity to each other if the Western companies sanctioned any one of them.[31]

The continuing global surplus of oil inhibited OPEC's power in its first years, however. Contributing to the oil glut were the many new deposits being developed across the MENA. These included sites in Libya, where oil was first struck in 1958; in the following decade smaller US oil companies helped develop the country's petroleum industry and Washington increased its ties to the Libyan monarchy of King Idris. Yet while the Middle East's share of world oil production surpassed the United States' as the largest region of oil production in 1963 and OPEC's membership had expanded to include Abu Dhabi, Indonesia, Libya, and Qatar by 1967, the global surplus of petroleum still outweighed the power of OPEC's growing market share in shaping oil prices.[32] In the mid-1960s OPEC had achieved little beyond ensuring that the MNOCs did not again lower the posted price of oil.

Meanwhile, Western governments increasingly acceded to anticolonialism in the MENA. The United Kingdom granted independence to Kuwait in 1961, leaving its formal influence in the Arab world to just a scattering of protectorates along the Arabian Peninsula. France granted independence to Mauritania in 1960 and, after a costly war, to Algeria in 1962, ending the French empire in the Arab world. Similarly, after the upheavals of 1958, Eisenhower and his successor, John Kennedy, determined that US efforts to marginalize

Nasser would only further alienate Arab popular opinion against the United States, and thus pursued a rapprochement with Egypt, restoring aid and seeking cooperation on shared goals such as curbing the rise of communist parties in the Arab world, which Nasser considered to be rivals. Kennedy in particular believed that the United States needed to establish better relations with non-aligned nations and encourage liberal modernization programs in the Third World lest their populations be driven into radical rebellion.[33]

Nasser, meanwhile, faced new challenges and opportunities. To his disappointment, the new Iraqi government did not join the United Arab Republic, instead privileging its autonomy and increasingly challenging Egypt's leadership of the Arab world. Even more detrimental to Nasser, in 1961 a coup in Damascus brought to power the Baath Party, a rival pan-Arab group to the Nasserists, which promptly withdrew Syria from the United Arab Republic. Domestically, Nasser increasingly adopted socialist policies for Egypt's economic development, funded in part by both Soviet and US aid.

Then, in September 1962, Yemeni military officers sympathetic to Nasser overthrew the conservative Imamate of North Yemen and established the first republic on the Arabian Peninsula. The Yemeni imam, Muhammad al-Badr, escaped capture, however, and rallied pro-royalist forces along the Yemeni border with Saudi Arabia, initiating a civil war. Nasser quickly championed the Yemeni republic as part of a reinvigorated pan-Arabist challenge to his monarchist rivals. "We are the ones who have launched the revolution so that we could be rid of the likes of [King] Saud, and so that we could be rid of feudalism and despotism," Nasser publicly declared. "Should we stand silent and watch reaction defeat the revolution in Yemen?"[34] Riyadh, alarmed that the capital of the most populous nation of the Arabian Peninsula had fallen to republicanism, began arming the royalists, while Cairo sent a growing number of Egyptian troops to defend the republican government. The threat Nasserism posed to the Saudi monarchy was driven home when three Saudi pilots defected with their plane, carrying arms intended for the Yemeni royalists, to Egypt, leading the Saudi government to ground its air force.[35] Overlooking the Saudis' concerns, however, Kennedy personally advised Saudi crown prince Faisal, the resolute and conservative half brother of Saud, not to waste Riyadh's limited resources on the conflict in North Yemen, as they were needed to institute reforms at home to prevent domestic unrest.[36]

To appease Kennedy, Faisal issued a ten-point domestic reform program and then proceeded to largely ignore it. Seizing on the fear that had gripped the Saudi leadership after the events in North Yemen, Faisal also increasingly consolidated power within the royal family at Saud's expense, who had periodically aligned himself with liberalizing reformers. Kennedy had hoped to withhold US arms to Saudi Arabia as leverage until Riyadh progressed in its reforms. Egyptian warplanes increasingly violated Saudi airspace in Egypt's efforts to support the Yemeni republicans, however, leading Kennedy to decide that he had to militarily support the Saudis without strings attached. The North Yemen Civil War thus led Kennedy to abandon his rapprochement with Nasser and instead unconditionally support Riyadh. Lyndon Johnson, who held Nasser in low esteem, further increased US cooperation with Saudi Arabia upon assuming the presidency after Kennedy's assassination in November 1963. A year later, Faisal forced Saud into exile and formally assumed the title of king.[37]

Faisal, in part responding to the Egyptian military buildup in Yemen, proceeded to rapidly grow the Saudi military, primarily through the purchase of British and US arms. Saudi arms purchases from the United States jumped in 1965 and increased each year of the decade after that. The Saudis updated their air force and missile defenses, increased the motorization of the army, and established new military bases. Faisal also increased arrests of suspected leftist and minority Shia dissidents, and in 1964 he established new antistrike laws providing for up to fifteen years' imprisonment. Despite the rocky start under Kennedy, the Saudi–US alliance reached an unprecedented level of cooperation under the Johnson administration.[38]

For Riyadh and Washington, events in the Arabian Peninsula during the mid-1960s continued to generate concern. The United States still looked to the United Kingdom to militarily defend the peninsula and its adjacent waterways, but the remaining string of British military bases and protectorates in the region were increasingly under assault by leftist nationalists. Inspired in part by the establishment of the republic in North Yemen, leftists began an armed struggle to end direct British rule in South Yemen in 1963 and indirect British rule in monarchical Oman in 1965.[39] In North Yemen the civil war continued, and while the Saudi-funded Yemeni royalists persisted in guerilla warfare that drained Egypt of both funds and domestic support, Sanaʻa came under increasing Egyptian control, and Cairo came under increasing Soviet influence. In 1965 Egyptian troops in North Yemen peaked at around seventy thousand, supported by Soviet arms and personnel.[40] The Saudi government felt compelled to undertake mass arrests and deportations of Yemeni migrant workers it feared sympathetic to republicanism. In late 1966 and early 1967, the Arabian Peninsula People's Union, an organization operating out of North Yemen and claiming to represent the Saudi people, carried out within Saudi Arabia up to thirty bombings against US and Saudi governmental and military instillations. The Saudis publicly executed seventeen accused perpetrators and deported hundreds more Yemenis.[41] Meanwhile, in Libya, Egyptian radio broadcasts and migrant teachers inculcated Pan-Arabism. The monarchy's financial corruption and US alliance increasingly angered Libyans as the economic benefits of their country's oil boom eluded them.[42]

Just as it had done with Saudi Arabia, the Kennedy administration, in keeping with its faith that modernization programs could help countries avoid a radical revolution like the one that had occurred in neighboring Iraq, pressed Iran to institute domestic reforms to better secure its regime. The shah responded in 1963 by launching the White Revolution, a state-led development and social engineering program that furthered his authoritarian reach into Iranian society. When Iranian troops killed hundreds of Iranian protesters that year, the Kennedy administration largely accepted the shah's claims that the violent crackdown was necessary to preserve his modernization agenda against communists and reactionary clerics.[43] This enabled Washington to disregard the significance of leftist and Islamist opposition to the shah in Iran. An important leader of the Islamist opposition was the Ayatollah Ruhollah Khomeini, a strong-willed and respected Shia religious leader who opposed the shah's Westernizing reforms and strengthening of relations with the United States and Israel. When the shah signed an agreement giving US soldiers, civilian staff, and family members of military missions diplomatic immunity as a quid pro quo for continued US arms, loans, and training of the Iranian armed forces in October 1964, Khomeini publicly declared that "the [Iranian] government has sold our independence, reduced us to the level of a colony. . . . If the religious leaders have influence, they will not permit this nation to be slaves of Britain one day, and America the next."[44] The shah responded by exiling Khomeini, who resettled in Iraq, where he conducted a media campaign against the shah and maintained coordination with his sizable supporters still in Iran.

The shah, meanwhile, was increasingly frustrated by the Johnson administration's efforts to limit his arms purchases due to its concerns about the Iranian government's finances. In 1966 the shah secured a US pledge to sell Iran McDonnell Douglas F-4E Phantom jet fighters, one of the most sophisticated planes in the world at that time, but initially fewer in number than he had requested. The shah responded by reaching an agreement with Moscow to purchase several squadrons of MiG-21 jet fighters, prompting the Johnson administration to increase the number of F-4s for sale to Iran in exchange for the canceling of the Soviet deal.[45] The experience reaffirmed the shah's desire for greater oil revenues to escape the restraints imposed by US aid to Iran. Later that year the shah complained to the US ambassador that the failure of the MNOCs to prioritize the expansion of Iranian oil production and profits showed "that Western oil companies and [governments] fail to appreciate [the] role Iran can and must play in" the Middle East.[46] The Saudis, meanwhile, jealously competed with Iran for market share.[47] The rivalry between the Iranians and Saudis, the two largest exporters within OPEC, exemplified the divisions within the organization and the frustrations of its members in failing to raise the rate of profit from oil sales.[48]

In 1962 the Kennedy administration approved the first major US arms sale to Israel, a delivery of Raytheon Hawk surface-to-air missiles. The Johnson administration further increased US military ties with Israel, and by 1965 the United States had become Israel's primary source of foreign arms as well as a significant source of aid. Multiple factors motivated the increase in US arms transfers to Israel under the two administrations: attempting to increase US leverage over Israeli foreign policy, encouraging Israel not to develop a nuclear arms program, offsetting ongoing Soviet arms sales to Egypt and Syria, and maintaining Jewish American votes for the Democratic Party.[49] Whatever Washington's rationale, however, the increase in US support to Israel alarmed Riyadh. "Those who opposed our principles continued to argue that U.S. assistance to Israel was proof of American opposition to all Arabs," Faisal told Johnson while visiting Washington in 1966. "This greatly hindered the actions of states which in fact would desire to cooperate with America." Faisal noted that he himself "had undergone tremendous abuse in the [Arab world] for his continuing with his visit to the U.S. in the face of the recent U.S. announcement of its arms sale to Israel. It was claimed that this proved that [he] and the U.S. were conspiring against Arab interests."[50]

Meanwhile, tensions between Israel and its Arab neighbors steadily escalated in the mid-1960s. Border clashes, Palestinian guerilla raids into Israel conducted from Arab states, and retaliatory Israeli strikes generated fear and anger on both sides, compounded by growing economic and political crises in Egypt, Israel, Jordan, and Syria. These came to a head in May 1967 when Nasser massed Egyptian troops near the Israeli border and declared a blockade of Israeli shipping in the Straights of Tiran. In response, Israeli military leaders pressed Israeli prime minister Levi Eshkol to commence a first strike against Egypt. Responding to inquiries from Israel on such a move, the Johnson administration sent mixed signals that increasingly tended toward a "yellow light." On June 5 Israeli armed forces launched a full assault on Egyptian forces, beginning the 1967 Arab-Israeli War.[51]

The Israeli military quickly devastated the Egyptian air force and routed Egyptian armies. When Jordan and Syria attacked Israel in solidarity with

Egypt, Israeli forces promptly defeated their militaries as well. Within six days the war was over, with the three Arab states accepting a cease-fire while Israeli armies possessed the formerly Egyptian-held Gaza Strip and Sinai Peninsula, Jordanian-held West Bank (including East Jerusalem), and Syrian-held Golan Heights, ending the territorial status quo of the last nineteen years. One million Palestinians in the occupied territories suddenly came under Israeli rule. The Israeli public was ecstatic over its stunning victory, while the Arab world experienced a severe psychological blow. The defeat especially undercut Arab confidence in Nasser and his program of secular Pan-Arabism.

The 1967 war caused unprecedented strain in US relations with the Arab world. Many Arab leaders and average citizens attributed Israel's victories to years of US diplomatic, economic, and military support to the Zionists. Throughout the Arab world, anti-US protests erupted. Algeria, Egypt, Iraq, Mauritania, Sudan, Syria, and North Yemen all broke diplomatic relations with the United States. While the Arab monarchies did not break relations with Washington, their rulers were angered by US support for Israel and fearful it could generate popular revolts against them. On the second day of the war these factors led Kuwait, Libya, and Saudi Arabia to join Algeria and Iraq in banning the sale of their oil to the United States and the United Kingdom, first to induce Western support for the Arab position in the conflict, and then to compel Western pressure on Israel to withdraw from Arab territory after the war ended. Arab oil exports were further disrupted or reduced by strikes and sabotage conducted by Arab workers, the closure of Arab oil pipelines, and Nasser's closure of the Suez Canal. Yet despite the growing importance of Arab supplies to the world oil market over the past two decades, the readily available supply of non-Arab oil was still sufficient to offset Arab production cuts, and the MNOCs diverted non-Arab oil to the United Kingdom and United States while redirecting Arab oil to make up the difference. Enduring a loss of revenue with no results to show for it, in September the Arabs lifted the embargo. Global conditions were still not yet ripe for the MENA states to dramatically alter the international political and economic order via the "oil weapon." But the desire of many Arabs to do so was manifest.[52]

From the 1930s to the mid-1950s US oil companies and Washington increasingly established a cooperative empire in the MENA in collaboration with local monarchs and European allies, one predicated on Western control over MENA oil and its global sale at relatively low prices. This order faced increasing challenges from the mid-1950s to the mid-1960s, however. US-allied Arab and Iranian monarchies increasingly organized to press for greater oil revenues to increase their still relatively minor economic and political power. Meanwhile, many nationalists escalated their opposition to US influence in the MENA and achieved withdrawals from US empire in countries such as Egypt and Iraq. After 1967 the persistence of the Arab-Israeli conflict, the hamstringing of US power caused by the Vietnam War, the continuing decline in British power, and a rapid shift to global overdemand for oil would combine to significantly challenge and transform US empire in the MENA.

Chapter 2

The Road to the Oil Shock

As the summer of 1973 drew to a close, US president Richard Nixon faced anger and distrust from the US public not only because of the unfolding Watergate scandal but perhaps even more so because of high rates of inflation and the contributing factor of rising oil prices. In a September Gallup poll asking Americans to name the number-one problem facing the United States, an unprecedented 89 percent said "the high cost of living."[1] Looking abroad, Nixon likewise confronted seemingly intractable problems, including a surge of threats from both hostile and allied Arab governments that they would cut oil production, and thus the West's supply of energy, if the United States did not move closer to Arab positions on the Arab-Israeli conflict. On September 5, Nixon gave a news conference on these issues. Nixon declared that he had given "highest priority" to resolving the Arab-Israeli conflict. However, Nixon also issued a warning to Arab governments considering continued increases in oil prices or expropriations of Western oil companies. "Oil without a market, as Mr. Mossadegh learned many, many years ago, doesn't do a country much good," Nixon said. "We and Europe are the market."[2]

Nixon's reference to the successful oil purchase boycott led by the MNOCs against Iran after it nationalized the AIOC, as well as the unspoken reminder of Mosaddeq's overthrow in a US-backed coup, would have been instantly recognizable to MENA leaders. Nixon's warning to the OECs of the MENA in the 1973 press conference was clear: if the governments of oil-exporting nations went too far in threatening Western access to cheap oil, the United States would inflict dire economic and political punishment on them. Yet whether

Nixon made his threat due to ignorance or his penchant for aggressive bluffing, the global circumstances that had facilitated Mosaddeq's overthrow in 1953 had now largely disappeared.

From 1970 to 1973 the relationship between the United States and the oil-rich MENA countries began to transform as the latter seized on a tightening global petroleum market to repeatedly raise the price of oil and significantly increase their petrodollar profits. The Nixon administration tolerated the initial, relatively modest price increases in MENA petroleum while failing to implement policies that would reverse the trend toward Western dependency on OPEC oil. The increase in petrodollar revenues facilitated a new role for oil-rich, US-allied MENA countries within the system of US cooperative empire, wherein these nations, above all Iran, purchased exponentially larger sums of US arms so as to serve as the new primary military defender of Western interests in the region as British forces withdrew. The United States had previously armed the militaries of oil-rich MENA allies, but the responsibilities of these countries and the lucrativeness of weapons sales to them for US corporations rose to a fundamentally different scale in the early 1970s.

Yet while the Nixon administration accepted a moderate increase in the cost of MENA oil, it opposed a major price rise that would harm the Western economies. Furthermore, it expected MENA allies to not challenge key US strategic prerogatives. In October 1973, the oil-rich countries would defy the United States on both counts. First, the Gulf countries would unilaterally raise the price of their oil by 70 percent, the opening salvo in a series of price hikes that ended the period of cheap global petroleum for over a decade. Second, the Arab countries, including US allies, openly threatened US influence in the MENA by launching an impactful oil embargo against the United States in response to its support for Israel during the latest Arab-Israeli war. These two overlapping events attacked the foundations of US cooperative international empire in the MENA and the larger geopolitical and economic order the United States had instituted over much of the world since World War II.

In late August 1967 the Arab League convened at Khartoum. The recent war with Israel had ravaged Egypt's economy, which was already weakened by the ongoing intervention in North Yemen and the cessation of US aid by the Johnson administration. Urgently needing to rebuild the Egyptian army but lacking the funds to do so, Nasser agreed to a rapprochement with Riyadh, acceding to Saudi demands that Egypt promptly withdraw its forces from Yemen (which it would do before year's end) in exchange for a pledge of regular distributions of aid from the oil-rich Arab countries to Egypt to strengthen it

vis-à-vis Israel.[3] Saudi Arabia, Kuwait, and Libya thereafter provided roughly
$250 million in grant aid annually to Egypt.[4] These funds helped Egypt pay
for a massive resupply of Soviet arms, which was accompanied by roughly four
thousand Soviet military advisers by the end of 1967.[5] The Khartoum Summit thus achieved greater unity among the previously feuding Arab powers,
but it also signified the geopolitical decline of Egypt and corresponding rise
of Saudi Arabia, as petrodollars became increasingly important for the continuation of Arab resistance to Israel.

Additional money committed by the oil-rich Arab states at Khartoum was
soon sent to Palestinian resistance groups. Private funding for Palestinian militias also came from wealthy citizens of, and the significant number of Palestinian laborers in, the Arab Gulf countries, whose incomes were either directly
or indirectly tied to the oil industry. Petrodollars served as the primary source
of funding for Palestinian groups, which increased their diplomatic and guerilla warfare attacks on Israel after 1967. Most Palestinian parties confederated
under the Palestine Liberation Organization (PLO), which under the leadership of Yasser Arafat obtained an increased international profile. The violent
resistance of the fedayeen (Palestinian guerillas) against Israel, widely covered
in Arab media, captured the imagination of many Gulf Arabs. At the same time,
however, the predominantly leftist, revolutionary ideology of the Palestinian
resistance, including for a minority Marxism, gave some Arab royals pause.
Many alleged the Arab monarchs provided aid to the Palestinians as a form of
protection pay from their acts of sabotage, terror, or assassination rather than
from political conviction. Whether for positive or negative reasons, however, the
oil-rich Arabs increasingly provided petrodollars to and political support for
the PLO.[6]

As the Gulf Arabs increased their support for the Palestinians, the British
further decreased their presence in the Arabian Peninsula. London determined
that the British military presence in the region was a counterproductive expense, endangering British interests in the region by inflaming Arab nationalist sentiment against regional allies while feeding rising British leftist protests
against the costs of empire. In November 1967 the British completed their
withdrawal from South Yemen despite knowing this would allow hostile leftists to take power. In January 1968, London announced it would grant independence to its last few protectorates in the Arabian Peninsula and withdraw
its remaining military forces from the region by the end of 1971. The Johnson
administration expressed outrage and then resignation that the British would
no longer provide a military defense of the Persian Gulf, reducing the Western
military presence there to only a US seaplane tender and two aging destroyers.

Mired in the Vietnam War, Washington concluded that it could not militarily replace the British in the region and thus would have to rely on local states to provide security for US interests.[7] In its final year, the Johnson administration, closely following London's lead, worked to establish a balance of power and regional cooperation between Iran and the Arab Gulf monarchies, believing this to be a prerequisite to local stability and a common defense of the region against Soviet influence.[8]

The year 1968 also witnessed an increasingly divided US public over the Vietnam War. By the end of that year the war had cost the United States more than twenty-five thousand lives and over $100 billion. A significant antiwar movement bred a growing radicalism within the US left and undermined the idea that the United States must contain communism abroad. Average Americans became increasingly polarized over the war, with those on both sides of the issue frustrated by the seeming endless nature of the conflict. As the ability of the United States to exert power overseas, and even the logic of doing so, fell into question, the Soviet Union reached a parity in nuclear arms, and its prospects of exporting communism to Third World countries like Vietnam appeared enhanced, alarming defenders of US Cold War orthodoxy.[9] In part due to concerns about the Vietnam War, in November Americans narrowly elected Republican candidate Richard Nixon to the presidency.

Nixon, a tenacious and ambitious man, had, through hard and often duplicitous work, risen from modest means in California to leader of the Republican Party, serving as a congressman, senator, and vice president under Eisenhower before securing the presidency. By inclination and circumstance, Nixon began his administration focused on foreign affairs. Nixon firmly believed that the primary job of the president was to conduct foreign policy, and that the United States must play an active, dominant role in international relations to secure US interests. Nixon entered the White House determined to extricate the United States from Vietnam while preserving the credibility of the US military and geopolitical alliances that upheld the larger system of US empire. For his primary assistant in conducting foreign policy, Nixon chose Henry Kissinger, a Jewish German refugee of Nazi persecution turned Harvard international relations professor, as his national security advisor. Both Nixon and Kissinger recognized that the United States, while still the dominant world power, had experienced a relative decline in military and economic power vis-à-vis both its adversary the Soviet Union and its allies in Western Europe and Japan as these regions had recovered from World War II. The Vietnam War had likewise demonstrated the limits of US power and had generated doubts about Washington's ability to uphold its foreign commitments.

Nixon and Kissinger sought to address these concerns while maintaining US dominance in the world. Containing the Soviet Union remained a primary goal for Nixon and Kissinger, but they also sought a good working relationship with Soviet general secretary Leonid Brezhnev and a lessening of tensions with Moscow, dubbed détente, that could help avert crises, lower US military costs, and aid in a favorable resolution of the situation in Vietnam. Western Europe and Japan remained key allies but were also watched over lest they develop independent policies that undercut US supremacy within the alliance.[10]

In the Third World, Nixon and Kissinger sought a shifting of the human and financial costs of regional defense away from the United States and to local allies. This strategy was rooted both in the view that the United States overextending itself in places like Vietnam needlessly sapped US strength and in the reality that the relative power of the United States had gradually declined since World War II. The United States would continue to defend Third World allies from a direct Soviet assault, as well as provide expertise and aid to allied countries. A greater share of the human and financial costs of defense, especially against internal or regional threats, would be placed on the local allies themselves, however, in order to better ration US power. This policy became known as the Nixon Doctrine. The Nixon administration considered the MENA as a region vital to US security but also prone to crisis.[11] In keeping with the Nixon Doctrine, the new administration sought to avoid increasing the US military presence in the MENA and to instead rely on regional allies to protect US interests.

By 1969 the shah felt more assured of his throne and believed he could soon establish Iran as a major global power. The securing of the F-4 deal and the closure of the US Agency for International Development office in Iran in November 1967 symbolized the increase in Iranian independence to manage its own military and development.[12] The shah now sought to prove that Iran no longer needed "Great Power tutelage" and to establish for his country military dominance over the Middle East and a European standard of living.[13] With the British withdrawing from the Persian Gulf and Iran's economy growing at nearly 10 percent annually, the shah felt poised to make his dream a reality.[14]

In the shah's view, only two obstacles remained to be overcome in establishing Iran as the dominant power in the Persian Gulf. First, the shah sought to persuade Nixon to end the Johnson administration's policies of limiting US arms sales to Iran and seeking a balance of power between Iran and the Arab Gulf monarchies, and instead secure US support for Iran as regional hegemon. The shah quickly gained ground on this front, as he deftly spoke to Nixon and Kissinger's geostrategic outlooks, convincing them that Arab radicals, particularly the new Baathist regime in Baghdad headed by President Ahmad Hassan al-Bakr that had seized power in a coup in 1968, threatened to vastly expand Soviet influence in the region and overthrow the remaining Arab monarchies, and that only Iran had the military capabilities and political will to act against such threats.[15] The second obstacle was that, despite Iran's high rate of economic growth, the Iranian government's spending far outpaced revenues, hindering the shah's ambitions for a simultaneous expansion of the Iranian military and economy. In March 1969 the shah repeatedly lamented in private to his minister of court Asadollah Alam about the Iranian "government's financial predicament" and the lack of funds for domestic development projects.[16] The shah needed more funds, and he sought them from oil sales, which constituted over half of the Iranian government's revenue.[17] Iranian oil production was still controlled by the IOP, however, and it resisted the shah's push for greater production and sharing of revenues.[18] Here, too, the shah looked to Nixon for assistance, but when the two met in April, Nixon maintained that he had no influence over the oil companies.[19]

Undeterred, the shah looked to US corporations outside of the IOP to support his bid for an increase in oil sales. US weapons, aerospace, automotive, electrical, and engineering companies all stood to gain if the economies of the MENA grew and were able to purchase more of their goods and services. Rising oil revenues for the MENA could thus benefit these US industries, and some US companies joined the shah in lobbying on behalf of higher oil revenues for Iran. General Electric wanted Iran to hire its services to install a massive electrification program that would include the construction of two new power plants for $100 million. At the same time, Planet Oil and Mineral Corporation, a smaller US company excluded from the IOP, sought to break into the Iranian oil extraction market.[20] Since 1959 the United States had imposed a quota system that limited the amount of foreign oil imports in order to protect domestic petroleum companies from competition by more cheaply produced foreign oil.[21] The shah, General Electric, and Planet Oil collaborated to persuade the US government to increase Iran's quota of oil exports to the United States by two hundred thousand barrels a day. The additional oil would be extracted by Planet Oil and enter the US market; in return, Iran would guarantee that all revenue earned from the oil quota increase would be placed in block accounts in New York and then spent solely on US exports like General Electric's electrification work. Herbert Brownell, an attorney general under Eisenhower, represented Planet Oil and used his connections to pitch the proposal to the Nixon administration. Writing to Kissinger in March 1969,

Brownell argued that the plan would measurably alleviate the deteriorating US trade balance while supporting "the maintenance of Iran as a bulwark of freedom" in a strategically vital region.[22]

The shah and his corporate allies' hopes for an increase in Iran's oil exports to the United States were encouraged by the White House's decision to appoint a cabinet task force to review and possibly increase US oil import quotas. Nixon showed minimal interest in economic issues beyond maintaining his political popularity; he once dismissively described economic policy as "building outhouses in Peoria."[23] Nixon soon privately shelved the possibility of liberalizing the quotas when he determined that increasing oil imports would be too politically costly with independent Texan oil producers.[24] Nixon did not want to upset the shah, however, and when Nixon and the shah met in October 1969, later records show the shah left understanding that Nixon would do everything he could to increase Iran's import quota.[25] Nixon had already written to Kissinger that he wanted increased Iranian revenue to come from the IOP rather than through an increase in Iran's quota, however, so it appears that Nixon may have overstated to the shah his willingness to help on the matter.[26] Nixon had also pledged to the shah, in this case with greater sincerity, that he would pressure the IOP to increase Iran's revenues.[27]

The shah continued to press the United States in the following months. Worried that Nixon might adopt an oil quota system that favored the Arab states over Iran, the shah argued to US ambassador Douglas MacArthur II in November that a "substantial part of money US oil companies paid for Kuwait [sic], Saudi, and Libyan oil went to Egypt to finance Nasser's vilification of the U.S.," which reminded the shah of US commercial interests before World War II exporting "tremendous amounts of scrap iron to Japan only to have it returned in finished form at Pearl Harbor."[28] In December the shah wrote to Nixon and continued his swipes at the Arab states, criticizing the consortium members for favoring increased production in "countries which do not need the money and which in many cases have several hundreds of million pounds deposited in foreign banks" while Iran needed to pay for economic and military development to counter increasing radical threats to the Gulf as the British withdrew from the Middle East.[29] But in January 1970 the Nixon administration found that its talks with the MNOCs to increase Iran's revenue were going nowhere, and informed Brownell that there would be no movement on Planet Oil's proposal "in the near future" and Iran should not expect support from the cabinet task force on oil imports.[30] When in February the shah conveyed to Nixon that he "was deeply disturbed" by Nixon's apparent "deception," Nixon attempted to bluff the MNOCs into helping Iran with the threat of an unfavorable decision on import quotas, a plan he had already decided to table, but the gambit does not appear to have been effective.[31] In April and again in July, Nixon was forced to write to the shah expressing sympathy for the shah's goals but admitting that an increase in Iran's quota would not be possible anytime soon.[32] The effort by Iran and its US corporate allies in non-oil sectors to achieve an increase in Iranian oil revenues had limited results in the first two years of the Nixon presidency. While valuing Iran as a client state, most of the members of Nixon's administration, including Nixon himself, were unwilling to take significant steps to increase Iran's oil revenues, and the IOP maintained a strong negotiating position against the shah.

Some of the key elements of the coming petrodollar economy, however, were taking form. US companies were increasingly noticing Iran as a potentially lucrative market if oil revenues went up, and some of them were forming networks with each other and with the Iranian government to try to capitalize on future opportunities. Nixon, moreover, while unwilling to take steps that might incur him a political cost, was sympathetic to the shah's desire for increased oil revenues.

The Nixon administration similarly confronted growing US ties and disputes with Saudi Arabia. Nixon appreciated Riyadh's opposition to communism and Arab leftists. Furthermore, by 1969 Aramco constituted the largest single US foreign investment in the world, and Aramco's repatriated profits combined with the United States' favorable trade balance with Saudi Arabia contributed over half a billion dollars to the US current account in 1968.[33] Yet like Iran, Saudi Arabia sought greater control over its oil. When Saudi prince Fahd, a half brother and trusted minister of King Faisal, came to Washington in October 1969, Aramco and Riyadh were engaged in one of their worst disputes over revenue, and Fahd requested the US government to pressure Aramco to accede to greater Saudi profits in order for Saudi Arabia to develop its still limited infrastructure and military to better serve as a force for stability in the region.[34]

The Saudi government also feared a new wave of Arab revolutionaries, and US inattention to them, in the aftermath of 1967. To the north of Saudi Arabia, the Baathist states of Iraq and Syria developed increasingly powerful armies through the purchase of Soviet weapons. To the south in Oman and South Yemen, Chinese and Soviet-supported revolutionaries called for the overthrow of reactionary regimes across the Arabian Peninsula. The Dhofari resistance increasingly adopted Marxist ideology and threatened to topple the Omani sultanate, and in June 1969 Marxist leaders secured control of the government of South Yemen, which proceeded to break relations with the United States.[35] The Nixon administration took little direct action against these radical groups and instead looked to the British and the Saudis to contend with them. The Saudis requested to purchase F-4 fighters in response to the mounting Iraqi, Omani, Syrian, and Yemeni threats.[36]

On September 1, 1969, Libyan military officers committed to Nasserism overthrew King Idris and established a republic. Despite the United States' previous support for Idris, the Nixon administration determined that the monarchy was unlikely to be restored even with US assistance and thus quickly recognized the new Libyan government in the hope of salvaging US influence in Tripoli.[37] The failure of the United States to defend another Arab monarchy disturbed the Saudi royals, who felt "increasingly encircled by 'Communist' or pro-Soviet radical nationalist regimes while the US in their view does nothing to support its moderate Arab friends," as one state official put it.[38] Fearing a military coup, the Saudi monarchy arrested up to two thousand people, including several military officers, by the end of 1969.[39]

The House of Saud also remained deeply concerned about the Arab-Israeli conflict, both on its own merits and for the challenge it posed to the Saudi rulers' legitimacy due to their close ties with the United States, now clearly Israel's primary benefactor. When meeting with Nixon, Fahd maintained that "Saudi strength derived to [a] large extent from [the] U.S." and that Saudi Arabia would continue to fight communism "because of its interest in democracy and freedom. However, everything depended on a just and fair Middle East settlement." Nixon assured his Saudi guests that after Vietnam, the Middle East conflict was his highest priority. Saudi foreign minister Omar al-Saqqaf, who accompanied Fahd, reiterated the point, however, that the "Saudis feel time is working against them. . . . They feel a rope around their neck. A Middle East settlement cannot wait too long."[40]

The Arab-Israeli conflict also worried US financial and petroleum leaders. On December 9 some of the most prominent of these met with Nixon to express their concerns. Among them were David Rockefeller, the chairman and chief executive of the New York City–based Chase Manhattan Bank, one of the largest financial institutions in the world and highly invested in the US multinational oil industry, and brother of Nelson Rockefeller, Republican governor of New York and former patron of Kissinger's; and Ken Jamieson, the chairman of Exxon. They expressed to Nixon their concern that if the United States was not seen moving toward progress on the Arab-Israeli impasse, the moderate Arab states would get swept along by the radical Arab states and either impose restrictions on US oil concessions in the region or nationalize US oil facilities outright. They feared this might occur as soon as the next Arab League summit on December 20. They recommended that a US envoy be sent to some of the moderate Arab states and perhaps Egypt with a new peace process proposal in hand to stave off the radical threat.[41]

The men had reason to worry. Ever since the coup that overthrew Idris, Aramco employees repeatedly received letters with Libyan postage stamps that violently denounced Americans. One such letter called on Arab workers to murder Americans and destroy their property, as "it is [America] that keeps saying that Israel is American and America is Israel. That American in front of you is thus no different from any Zionist enemy. . . . Death is much better than the kind of life our American enemies want for us."[42] The US oil companies and their financial backers knew firsthand that Washington's support for Israel was generating anti-US sentiment that endangered their enormous investments and the lives of their employees. They pushed Nixon to solve the Arab-Israeli conflict so as to eliminate a major source of anti-Americanism among Arabs.

Nixon wanted to resolve the Arab-Israeli crisis, viewing it as the main reason for Soviet influence in the Arab world. But he also wanted to maintain Israel's military superiority over its Arab neighbors to demonstrate that the benefits of an alliance with Washington were superior to those of aligning with Moscow. The opposing views of Kissinger and Secretary of State William Rogers accentuated Nixon's dual outlooks. At a National Security Council (NSC) meeting held the day after the Rockefeller group met with Nixon, Rogers argued that "our position [in the Middle East] has deteriorated because we are seen as the principal supporters of Israel. . . . We are never going to escape from this problem unless we discontinue our support for Israel." Kissinger countered that it was possible the United States would not gain any significant or lasting benefits from the Arabs if Washington sacrificed its standing with Israel, and instead suggested that "the longer Israel holds its conquered Arab territory, the longer the Soviets cannot deliver what the Arabs want. As that time drags on, the Arabs must begin to conclude that friendship with the Soviet Union is not very helpful." Nixon straddled both arguments, saying that if he was going to "squeeze" Israel, the United States "ought to get as much as possible in return for it. The Soviets should not come out ahead. The Arabs played a substantial part in bringing on the [1967] war, and the Soviets should pay some price for picking up the pieces."[43]

Nixon initially put Rogers in control of a new Middle East peace initiative. In October 1969 Rogers privately put forth a plan to the Soviet Union, Egypt, Israel, and Jordan that called for an end to hostilities, a return to pre-1967 borders, and negotiations on the status of refugees and Jerusalem. Unbeknownst to Rogers, however, Nixon did not press Israel to accept the deal, and even authorized Kissinger to encourage the Israelis to publicly criticize the plan. Rogers publicly described the plan in a speech on December 9, the same day that David Rockefeller met with Nixon. To Rogers's disappointment, Egypt was noncommittal and Israel rejected the plan outright. As the stalemate persisted into early 1970, low-level fighting between Egypt and Israel escalated. Unable to counter Israeli air raids utilizing US-supplied F-4s, Egypt petitioned for and received an influx of Soviet missiles, planes, and nearly twenty thousand military advisers. These advisers included Soviet pilots who manned Egyptian planes. For the first time, Moscow extended SA-3 surface-to-air missiles and Soviet pilots to a noncommunist country. While Rogers managed to negotiate a cease-fire between Israel and Egypt, tensions remained high when, on September 28, Nasser suffered a fatal heart attack. Shocked Arab nationalists mourned the unexpected death of their battered but still reigning leader.[44]

Nasser was succeeded by his vice president, Anwar Sadat, a heretofore underestimated politician unafraid of striking out boldly on new paths. Sadat was determined to revive the languishing Egyptian economy, and to this end he began to implement a partial liberalization of Egyptian policies away from the growing autarky under Nasser, with the intent of drawing into Egypt more Western investment and Arab petrodollars. To entice a return of foreign capital, in 1971 Sadat enacted laws that protected foreign companies from nationalization and established "free zones" where they would have tax privileges.[45] That year Sadat also began to repeal numerous restrictions on the ability of Egyptian citizens to work abroad and replaced them with new incentives so as to increase the number of Egyptian migrant workers, particularly to the oil-rich Arab states, and thus increase the sum of petrodollar-funded remittances to Egypt.[46]

Sadat was also determined to regain the Egyptian territory seized by Israel in 1967. Sadat successfully solicited additional aid from the oil-rich Arab countries, which Egypt used to purchase even larger sums of Soviet arms.[47] But Sadat also pursued a rapprochement with the United States, convinced that it held the key to retrieving Egypt's lost territory. The Nixon administration continued the Johnson administration's policy of large US arms transfers to Israel and in its first four fiscal years would provide Israel with $1.7 billion in aid, up from a little over $400 million in the previous four years. Nixon also followed through on the delivery of F-4 jet fighters to Israel authorized by Johnson, providing the Israeli air force with a qualitative edge over its Arab counterparts while leaving it increasingly dependent on the United States as France, Israel's previous source for aircraft, realigned itself toward the Arab world in the mid-1960s.[48] Sadat reasoned that Israel's increased reliance on the United States meant that Washington alone held the leverage necessary to induce Israeli concessions. In May 1971 Sadat met with Rogers and told him of his desire for a land-for-peace settlement with Israel and pledged that he would expel most Soviet advisers if the United States brokered an interim agreement between Egypt and Israel. Rogers and Nixon were enthusiastic about Sadat's proposal. Moscow, however, seeking to prevent a loss of influence in Cairo, induced Sadat later that month to sign the Soviet-Egyptian Treaty of Friendship and Cooperation, which, while falling short of a mutual defense agreement, was the first such treaty of military cooperation the Soviets had extended to a noncommunist nation.[49] Israel used the treaty as part of its justification for refusing to negotiate with Sadat, and Rogers's peace initiative once again stalled.[50] In a gambit to gain greater support from Nixon vis-à-vis Israel, in May 1972 Sadat unilaterally expelled the nearly twenty thousand Soviet military advisers based in Egypt. Despite this, Nixon told Sadat that he could not seriously revive the Arab-Israeli peace process until after his reelection in November.[51]

As tension lingered in the Middle East, Western demand for MENA oil, which now provided almost all spare capacity in the global market, continued to grow. In 1971 OPEC's share of world oil production exceeded 52 percent, while the US share fell below 20 percent.[52] The countries of the MENA had finally accumulated a large enough share of the oil market, as well as enough technical expertise and political unity, to take control of the pricing and production of petroleum. Muammar Qaddafi, the new revolutionary leader of Libya, who embraced a mix of Pan-Arabism and Islamism, was the first to break through the old order. In September 1970 he negotiated a significant increase in the posted price of Libyan oil and an increase in Libya's share of revenues from 50 to 55 percent from the Western oil companies operating in his country. The shah then demanded the IOP to also increase the posted price of Iranian oil and Iran's share of revenues from 50 to 55 percent, something it acceded to in November. This proved to be a major blow to the power of the MNOCs, which then felt compelled to make the same offer to the Arab Gulf states. At the start of 1971 Libya then made new demands for an increase in price, which was soon joined by other OPEC members, setting off another tense round of negotiations between host countries and the MNOCs.[53]

The rapid escalation in oil prices and threats of oil cutoffs from OPEC members if their demands were not met prompted a response from the Nixon administration. The White House sought to attain both the uninterrupted flow of oil and a stabilization of oil prices but prioritized the former, accepting that an additional price increase was likely and more fearful of the possibility that the OECs might attempt to nationalize US oil companies. Nixon wrote to the shah expressing his concern about the situation and asked that he "contribute constructively . . . to arrive at an equitable solution to this pressing problem," arguing that "the consuming countries need a secure source of oil available on reasonable terms, and the producing countries have every right to expect a fair income from their most precious resource." Nixon sent State under secretary John Irwin to Iran, Kuwait, and Saudi Arabia, where Irwin impressed upon their leaders the need for stable prices and supply, while acknowledging that inflation likely justified some price increase for oil.[54] Seeing no way to prevent increased revenue sharing with the host governments, the MNOCs determined that their only hope for maintaining their large profits was to abandon the effort to control pricing and production and instead raise costs for consumers while placing the blame on the MENA states.[55] In February the MNOCs agreed to revenue sharing changes and an increase to the posted price that increased host governments' revenue per barrel of Gulf oil by nearly 40 percent under the Tehran Agreement, and in April to similar changes that increased host governments' revenue per barrel of Mediterranean oil by over 45 percent under the Tripoli Agreement; both agreements were to last five years and included set annual increases to meet anticipated inflation.[56]

The Tripoli and Tehran agreements temporarily stabilized the price structure, but they did not prevent the MNOCs from further losing control over the oil industries in the MENA. In between the Tripoli and Tehran meetings, Algeria unilaterally took control of over 51 percent of the French oil operations in the country. "Until now," Algerian president Houari Boumediene declared, "the riches of the third world have served the interests of the rich nations." Now, Boumediene maintained, Algerian oil wealth would be utilized to develop an egalitarian high standard of living for Algerians under socialism. Yet whether leftist republicans or conservative monarchs, leaders of OECs followed Algeria's lead in nationalizing the MNOCs operating within their countries. Over the next two years Tripoli seized controlling shares of oil companies operating in Libya, Iraq nationalized the IPC outright, and the Saudis negotiated an immediate 25 percent "participation agreement" with Aramco that would gradually give Riyadh majority control over the company by 1983. The shah likewise secured Iranian control over operations of the oil industry from the Western-dominated IOP. "Finally I won out," the shah declared. "Seventy-two years of foreign control . . . ended."[57]

As the oil market abroad began a seismic shift, Nixon put off reform of US domestic energy policies due to political considerations, a decision that compounded US vulnerability to OPEC. In March 1970 the Council of Economic Advisers warned Nixon that the United States would face a serious fuel shortage in the next five years if significant action was not taken to reform the country's energy sector, where demand would soon outstrip existing supplies. Nixon, however, believed that brownouts and heating shortages would be less politically costly to him than any effort on his part to champion new legislation to increase domestic energy production, efficiency, or conservation, so he insisted that no action be pursued until after the 1972 election. To meet growing demand, in 1972 Nixon partially relaxed the quotas limiting imported oil, which rose to 29 percent of US consumption. While only 11 percent of US oil consumption came from the Middle East that year, the United States no longer maintained energy production levels that could offset a cutoff of MENA supply.[58]

Other economic decisions made by the Nixon administration contributed to the US economy's vulnerability to foreign oil price increases and inflation. By the end of 1970 the US unemployment rate breached 6 percent.[59] Fearing for his reelection prospects in 1972, Nixon over the next two years cut taxes and increased government spending to promote economic growth and higher employment while implementing wage and price controls to inhibit inflation. These measures largely appealed to voters, but the combination of high economic growth and wage-price controls masked rising inflationary pressures and discouraged conservation of oil.[60]

Additionally, in August 1971 the Nixon administration ordered a suspension of the convertibility of the dollar into gold and imposed a 10 percent import tax. Since the end of World War II the United States had linked the value of the dollar to gold, with other Organisation for Economic Co-operation and Development (OECD) members fixing their currencies' exchange rates to the dollar by 1958, an order called the Bretton Woods system. The maintenance of fixed exchange rates had relied in part on capital controls imposed by the United States and allied nations. By the 1960s, however, the dollar had become overvalued. Over the decade, banks outside the United States in countries with fewer regulations on foreign currencies acquired and lent growing sums of dollars, a system called the Euromarkets (the system had its origins in European financial centers like London, hence the "Euro" part of the name, but quickly came to include banks operating outside Europe as well). By the early 1970s the massive volume of dollars within the Euromarkets left the US currency subject to increasing speculative attacks by investors, increasing the cost of US and allied efforts to maintain the dollar's value. At the same time the overvalued dollar hurt the competitiveness of US exports, which already faced increased competition from the recovered industries of Western Europe and Japan. Nixon believed a decline in US exports portended a decline in US economic supremacy, and thereby US geopolitical supremacy, and he tired of the domestic costs of defending the dollar against speculators. Nixon thus sought to compel Western European countries and Japan to negotiate a devaluation of the dollar vis-à-vis their currencies in exchange for the lifting of the import tax, something they reluctantly acceded to in December, when the dollar was devalued on average by about 10 percent against the major OECD currencies. Nixon's decisions marked a shift in US policy away from accepting domestic sacrifices to safeguard allies' economies and toward emphasizing commercial competition with Western Europe and Japan, a precedent that would have important ramifications in the OECD's looming showdown with OPEC.[61]

The increase in oil prices combined with continuing growth in market share brought unprecedented wealth to the oil-rich countries of the MENA, the two largest exporters being Saudi Arabia and Iran. Oil revenues for Saudi Arabia in 1972 hit $2.7 billion, triple the amount of 1969; Iran's oil revenue grew at nearly the same rate, hitting $2.4 billion in 1972.[62] The shah was "in a euphoric state" at the conclusion of the Tehran Agreement, telling court minister Alam that "the oil problem is solved" and "Iran's leadership of the Middle East [is] acknowledged throughout the world."[63] The increase in petrodollars would finance the shah's increasing arms purchases, facilitating his aim of establishing Iran as the military hegemon of the Persian Gulf. Only through large military expenditures, the shah argued, would Iran avoid being "prey to a miserable little dwarf like Iraq."[64]

The increase in petrodollars to oil-rich MENA allies and their willingness, especially in the case of Iran, to use them to purchase US arms dovetailed with the Nixon Doctrine's imperative to shift the costs of defending US interests in the Third World to regional allies. On November 7, 1970, Nixon approved National Security Decision Memorandum (NSDM) 92, which reaffirmed Iran and Saudi Arabia as the United States' two key allies in the Persian Gulf.[65] By shifting the defense of the Persian Gulf to local allies, Nixon sought to reduce expenses and avoid getting drawn into future conflicts as the United States had in Vietnam.

NSDM 92 also directed the NSC to "review plans for U.S. technical and educational assistance and cultural exchange in [the Persian Gulf] through *private* as well as public programs consistent with the strategy of promoting orderly development and local responsibility for maintaining stability."[66] The Nixon administration's favoring of private over public development for oil-rich allies like Iran and Saudi Arabia reflected both its desire to reduce US foreign aid expenses without compromising US security interests and its distrust of liberal modernization programs overseen by the US government (a growing sentiment in the wake of notable liberal development failures at home within certain Great Society programs and abroad in places like Vietnam over the course of the 1960s) and favoring of neoliberal, market-driven development models instead. Iran and Saudi Arabia did not run their economies on neoliberal lines; the key sectors of the economy, including oil, as well as the development plans of the two countries were controlled by the state.[67] Iran and Saudi Arabia did, however, regularly partner with US corporations to develop their economies, something that Washington generally assumed would strengthen governments and societies; and because of rising petrodollar revenues, they were able to pay for these services without US governmental aid. From the perspective of the Nixon administration, petrodollars enabled its oil-rich MENA allies to pursue the benefits of modernization in collaboration with and to the mutual benefit of US corporations without the drawbacks of US governmental aid and management.

Nixon viewed Iran as his main military ally in the region. NSDM 92 noted that while both Iran and Saudi Arabia were important to maintaining US regional influence, "the preponderance of Iranian power" had to be recognized.[68] Meeting with Ambassador MacArthur in April 1971, Nixon asked if Iran could fill the vacuum created by the British withdrawal from the Persian Gulf, noting "that the Department of State and some of his staff had suggested that this might be placing too great a burden on Iran." MacArthur maintained that Iran was economically sound and that while "frequently the Shah tended to inflate his [military] requirements," the US embassy ensured that he did not overspend. MacArthur furthermore argued that the "U.S. could not fill the vacuum [in the Persian Gulf]. If Iran does not, then it would be filled with radical Arab states, probably supported by the Soviet Union." Nixon agreed that "Iran was a key country in the area and would serve as a crucial force during the turbulent period facing the area. . . . Our relations with the Shah must be carefully nurtured and strengthened."[69]

The Arab monarchies, however, were wary of the expansion of Iranian power as the British withdrew from the Persian Gulf. London and Washington successfully mediated most territorial disputes between Iran and the Arab states, and in 1971 the British formally granted independence to Bahrain in August and to Qatar in September. However, on November 30, on the eve of the United Kingdom granting independence to the Trucial States and with-drawing the last of its military forces from the Persian Gulf, Iran militarily seized Abu Musa and the Tunbs, small islands in the Persian Gulf claimed by both Iran and the Trucial States. The Arab nations uniformly denounced Iran's actions, but they did not attempt to retake the islands. Yet while the shah's successful use of force in resolving the territorial dispute dismayed Arab lead-ers, it impressed Nixon that Iran was the new dominant regional power.[70]

Subsequent events underscored to the Nixon administration the value of Iran. In early December war broke out between India, backed by Moscow, and Pakistan, backed by Washington. Islamabad immediately asked Nixon for arms, but while he wished to support Pakistan, he also knew the US pub-lic and Congress largely disfavored such a move. Nixon instead asked for, and received, the shah's agreement to clandestinely supply US arms in Iran to Pakistan, with the understanding that the United States would replenish Iran's arms afterward. Authorizing such a third-party transfer of US arms was illegal under US law unless the president formally declared that the United States itself would transfer the same weapon to the same country, but Nixon chose not to do this, as he wanted to avoid paying the domestic political cost.[71]

Iran's arms transfer to Pakistan was an early example of the White House utilizing the emerging petrodollar economy to flout the will of US voters and violate US law for foreign policy objectives. It also constituted an example of how rising oil wealth helped a US ally defend shared geopolitical interests with-out requiring a direct US role, as envisioned under the Nixon Doctrine. Al-though Pakistan suffered a swift military defeat at the hands of India, Nixon appreciated the shah's assistance.

The Soviet Union also increased its influence in Iraq, however. The new Baathist government in Baghdad initially sought an improvement in relations with the United States, but the Johnson administration rejected its overtures.[72] This, coupled with the Nixon administration's increase of arms to Iran, ongo-ing disputes with Iran over possession of the Shatt al-Arab and Iranian sup-port for the Kurdish insurgency in Iraq, and the IPC's refusal to meet Iraqi terms, led the Baathists to change strategy and pursue a pro-Soviet policy. The move was spearheaded by Saddam Hussein—the Iraqi vice president and cousin of President al-Bakr—a politically cunning and ruthless man whose influence within the Baath Party rivaled that of al-Bakr. The shift was welcomed by Mos-cow. In April 1972 the Soviet Union signed a treaty of friendship with Iraq similar to Egypt's and shortly thereafter approved a massive sale of arms that would double the size of the Iraqi armed forces over the next four years. Mos-cow in recent years had also advocated nationalization of MNOCs as superior to price rises and boycotts as a measure against Western imperialism, and strongly supported Iraq's decision to nationalize the IPC, providing technical support and guaranteeing purchases of Iraqi oil exports with hard currency until Iraq reestablished its sales to the broader world, thus stymieing retaliatory measures by the MNOCs.[73]

Nixon looked to Iran to replace the British as a military counterweight to Soviet-armed Iraq and a credible extension of US power in the Middle East more generally. US industries sought to sell arms and infrastructure projects to Iran. And the shah, eager to boost the capabilities of Iran's military, increasingly had revenues to make this happen. When Nixon visited Tehran in May 1972, the shah outlined the varied regional threats to Western interests that Iran was combatting: weakening Iraq by aiding the Kurdish resistance there, supporting Pakistan against Soviet-backed India, and assisting the Omani sultan Qaboos bin Said against communist-backed rebels. Iran alone could defend the Persian Gulf, the shah intimated, as the Saudi government was in "great danger" and "very backward" and its soldiers were "lousy fighters." Nixon responded by asking the shah to "protect me" and agreeing to sell Iran some of the most advanced nonnuclear US weapons, including the Grumman F-14 Tomcat and McDonnell Douglas F-15 Eagle jet fighters and laser guided missiles, to aid him in his role as the West's guardian of the Persian Gulf.[74] The shah came away from the meeting feeling Nixon had "agreed to every request that was put to him" by the monarch.[75] And Nixon kept his word, instructing Defense and State to move quickly on the sale of F-14s, F-15s, and laser guided bombs to Iran and that "decisions on the acquisition of military equipment should be left primarily to the government of Iran. If the Government of Iran has decided to buy certain equipment, the purchase of US equipment should be encouraged tactfully where appropriate."[76]

The occasion for Iran to use US arms soon emerged in Oman. In the second half of 1972, the Omani sultanate increasingly looked to Iran for support in its war against the Marxist insurgency in the Dhofar region. In August the shah utilized US planes to deliver US arms, using Lockheed C-130 Hercules military transport planes to deliver a cache of weapons to Oman, including three Bell 206 JetRanger helicopters. By October Oman secretly accepted the introduction of 150 Iranian special forces soldiers, beginning a direct role for Iran in the Dhofar conflict. The shah initiated this military intervention without seeking prior approval from Washington, as he sought to demonstrate Iranian independence in protecting its national interests in the Persian Gulf, but the move was in keeping with the logic of the Nixon Doctrine and was met with US approval.[77]

Nixon desired a strong Iran primarily for geopolitical reasons, but his administration also recognized the economic benefits of Iran's arms purchases
from the United States. One NSC staffer, Harold Saunders, noted to Kissinger
that "salesmen from England, France, and Italy [are] putting the hard sell on
the Iranian armed forces to buy their equipment" while the United States had
been "hesitant to push US equipment . . . [since] there is a point of view in
some echelons of our government to the effect that we should prevent Iran from
overbuying." But now "the President's policy is to sell Iran what Iran feels it
needs and to encourage the purchase of US equipment since that helps our
balance of payments."[78] And buy the shah did. In early 1973 Iran announced
that it would be purchasing over $2 billion in US arms that year, including
additional F-4 fighters. The shah also expressed interest in future purchases of
the F-14 fighter and Hughes Phoenix air-to-air missile.[79] Petrodollars had
facilitated the transition from Great Britain to Iran as the primary military
defender of Western interests in the Persian Gulf, and they were bringing far
larger revenues to US arms manufacturers.

While the Nixon administration viewed Iran as its primary military ally in
the region, it also worked to promote stronger ties with the Arab monarchies
to ensure US security interests, efforts facilitated by record oil profits. In the

Figure 1. The shah and Richard Nixon at the White House, July 24, 1973. Courtesy of Richard
Nixon Presidential Library.

first three years of Nixon's presidency, the value of arms sale agreements with Saudi Arabia averaged $28 million; in 1972 it hit $330 million, and in 1973 rose to $689 million.[80] In 1971 Nixon approved US weapon sales to Kuwait to counter threats posed by the British withdrawal, Iraqi claims to Kuwait, and unrest among the large Palestinian population in the country. In arguing for the arms sales, the Nixon administration noted that Kuwait's strong balance-of-payments status meant it could readily afford to make such purchases with little threat to its economy.[81] On August 18, 1972, the NSC implemented NSDM 186, which took the logic of NSDM 92 of promoting US arms sales to Iran and Saudi Arabia to enhance regional security while reducing US burdens and extended it to the lower Persian Gulf states.[82]

The benefits to the United States from increased MENA oil revenues were not limited to increased arms sales. As Kissinger noted to Nixon in a memo preparing him for his meeting with King Faisal in May 1971, Saudi Arabia was the "wealthiest state in the Arabian Peninsula," and it was hoped the Saudis could be encouraged to "be more active in support of moderate governments in Northern Yemen, Oman, and the Persian Gulf . . . [and] to continue their financial aid to [Jordan's] King Hussein." Kissinger also noted that the Saudis had been a "constant" supporter of the dollar, which would be increasingly important as Saudi Arabia's foreign exchange reserves were expected to rapidly rise as its oil profits increased.[83]

By mid-1971 many of the elements characterizing a new petrodollar order between the United States and the MENA had taken shape. US allies in the region used rising oil revenues to purchase vastly increased amounts of US arms to defend themselves and Western interests in the region. The US government likewise looked to oil-rich allies to provide financial and military assistance to oil-poor MENA allies. And the US government and some businesses increasingly looked to oil-rich MENA countries as an important supporter of US exports and the strength of the dollar.

Yet Israeli-US relations remained a significant concern for the Arab world. When Faisal met with Nixon in Washington in May 1971, the Saudi king maintained that Zionism was in alliance with communism, working to drive apart the Arab world and the United States. Faisal stated that he would accept a settlement that restored Arab-Israeli borders to their status before the 1967 war and argued that such "an expeditious settlement could deal a fatal blow to Communist influence in the area," but if the status quo was "allowed to drag on, then the Communist influence in the area will become too strong for us to cope with." Nixon told Faisal he agreed on the urgency of a settlement but offered few specifics.[84] In the following months the Arab–Israeli conflict would continue to fester.

In November 1972 Nixon won reelection with a decisive 60 percent of the popular vote. Nixon's success owed to a variety of factors. His Democratic challenger, US senator from South Dakota George McGovern, ran a politically disastrous campaign that hemorrhaged centrist Democrats. Nixon's expansionist economic policies of the past two years had brought unemployment down to 5.6 percent by the election, while Nixon's implementation of price and wage controls during the same period kept inflation in check.[85] Nixon had also significantly drawn down US ground troops from the Vietnam War by 1972, a conflict that had killed over fifty-eight thousand Americans and millions of Southeast Asians. In January 1973 the United States signed the Paris Peace Accords, securing the withdrawal of US military forces from the Vietnam War and a short-lived cease-fire between North and South Vietnam.

Yet Nixon's triumph in 1972 also contained the seeds of his political downfall, the several-year-long period of recurrent recession coupled with persistent inflation, dubbed stagflation, that would soon befall the United States, and a significant drop in Americans' confidence in their political and economic institutions. Nixon's efforts to cover up the role of his administration in the Watergate burglary began in the summer of 1972, and while the incident was little noticed during the election, by the summer of 1973 it was a major public scandal. The policies pursued in 1971 and 1972 of economic stimulus, unsustainable price and wage controls, and devaluation of the dollar all contributed to a rapid increase in inflation, with US consumer prices rising from a little over 3 percent in mid-1972 to 8 percent in mid-1973.[86] Finally, the neglect of the energy sector through 1972 set the conditions for the 1973 oil crisis.

In 1973, 16.5 percent of the world's oil was produced in the United States, while over 55 percent was produced by OPEC, which since 1969 had added Algeria, Ecuador, Nigeria, and the United Arab Emirates (UAE) to its ranks.[87] The Middle East was now the only major source of surplus capacity in a tight oil market for the noncommunist world, giving the MENA countries significant control over global supply and prices. In April, Nixon belatedly launched a two-prong effort to address the emerging energy crisis, in the domestic realm calling on Congress to pass legislation to increase US energy production, while in the international realm ending limits on US oil imports, which had now caught up in cost with controlled US domestic prices. Legislation moved slowly, however, so with US oil consumption continuing to grow while existing domestic production was already at full capacity, the difference was made up by imported oil, which rose to 35 percent of total US consumption that year, roughly half of it from the Middle East. The Nixon administration thus relied on its oil-exporting allies, particularly Saudi Arabia, which had the greatest ability to swing its levels of oil production due to its vast reserves and small governmental budget, to increase their output of oil so as to exceed global demand and thereby keep down prices. Production cuts by Iraq, Kuwait, and Libya, combined with rising US imports, however, kept global petroleum supplies tight and market oil prices rising.[88]

As the sparsely populated Arab countries increasingly accumulated petrodollars faster than they could spend them, their monetary reserves ballooned, making the financial decisions of these nations increasingly impactful globally. The system of fixed exchange rates reached in December 1971 by the Western countries suffered repeated setbacks as speculators abandoned currencies they judged to be overvalued. In June 1972 these speculative attacks led the British to float the value of sterling; in January 1973 Italy floated the lira for the same reason. In February speculators began fleeing the dollar, prompting the United States, Japan, and the Western European countries to negotiate a devaluation of the dollar of about 10 percent. This failed to stop speculation against the dollar, and on March 1 holders of dollars flooded the West German foreign exchange markets with $2.7 billion that they sought to convert to deutsche marks in anticipation of a further devaluation of the US currency. Notably, an estimated 25 percent of these dollars came from MENA central banks. Petrodollars were now playing a major role in the volatility of the international monetary system. Furthermore, the events of March 1 led US, European, and Japanese leaders to accept the floating of the dollar. While many at the time anticipated and desired that the dollar would soon be restored to a fixed rate, this would not occur. March 1973 would mark the effective end of the Bretton Woods system, a result brought about in part by petrodollar flows.[89]

As Arab monetary reserves continued their rapid growth, their potential impact on the international monetary system grew apace, a fact increasingly discussed in the West in the aftermath of the March run on the dollar. Secretary of the Treasury George Shultz, a neoliberal-oriented economist, welcomed the end of fixed currencies, believing the market would more efficiently determine the value of moneys, a stance at odds with most other countries' finance ministers and even many officials within the Nixon administration. In mid-1973 Shultz likewise argued that Gulf Arab monetary reserves, projected to reach $100 billion by 1980, could be effectively managed by financial markets. Shultz reasoned that Arab investors would increasingly seek long-term investments rather than short-term holdings so as to profit from a higher rate of return. This would provide useful capital to Western industries while preventing rapid movements of Arab petrodollars that could destabilize currencies. Shultz also contended that the United States "can compete with any nation in investment opportunities" and that petrodollar funds could improve the US balance of payments.[90]

Others were not as sanguine. The staff of the NSC cited "the potential disruption to the world monetary systems which large accumulated Arab reserves could cause" as one of the reasons to pursue low oil prices. Gottfried Haberler of the American Enterprise Institute warned Shultz that the oil-importing nations might soon engage in trade wars in an attempt to pay for the rising cost of energy. Others cautioned that if Western economies and currencies weakened, the Arabs might reduce production of oil rather than acquire surplus petrodollars that had no profitable place to go. "It may be that oil reserves in the ground are more valuable in the long run than financial reserves in a foreign bank," Saudi deputy minister of petroleum Prince Saud bin Faisal publicly proclaimed. Even Shultz privately described the projected growth of Saudi monetary reserves as "startling" to Nixon in April, and he promoted US policies that would bring down the price of oil and thereby the "rent" acquired by Arab producers.[91]

To address both oil prices and petrodollar flows, Treasury and the NSC embraced a strategy of interdependence, particularly with Saudi Arabia. Under this logic, the United States would promote deeper Saudi-US military ties and Saudi investments in the US economy and purchases of US goods and services. These would bring significant geopolitical and developmental benefits to Saudi Arabia, but Washington would also "convince the Saudis that oil production levels cannot be allowed to fall short of U.S.-Allied needs without disrupting other elements of our relations they value," explained an August NSC memorandum for Kissinger. At the same time, such Saudi investments and purchases would help ensure that Arab petrodollars would return to the US economy and stabilize the international monetary system. Petrodollar interdependence would thus support US energy and financial interests. There was one area where the NSC sought to avoid linkage, however, in keeping with Kissinger's strategic outlook. "Insofar as possible, *we should try to disassociate oil from our* Israeli policy," the NSC argued.[92]

At the same time, Saudi Arabia increasingly attempted to use both its growing dominance in the global oil market and its new petrodollar wealth as leverage with the United States. In September 1972 the Saudis proposed a special oil sale arrangement with the United States, similar to the one previously proposed by Iran, where the revenues of increased Saudi oil exports to the United States would be guaranteed to be spent or invested there. Rogers noted that given world market conditions, there was little to no market incentive for the Saudis to secure sales to the United States when it could easily sell the oil closer to home. Rather, the Saudis appeared to be attempting to increase Saudi Arabia economic integration with, and thus influence over, the United States.[93]

Nixon ignored the proposal, but the United States' economic interdependence with Saudi oil and petrodollars grew regardless. When Zaki Yamani, the urbane Saudi minister of petroleum and trusted adviser of Faisal, and his deputy, Prince Saud bin Faisal, met with Kissinger in April 1973, Yamani warned that while Saudi Arabia had increased its oil production beyond its own needs due to "a sense of responsibility" to meet rising Western demand and keep prices down, the Saudis were isolated and "under heavy pressure from the rest of the Arab world" to reverse course and allow a doubling of oil prices until the United States addressed Arab concerns regarding Israel, and he was not sure how long they could withstand this pressure. Yamani implied that such an increase in oil prices would be a major drain on US balance of payments, and Saud added that "other Arabs—even Europeans talking to Saudi Arabians—asked why Saudi Arabia should only talk with the US and only invest its oil revenues in the US." Both Saudi oil production and petrodollar flows to the United States were at risk, Yamani and Saud implicitly threatened, if the United States did not change course on the Arab-Israeli conflict.[94]

In early 1973, Nixon expressed a determination to revive the Arab-Israeli peace process and to apply pressure on Israel to make concessions. The growing Watergate scandal, however, soon diverted Nixon's attention from this pursuit; indeed, the investigations into the administration's crimes increasingly distracted Nixon from policy matters generally, leaving his subordinates greater latitude, even necessity, to act independently. Kissinger, meanwhile, demonstrated no urgency in addressing the Arab-Israeli dispute. He believed the Arabs were unlikely to launch another war since they knew they would lose, and he did not think negotiations of substance could occur until after the next Israeli elections, set for late October. Kissinger held fruitless talks with Egyptian national security adviser Hafez Ismail in February, while in March news leaked that Nixon had secretly pledged to provide additional jet fighters to Israel.[95]

Contrary to Kissinger's assumptions, the United States' continued neglect of the peace process and arming of Israel pushed Sadat in late April to reach a secret agreement with Syrian president Hafez al-Asad to launch a joint Egyptian-Syrian assault on Israeli positions in the occupied territories within six months. In preparation for battle, Sadat mended relations with Moscow, securing new arms deliveries, including SCUD ballistic missiles, as well as the return of two thousand Soviet military advisers; Syria likewise received a steady flow of Soviet arms including MiG-21 jet fighters and SA-6 surface-to-air missiles. Sadat did not expect to defeat Israel but hoped a limited war would result in Egypt recovering some of its land and pride while shaking the status quo that left Israel and the United States uninterested in negotiations. Sadat knew a war with Israel was a gamble due to its military strength. Sadat also knew, however, that a continued stalemate would leave Egypt's economy on a war footing it could not afford, impoverishing his country while cultivating popular frustration about Israel's continued occupation of the Sinai, which could lead to his overthrow.[96]

While not initially privy to Sadat's war plans, Faisal was also losing patience with Washington. While he had privately pressed Nixon for action before, Faisal had resisted calls from the other Arab states to publicly raise the threat of the "oil weapon" through 1972. Angered by continued US inaction, diplomatically pressured by other Arab governments, and fearful that a lack of response would undermine the Saudi monarchy's popular legitimacy and expose the kingdom to the violence of Palestinian militants and general domestic unrest, while now possessing a new level of influence over global oil supply, in 1973 Faisal determined it was both necessary and possible to press the United States harder. Yamani's warning to Kissinger was Faisal's initial escalation. When this failed to move the Nixon administration, in May Faisal told executives of Aramco that if the United States did not soon change its policies toward Israel, "American interests [would be] thrown out of the area" and "you will lose everything." The oilmen frantically relayed the threats to the White House, but Kissinger and other administration officials viewed the warnings with skepticism. That summer Faisal made the rare move of interviewing with the US press, including the *Washington Post*, *Christian Science Monitor*, *Newsweek*, and NBC Television, where he warned that continued Saudi oil exports to and friendship with the United States were conditioned on a change in the US government's stance toward the Arab-Israeli conflict.[97]

While skepticism remained within the Nixon administration regarding Faisal's commitment to his threats, US officials did seek to reassure the king about the US commitment to Saudi Arabia. The White House tried to assuage Faisal's concerns by pointing to US military and development projects with Saudi Arabia, ventures made possible by rising petrodollar profits. In the spring of 1973 the Nixon administration made available the sale of the F-4 fighter to Saudi Arabia, a decision strongly protested by Israel as a threat to its security since the warplane had provided it with air superiority over the Arabs.[98] Writing to Faisal on August 31, Nixon sought to affirm "the constancy of our strong interest in Saudi Arabia's security and welfare," something that "our recent statement of willingness to sell F-4 Phantom aircraft whenever your air force is ready to receive them" demonstrated. Nixon further wrote that "we see Saudi Arabia on the threshold of a period of great economic growth and development and I believe American technical and managerial experience could make a significant contribution. . . . I am pleased that a number of American firms are studying possible joint ventures which would help diversify Saudi Arabia's economy."[99] The Nixon administration hoped that petrodollar projects would preserve Saudi-US relations while the peace process remained stalled.

Eight days before the transmission of Nixon's letter, however, Sadat had privately informed Faisal that Egypt might soon go to war against Israel, and Faisal had responded by pledging to deploy the oil weapon as well as increased petrodollars to Egypt to support such a campaign. On September 5 Nixon gave his press conference pledging a prioritization of the Arab-Israeli peace process while warning Arab producers against higher oil prices. Eleven days later OPEC demanded that the MNOCs conference with them in Vienna starting October 8 to renegotiate the posted price arrived at under the Tehran and Tripoli agreements.[100] Then, on October 6, Egyptian and Syrian forces attacked Israeli positions in the Sinai and the Golan Heights.

The surprise Egyptian and Syrian attack caught Israel and the United States off guard, and in the first few days the Arab armies scored impressive victories and pushed back the position of Israeli forces. For Kissinger, who had recently been confirmed as secretary of state while also retaining his job as national security advisor, the overarching concern was to prevent the regional war from escalating into a crisis between the two superpowers over their support for the opposing sides. Kissinger thus worked frantically to achieve an early cease-fire. To his dismay, on October 10 the Soviets began military resupplies to Egypt and Syria. On October 12, Israeli prime minister Golda Meir, her forces still in a precarious position, reluctantly agreed to a US proposed halt in the fighting. Sadat, however, rejected the cease-fire, instead holding out for Israeli assurances for a lasting peace settlement involving a full Israeli withdrawal from the lands it seized in the 1967 war.[101]

As the war entered its third day, the MNOCs and OPEC began their negotiations in Vienna. The MNOCs opened with a bid to increase the posted price of oil by 15 percent. OPEC countered with a proposal to raise the price by 100 percent. Stunned by the unprecedented demand, the oil company executives requested the advice of the governments of the United States, Japan, and Western Europe. Their response was to refuse anything close to OPEC's demand. On October 12 the oil executives asked OPEC for a couple of weeks to formulate a new offer. After spending the night unsuccessfully trying to force an offer out of the MNOCs, Yamani coldly told the oil executives that they would hear of his next move over the radio and then adjourned.[102]

Meanwhile, the war in the Middle East raged. The Israelis desperately called for a US military resupply of their own, warning that Israel's survival possibly depended on it. On October 12, however, the chairmen of Aramco sent a message to Nixon warning that "the terms demanded by OPEC at Vienna are of such a magnitude that their impact could produce a serious disruption in the balance of payments position of the Western world" and that they had been told that in terms of oil production cutbacks a "substantial move will be taken by Saudi Arabia and Kuwait in the event of further evidence of increased U.S. support of the Israeli position." Despite this warning, Nixon and Kissinger determined that they could not take any chance in allowing Soviet arms to bring about the defeat of a US ally, and on October 13 began an airlift of US arms to Israel via US military planes. By October 15 the Israeli army had regained the initiative on both the Egyptian and Syrian fronts. The resultant Arab outcry against the United States was intense, but Kissinger continued to profess that Saudi Arabia was unlikely to cut off US oil imports.[103]

On October 16, Arab and Iranian oil officials, including Yamani, reconvened in Kuwait City and announced that they would unilaterally raise the posted price of their oil by 70 percent. The move caused a massive increase in the price of petroleum around the world. Furthermore, by declaring the price hike unilaterally, rather than through negotiations with the MNOCs, the MENA nations had successfully inaugurated a new era in which they, not the West, controlled their oil resources. The coinciding Arab-Israeli War, by raising fear of Arab oil production cutbacks, strengthened OPEC's bargaining position. But the key factor in the new price increase was the change in the global oil market. By 1973, it was clear that the MENA countries were now the only ones with significant excess oil capacity, while global oil demand had continued to rise. At the same time, the nations of the MENA had secured the control of their oil through either nationalization or negotiated shared control with the MNOCs. In October 1973 the leaders of the oil-exporting MENA states realized they no longer needed to negotiate price or production levels with the MNOCs, and they were jubilant. "This is a moment for which I have been waiting a long time," Yamani told a fellow delegate. "We are masters of our own commodity."[104] The new terms of pricing meant the OECs would make unprecedented and enormous profits in the coming months and years. The petrodollar economy had begun in earnest.

The day after announcing their 70 percent price hike, the Iranian delegation departed Kuwait City while the Arab officials reconvened to discuss the unleashing of the oil weapon in retaliation for the US military resupply of Israel. The Iraqi delegation proposed that the Arabs unite in withdrawing all funds from US banks, nationalizing all US property in the Arab world, and instituting a total oil embargo against the United States. The other Arab participants feared such drastic economic warfare against the United States would take them into too unpredictable and dangerous territory, however, and rejected the Iraqi proposal, prompting the Iraqis to leave the meeting. The remaining Arab delegates joined in announcing that they would cut their oil production by 5 percent from September levels and continue to cut production by an additional 5 percent each month until Israel had withdrawn from all Arab territories. Countries deemed to be favoring Israel would receive steeper drops in exports, while countries deemed to be playing a positive role would receive normal export levels. Despite this proclamation, on October 19 the Nixon administration proposed a $2.2 billion aid package for Israel to Congress. Within the next two days, Abu Dhabi, Algeria, Bahrain, Dubai, Kuwait, Libya, Qatar, and most importantly Saudi Arabia ordered a complete oil embargo against the United States. The relative decline in US oil output and the 70 percent increase in the posted price for Gulf oil meant that the embargo and production cuts would cause significant economic pain in the West while unprecedented petrodollar profits would continue to be accrued by the Arab countries.[105]

While angered by the Arab embargo, Kissinger's first order of business remained the establishment of an Arab-Israeli cease-fire, something Brezhnev and Sadat increasingly desired as Israeli forces threatened to overtake the Egyptian Third Army. On October 20 the Soviet Union and the United States issued a joint resolution calling for an immediate cease-fire to be followed by vaguely defined negotiations. On October 22 Egypt and Israel accepted the cease-fire, followed by Syria the next day. But the Israeli army instituted a blockade of the Egyptian Third Army, leading Brezhnev on October 24 to message Washington with a warning that if the United States did not join in restraining Israel, the Soviets would consider a unilateral Soviet intervention. In response, Kissinger held an emergency meeting of top presidential advisers without Nixon, who was asleep and emotionally spent from escalating Watergate charges. In Nixon's name, Kissinger replied back to Moscow warning a unilateral Soviet intervention "would produce incalculable consequences" and ordered the US military to raise its nuclear threat level to make clear Washington's resolve. Fortunately, the Soviets did not escalate the crisis further, and a lasting cease-fire between Egypt and Israel took hold in the following days. Still, the war had once again demonstrated how the Arab–Israeli conflict could spiral into a superpower crisis, and it had taken the lives of an estimated twelve thousand Egyptians, three thousand Syrians, and twenty-three hundred Israelis.[106]

And while the war was over, the price of oil remained high and the Arab oil embargo against the United States in place. On October 23 Fahd had messaged Kissinger, reiterating the Saudi position that "the embargo on oil for the United States will continue in force as long as Israel occupies Arab territory beyond its borders as they existed before the June 1967 war." Three days later at a State meeting on the embargo and the larger problem of rising global oil prices, Kissinger confessed "I don't know what the answer is" before lamenting that "I know what would have happened in the nineteenth century. But we can't do it. The idea that a bedouin [sic] kingdom could hold up Western Europe and the United States would have been absolutely inconceivable. They would have landed, they would have divided up the oil fields, and they would have solved the problem."[107] Yet while Kissinger waxed nostalgic about the high imperialism of the nineteenth century, what he mourned was the end of the US imperial order in the MENA of the mid-twentieth century, one where Western power imposed low oil prices and compliant local clients. Now, unprecedented sums of petrodollars were bringing the oil-rich MENA countries significant economic and political strength, and even traditional allies like Saudi Arabia were defying US power. The old system of US empire in the MENA had been dramatically overturned. Whether the United States and any oil-exporting MENA countries could reach a new accord stood as an open, and pressing, question.

Chapter 3

Pursuing Petrodollar Interdependence

Kissinger's patience had run out. For over three months he had pressed the Saudi government to end the Arab oil embargo against the United States. In late January 1974 Kissinger thought he had obtained a solid pledge from the Saudis to this effect. But on February 3 he received word from Faisal that, due to the insistence of nearly every other Arab country, the embargo would not be lifted until Syria regained some of its territory from Israel. The next day Kissinger instructed US ambassador James Akins to tell the Saudis that "in view of the number of unfulfilled past assurances received from Saudi Arabia, we will accept no further assurances. In particular, we want no letter from [the] Saudis that [the] embargo will be lifted when [a] Syrian-Israeli disengagement agreement [is] concluded and implementation begun. You should leave [the] Saudis with no doubt that President [Nixon] will not authorize a further American effort to achieve Syrian-Israeli disengagement unless embargo and production restrictions are lifted." In a shocking breach of diplomatic protocol, Kissinger also directed Akins to tell the Saudis that unless they ended the embargo, "we would have no alternative but to make public [diplomatic] exchanges received from [the] Saudis" to prove to the world that they had assured the US government of an imminent end to the boycott.[1]

Meeting with Saudi foreign minister Omar al-Saqqaf on February 5, Akins shared Kissinger's message. Stunned, Saqqaf alternated between painfully long lapses of silence and expressions of outrage. Saqqaf told Akins that "this hostile reaction from Washington could only be interpreted as Washington's acknowledgement that it does not really intend to put pressure on Israel." He then asked Akins if "the United States had any idea of what it was about to lose. . . . Did not the United States understand what its political and economic interests were. . . . Or was it just that the United States was even more totally enslaved to Israeli wishes and Zionist pressures then [sic] the Arabs had believed?" Saqqaf declared that the Saudis would have to start a reassessment of their relationship with the United States. "The US–Saudi military association will have to be reviewed—this will cause no problem; many European countries are anxious to replace the Americans," Saqqaf stated. "Saudi Arabia will have to consider starting withdrawing its funds from American banks, and the United States can forget about participating in any of the large development programs in the Kingdom." Recalling their frequent conversations on the last of these, Saqqaf told Akins this loss particularly pained him, since he "agreed . . . completely on the desirability of forming a giant economic cooperative organization including the United States, Saudi Arabia and other Arab states. The United States would have been given a preferred position in Saudi Arabia, since it has the largest economy, the most developed technology and the most trustworthy businessmen." But Saqqaf lamented "it seemed this was now finished if the United States really is taking the position implied in the message." The Saudis would instead accept the proposals of the European countries and Japan for industrialization and investment programs in return for Arab oil. "We can live without you altogether, you know," Saqqaf concluded.[2]

The 1973 Arab-Israeli War and the Arab oil embargo against the United States caused Arab-US relations to reach a new low. The damaged ties came at a particularly bad time for the US government, as the oil shock and mounting petrodollar surpluses had significantly increased the importance of the oil-rich Arab states, especially Saudi Arabia, in determining the global supply and cost of energy and the health and shape of the international financial system. Recognizing this, the Nixon administration focused its energy on repairing relations with Riyadh, seeking to first end the Arab embargo and then to reintegrate the Saudi Kingdom into the US empire. The House of Saud likewise evinced a strong desire to repair its relations with the United States in order to advance its foreign agenda and domestic development. Yet despite this shared desire to diplomatically reengage, the deep mistrust stemming from the events of October 1973 took months for both the Saudi and US governments to even partially overcome, and serious fears that relations could dissolve into a war between the two persisted for years.

To a large degree, Saudi Arabia and the United States gradually regained trust in each other through joint projects that utilized Saudi petrodollars. These included the significant growth of long-term Saudi investments in US private financial institutions and the US government and Saudi purchases of US goods and services, particularly for Saudi Arabia's industrial and military development. This system of petrodollar interdependence met immediate concerns of both parties, such as providing the Saudis with secure places to invest and appreciate their revenues while providing the United States with needed funds. More broadly, however, Riyadh and Washington sought to develop petrodollar interdependence between each other in the service of indirect goals, most prominently Saudi oil supply and price policies for the Americans and US action on Arab demands regarding Israel for the Saudis. Saudi-US petrodollar interdependence would take time to develop, and petrodollar ties did not guarantee a meeting of minds. Indeed, despite the deep and uninterrupted petrodollar links between Iran and the United States during the mid-1970s, the shah would be a hawk on oil prices, to the frustration of US officials. But pursuing petrodollar interdependence went a long way in restoring Saudi Arabia to the system of US empire while radically transforming the former's role within the latter, as Saudi Arabia's importance shifted from providing the West with low-priced oil to supplying the United States with large sums of petrodollars that provided vital funds to the US economy.

At the conclusion of the 1973 Arab-Israeli War, restoring the fealty of erstwhile Arab client states, especially Saudi Arabia, to the United States preoccupied the Nixon administration. A CIA assessment sent to Kissinger on October 25 reported that there was a real chance that the Saudi and other Arab governments might utilize their petrodollars in addition to the oil embargo to pressure Washington to act on Arab positions in the Arab-Israeli conflict. These measures included replacing the United States with other countries as a supplier of arms, a total boycott of all US trade, fuller cooperation with "fedayeen terrorists," and "a determined effort in the international money market to weaken the US dollar." The CIA analysts noted that historical ties and interests shared with the United States would constrain the enthusiasm of traditional US allies in the Arab world for such measures, but concluded that "nonetheless, if the cease-fire does not result promptly in negotiations that give promise of movement toward at least the immediate Arab objective—acceptance by Israel of the principle of withdrawal from the territory occupied in 1967—these courses will be considered seriously."[3]

The existing Arab oil production cuts and price increases alone already brought significant economic pain to the oil-consuming countries. Increased oil prices contributed to accelerating rates of inflation in the United States, which rose from a rate of 7.8 percent in October 1973 to 12.3 percent in

December 1974. For the same period, the US unemployment rate rose from 4.6 percent to 7.2, as higher costs and uncertainty contributed to an economic recession.[4] The direct cost of OPEC's price increase, while high for the United States, was far higher for its largest allies. Japan was the world's largest importer of oil, and whereas before the latest Arab-Israeli war the United States relied on imported oil for 17 percent of its total energy consumption, for the European Economic Community (EEC) this figure ranged from 42 percent for West Germany to 93 percent for Italy.[5] The oil-consuming countries launched varied campaigns to develop domestic oil or alternative fuel sources and more efficient energy use; in November Nixon proposed such measures under the title "Project Independence" with the goal of achieving US energy self-sufficiency by 1980. But such programs would take years to develop, and for most countries would not eliminate the need for imported petroleum. For at least the short term, oil-importing countries either would have to pay higher sums for foreign oil or cut back on energy use, both of which endangered economic growth.

Meanwhile, the oil shock had worsened relations between the United States and its European and Japanese allies, relations already strained by the collapse of Bretton Woods. Far more dependent on Arab oil than the United States for the basic functioning of their economies, the Western allies broke with US policies in an effort to secure petroleum imports. Within the North Atlantic Treaty Organization (NATO), Portugal alone had allowed landing rights to US planes supplying arms to Israel during the war, and in November the EEC called on Israel to withdraw to the pre–1967 war borders. The Europeans and Japanese likewise entered into bilateral trade deals with the Arab world and Iran to secure petroleum, a rational strategy on an individual level but one that placed greater bargaining power with the oil exporters and thus achieving a collective increase in the price of petroleum imports. Kissinger feared that the Western alliance was eroding, that autarky was reemerging, and that US leadership on the Arab-Israeli peace process would be increasingly challenged.[6]

Faced with simultaneous rifts with its Arab and Western allies, the United States also had to contend with efforts by the Europeans to seize upon Arab dissatisfaction with Washington to displace the latter's influence in the MENA. Seeking to secure access to oil imports from the Arab states and export sales to secure MENA petrodollars to offset the price increases for petroleum, Western Europe and Japan proved increasingly willing to challenge US security and trade ties with the Arab states. France, which was particularly opposed to many US policies within the Atlantic alliance and since 1967 had shifted to a strategy of improving Arab ties, proved especially eager to undercut US influence. While France already had strong ties with Algeria and Iraq, it also worked to increase its sway, at US expense, in traditionally US spheres of influence like Saudi Arabia. In November US Defense under secretary William Clements noted that $2 billion worth of equipment to modernize the Saudi navy and national guard was lying idle in the kingdom due to the rupture in Saudi-US relations. "The Saudis are beginning to think we're not serious about them," Clements lamented. "They're beginning to flirt with the French. The French Defense Minister has been over there and the French are busting a gut to take over from us in Saudi Arabia."[7]

The US government had traditionally opposed European efforts to reduce US economic and political influence in the Arab world; with the Europeans competing with the United States for critical supplies of oil and capital from the region and challenging core US diplomatic initiatives like the management of the Arab-Israeli conflict, preventing the loss of US ties with Arab states took on added weight. European efforts to displace US influence in Saudi Arabia were particularly threatening since the Nixon administration considered Riyadh the key to ending the Arab oil embargo, lowering oil prices, and restoring US power in the larger Arab world. Saudi Arabia was the world's largest oil exporter, and unlike Iran, its population and domestic infrastructure were sparse. For these reasons, the Saudis earned far more than they could spend from their oil exports, leaving them with less incentive to press oil prices higher and greater swing capacity in determining the world's oil supply. Iran remained the most important US military proxy and importer of US goods and services in the MENA, roles uninterrupted by the Arab-Israeli conflict and in fact significantly enhanced by its rising petrodollar revenues. The Nixon administration likewise favored greater interdependence with Kuwait, the UAE, Qatar, and even the "radical" states of Algeria, Iraq, and Libya. But Saudi Arabia held the ultimate importance for both ending the oil embargo and lowering oil prices.

To improve relations with Riyadh, Kissinger, who had previously spent little time on MENA affairs, threw himself into a frenzy of direct negotiations with Arab and Israeli leaders that came to be called "shuttle diplomacy." He argued to the Saudis and other Arab leaders that his peace efforts demonstrated the United States' good faith. At the same time, he routinely insisted that further progress on the Arab-Israeli peace process depended on the end of the embargo, both to prevent a US domestic backlash against the Arab countries that would hinder the Nixon administration's ability to champion Arab positions and to preserve the geopolitical stature of the United States. Speaking to some of his national security peers during a meeting in late November, Kissinger expressed his belief that the United States could not reinforce the demands of the radical Arab states or the Soviet Union. "[Faisal's] problem is he is a friend of the United States, but he is pressured by radicals," Kissinger argued. "So he is leapfrogging the radicals so he isn't embarrassed by his U.S. relationship."[8]

Faisal shared Kissinger's desire for an end to the oil embargo and a return to cooperative relations between Riyadh and Washington, but he insisted there first be tangible US action on Arab claims in the Middle East conflict. Meeting with Kissinger on November 8, Faisal was polite but firm, stating that while "nothing would please him more than to be able to maintain and even increase oil supplies to his American friends . . . he was under pressure from the radicals. He pointed out that all Arabs were united on the basic issues and he hoped we would move as expeditiously as possible toward a settlement."[9] Three days later, Yamani told Kissinger "that the major problem facing him was the fact that the King [Faisal] was so terribly angry at the United States that it will be difficult to get his approval to proceed [on reductions in the oil embargo] . . . a complete lifting of the embargo was impossible at this time and that the United States would have to pay the price of her support to her Israeli friends."[10] Six days after that, Kissinger received a report from Saudi royal adviser Kamal Adham claiming that Faisal had recently told Sadat that if current US negotiations stalled, Saudi Arabia would press for renewed warfare against Israel to create instability in the region and force superpower attention back on the issue of the Israeli-occupied Arab territories.[11]

To underscore Riyadh's determination and newfound capabilities in the wake of the petrodollar boom, Saudi officials emphasized their country's ability to resist US economic coercion and replace US trade. When Republican representative from Connecticut Robert Steele and Democratic representative from California Leo Ryan visited Saudi Arabia in November, Yamani warned them that "any effort by the United States to boycott machinery exports to Saudi Arabia would fail. The Japanese were eager to sell machinery to Saudi Arabia. The Saudis prefer to continue to purchase machinery from the United States, but they would purchase from the Japanese if they had to." Another Saudi minister made a similar argument to them regarding a potential US grain boycott, noting that "there are other countries willing to supply wheat to Saudi Arabia."[12]

Seeking to press the Saudis, Nixon wrote to Faisal on December 3, reemphasizing his "concern that the American people will not understand the continuation of [the embargo] while their Government is making a major and difficult effort over the weeks and months ahead to promote the just peace that the Arab world seeks. . . . I fear that [US] public opinion will not permit us to play the sustained role which you and we agree is our responsibility."[13] Faisal did not budge, however, and when Yamani met with Shultz in Washington on December 10, he told him that while the Arab oil producers were "anxious to find some justification for removing the [oil] embargo" and to collaborate with the United States on issues like ensuring the stability of the international monetary system in dealing with the massive projected Arab monetary surpluses, the United States needed to take action on the Arab-Israeli conflict and help save the Saudis "from this painful dilemma" that undercut "the traditional Saudi friendship for, and mutual interests with, the U.S."[14] Again the Saudis alluded to their US counterparts that their new petrodollar power could be used in collaboration with or opposition to the United States.

While the Americans and Saudis remained at an impasse, the shah collaborated with Arab leaders to introduce a large new oil price hike. On December 23 the shah announced that the Persian Gulf producers would double the price of their oil to $11.65 a barrel at the start of 1974. "The industrial world will have to realize that the era of their terrific progress and even more terrific income and wealth based on cheap oil is finished," the shah lectured reporters. "If you want to live as well as now, you'll have to work for it. Even all the children of well-to-do parents who have plenty to eat, have cars, and are running around as terrorists throwing bombs here and there—they will have to work, too."[15] The shah had not joined the Arab oil embargo, but he remained a leading oil price hawk, determined to obtain the petrodollar revenues needed to rapidly develop his country regardless of Washington's desire for price restraint.

At the start of 1974 Persian Gulf oil, which supplied 43 percent of noncommunist petroleum consumption and had an outsize effect on global oil rates, had nearly quadrupled in price in two and a half months.[16] High oil prices and petrodollar revenues were the new normal, and it was anyone's guess as to what ceiling, if any, there was for petroleum costs. US ambassador to Iran Richard Helms, corresponding with Kissinger in the wake of the news, captured the sense of shock. "It can be said without exaggeration that the non-Communist world is in a fair way to being shaken to its economic foundations," Helms wrote. "The leaders of these [OPEC] countries know they have the whip hand, remember every denial or indignity of the major oil companies over the years, and are in no mood to have commodity prices float freely in the market while crude oil prices do not. . . . I would like to suggest that finding the answers [to dealing with OPEC] will require your personal leadership . . . to devise an approach to a problem which in the short term at least is the most important economic challenge faced by the industrialized world since World War II."[17]

Kissinger told Ambassador Helms that at the earliest opportunity he should impress upon the shah that Nixon "is greatly concerned over the destabilizing impact that the price increases . . . will have on the world's economy and the catastrophic problems it could pose for the international monetary system. . . . It will have severe repressive effect on the economies of oil consumers which could cause a worldwide recession and which eventually would benefit no one including oil exporters." The shah was unmoved, however, and merely deflected blame for the price hike on other members of OPEC.[18] Kissinger wrote directly to Saqqaf on December 28 that "I cannot express too strongly my disappointment and dismay" at the Arabs' decision to continue the oil embargo and that "it is absolutely essential that the oil embargo and oil production restrictions directed against the United States be ended immediately." Furthermore,

Table 1. Oil export revenues of MENA members of OPEC, 1967–1988 (billions of US dollars, 2018 constant value)

	Saudi Arabia	Iran	Libya	Kuwait	Iraq	UAE	Algeria	Qatar	Total
1967	10.4	13.1	8.8	9.9	4.6	2.0	4.0	1.5	69.0
1968	14.6	12.2	13.4	10.0	5.5	2.4	4.2	1.5	78.0
1969	14.4	12.7	14.8	10.1	5.3	2.8	4.1	1.5	79.2
1970	15.6	15.3	15.4	10.2	5.1	3.4	4.4	1.5	83.6
1971	23.6	21.7	16.7	15.0	6.7	5.2	3.8	1.9	106.7
1972	32.9	21.9	17.6	17.0	6.2	6.7	6.2	2.3	122.6
1973	50.7	31.8	22.5	20.2	10.4	9.8	8.6	3.5	168.8
1974	180.6	106.4	42.0	53.8	33.3	32.2	21.7	10.1	490.1
1975	137.6	91.7	31.6	40.1	38.4	31.8	20.1	8.2	408.7
1976	168.3	101.1	42.1	40.1	40.6	37.0	21.1	9.4	468.4
1977	179.3	97.7	47.2	36.9	39.6	38.3	23.0	8.5	478.7
1978	155.3	83.5	38.1	36.8	42.0	33.3	22.5	8.9	428.0
1979	217.5	66.4	55.2	59.8	74.0	44.5	30.3	12.8	567.2
1980	309.3	35.7	66.8	57.8	79.6	59.1	39.6	13.9	667.8
1981	307.9	27.7	41.2	39.3	27.7	51.8	36.1	12.9	550.0
1982	190.5	48.6	35.6	23.6	25.8	41.5	29.0	9.4	409.1
1983	113.0	51.1	31.1	25.4	19.4	32.8	24.3	6.6	308.7
1984	87.8	38.0	26.5	26.6	22.0	29.1	23.7	8.0	266.6
1985	60.4	30.3	28.3	22.0	26.2	25.4	22.5	5.8	225.6
1986	41.4	13.5	17.3	14.6	15.8	15.7	11.8	3.4	138.1
1987	45.1	20.8	13.9	16.6	24.6	17.5	14.5	3.7	161.1
1988	42.8	17.8	12.9	14.5	24.0	16.2	12.1	3.2	147.8
Total	2,399.0	958.9	639.0	600.4	576.7	538.5	387.7	138.5	6,423.9

Source: Organization of the Petroleum Exporting Countries, *Annual Statistical Bulletin* (2018).

he wanted the Saudis to know that "the drastic and unjustifiable price increases announced in Tehran on December 23 . . . [and] their predictable and disastrously destabilizing effect on the free world's economic and monetary system is of the deepest concern to us."[19] Nixon sent a letter to Faisal covering the same points in a politer tone the same day.[20]

The Saudi government again refused US entreaties. "If the Saudis were to lift the boycott now," Saqqaf told Akins on December 30, "it would appear as complete surrender to American pressure. Israel's American defenders would boast that they had brought Saudi Arabia to its knees . . . and therefore there was no reason to make any concessions to them. And the reaction in the Arab world against the King and against Saudi Arabia would be even stronger." Akins expressed to Kissinger his sense that "the Saudis are feeling very uneasy. The Israelis may be bothered by a Masada complex; here it is more 'Goetterdaemmerung,' or mixing my periods, a feeling that the Saudis are Samson in the Temple of Gaza; if pressures on them become intolerable (and they still are also clearly afraid of a [US] military attack), they will be destroyed, but the world will also suffer horribly."[21] From Akins's vantage point, Saudi-US relations had reached dangerously low levels; Saudi leaders had accepted annihilation at the hands of the United States as both possible and preferable to conceding to Israeli demands, a less dignified course that might well lead to their overthrow by radicals anyway.

In January 1974, as Kissinger continued his diplomacy, CIA analysts estimated that "the [petroleum] producing countries' oil revenues will reach about $95 billion in 1974—three and a half times as much as last year" and that "the receipts of Saudi Arabia, Kuwait, and the other small Persian Gulf states will far exceed their spending capability."[22] Given the massive sums of money involved, the issue of how the oil-rich countries would spend and invest their petrodollars increasingly took on a level of seriousness comparable to the issue of how the oil-importing countries would cover their rising energy costs. Depending on how they were used, petrodollars might either significantly strengthen or damage the United States' global position.

The Treasury Department determined that financial interdependence between the United States and the petrodollar states would help persuade the latter to end the oil embargo, refrain from future attacks on the US economy, and even moderate their pricing of oil. The rationale behind this plan was laid out in a January 1974 Treasury research report. The report recognized that in addition to the "oil weapon," the projected surpluses of the members of OPEC constituted a second potential weapon that could be aimed at disrupting financial and exchange markets, though it contended unintended mismanagement of funds by OPEC finance ministers posed the more probable threat to the smooth functioning of global markets. To mitigate either possibility, the paper recommended that the United States "encourage OPEC countries to invest heavily in financial institutions such as brokerage houses, investment banks, and market-making operations so that they will have a stake in the smooth functioning of the markets and that disruptive activities will be doubly costly—in the first instance to the value of their security portfolios and in the second instance to the value of their direct investment." Furthermore, "as the OPEC countries accumulate financial assets [in foreign countries] . . . their stake in the continued economic growth and stability of these countries will increase. To the extent that OPEC members are concerned about the aggregate size of their wealth, they will be significantly less likely to attempt to disrupt the economies where they hold assets. Therefore as their wealth increases, the probability of their pursuing policies designed to hamper other economies like cutting off their oil—is likely to decline." In short, the Treasury Department believed interdependence between the economies of the United States and of the members of OPEC would significantly reduce the chance that the latter would pursue economic policies that harmed the United States, including access to affordable oil, out of self-interest.[23]

In keeping with this reasoning, in January 1974 Treasury made it a top objective to "achieve major Middle Eastern Countries' investment in the United States, utilizing dollars earned by oil exports; and develop a national program for attracting such investments to the United States."[24] Other departments shared Treasury's goal of petrodollar interdependence for related reasons. The Commerce Department emphasized that the oil producing nations' desire to obtain US technology could lead them to both invest in related US businesses and purchase US exports, bringing needed capital and sales revenues, a "valuable current account receipt offsetting our rising oil import costs."[25] Defense, the NSC, and State focused on the potential of technology and arms sales to MENA states as a means to forge stronger US ties with client states in the MENA while simultaneously making these clients militarily and politically stronger. As early as December 1973, Kissinger sounded out Saudi officials about establishing a "new mechanism" for "cooperative arrangements" for things like technology transfers.[26] There thus existed a broad consensus across the Nixon administration that US interdependence with petrodollar states would serve US interests. Increasing petrodollar interdependence would work in tandem with progress on the Arab-Israeli peace process as a primary means of restoring US influence over the oil-rich Arab states.

As an economic and geopolitical superpower, the United States had long attracted business from both conservative and radical Arab states, yet the Arab-Israeli conflict threatened its continuation. The Arab monarchies remained deeply fearful of possible US reprisals against them due to the ongoing oil embargo. In February 1974 the US consul in Zurich, having talked with "a rather large sample of the banking community," reported to the State Department that "the amount of Arab money handled in various ways by Swiss banks is enormous" and that, along with the mark and yen, bankers reported that "dollar investments are favored by Arab customers because of their general belief in the relative strength and stability of the United States, the American economy, and the dollar." These bankers also reported, however, that the Arabs sought to "camouflage" their investments in US institutions so as to make them untraceable, a precaution taken to avoid the seizure of their assets in the case that Arab-US relations further deteriorated.[27] Both practices inhibited interdependence and might eventually lead US financial institutions to reject additional Arab deposits. Furthermore, it was conceivable that the Arabs, if sufficiently angered or frightened, would pull out of US financial institutions entirely, both domestically and in the Euromarkets .[28] Such an outcome could severally harm the value of the dollar, the US economy, and global finance, and even a partial avoidance of US financial institutions could lead the Arabs to further decrease oil production due to the shrinking of attractive places to invest their petrodollars. For economic interdependence to be firmly reestablished between the Arab world and the United States, political relations needed to improve.

Despite the growing consensus in early 1974 within the Nixon administration over the desirability of US petrodollar interdependence with Saudi Arabia, disagreements over the Arab-Israeli peace process and the oil embargo continued to frustrate this goal. In mid-January, Kissinger successfully negotiated the first Sinai agreement, which disengaged Israeli troops from part of Egypt's territory. Kissinger expected this achievement would provide the Saudis with sufficient standing to end the Arab embargo. But on February 3 Kissinger received word from Akins that King Faisal had found no support from the other Arab states, excepting Egypt and Qatar, for his proposal to end the embargo, and instead encountered strong pressure from Abu Dhabi, Algeria, Kuwait, and Syria that the embargo should not be lifted until an Israeli disengagement began on the Syrian front. Iraq and Libya argued against ending the embargo at any time. Faisal thus maintained that the United States must achieve a disengagement on the Syrian front before an end to the Arab embargo could be achieved.[29] It was this message from Faisal that prompted the angry words questioning the very viability of the Saudi-US alliance from

Kissinger and subsequently from Saqqaf at the start of this chapter. Responding to the fallout in Saudi-US relations, on February 7 Nixon met with Saudi ambassador Ibrahim bin Abdullah al-Sowayel. Nixon asked the ambassador to relay to Faisal that the embargo hindered his ability to conduct peace negotiations because it gave his domestic enemies fodder to claim he was doing so under pressure. At the same time, Nixon also argued that "I want a world where we would trade with you" and "there are two threats in the [Middle East]—the radicals and the Soviet Union. It is in both our interests for the United States . . . to keep these two forces under control."[30] By implication, Nixon suggested the embargo stood in the way of mutually beneficial petrodollar ties in the economic and military realms.

Hoping to bring down oil prices and reverse the erosion of the Western alliance, Kissinger proposed organizing an oil consumers' cartel among the OECD countries, using their collective purchasing power to drive down the price of petroleum. As part of this approach Kissinger sought agreement among the MDCs not to pursue bilateral deals with the members of OPEC in the pursuit of either oil or petrodollars via investment and trade. To this end, in February 1974 the United States held the Washington Energy Conference with Japan, West Germany, the United Kingdom, France, Italy, Canada, the Netherlands, and Norway. Japan and the European countries refused to offend OPEC and risk a drastic cutoff of their energy by adopting the confrontational approach Kissinger proposed, however, so the conference concluded with the signing of a mild agreement, devoid of enforcement measures, calling for increased cooperation in the OECD. France refused to sign even this statement. The OECD nations promptly ignored their pledges and continued their mutually harmful competition for MENA oil and petrodollars. Meanwhile, the Arab embargo against the United States continued, and shortages of gasoline were leading to long lines at fueling stations across the country. Some of the automobile lines stretched for a mile, leaving cars to burn fuel while idling and drivers irate. In Gary, Indiana, one motorist shot and killed a station owner for refusing him gas after cutting in line.[31]

With no meaningful OECD cooperation, the Nixon administration needed Saudi assistance more than ever. Fortunately for the White House, Saudi resolve on the continuation of the embargo was weakening. Nixon continued to hold out the prospect of stronger petrodollar ties in exchange for the lifting of the embargo, telling Saqqaf on February 19 that what was "on the line" was his administration's ability to "get Israel to be reasonable" and provide "our help, economically, industrially, culturally" for Saudi Arabia. On March 2, Kissinger visited Riyadh and likewise held out the incentives of US commitment to the peace process and petrodollar interdependence, telling Faisal that "we will pursue our policy of bringing peace in the area, and simultaneously we are prepared to strengthen our relations with the Kingdom of Saudi Arabia." For the latter, Kissinger declared that the United States was "prepared to begin talking about long-term cooperation in the military field, in the economic field, and in the scientific field. . . . We are prepared to send a mission to Saudi Arabia to deal with questions of economic and technical cooperation on a long-range basis. . . . Our objective is to work with Your Majesty and to strengthen our friendship on a long-term basis." Faisal responded warmly to these proposals, affirming that "we will welcome this with the greatest pleasure" and that "these steps are bound to widen and strengthen relations between us." Faisal still pushed for a disengagement on the Syrian front before an end to the embargo while Kissinger promoted the reverse order, but the discussion was cordial.[32]

Kissinger felt increasingly optimistic that promises of increased economic and military cooperation with the United States would finally induce Saudi Arabia to end the embargo. "We are going all out now with the Saudis," Kissinger told Clements on March 7, 1974. "I worked it out with the King [Faisal]. . . . We are going to send out a military mission and an economic mission. . . . The King liked the idea."[33] On March 11 Kissinger told Nixon, "We had approached the Saudis on bilateralism and their response has been so enthusiastic, in fact so wildly enthusiastic that I can't help but believe this must effect [sic] their decision on the embargo." Along with "a military relationship and a long-term economic relationship," Kissinger noted, the Saudis would have "the commitment of the U.S. strategically to them against their enemies in Iraq and South Yemen and so forth" as well as against internal enemies.[34]

On March 18, Saudi Arabia, along with all other Arab states except Libya and Syria (the latter having only marginal oil exports), agreed to end the oil embargo against the United States in spite of the fact that Kissinger had not yet achieved an Israeli disengagement in Syria. Saudi Arabia also pledged to raise its oil production and successfully pressured the other members of OPEC not to raise the official price of oil by 15 percent for the next three months, a measure all the other members of OPEC supported.[35] The Saudi Kingdom had finally acted to improve the United States' political standing in the MENA and to moderate OPEC's pricing decisions. Saudi Arabia faced considerable hostility for these acts from other Arab and OPEC governments, and the US embassy in Jiddah noted that the Saudis expected US support because of its efforts.[36] To this end, on April 5 the Saudi and US governments publicly announced their decision to establish joint commissions for economic and military development in Saudi Arabia.[37] On May 31, after arduous negotiations, Kissinger achieved an Israeli withdrawal from a portion of the Golan Heights it had seized from Syria.

On June 8 Prince Fahd oversaw the official signing of two joint commissions, one economic and one military, in Washington. "It is our thought that a close economic relationship will provide a more tangible basis for cementing US-Saudi relations," Kissinger wrote to Nixon on June 6. "One of our concerns is to avoid a reposition of the oil embargo, but we are also seeking Saudi support for our approach to Arab-Israeli negotiations."[38] The two agreements were the first of their kind between the United States and an Arab country. The US contingent of the joint military commission was headed by Defense and the economic commission by Treasury.[39] Three days earlier Fahd privately met with Kissinger, expressing his concern that the Soviet Union was attempting a "pincer movement" around Saudi Arabia via Iraq and South Yemen and the need for Saudi Arabia to strengthen itself against this threat. Kissinger assured Fahd that Saudi requests for US arms would be favorably received.[40]

On June 10 Nixon and Kissinger started a nine-day trip to Egypt, Saudi Arabia, Syria, Israel, and Jordan aimed at strengthening the peace process and

Figure 2. Richard Nixon, Crown Prince Khalid (partly obscured), Alexander Haig, Henry Kissinger, Prince Abdullah (partly obscured), King Faisal, Prince Fahd, and Prince Sultan in Jeddah, June 15, 1974. Courtesy of Richard Nixon Presidential Library.

US economic ties with the region. In Saudi Arabia, Nixon privately under-scored to Faisal "the seriousness of our new joint 'active partnership' with Saudi Arabia," suggested the Saudis could order US weapons for secret transfer to allied countries like Egypt and Pakistan to get around congressional arms trans-fer restrictions, stated "the United States was keenly interested in Saudi Ara-bia playing the role of 'watch man' vis-à-vis the small states of the Gulf," and concluded with a plea for a Saudi "favor of influencing the oil producing coun-tries to reduce the price of oil." Faisal in turn expressed his support for Nixon and "the new policy for a just peace in the Middle East worked on so tire-lessly by brilliant Dr. Kissinger" and promised to continue to counsel price restraint to the other oil-producing countries.[41]

In mid-1974 responsibility for the Nixon administration's campaign to strengthen Saudi-US petrodollar interdependence and lower the price of OPEC oil increasingly rested on William Simon, a staunch neoliberal, former executive bonds salesman, former director of the Federal Energy Office, and, as of May, replacement of Shultz as Treasury secretary. Simon was eager to implement the new economic cooperation agreement with Saudi Arabia. He strongly endeavored to lower US oil prices, and even more than most, Simon believed Saudi Arabia was the key to lowering the cost of petroleum. Simon held this conviction in part because of Saudi Arabia's primacy in world oil exports, but also because he correctly gauged that the Saudi monarchy was far more disposed to lower prices than the shah. Simon earned the personal ire of the Iranian leader when he testified before Congress in February 1974, heatedly countering statements the shah had publicly made on the CBS news program *60 Minutes* that the United States was not in fact short of oil and that US oil companies were breaking the Arab embargo by rerouting tankers at sea. Simon described the shah's views as both "irresponsible and just plain ridiculous" as well as "insane."[42] After this media spectacle, Simon was persona non grata in Iran; later that year the shah would privately vent his displeasure to British officials when he "dismissed Simon as a 'stock-broker.'"[43]

Considering the shah a lost cause, Simon aimed to pit Saudi Arabia against Iran. During OPEC's meeting in June, only Saudi Arabia pushed for another three-month oil price freeze; all the other members, led by Iran, desired a price increase. Yamani prevailed in persuading the other members of OPEC to ac-cept the Saudi position.[44] Simon, however, hoped that he could persuade the Saudis to force OPEC to accept oil price reductions in the future. At the be-ginning of July, Simon privately tried to convince Yamani that the Saudis were "strengthening their enemies—the high price [of oil] now helps the others [members of OPEC], not them."[45] A few days later, just before he arrived in the Middle East for his first visit to discuss economic policy, Simon made his case public in an interview with *American Banker*. "The shah is a nut," Simon told the newspaper. "He wants to be a superpower. . . . He is putting all his oil profits into domestic investment, mostly military hardware. . . . Maximization of the oil price is in his best interests, as he sees it." Then, the hard sell to Saudi Arabia: "But it is not in the Saudis' interest. It is crazy from their point of view. The Saudis' helping keep oil prices high is making Iran, their natural rival, strong."[46]

The international banking system's ability to continue to recycle petrodollars also concerned Simon. Western banks had a conflicted outlook on petrodollars. On the one hand, many banks eagerly acquired petrodollars so as to capitalize on rising global demand for loans, many taken out by countries to pay their rising oil-import bills. In the first half of 1974 Japan alone borrowed $9.4 billion. In 1974 new OPEC deposits to banks in the Euromarkets would total roughly $24 billion, a sum equal to over 40 percent of all net international lending by Euromarkets banks that year. This contributed significantly to the rapid growth of the Euromarkets in 1974, the net size of which grew by an estimated $55 billion to a total of $210 billion.[47] On the other hand, banks worried about two significant problems that might make significant levels of petrodollar recycling unfeasible. The first problem was that Arab lenders tended to insist on depositing their petrodollars on terms that ensured high liquidity, often stipulating that they be allowed to withdraw their funds only a week or less after deposit. Most bank loans, however, were scheduled on a far longer time frame. The risk of bank failure grew as bank holdings increasingly consisted of petrodollar deposits that the Arabs could quickly withdraw. Critically, the Arabs insisted on high liquidity in part to allow themselves the possibility of quickly withdrawing their funds and avoid a US seizure if Arab-US relations further deteriorated. The second problem was that Arab investors, seeking security, tended to lend to only the largest banks (such as Chase and First National City Bank, the latter renamed Citibank in 1976, both based in New York City), and capital markets in 1974 were unstable and insecure. This meant that the larger banks receiving the majority of petrodollars might determine that lending to smaller banks was too risky, creating a situation where the larger banks no longer wished to acquire petrodollars and the smaller banks could not obtain access to them, potentially precipitating a credit squeeze and global economic crash.[48]

In June 1974 bankers from Europe, North America, and Japan gathered for an international monetary conference in Williamsburg, Virginia. The bankers largely focused on their fear and dismay that Arab deposits continued to be largely short term. One economist for a major New York bank recalled being ridiculed by the head of its foreign department for asking how much one-year money the bank had received from Arab investors. "One-year money!" the banker replied incredulously. "I wish I could get it for more than 24 hours."[49] The consensus among the bankers was an increasing unwillingness to accept additional short-term deposits; the banks would not risk such an imbalance between their short-term deposits and long-term loans, even though this meant a drying up of credit for businesses and countries. Simon feared disaster. "With all the [oil] states with money and nowhere to spend it, the banks and financial markets are in trouble," Simon told Nixon on July 9, right before his trip to the Middle East. "The financial markets are close to panic. There are major corporations which are unable to borrow."[50] Simon sought to persuade the Arab countries to increase their long-term investments so that banks would continue to offer loans to other customers.

A related issue for Simon was how to fund the rising US federal debt. He preferred to reduce the federal debt by cutting the budgets of government social programs. Simon strongly opposed reducing the deficit by raising taxes; he believed higher taxes would discourage business investment and slow economic growth, and felt taxes instead needed to be lowered. In the same July 9 conversation with Nixon in which he discussed the recycling problem, Simon urged Nixon to "demand restraint. Taxes cut . . . take $5 billion out of social security . . . send a bill up, say government spending has gone on long enough. Send up five bills like that."[51] Congress would not implement the tax or spending cuts Simon desired, however, something Nixon quickly pointed out, so he was forced to pursue a third option: increase government borrowing. Simon felt that Treasury borrowing in the US domestic capital market presented its own problem, because it took away funds that would otherwise be potentially available to private borrowers.[52]

A partial solution to this problem was for Treasury to borrow petrodollars directly from Arab central banks. This way, the US government could fund some of its debts without crowding out private borrowers in the US domestic economy. Simon harked back to his days as a Wall Street bond broker and prepared to sell the Arab countries, particularly Saudi Arabia, special US Treasury securities outside of the normal auctions held by the Federal Reserve Bank of New York, something previously done with countries such as West Germany.[53] "The advantages to us [of selling special US Treasury securities to Kuwait and Saudi Arabia] would be that we could know in advance when large amounts would be coming to us and we would achieve some lowering of interest rate levels in the U.S.," Simon wrote to Nixon. "The advantage to them would be that by dealing directly with the Treasury they could avoid the adverse price movements which would harm them when they tried to move large amounts into or out of the private markets."[54] In addition to economic rationales, Simon was also aware that political considerations could provide an additional incentive. "For the Saudis the close relationship with the U.S. assures them of a great-power supporter against hostile neighbors," Simon noted to himself in preparing for his trip, "and the hope of obtaining the best available technology and skills for the rapid economic development of their country."[55] US geopolitical power, in short, could serve to shore up US economic power through inducements to the Saudis.

Simon visited Egypt, Israel, Kuwait, and Saudi Arabia during his July 1974 trip. On the matter of oil, Simon warned Saudi ministers that "Saudi Arabia has probably 150 years of production left, where Iran has only 15 years. Maybe Iran will build its industry and then when the oil runs out, they can take you [over militarily] and get the oil back."[56] The warning seemed effective; Simon believed there was a good chance of a "significant reduction" in oil prices in the next few months if "we play our cards right." The Kuwaitis stated that they did not see a benefit to lowering oil prices, but the Saudis did. "The Saudis recognize that it is not in their interest to hold prices up today by withholding Saudi production when the probabilities are that the current benefit goes to Iran and the large Saudi oil reserves will end up being sold at much lower prices in the future," Simon wrote to Nixon after his trip.[57]

The possibilities for developmental cooperation likewise impressed Simon. He reported that when the Saudi delegation came to the United States in June, "the Saudis were skeptical that cooperation with the U.S. Government on industrialization could really amount to much. . . . They suspected we were just going to offer the services of private U.S. companies which they figure are already fully available to them. Now after our various discussions . . . the Saudis are now enthusiastic over the benefits obtainable from direct cooperation with the U.S. government." It was determined that a number of US officials would work full time in Riyadh to oversee the development of economic, industrial, and petroleum sectors.[58]

On the more immediate issue of financial cooperation, Simon also found great reason for optimism. "Considerable mutual benefit can be—and will be—derived from the services which the U.S. can offer the oil producers in relation to their financial investments abroad," Simon wrote after his trip. "We found both the Saudis and the Kuwaitis more than willing to cooperate with us. They feel—I think rightly—that in this area they are both responsible and conservative." Furthermore, Simon left "confident that [Kuwait and Saudi Arabia] will decide to purchase a considerable amount of our special [Treasury securities] issues primarily for economic reasons, *but probably also to some extent to demonstrate their desire to cooperate with us.*"[59] While Simon was loathe to admit it publicly, he privately conceded that the "free market" alone was not determining the flow of petrodollars; US political inducements influenced decisions too. The basis of US empire in the Arab world had transitioned away from cheap oil and toward petrodollar funding.

Simon's visit to Riyadh reaffirmed his conviction that the Saudis were the key to lowering oil prices, but he also came away convinced that Saudi action in this area would be seriously constrained unless the United States placed greater pressure on Iran to not contest Saudi measures to raise production and lower costs. During his visit, Simon secured a pledge from the Saudis to increase their oil output through additional auctions, a measure that could reduce global prices if not offset by production cuts elsewhere. Saudi Arabia faced intense pressure from Iran and other members of OPEC not to go through with the auctions, however.[60] Upon his return to Washington, Simon told Nixon that he was particularly worried about balance-of-payments problems ensuing across the world if oil prices remained high. "Faisal says he has gone as far as he can without our help," Simon told Nixon. "The shah is threatening to cut production." Nixon responded that the shah "is our good friend, but he is playing a hard game on oil." Simon repeated that Faisal needed US help with the shah in order to counter price hawks within his own government. "The shah has us," Simon insisted. "No one will confront him. . . . This issue will ultimately require strong action by the United States." Nixon agreed a strategy toward Iran should be developed and directed Simon to collaborate with Kissinger.[61]

Simon had a strategy in mind: withhold US arms sales to Iran if the shah did not moderate on oil prices. On August 3 Simon made his case to Kissinger, arguing that high oil prices were unmanageable and, if allowed to persist, would "force a massive political realignment. . . . Europe is becoming dependent on the Arabs both for oil and for money."[62] Kissinger shared Simon's desire to lower the price of oil; he would say two weeks later that "we have to find a way to break the [OPEC] cartel. . . . It is intolerable that countries of 40 million can blackmail 800 million people in the industrial world."[63] Yet Kissinger regarded the potential helpfulness of the Saudis with far greater skepticism than Simon. "You must also know there is a real chance for another Arab-Israeli war," Kissinger told Simon. "Are the Saudis really prepared to cooperate in getting lower prices, and how far?" Simon maintained that "if production doesn't get cut, oil prices would drop by 30%." He then argued that "we would consider production cuts an unfriendly act, and for Iran, we could cut military supplies." Kissinger said he was willing to talk privately with the shah, but he believed the other members of OPEC were likely to side with Iran rather than Saudi Arabia. If the United States cut its arms sales to Iran, the Europeans could sell arms instead, and if the United States became dependent on Saudi Arabia for oil by alienating the shah, the Saudis would further squeeze the United States regarding Israel. The United States must first secure the cooperation of the Europeans. "Then we can do some confronting," Kissinger said. "But it will only work if we are willing to use force." Simon expressed skepticism that the Europeans would support the United States in a confrontation with OPEC. "If you are right," Kissinger responded, "we don't have the strength to do it alone, against the Arabs, the Europeans, the Japanese, and in a possible Israeli crisis, the USSR." Federal Reserve Board chairman Arthur Burns seconded Kissinger that "withholding arms from Iran won't help. Getting the consumers together would work." Sidelined, Simon demurred and lent his support to coordinating with the Europeans.[64]

Six days later, on August 9, facing impeachment by Congress over his role in the Watergate scandal, Nixon resigned from office, and Vice President Gerald Ford ascended to the presidency. Ford had been a long-serving Republican representative for Michigan and had been the House minority leader for nearly a decade when he was tapped to replace Spiro Agnew as vice president after Agnew's resignation over acts of bribery and fraud. Ford held a traditional conservative outlook on the economy, and while he had limited experience in foreign relations, he ascribed to the Cold War belief in the necessity of maintaining US power globally.[65]

Ford retained Kissinger and Simon as cabinet members, and their debate over Iran quickly resumed. During a meeting on August 13 Simon again pressed for greater US pressure on Iran regarding oil prices to bolster the resolve of the Saudis, and questioned if the Europeans could truly replace the United States as an advanced arms provider. Kissinger and his deputy Brent Scowcroft maintained that they could; the French Mirage jet fighter, for example, could replace the US F-14 for Iran's purposes. Simon then argued that Iran should be told it risked its alliance with the United States if it was not more forthcoming on oil prices. "I don't think we have anything to lose by leaning on the shah," Simon said. Kissinger would have none of it. "Bill, we have plenty to lose," the secretary of state rejoined. "He is the one non-ephemeral political force in the area. The idea that Saudi Arabia will be our reliable source for the rest of 1974 is not reasonable." Kissinger stated he was willing to express

US concerns to the shah, but he would not risk alienating Iran while he had little leverage over the Arab oil producers.[66] Furthermore, as Kissinger told Ford four days later, he believed that the shah "is our real friend" in opposing the Soviets and that "we can't tackle him without breaking him" on the issue of oil prices.[67]

To gain more leverage in the MENA, Kissinger hoped to intimidate the Arabs in the short term and potentially hold major US projects under the joint commissions as hostages in the long term. In the short term, Kissinger stated in a principals meeting that he was telling every Arab official he saw "that the United States simply won't accept another oil embargo," with the intent of spreading the threat widely as a deterrent. "I simply don't think we can take another embargo," Kissinger explained to his colleagues. "It would lead to economic collapse in Europe. It would lead to the collapse of NATO. If it comes to that. . . ." At this point in the documentary record, Kissinger's words remain classified for two lines, as well as six and a half lines of following discussion among Burns, State assistant secretary Thomas Enders, and Kissinger. The possibility that they discussed potential plans for invading oil-rich Arab countries in response to a new embargo is plausible; at the very least, the declassified record makes it clear that Kissinger considered the oil situation so serious that he intended to frighten Arab leaders to preclude them from even considering another embargo.[68]

In the longer term, Kissinger hoped the joint commissions would establish prized development projects in the Arab countries and Iran that would be funded by Arab and Iranian petrodollars but dependent on US expertise and technology. Once under way, Kissinger believed these projects could be used as leverage over Arab leaders and the shah; the ventures would only continue so long as the oil-rich states did not challenge core US interests. To that end, Kissinger stressed that the joint commissions needed to get under way as quickly as possible. The failure of the Europeans and Japanese to join the United States in confronting OPEC made this all the more imperative. "The United States' strategy should be first to preempt as much as possible in the bilateral field," Kissinger declared. "We've got to get going on the Commissions in Saudi Arabia and get started in Iran. . . . We need to preempt the goddamn Europeans." Simon and State deputy secretary Robert Ingersoll insisted the joint commissions were making good progress, but Kissinger pointedly expressed impatience. When Ingersoll mentioned holding a meeting the day prior to get the commissions' work moving, Kissinger snapped "I don't want to talk about any goddamn meeting. Is anything being built there that they won't want to give up? . . . Until we can create a physical nexus for our relationship, we have nothing. . . . In Saudi Arabia and Iran the Commissions can be useful. But not just by having meetings. They have to do something." Kissinger stressed that he did not care about the utility of the projects; they just needed to be projects that foreign leaders highly valued so that the United States could gain leverage over them. One project proposed for Saudi Arabia included a multilateral institute on fertilizers, but the plan was tied up in the US Agency for International Development, which insisted it needed sufficient time to develop it well. "I need assets in Saudi Arabia," Kissinger seethed. "I don't give a damn about a well distributed world fertilizer industry. . . . If we can put a nuclear plant into Egypt in eight years and do something in fertilizers in Saudi Arabia, then we have a strategy. Then we have something they don't want to lose. I want a confrontation, believe me. But I need chips."[69]

Kissinger prevailed over Simon for the time being; the Ford administration did not seriously press the shah on oil prices in 1974. Instead, the shared goal of State and Treasury to increase petrodollar interdependence with Iran and Saudi Arabia went ahead full speed. Through the second half of 1974, Saudi Arabia began approving US investment, development, and military proposals, and in November, Iran and the United States inaugurated the Joint US-Iranian Commission on Cooperation to expand ties in "political, economic, defense, cultural, scientific, and technological fields."[70]

The Saudi government ultimately decided not to go forward with the oil auctions it had agreed to with Simon, in part due to pressure from Iran. At the September meeting of OPEC, however, Saudi Arabia again overruled the desire of all other members to raise prices and forced an agreement to maintain the posted price at $11.65. At the December meeting, the Saudis went even further, achieving a reduction of the posted price to $11.25 (though the OPEC governments imposed an increase in royalties and taxes on foreign oil companies that more than offset the price decrease).[71] These were not the large price cuts that Simon and others had hoped for, but the Saudis had almost singlehandedly, and in the face of significant opposition, put the brake on OPEC's oil price increases, and had even achieved a slight reduction by the end of 1974. The impact of inflation meant that the real cost of oil was further decreased over time. As a result, petrodollar surpluses in the OECs and corresponding deficits in oil-importing countries did not grow as large as earlier feared, bringing partial relief to the international monetary system and the economies of the industrialized countries, just as Simon had hoped.

Rising US exports to the OECs also helped offset the rising cost of oil imports while improving political ties. From 1973 to 1974 US exports to Iran rose from $772 million to $1.73 billion, to Saudi Arabia from $442 million to

$835 million.[72] By 1974 Iran and Saudi Arabia were the two largest econo-
mies among the oil-rich MENA states and the two largest oil exporters within
OPEC, whose combined oil production constituted 48 percent of OPEC's
total output.[73] By retaining or restoring working relationships with Iran and
Saudi Arabia, the United States kept the two most influential countries in the
petrodollar order within its sphere. On a smaller order, US exports to Algeria,
Iraq, and Libya also rose, and relations moderately improved as well. In November 1974 Algeria restored diplomatic relations with the United States. Iraq
officially maintained its diplomatic break with Washington but privately courted
US businesses.[74] And in early 1975, Qaddafi ended Libya's oil embargo against
the United States, if not his anti-US rhetoric.[75]

The outlook of the international financial system also improved over late
1974 and early 1975. While some economists in the summer of 1974 predicted
the accumulated surplus of the OECs could exceed a trillion dollars by 1985,

Table 2. US exports to the MENA, 1967–1988 (billions of US dollars, 2018 constant value)

	Saudi Arabia	Iran	Other Arab OPEC	Arab non-OPEC	Israel	MENA total
1967	1.3	1.8	2.2	2.2	1.5	9.0
1968	1.4	2.0	2.5	2.2	2.0	10.0
1969	1.1	2.4	2.3	2.5	3.1	11.4
1970	0.9	2.1	2.0	2.4	3.8	11.3
1971	1.0	3.0	2.1	2.7	4.4	13.2
1972	1.9	3.4	2.5	2.7	3.4	13.8
1973	2.5	4.4	3.4	4.2	5.4	20.0
1974	4.3	8.8	6.5	6.7	6.1	32.4
1975	7.0	15.1	9.6	8.7	7.2	47.7
1976	12.2	12.2	9.7	9.5	6.2	49.9
1977	14.8	11.3	9.8	9.6	6.0	51.5
1978	16.8	14.2	9.8	9.5	7.4	57.7
1979	16.9	3.5	11.1	10.2	6.4	48.1
1980	17.6	0.1	12.1	11.3	6.2	47.3
1981	20.2	0.8	13.5	12.4	7.0	53.9
1982	23.5	0.3	11.6	13.1	5.9	54.4
1983	19.9	0.5	8.3	12.2	5.1	46.0
1984	13.5	0.4	7.5	11.2	5.3	37.9
1985	10.4	0.2	6.0	9.1	6.0	31.8
1986	7.9	0.1	5.7	7.9	5.1	26.7
1987	7.5	0.1	5.8	8.0	6.9	28.3
1988	8.1	0.2	7.7	8.3	6.9	31.1
Total	210.5	86.9	151.6	166.8	117.5	733.3

Source: US Bureau of the Census, *Statistical Abstract of the United States*, various years.

in February 1975 the *New York Times* reported there was widespread belief among economists that the surplus would peak at $300 billion in the late 1970s or early 1980s and then decline, easing concerns about financial imbalances in the global monetary system. The drastic change in outlook was due to the declining real price of oil and the unexpected volume of imports the members of OPEC were able to purchase in so short a time.[76] Western bankers likewise largely came to celebrate petrodollar funds as Arab investors noticeably increased their long-term investments.[77] "Private bankers are more confident now than last year" a panel of executives from Bank of America, Citibank, and Chase as well as a consultant to the US Council of the International Chamber of Commerce privately informed Treasury in 1975. "More recent estimates of probable OPEC financial accumulation . . . appear much more manageable than earlier estimates." Nor did they expect any problems to arise from the new Arab investors. "Most of the OPEC financial accumulations will be by Kuwait, Saudi Arabia, the United Arab Emirates," the panel stated. "These are all very conservative governments, and conservative investors. Not interested in takeovers, but in portfolio and real estate investments . . . they recognize their lack of infrastructure and management capability."[78]

Yet while petrodollar ties were mending the Saudi-US alliance, the trauma of 1973 still haunted the relationship, leaving both sides with an enduring sense of uncertainty and apprehension. When *Business Week* published an interview with Kissinger in early January 1975, it included a part where the interviewer asked if military force was the only solution to breaking up OPEC. Kissinger was quoted as responding that such a move would be "a very dangerous course. We should have learned from Vietnam that it is easier to get into a war than to get out of it," but also adding that "I am not saying that there's no circumstances where we would not use force. But it is one thing to use it in the case of a dispute over price; it's another where there is some actual strangulation of the industrialized world."[79] Riyadh privately expressed great alarm at the latter half of Kissinger's statement. Yamani told Akins that "he had never seen the King [Faisal] so depressed, so worried and so questioning of his relationship with the United States" and warned that the Saudis could sabotage their oil fields and deny the United States supplies for ten years if faced with invasion.[80] Akins also believed that European and Japanese ambassadors and other diplomatic officers were playing on Saudi fears of a US invasion in an attempt to garner larger shares of government arms purchases and engineering contracts at America's expense.[81] In response to Saudi anxieties, the Ford administration sent repeated messages disavowing any military intentions toward the Arab world and reaffirming the United States' commitment to the kingdom, including a personal letter from Ford to Faisal.[82] Yet three days after sending Ford's letter, Kissinger argued to the members of the Special Actions Group that if another Arab-Israeli flashpoint led the Arabs to launch a "total oil embargo of the West, we have to have a plan to use force." Kissinger believed the United States might indeed need to militarily occupy an Arab country under these circumstances. "I'm not saying we have to take over Saudi Arabia," Kissinger continued. "How about Abu Dhabi, or Libya?" Clements, however, appeared to favor an invasion of Saudi Arabia, and Kissinger seemed open to the possibility.[83]

Kissinger sought to avoid such an outcome, however, and he and Simon continued to believe petrodollar interdependence held the best hope of achieving this. "We've got to come up with ways to soak up their dough," Kissinger told an approving Simon in early February, again emphasizing that he did not care how the Arabs deployed their money so long as it created interdependence with the United States. "If those Bedouins want to use all of their money to build soccer stadiums, that's fine with me. . . . We should absorb as much of their money as we possibly can. . . . Our principal objective should be to maximize their dependence on us."[84] Yet it also remained clear to Kissinger and Simon that the persistence of the Arab-Israeli conflict threatened to undo all their efforts at petrodollar interdependence with the Arab world. The risk of another major war needed to be neutralized, and to do that, Kissinger and Simon understood, Egypt needed to be brought into the US system of empire. To achieve this end, as well as other objectives vis-à-vis the larger Third World, the two once again perceived major roles that petrodollars could play.

Chapter 4

The Triangle to the Nile

"As you undoubtedly observed while you were in Egypt, the economy of that country had been brought to an advanced state of deterioration by the socialist controls of Nasser," Simon wrote to Nixon in July 1974. "Now Sadat and his able economic 'czar' [Abdel Aziz] Hegazi, appear dedicated to freeing-up the economy and bringing in foreign private initiative as fast as political realities permit." Simon, excited by this prospect, argued that "the public evidence of the extent of the U.S. Government commitment to cooperation will undoubtedly make it easier for Sadat to move even faster in the direction of liberalization." Simon had already begun a series of Egyptian-US initiatives, including an agreement "to try to set up jointly a new institute to do project feasibility studies which can be used to attract investment not only from the U.S. but from oil-surplus countries." Simon expressed enthusiasm about Egypt's prospects, "for I believe there will be attractive investment opportunities to make use of the large quantity of under-utilized educated Egyptian manpower as Socialist controls—which seem alien to Egyptian nature—are shuffled off."[1]

While Simon was optimistic about the future potential of the Egyptian economy, the sharp rise in world petroleum prices hit oil-poor LDCs like Egypt especially hard. If they could not offset the higher cost of oil imports with foreign aid, exports, loans, or remittances, the already comparatively weak economies of LDCs would decline, bringing additional hardship or even destitution to much of their populations. Despite the dire circumstances, the Nixon and Ford administrations pursued policies that hindered relief reaching the most impoverished peoples of the world. The US government successfully undermined international efforts by the International Monetary Fund (IMF), the World Bank, the Non-Aligned Movement, and the Group of 77 to increase foreign aid from and improve terms of trade with the MDCs as part of a dubious campaign to bring down oil prices, increase foreign aid contributions from oil-rich countries, and promote private control of capital.

Yet while the Nixon and Ford administrations weakened efforts toward MDC support to the LDCs, they also worked to steer Arab and Iranian aid and investment in ways that drew LDCs more closely to the US system of international empire and global capitalism. Due to its strategic value and regional ties, Egypt constituted a top priority of US efforts to direct petrodollars to oil-poor LDCs. Egyptian and US government officials believed that petrodollars could facilitate the strengthening of Egyptian-US ties in two ways. First, the Nixon and Ford administrations hoped to induce oil-rich countries to provide increased aid to Egypt, which would demonstrate the value of the United States as an ally and assist Cairo's reorientation away from Moscow and toward Washington. Second, Simon and other officials believed that if the Gulf countries invested petrodollars in Egypt, this would help lead that country away from the stagnation of a closed, state-run economy and into a new era of prosperity created through private enterprise and global trade. They also recognized that US companies could benefit from the opening of Egypt's market and the investment of petrodollars. Egyptian and US officials began to use the term "tripartite" or "triangular investment" to describe the goal of combining oil-rich Arab investment funds with US technology and service expertise to produce profitable private ventures in developing sectors of the Egyptian economy such as industry, agriculture, tourism, finance, and mineral extraction. Triangular investment, as envisioned by its advocates, would recycle Arab petrodollars back into the world economy with a profit to the Gulf states, bring needed development to Egypt, and provide US companies with lucrative new sales and investments. Israel, however, would vigorously oppose Washington's efforts to establish stronger economic and military ties with Egypt, and Israeli efforts would cause new strains in Arab-US relations and contribute to an increase in US aid to Israel to help assuage its petrodollar-linked fears.

In the modern era, LDCs have regularly looked to acquire loans from MDCs as part of their efforts to develop their economies and eventually ascend to a more-developed state. During the nineteenth and early twentieth centuries, private Western banks (at first primarily British but over time increasingly US firms), seeking profitable outlets for their savings, lent to the governments and businesses of sovereign LDCs with the expectation that the capital would be profitably utilized, enabling the LDCs to repay the banks the original loan with interest. The Great Depression led to a wave of loan defaults by LDCs (and MDCs), however, and for over three decades thereafter private banks virtually ceased new lending to the nations of the Global South. In the aftermath of World War II, loans to Third World countries instead primarily came from the US government, the IMF and World Bank, and to a lesser extent the Soviet Union. Unlike private lending, governmental loans were extended not for profit but as a form of assistance for reasons of state and international order, to secure allegiances in the Cold War and advance particular visions of modernity. These governmental loans constituted a critical source of currency for many LDCs, funding programs for industrialization and raising the standard of living. In the mid-1960s a gradual revival of private Western lending to select Third World countries began, providing these countries with a new source of development funds.[2]

The rise in petroleum prices threatened the efforts of oil-poor LDCs to continue their development programs. Given the pivotal, often irreplaceable role of petroleum in modern economies, oil-importing countries either had to find a way to offset the increased cost of petroleum or reduce their consumption and experience a decrease in economic growth. But in contrast to oil-poor MDCs, oil-poor LDCs usually lacked comparable currency reserves, capital, powerful banks, or competitive export industries that could provide the funds needed to counterbalance the rising cost of oil imports. Unless new sources of wealth could be obtained by the oil-poor LDCs, their development programs would stall, their economic strength relative to the MDCs and oil-rich LDCs would decline, and their living standards would stagnate, with millions of people living in extreme poverty bearing the stark consequences.

Institutionally committed to assisting countries with balance-of-payments difficulties and development needs, respectively, the IMF and the World Bank proposed programs to utilize petrodollars and MDC funds to alleviate the economic challenges of the LDCs caused by the oil shock. Johannes Witteveen, the IMF managing director and former Dutch politician, proposed creating a new IMF facility that would borrow money from OECs and MDCs and lend the funds to oil-importing countries with large current account deficits in the wake of the oil shock. Witteveen intended for the facility to primarily assist LDCs, with the possible addition of MDCs with serious balance-of-payments difficulties.[3] Witteveen sought to acquire as much money as he could for the fund, which came to be called the "oil facility."[4] Robert McNamara, the president of the World Bank and former US defense secretary, held similar concerns as Witteveen regarding the oil-poor LDCs. McNamara had already redirected the World Bank to make the eradication of poverty, rather than infrastructure projects, a central tenet of development.[5] With the onset of the oil shock, McNamara directed his staff to sound out Saudi Arabia on its views for possible collaboration on how to address the problem of oil-poor LDCs running heavy current account deficits.[6] Like Witteveen, McNamara would pursue an increase in funds from both the OECs and MDCs to assist the oil-importing LDCs.

The Nixon and Ford administrations, led by Treasury, opposed the IMF and World Bank proposals. First and foremost, the administrations firmly argued that the United States, either bilaterally or through international institutions, should not increase public lending to offset rising oil costs for LDCs, as a freeze in US aid might force down the global price of oil. Treasury outlined the strategy in a January 1974 memorandum. It projected that most LDCs would exhaust traditional means of paying for oil imports by the end of the year. They were thus likely to seek increased financial assistance from the United States, a reasonable assumption since most LDCs remained reliant on public sources for loans. The memorandum "recommended that the U.S. establish a general policy position that its economic and financial assistance to the LDCs (including debt rescheduling) should not and cannot be increased to cover the additional costs of oil imports" in the hope that a failure to secure financing for oil bills "could result in LDC efforts to have the Arab OPEC countries reduce oil prices."[7] The plan in effect aimed to pit the poorest countries in the world against the newly cash wealthy but still less developed OECs for the economic benefit of the United States. The US plan was soon recognized by other countries. As the chancellor of the duchy of Lancaster Harold Lever put it to British prime minister Harold Wilson, "The other [oil] consumers feel that the Americans' present position still hinges around their earlier unrealistic policy of trying to bring about a major roll-back of the [oil] price. . . . The Americans give the impression that they hope to squeeze the [oil] price by leaving the less developed countries short of cash."[8]

The Nixon and Ford administrations also opposed the IMF and World Bank plans on the grounds that the OECs would be lending their petrodollars on insufficiently concessionary terms. The administrations generally advocated for an increase in OEC aid to other LDCs, for while it would not bring down the price of oil, it did shift some of the cost of the price increase back to members of OPEC, and it could reduce demands on US foreign aid. OEC aid was particularly valued if sent to US strategic allies. Treasury argued that the contribution of the OECs to the proposed IMF oil facility was not concessionary enough since it would be a loan repaid with interest.[9] Similarly, Treasury opposed the World Bank's campaign to increase its capital, and thus lending capacity, by selling more bonds to OECs, since, as one Treasury memo argued, the OECs received "political credit for helping the LDCs" with its purchase of World Bank bonds, despite them being a "basically commercial investment," which meant there was "reduce[d] political pressures on the oil countries to provide the highly concessional assistance most needed by the LDCs."[10]

Finally, Treasury officials' adherence to free market ideology and disdain for New Deal or Great Society–esque programs generally and the strategic pursuit of petrodollar interdependence specifically led them to see the United States as being in competition with the IMF and World Bank for obtaining Arab and Iranian capital and determining its use. For example, Paul Volcker, a conservative economist who had worked for federal and private banks and now served as a Treasury under secretary, wrote to Shultz that one of the reasons to oppose the oil facility was that it would turn the IMF into a "'welfare' institution."[11] An August 1974 Treasury memorandum expressed concern that the World Bank's growing accumulation of petrodollars via the sale of bonds challenged both inflows and outflows of US capital. "The Bank bonds are basically directly competitive with Treasury issues, and funds not invested in such bonds would tend to reach the U.S. market directly or indirectly," a Treasury official argued. Furthermore, "the Bank's growing dependence on borrowing from governments is changing the nature of the World Bank—further eroding its support for the private sector in LDCs and for the sound financial policies needed to have full support from private capital markets. . . . [It] is also giving the lending governments much increased influence on the Bank. . . . For example, it appears Libya has pressed the Bank strongly, and perhaps successfully, to move into mineral development in Africa through support of public sector enterprises for projects which U.S. private concerns were trying to organize."[12] At odds with the approaches of the IMF and World Bank, Treasury worked to steer petrodollars toward the US government and private banks, which it felt would make wiser decisions guided by market principles.

In early 1974 both Shultz and Volcker corresponded with Witteveen in an attempt to dissuade him from developing an oil facility on near-market terms. The Treasury officials argued that the poorer countries were unlikely to be able to repay even semiconcessional loans, that what was instead needed was either grant assistance from the OECs or a rollback in oil prices, and that an increase in near-market IMF lending would diminish the pressure on the OECs to provide grant aid or lower prices. Responding to Shultz's entreaties in March, Witteveen wrote a passionate defense of the proposed oil facility. He maintained that there was good reason to expect the LDCs to be able to repay loans, but argued that even with the risk of some defaults, IMF lending remained preferable to LDCs borrowing in private markets at higher costs and asked Shultz "whether we can reasonably withhold assistance from our poorest members, and thus adversely affect their credit-worthiness and development programs, in the uncertain hope that this might lead to lower oil prices or sufficient concessionary aid."[13] Witteveen's letter contested the economic and moral validity of Treasury's strategy to squeeze the LDCs, but the Nixon administration remained opposed to the IMF plan.

Undeterred, Witteveen traveled to the Middle East in April to solicit petrodollar pledges, ideally on concessional terms, for the oil facility. Arriving in Riyadh, Witteveen and his assistants found the small city inundated with more private bankers and government finance ministers than there were hotels to house them, leading presidents of banks to rent cabs and sleep in the back seat for a hundred dollars a night. The Saudis did ensure the IMF officials received a shared hotel room with cots, though it was run down and infested with cockroaches and bedbugs.[14] The situation underscored both the high level of international competition for Saudi petrodollars and the degree to which they could be used for development domestically. For their part, the Saudi leadership considered their petrodollars as something to be used for Saudi Arabia's economic or political interests, not for charity. The governor of the Saudi Arabian Monetary Agency, Anwar Ali, pledged roughly $1.2 billion for the oil facility with the possibility of additional funding, but he insisted on interest only slightly below market rates and made clear that he was "actively interested in the possibility of Saudi Arabia appointing an Executive Director [to the IMF]—hence his willingness to lend to the Fund."[15]

In Kuwait City, Witteveen encountered even greater skepticism about the proposed oil fund. Questioning the need for IMF mediation and bristling at popular accusations that the Arabs were depriving the world of capital, Kuwaiti minister of finance and oil Abdul Rahman al-Ateeqy pointedly contended that Kuwait's surpluses were already invested abroad or granted as aid. "Kuwait had always adopted an attitude of constructive cooperation, and yet the Arabs were reviled in the rest of the world," Ateeqy protested. "The world would have to realize that if the Arabs were treated as devils, they would start to act accordingly." While the United States feared the oil facility would maintain high oil prices, the Kuwaitis feared the oil facility was a Western trap. The Kuwaitis reasoned that if the oil-rich countries were expected to bear the majority of the burden of committing loans to the oil-poor LDCs, and the oil-poor LDCs then defaulted on the loans, the oil-rich LDCs would be sacrificing their petrodollar wealth to prop up the oil-poor LDCs while the Western countries sacrificed little to nothing. "This would benefit the industrial world," Ateeqy argued, "the very countries that had exploited the Arabs for so long."[16]

When the IMF oil facility was established on June 13, 1974, it was funded by Kuwait as well as the other OECs of Iran, Nigeria, Oman, Saudi Arabia, the UAE, and Venezuela and the MDCs of Canada and the Netherlands. A second oil facility was approved by the IMF in 1975, with Belgium, Sweden, Switzerland, and West Germany joining in making contributions. The United States declined to offer any funds to either facility, however, as it stuck to the strategy of squeezing the LDCs. For their part, the OECs provided relatively small loans and insisted on repayment with interest only slightly below market rates. The two oil facilities contributed roughly $7.9 billion in loans to countries with balance-of-payments difficulties, a sum dwarfed by the estimated $140 billion surplus accumulated by the members of OPEC between 1974 and 1976.[17] The IMF thus played only a minor role in petrodollar recycling.

The United States and the OECs likewise frustrated McNamara's vision for the World Bank. On the plus side, in the year and a half after the oil shock the members of OPEC provided nearly 80 percent of new loans to the World Bank. The OECs insisted on relatively high rates of interest, however, and during 1975 their purchases of World Bank bonds declined significantly. Ultimately, for the period from 1974 to 1981, OPEC members lent only 1.4 percent of their current account surplus to the World Bank, preferring to place their petrodollars in Western banks and investments that promised a higher return. The United States, meanwhile, worked to limit the World Bank's capital base, which would in turn limit its lending capabilities. In early 1974 McNamara launched a campaign to double the World Bank's general capital stock to $40 billion, but US resistance forced him to accept an increase of only $8.5 billion after two years of negotiations.[18] McNamara was deeply frustrated by US resistance to his efforts to support oil-poor LDCs. "The [US] Treasury's position," McNamara angrily told his staff in January 1976, "seemed to be that the needs of the LDCs had been exaggerated, that the LDCs don't deserve external assistance, that the external world cannot afford such assistance and that, in any event, private finance is doing a better job."[19]

Drawing on its leadership role within the Third World movement, oil-exporting Algeria championed a radical strategy to improve the standard of living of the oil-poor LDCs. The Algerian government utilized the Non-Aligned Movement, an organization founded to protect the right of countries to remain neutral in the Cold War and whose membership in the early 1970s comprised most Third World countries (including all Arab states, but not Israel or Iran), as its initial forum. Since 1967 the Algerian government had led an effort to shift the focus of the Non-Aligned Movement from defending the right to neutrality within the East-West struggle to addressing the issue of economic inequality in North-South relations. When Algiers hosted the fourth Non-Aligned Movement summit in September 1973, the Algerians guided the passage of resolutions that encapsulated their platform. The meeting's declaration maintained that "imperialism is still the greatest obstacle to the emancipation and progress of the developing countries" and that "neo-colonialist exploitation . . . accounts for the considerable and ever-increasing disparity between the industrialized countries and the under-developed world." The United States was implicitly cast as an imperial power for "the unleashing of criminal wars such as those affecting the peoples of Indochina and the Arab peoples," the latter an allusion to US support for Israel. The declaration maintained that overcoming the widening inequality produced by neocolonialism lay in organizing natural-resource cartels modeled on OPEC and a significant increase in multilateral aid to the least developed countries, administered by the United Nations and funded by the MDCs. In this way the Non-Aligned Movement laid the responsibility for the economic problems of oil-poor LDCs on the MDCs rather than the oil-rich LDCs, and therefore maintained that the cost of economically uplifting the oil-poor LDCs should be borne by the MDCs rather than the oil-rich LDCs.[20]

Algerian president Boumediene then seized upon global concern about resources in the wake of the oil shock to successfully petition for a special session of the United Nations on raw materials. In April 1974 at the UN Sixth Special Session, Boumediene spoke on behalf of the Group of 77 (G-77), a caucus of Third World countries that paralleled the objectives of the Non-Aligned Movement within the UN. Boumediene maintained that OPEC should serve as a model for other LDCs on how to nationalize resources like bauxite, copper, and iron-ore and increase their export price through the creation of cartels. "The raw-material-producing countries insist on being masters in their own houses," Boumediene declared.[21] The oil-poor LDCs continued to overwhelmingly embrace Algeria's vision, and they and the OECs used their majority in the UN General Assembly to approve the *Declaration on the Establishment of a New International Economic Order* (NIEO), which called for the correction of economic inequality between the Global North and the Global South through increases in the price of raw material exports, nonreciprocal trade preferences, and increased and nonconditional MDC aid for the LDCs. The UN resolution was nonbinding, but in the following months the Group of 77 held additional conferences that developed concrete proposals for changes to international agreements and possible plans for the members of OPEC to finance the start of new natural resource cartels. Saudi Arabia also insisted to the United States that multilateral talks on the possible reduction of the price of oil would have to be linked to discussions on stabilizing the price of other raw materials. The petrodollar windfall of the OECs served as both an inspiration to the advocates of the NIEO and a possible tool to bring it about.[22]

The cartelist, statist, and often anti-US rhetoric of NIEO proposals was not well received by the Nixon and Ford administrations. At first Kissinger pursued a strategy of noncooperation with the NIEO movement. By 1975, however, he had shifted tactics and initiated limited US engagement with the Group of 77, supporting talks on some raw materials and other NIEO issues tolerable to Washington but not others in an effort to divide the Third World across ideological and resource lines. By appearing constructive and offering concessions to some countries but not others, Kissinger hoped to foment divisions among the LDCs' moderates and radicals, oil rich and oil poor. To this end, Kissinger reminded the oil-importing LDCs of the economic pain they experienced from high oil prices, while also leveraging the benefits of petrodollar interdependence with the United States to dissuade OECs from committing themselves too strongly with the demands of the oil-poor LDCs. As Kissinger noted to Yamani, "You want security for your investments. We want security of [oil] supply. You want a reasonable price for your oil. . . . We have an interest in a number of issues associated with development." Ultimately the OECs proved unwilling to risk those ties with the United States and other Western countries on behalf of other LDC cartels. The Arab countries and Iran, regardless of their government, pursued their development by spending or investing most of their petrodollars in the West, and they accepted the deadlock of NIEO negotiations rather than seek a serious confrontation with the Western powers. Furthermore, oil was an uncommonly important, and often unexchangeable, raw material for modern economies whose supply was concentrated in a relatively few Third World countries, whereas other natural resources tended to be more interchangeable or globally diffuse. This accounted heavily for the failure of other raw material cartels to emerge in the wake of the oil shock; indeed, the relative market value of many natural resources declined during the 1970s.[23]

In sum, whether through the IMF, the World Bank, or the NIEO summits, international efforts at instituting an international, large-scale, and progressive program for funding LDC oil imports failed. These programs were unable to overcome the opposition of the US government and the disinterest or caution of the Arab monarchies and Iran. Oil-poor LDCs would have to either reduce their consumption of petroleum or offset the rising cost of oil imports by primarily traditional means: selling exports and labor and attracting investments in the free market and obtaining strings-attached aid from the MDCs and OECs.

While working to freeze total US foreign aid, the Nixon and Ford administrations encouraged the OECs to provide aid to and invest in oil-poor LDCs, especially those of strategic interest. Egypt quickly emerged as one of the top LDCs on whose behalf Washington lobbied for petrodollar transfers from the oil-rich Arab states and Iran. In the wake of the 1973 war, Kissinger now considered Egypt vital to preventing another Arab-Israeli war and its attendant risks of a complete breakdown in Arab-US relations, an even more severe oil embargo, and a military crisis with the Soviet Union. Upon meeting Sadat in December 1973, Kissinger also grasped that the Egyptian president sought a partnership with the United States, presenting him with the irresistible opportunity to switch the Cold War alignment of the most populous and militarily powerful Arab nation while addressing the Arab-Israeli conflict on US terms.[24] Upon his first visit in July 1974, Simon likewise became enthralled with Egypt for an additional reason: to "make it easier for Sadat to move even faster in the direction of [economic] liberalization" and "shuffle off" socialist controls. To that end, Simon "agreed to set up jointly a new institute to do project feasibility studies which can be used to attract investment not only from the U.S. but from oil surplus countries."[25] The United States sought to assist Egypt in obtaining MENA petrodollars to fund projects that would liberalize the economy, hire US companies and purchase US products, and politically tie Cairo to Washington.

Sadat's outlook aligned with that of US officials. In addition to US support in negotiations with Israel, Sadat desperately desired US assistance in improving Egypt's finances. Acquiring foreign currency had become an urgent task. The burdens of war and a stagnating economy had caused Egypt to run critically low on foreign currency reserves in the late 1960s, and by the spring of 1974 Egypt had accumulated $15 billion in foreign debt, an equivalent of six years of export earnings. Without foreign currency, Egypt would be unable to import arms to counter Israel, basic supplies like grain needed by its population, or technology and services to develop Egyptian industry and agriculture. Egypt also urgently needed new sources of foreign currency to avoid defaulting on its existing foreign debts; default, many feared, would significantly worsen Egypt's ability to attract additional foreign capital. Sadat calculated that after the 1973 war he now had a golden opportunity to press the petrodollar-rich Arab countries to provide Egypt with massive infusions of capital to sustain Egyptian military and diplomatic pressure on Israel. This capital would be used to purchase advanced technology and services from US and other OECD corporations, as well as to attract additional Western investments through joint ventures. This triangular investment would then enable Egypt to develop its industrial and agricultural sectors and achieve higher levels of domestic production and export sales, restore its balance of trade, and escape the cycle of growing debt.[26]

Shortly after assuming the presidency, Sadat had begun a gradual relaxation of governmental controls over the economy and other incentives to encourage foreign commercial exchange and investment. In the aftermath of the 1973 war, Sadat sought to further advance this economic course. It is important to note that Sadat's regime did not seek to reverse all government controls over the economy, however. The Egyptian government continued to own and run most sectors of the economy, directly employed a large portion of its population, placed official limits on income, and set prices for key commodities that it also subsidized. While some within the Egyptian government sought to liberalize these aspects of the economy as well, most remained committed to socialist planning, with Sadat's apparent support. Most Egyptian officials pursued the opening of Egypt to foreign investment and trade strictly as a measure to obtain foreign currency, not as a step toward a general liberalization of Egypt's economy along capitalistic lines.[27]

For shifting away from the Soviet Union, Cairo expected the United States to not only facilitate triangular investment to Egypt but provide direct economic and military aid, too. The Nixon administration strongly desired to grant Egyptian aid requests in order to further pull Egypt into the US sphere of influence. The Nixon administration faced strong congressional resistance to any new major assistance program to Egypt, however, owing to both the Arab-Israeli conflict and growing US opposition to foreign aid programs in general. The Nixon administration thus moved gradually in increasing US aid to Egypt. In January 1974 it announced a commitment of $8.5 million for Egypt after the first separation of Egyptian and Israeli forces, and in March requested Congress to approve $250 million in aid to Egypt for fiscal year 1975.[28]

In early 1974, however, Moscow, observing Sadat's shift toward the United States, withheld assistance to Egypt to force Cairo back into the Soviet camp. With the Egyptian economy and military seriously weakened from the 1973 war, the lack of significant and immediate support from either superpower placed Sadat's government under extraordinary strain. Even before the end of the Arab oil embargo, on March 2 Kissinger suggested to Faisal that he transfer some US weapons to Egypt "to reduce Soviet influence there" and maintain their capability in the face of the Soviet arms cutoff. Kissinger explained that the transfer of US weapons to Egypt through Saudi Arabia, rather than directly, was at the moment necessary since "we have temporary domestic difficulties" (i.e., congressional opposition to the United States arming Egypt).[29] On April 1, 1974, US ambassador Hermann Eilts reported to Kissinger that Egyptian foreign minister Ismail Fahmy had made to him an impassioned plea for US economic aid. Fahmy told Eilts that Moscow had "made it crystal clear that any further Soviet help, military or economic, is conditioned on Egyptian endorsement of direct Soviet participation in all further [Arab-Israeli] peace talks" and that the Soviets "are 'squeezing Egypt' and Egypt is feeling the pinch. In the past four months the president [Sadat] and he have drastically reoriented Egyptian policy [toward the United States]. They have done so at great political and personal risk to themselves and have as yet gotten little from the [US government] in return. . . . He hopes the [US government] realizes that the disengagement agreement [between Egypt and Israel], while helpful, is no (repeat) no answer to Egypt's serious political and economic requirements."[30] Three days later Fahmy again warned Eilts that "Egyptians at all levels will shortly begin to contrast what Egypt has been getting in past twenty years from Soviets with meager US support to date. If there are any commodity shortages in Egypt, as there currently are because [the] Soviets have refused to provide needed economic help except on [a] cash basis, these will be laid at the door of Sadat's and his policy shift."[31] On April 20 Sadat told Eilts that obtaining US arms in order to diversify Egypt's weapons sources was an urgent matter and that he hoped the United States would be responsive.[32] It was clear that the Egyptians considered economic and military assistance to be vital requirements for an Egyptian-US alliance; progress in the Arab-Israeli peace process alone would be insufficient.

The State Department, eager to encourage Egypt's political reorientation toward the United States but also aware that Congress would prevent a quicker allocation of aid than Egypt desired, looked for alternative means of assistance that bypassed the legislative branch. Many proposals incorporated Arab petrodollars. As early as January 1974 State suggested encouraging the World Bank to "provide a framework in which Western and Arab money would be combined with Western technology to make Egypt one of the fastest growing LDCs."[33] In late January, State began secretly serving as an intermediary to avoid the dissolution of the first major triangular investment project in Egypt that had been established a week before the outbreak of the 1973 war: the construction of the SUMED pipeline, which was to be cofinanced by Arab and

US lenders (including Chase) and constructed by the California-based Bechtel Corporation. Pricing and financing disputes between Bechtel and the Egyptian government threatened to scuttle the entire venture, an outcome Fahmy told Eilts "would be catastrophic." In response, Eilts pressed both Bechtel and the Egyptian government to achieve a resolution.[34] While Bechtel ultimately reduced its role from building the pipeline to acting as a management supervisor (the actual construction would be taken up by Italian firms), State's mediations may have prevented a complete collapse of the plan and preserved hopes for future joint Arab-US investment in Egypt.[35]

On May 1, while in Egypt, Kissinger told Sadat that his immediate arms assistance requirements from the United States "could be sold to Kuwait and/or Saudi Arabia and be transferred to Egypt by one or another of these governments." Later arms sales, credits, and grants could then be made directly between the United States and Egypt. Kissinger explained that he wanted to pursue a gradual increase in arms transfers to Egypt, beginning with indirect transfers, in order to blunt the effectiveness of Israeli lobbying. "We should sell those items first which are not likely to create public furor," Kissinger explained to Sadat. "We can permit the Saudis to purchase [F-4] Phantom [fighters] since there has already been talk of Phantom sales for Saudi Arabia."[36] Saudi petrodollars could thus serve to facilitate the transfer of US weapons to Egypt that Congress might not be ready to approve. Notably, Harold Saunders, now a State deputy assistant, had earlier expressed his concern to Kissinger that since such transfers of US arms between another Arab country and Egypt would legally require notification of Congress and would also inevitably be observed and publicized by Israeli intelligence, such indirect transfers might create more anger in US public opinion than a concerted campaign by the administration to develop support for a direct arms transfer to Egypt, but Kissinger raised the indirect arms transfer scheme with Sadat anyway.[37]

Treasury also became involved in petrodollar recycling schemes for Egypt, and while both Kissinger and Simon recognized the political opportunities that could be achieved through petrodollar recycling to Egypt, Simon also focused on the opportunities created by petrodollars to change Egypt's economic structures. Treasury saw in Sadat a desire to liberalize Egypt, but also believed he needed "considerable financial aid if he is to open up the economy." While amenable to US assistance to Egypt, Treasury also recognized that "many of the Arab oil producers have publicly indicated their willingness to provide substantial financial assistance for Egyptian development if feasible projects can be found. Our assistance in identifying projects will thus help the oil producers make good on their pledge of shouldering a share of the aid burden." To pursue this goal, Simon planned to propose to Egypt the establishment of "a Project Development Institute to identify growth areas and viable projects to absorb the capital provided by Arab oil producers. The Institute could contract out to private firms in the U.S. or other countries for project feasibility studies."[38]

Yet while Treasury anticipated petrodollar investments could help smooth Egypt's economic liberalization, Treasury also considered economic liberalization measures as necessary to attract petrodollar investment in Egypt. Specific proposals Treasury desired Egypt to pursue included the decontrol of prices and interest rates, allowing more public enterprises to compete for goods and capital, and depreciating the Egyptian currency, which they considered artificially overvalued.[39] Treasury supported such economic liberalization as a point of principle, but it also believed that this program was particularly important for Egypt if it was to attract sufficient amounts of petrodollar investments. It also appears Treasury underestimated the level of resistance many of these proposed changes would encounter from Egyptian officials who desired both foreign capital and government intervention in most aspects of the economy.

Governmental efforts to promote foreign investment in Egypt and economic cooperation between Egypt and the United States appeared to make steady progress in the first half of 1974. On February 11 Sadat established the Agency for Arab and International Cooperation to attract foreign investment. In April Sadat publicly announced his plans for an "opening" (*intifah*) of Egypt to foreign investment and trade through a relaxation of governmental controls.[40] The same month Sadat publicly declared that Egypt would end its reliance on Soviet military equipment by purchasing Western arms with the assistance of the oil-rich Arab states.[41] On May 31 Egypt and the United States formally formed a joint cooperation committee to improve economic relations between the two.[42] On June 10 Egypt passed Law 43, which opened previously protected areas of the Egyptian economy to foreign investment, allowed the entry of foreign banks, and provided taxation and repatriation incentives to foreign investors.[43] Four days later, Nixon, visiting Cairo, reiterated the United States' commitment to providing Egypt with aid and private investment and announced an agreement to provide Egypt with nuclear technology for peaceful energy purposes.[44]

All of this set the backdrop for Simon's visit to Egypt in July. While encouraged by recent Egyptian laws and rhetoric aimed at liberalizing the economy and attracting foreign investment, Simon believed far more could be done. Meeting with Egyptian government officials, Simon and his assistants emphasized the need to improve Egypt's credit rating by paying off outstanding debts, to simplify tax codes, and to allow a larger percentage of profits to be repatriated by foreign companies.[45] Simon also told Hegazi of his idea to establish the Project Development Institute as part of the Joint Cooperation Committee to identify and create feasibility plans for projects within Egypt that would attract foreign investment from both Arab and US sources. Treasury planning materials for Simon's visit instructed him to emphasize to Hegazi that "the Project Development Institute . . . could uniquely combine oil producing capital, U.S. know-how and private capital, and Egyptian land and personnel."[46] Hegazi publicly agreed during Simon's visit to establish the Project Development Institute.[47] Hegazi and Simon also signed a bilateral investment-guarantee agreement that stipulated that Washington could take up claims with Cairo on behalf of US companies if they felt they did not receive satisfactory treatment in the case of a dispute with the Egyptian government. On the same day of the agreement's signing, Egypt also announced it was allowing Chase, Citibank, American Express Company, and Bank of America to open banking offices in the country, the first foreign banks allowed to do so in seventeen years.[48]

Cairo recognized that promises of petrodollar financing would go far in attracting US business, and it worked to promote this idea. When the US-Egyptian Joint Commission met at the offices of the US Department of Commerce on August 15 to discuss measures to further advance investment and trade between the two countries, the Egyptian delegation raised "the concept of 'tri-partite' investment, which would combine U.S.-Egyptian investment projects with capital from third countries—most probably from Arab oil-producing areas. . . . In this way, the technical information and skills of the U.S. private sector can make a vastly greater contribution to Egypt than if the U.S. partners had to provide all of their own capital." The Egyptian delegation offered to connect US investors to such third-party capital as an additional inducement to do business in Egypt. The US officials agreed to help make US businesspeople aware of opportunities in Egypt and pass along information from the Egyptian government. The Joint Commission also "agreed to form a 'joint business chamber' type organization to provide a continuing forum in which U.S. and Egyptian businessmen can meet on their own terms, to discuss matters of mutual interest."[49]

When Ford succeeded Nixon as president, the US effort to utilize Arab petrodollars to build its empire by boosting private US business interests and drawing Egypt into the US orbit continued. In the first days of Ford's presidency, Kissinger impressed upon Ford the importance of both the Middle East conflict in general and Egypt in particular to US interests. "The Middle East is the worst problem we face," Kissinger told Ford the morning of August 12.

"The oil situation is the worst we face. . . . We can't afford another embargo. If we are faced with that, we may have to take some oil fields." At the present, Kissinger argued that "the critical issue is Egyptian military equipment. The Soviet Union is turning them off. If that continues, the military will have to turn out Sadat or go back to the Soviet Union." To preserve Sadat's government and its tilt toward the United States, the Ford administration needed to offset the loss of Soviet arms. Kissinger noted that an initial step toward this was "equipping them [with US arms] through Saudi Arabia. The first step would be to send it to Saudi Arabia and let Egyptian troops train in it. . . . Saudi Arabia is willing to use 200 million [presumably dollars] for Egypt."[50] That evening, the visiting Fahmy again impressed upon Kissinger Egypt's need for US arms in the wake of the Soviet freeze. Kissinger attempted to placate him with assurances that US arms would soon arrive to Egypt through Saudi Arabia.[51] The next day Kissinger provided Ford with a list of weapons that the United States could provide Egypt through Saudi Arabia, and again encouraged Ford to approve it. "You think we should go ahead then?" Ford asked. "I think we should," Kissinger answered. "Egypt is in a difficult situation. If we can't encourage the switch away from the Soviet Union and they turn back, there will probably not be another opportunity in our generation." "I think we should do it," Ford agreed.[52]

Treasury and Commerce likewise continued their push to attract Arab petrodollars for Egyptian-US projects under Ford. By the fall of 1974 many US companies expressed interest to Treasury about entering the Egyptian market: AT&T and Western Electric were interested in providing telecommunications technology, Northrop in establishing a research foundation, Genesco a textile plant, Union Carbide a petrochemical complex, and Occidental Petroleum phosphate mines and fertilizer plants. Concerns did loom in the minds of Treasury officials; the Egyptian government did not seem capable of producing the satisfactory feasibility studies needed to attract most investors, did not seem to understand the purpose of the US-proposed Project Development Institute to assist them in creating investment proposals, and struggled to pay off or even comprehensively catalog its foreign debts.[53] But Treasury pressed forward in its efforts with Egypt and by November had developed the term "triangular investment" as a useful shorthand. "We have spent a good deal of time focusing on individual jointvventure [sic] projects and on the concept of triangular investment, which involves bringing together U.S. technology, Egyptian projects and other Arab financial resources," Treasury official Gerald Parsky wrote to Kissinger in a November status update on activities of the US-Egyptian Joint Cooperation Commission. "This latter concept interests the Egyptians very much."[54] The same day, Parsky also wrote to Shultz, now a vice president at Bechtel, about Shultz's upcoming trip to Egypt. Parsky described to Shultz his efforts toward "developing the concept of tripartite or triangular investment." Parsky also asked Shultz "for any thoughts you have after your talks [in Egypt]—especially the feelings of the government about our efforts. . . . Of particular interest, of course, will be opportunities for U.S. business to play a major role for the mutual benefit of our two countries."[55]

Yet despite the liberalization efforts of the Egyptian government, foreign investment from both the West and the Arab world remained minimal by mid-1975. Faced with this reality, Cairo pushed the Ford administration to both increase US aid and lobby oil-rich countries and MDCs to increase their aid to Egypt. Despite unprecedented levels of aid from the oil-rich Arab countries already being sent to Egypt, in May 1975 Egypt told the United States that it needed an additional emergency aid package of $1 billion for import financing; if this sum was not quickly delivered, Cairo would have to either default on foreign loans, thus further damaging Egypt's creditworthiness and economic prospects, or severely cut back on imports, which could lead to political unrest that would threaten the Sadat regime. State noted that "the Egyptians turned to the United States, rather than the [World Bank] and IMF, to represent their case for [the emergency] non-project aid to the other potential donors because they evidently feared that a consortium managed by the international agencies would attach politically troublesome economic reform conditions to its pledges."[56] While the Ford administration agreed with the IMF and World Bank that Egypt needed to undertake additional economic reforms, it also desired to incur political favor from the Egyptian government and to support the stability of Sadat's regime. In this instance, the Ford administration favored its political calculations over its economic concerns and proceeded to lobby on Egypt's behalf for foreign aid without economic restructuring stipulations.

The Ford administration first lobbied Iran and Saudi Arabia to join the United States in forming an aid package in which the three countries would each contribute roughly $250 million for fiscal year 1975. This "nucleus group" would then use their pledges as an inducement to encourage other Western and oil-rich countries to add contributions. The Saudi government quickly agreed to the plan, provided the Saudis could make their contribution bilaterally and it was impressed upon Egypt not to expect expanded aid to be repeated the following year lest it become a habit; the United States readily agreed.[57] The Iranian government expressed less enthusiasm about the plan, complaining that while it supported Sadat, the recent decline in the real value of oil revenues due to inflation made it harder for Iran to be as generous in foreign aid.[58] Iran eventually went along with the plan, pledging $150 million and an additional $100 million conditioned upon Egyptian procurement of Iranian goods, while Saudi Arabia quickly dispatched its $250 million in aid. In addition to $250 million from the United States, West Germany and Japan also each pledged $50 million.[59] The Ford administration had facilitated a critical petrodollar aid package to Egypt, helping to preserve Sadat's government and Egypt's economic prospects, while at the same time demonstrating the benefits of a closer relationship with the United States.

But where the US government saw potential to utilize petrodollars in aligning Egypt and others toward itself, the Israeli government saw an existential threat. Israel realized that petrodollars were reshaping the balance of economic and military power between it and the Arab world to Israel's disadvantage, and sought US assistance in offsetting this. To strengthen its bargaining position, Israel tied its cooperation in the peace process to US assistance.

The Israeli economy languished in the mid-1970s. The oil price surges contributed to Israel's energy bill rising from an average of 1 percent of GNP in the 1960s to over 7 percent from 1973 to 1979. Israeli defense expenditures also ballooned in response to the 1967 and 1973 wars and the arms race with the Arab states, as petrodollars funded the Arab arsenals. The rise in petrodollar profits thus raised the specter of both an augmented Arab military threat and an Israeli economic collapse from unsustainable military expenses. During the October 1974 Rabat Summit, not only did the Arab League unanimously declare the PLO the sole representative for the Palestinians, but the oil-rich member countries also pledged annual aid of $1 billion each to Egypt and Syria, $300 million to Jordan, and $50 million in annual assistance to the PLO for the next four years, in addition to any previously existing aid agreements. Both the oil shocks and increased defense expenditures contributed to high levels of inflation in Israel as well. The Israeli government thus urgently sought both military and economic assistance to counter the rising power of the Arab countries.[60]

At first, Israeli officials emphasized to Washington an alleged contrast between the large flows of Soviet weapons to the Arabs and the paltry arms deliveries from the United States to Israel. In August 1974, for example, Israeli deputy prime minister and minister of finance Yigal Allon harangued Simon about "the Soviet arms build-up in Syria and Iraq and to a lesser extent in Egypt" and stated that "he was surprised . . . to see how unprepared the U.S. is to meet challenges around the world and is unable to help friends and allies with needed minimum supplies of conventional arms." Allon insisted that he could not go to any peace conference "so long as Israel's bilateral military, economic, and political problems with the U.S. are not solved," and said that "war can be averted if a balance of military strength is maintained."[61]

As US arms sales to Arab countries grew, the Israeli government not only continued to demand increased US aid but also pushed the United States to limit arms sales to the Arab countries, emphasizing perceived disparities between US arms deliveries to Israel and those to Saudi Arabia. In February 1975, for example, Israeli ambassador Simcha Dinitz began a meeting with Kissinger and Scowcroft with a protest over the delay in receiving a letter of offer for the US sale of F-15 fighters to Israel, but he quickly shifted into a complaint about Saudi Arabia. The United States, Dinitz maintained, delivered arms to the Saudis more promptly than to the Israelis, was heedlessly selling some of its most advanced arms to the Saudis, and was not taking sufficient precautions to prevent the Saudis from transferring US arms to Egypt. At one point in his protestations, Dinitz stopped and observed that he had visibly upset Kissinger. "I get upset," Kissinger retorted, "because whenever I want to talk about the [peace process] negotiations, to get you in a good mood you want weapons."[62] Dinitz clearly registered to Kissinger the Israelis' concern that the Saudis were acquiring too many weapons and that they might be transferred to Egypt, endangering Israel's military supremacy over its Arab neighbors. Furthermore, Kissinger was well aware of, and frustrated by, the Israeli strategy to link cooperation in the peace process to US military and economic assistance to Israel.

Yet while the Israeli government attempted to use the peace process to extract US aid, the US government attempted to use US aid to extract Israeli concessions in the peace process. Nixon, Ford, and Kissinger all used US aid as a carrot to reward Israeli territorial withdrawals and to balm concerns over strengthening Arab-US relations. The three also readily used the threat of withholding US assistance as a stick to prod Israel forward in the peace negotiations when they deemed the Israelis to be too intransigent.[63] In 1974, however, Israel received more carrot than stick. In part due to Israel's massive rearmament needs during and after the 1973 war, in part due to US efforts to keep Israel progressing in the peace process, and in part to assuage Israeli fears about rising Arab petrodollar power, the United States provided Israel with an unprecedented, near $2.6 billion in aid in 1974, a sum larger than the total amount of US aid provided to Israel during the first five years of the Nixon administration ($1.9 billion) or of all US aid to Israel from 1961 to 1973 ($2.5 billion). Furthermore, whereas all US military aid and most economic aid to Israel had previously been provided in the form of loans, the 1974 aid package included $1.5 billion in military grant aid.

The year 1974 marked the beginning of a dramatically new era in US aid to Israel; whereas before the United States had been only a modest financial contributor to the Israeli government, from 1974 to 1980 US aid would supply 85 percent of the Israeli defense budget.[64] This dramatic shift was in part the result of Israel's and the United States' responses to the new petrodollar economy.

The dramatic increase in US aid to Israel displeased most Arabs, and Cairo had particular reason to be dismayed at the end of 1974 when it compared the actual US disbursement of $2.6 billion to Israel during that year with the $250 million in nonmilitary aid the United States had pledged to Egypt for fiscal year 1975. In December 1974, Saudi acting foreign minister Muhammad Masud confidentially informed Akins that Egyptian security adviser Ashraf Marwan had recently visited with Faisal and Fahd and told them that "the Egyptians were becoming increasingly disillusioned with their new relationship with the United States. They [the Egyptians] had broken with the Russians at the urging of the United States and Saudi Arabia, but what had they achieved? The United States had made promises of economic and military support and had given nothing. They had promised that Israel would withdraw further from the occupied Arab lands, yet it was increasingly evident that Israel would not do this." Akins believed that "at least some Saudis . . . are concluding that our words of conciliation and our 'special relationship' [with Saudi Arabia] are merely covers for aggressive plans" and that Marwan's complaints had made a strong impression on Faisal.[65] On December 18 Faisal sent a strongly worded letter to Ford echoing the Egyptian complaints. "What benefits did the Egyptian Arab Republic obtain by changing its position toward the Soviet (Union)?" Faisal pointedly asked. Faisal contrasted the lack of US support to Egypt with US assistance to Israel and stated that while he was grateful for the efforts of the United States in the peace process, "I assure you that the delay in reaching a complete withdrawal from all the Arab territories, and in giving the Palestinian people its right to self-determination and to return to its fatherland, shall undo all the efforts that have been made, and the reaction in our Arab world will be intense toward the United States."[66] Faisal clearly feared that an imbalance in US aid and a failure to oversee progress in the peace process could undo Saudi efforts to create a Saudi-US aligned Arab bloc, and could even force Riyadh back to a position of hostility toward Washington.

Ford wrote back to Faisal stating that while progress had not occurred as quickly as he wanted, significant steps had been made in the first withdrawals of Israeli forces from Egyptian territory and in establishing the resumption of US aid and economic development plans for Egypt. Further advances could be made soon, Ford insisted, so long as Faisal continued to support US efforts.[67]

The Ford administration did not want to see the Saudi-US–led Arab bloc break apart any more than the House of Saud did, but pressure increasingly mounted for further US action. A CIA assessment sent to Scowcroft on March 14, 1975, stated that "if progress [on the peace process was] not quickly achieved . . . or at least an assurance gained that it could be effected soon, the odds are high that Egypt, in conjunction with Syria, would reopen the war."[68]

This was the backdrop when Kissinger failed to achieve a second Egypt-Israeli agreement in March 1975. Israeli prime minister Yitzhak Rabin refused to return a pair of strategic passes to Egypt without a formal pledge of non-belligerence; Sadat refused to make any deal without the return of the passes and stated that for purposes of political cover in the Arab world he could only pledge to not resolve the Arab-Israeli conflict through military force. Despite pressure from Ford and Kissinger to accept the Egyptian formula, Israel refused. At this point, Ford publicly declared that his administration would reassess its Middle East policy, making clear that he blamed Israel for the breakdown of the peace process and hinting that the special relationship between Israel and the United States might suffer for it.[69] At an NSC meeting on March 28 the Ford administration expressed consensus that aid and policy coordination with Israel would be restricted while cooperation with the Arab countries would continue relatively unchanged. The NSC voiced concern that if the United States failed to persuade Israel to resume the peace process along lines minimally acceptable to Egypt, another war would break out. The likely result would be a significant loss of US influence in the Arab world, another Arab oil embargo, and the movement of Soviet military forces into the region.[70]

Vice President Nelson Rockefeller, back from a visit to Saudi Arabia to attend the funeral of King Faisal, who had been assassinated by a nephew three days earlier for unclear reasons, participated in the NSC meeting. Faisal's unassuming half brother Khalid succeeded him as king, but Fahd, who would become crown prince, was understood to now be the guiding force behind Saudi policy. Rockefeller reported that while attending the funeral, Fahd told him that "unless there is a 'just, equitable and lasting peace within one year'—and those are his exact words—the Soviets will move back in, the radicals will be reinvigorated and rearmed by the Soviets while the moderates will move away from the US and establish a close relationship with Western Europe. The Europeans have arms they want to sell, we have the money to buy. . . . The Arabs will keep building their military strength as long as it takes from the USSR and Western Europe and in time we will crush Israel." Rockefeller added that Fahd "is right about the Western Europeans. The French sent their Defense Minister to the funeral with a list of items for sale and models of aircraft and tanks. This offended the Saudis."[71] Yet if the French had proved tactless, they also demonstrated that the Europeans offered the Saudis alternate patrons. From the vantage point of the Ford administration, the Israelis had dangerously imperiled the new order of petrodollar interdependence between the United States and the Arab world.

The Ford administration suspended all new economic and military agreements with Israel, hoping the pressure would lead the Israelis to reverse course before the outbreak of another war. At first Rabin resisted, knowing his bargaining position with Washington was enhanced by the recent growth of pro-Israel Jewish activism in the United States. After the 1973 war many Jewish Americans feared that Arab oil power might lead other Americans, and in turn the US government, to sacrifice Israel in pursuit of economic interests; the National Jewish Community Relations Advisory Council set up a $3 million emergency fund for a public relations task force in response. This task force led the media and congressional campaign against Ford's reassessment.[72] On May 21 Ford received a letter from seventy-six senators calling on him to be "responsive to Israel's economic and military needs."[73]

The Ford administration stood fast, however, and in June Rabin and his cabinet determined that they should reengage in the peace process along US

Figure 3. Anwar Sadat and Gerald Ford at the White House, October 27, 1975. Courtesy of Gerald R. Ford Presidential Library.

lines. Sadat also made concessions, agreeing that US civilians could be stationed at observation points in the Sinai to further ensure that Egypt would not resume hostilities. On September 4 Egypt and Israel formally signed the Sinai II Accord, which granted most of the territorial concessions Egypt had insisted upon in return for a commitment to solving the Arab-Israeli dispute without military force. To ensure Israeli cooperation, however, Kissinger also pledged about $2 billion in additional aid to Israel.[74] The Ford administration had managed to keep the peace process moving.

Yet the protracted struggle over the Sinai II agreement underscored how Israel's fears, in part due to Arab petrodollar power, could potentially lead to a new conflict in the region that would undo the fragile new Saudi-US Arab bloc, a coalition largely linked together by petrodollars. The episode also underscored how the United States was supplying both sides of the Arab-Israeli arms race, just one of the many trends in the region being rapidly reshaped by rising petrodollar revenues.

Chapter 5

The Petrodollar Economy

Cecil Andrus, Democratic governor of Idaho, was determined to see the shah. In April 1976 Andrus led a trade mission for his state to Iran, composed of ten Idaho business leaders, including the chairman of the American Potato Company and other executives from nuclear power, oil refining, construction, mining, livestock, irrigation, and agricultural companies, as well as Republican senator from Idaho James McClure. A month before his trip, Andrus requested a letter of introduction to the shah from President Ford to arrange a meeting.[1] The Ford administration had a policy against granting presidential letters for private US business travel abroad, however, and politely declined the request.[2] Andrus wrote again to Ford, stating that while he was sure it was a State Department position not to grant presidential letters, Andrus was also "certain that you [Ford] would not have allowed the State Department to dictate to you whether or not you could write a letter of introduction on behalf of a governor, a United States Senator and ten prominent business executives to a foreign leader." Andrus then repeated his request for a presidential letter.[3]

The Ford administration appreciated Andrus's past support for the president's initiatives, so White House officials attempted to get around the issue of the presidential letter by having Ambassador Helms arrange a meeting for Andrus with the shah. Helms had his own policy against personally arranging private meetings with the shah, but Scowcroft, now national security advisor after Ford decided to have Kissinger focus solely on his role as secretary of state the previous November, wrote to Helms that "this is a very unusual case. . . . I—and I am sure the President—would be very grateful for any help you might feel able to provide."[4] Helms "pulled out all [the] stops with Minister of Court Alam" and successfully secured the meeting.[5] "The shah undoubtedly [now] knows more than he needs to about raising potatoes," Scowcroft wrote to Helms afterward, "but I want you to know once again how much we appreciate the way you came through on an awkward one."[6]

The Idaho trade mission to Iran emblemized major trends of the new US-led petrodollar economy. This order produced new points of contact and cooperative networks among Americans and Arabs and Iranians, broadening the number of individuals and kinds of actors involved in MENA-US relations. US corporations and MENA governments developed an unprecedented symbiotic relationship with each other, as a variety of US economic sectors and communities from nearly all regions of the United States came to rely on petrodollars as a major source of capital and oil-rich regimes counted on US goods and services to undertake rapid economic and military modernization drives. These ventures further drew the MENA into the system of global capitalism and consumption. All of these trends contributed to Washington's goal of securing and expanding its empire in the MENA through interdependence. At the same time, the petrodollar boom transformed US empire and the role of oil-rich MENA allies within it. Instead of supplying cheap oil, MENA allies provided petrodollars. Instead of relying on British forces, rapidly militarized regional allies, especially Iran, would defend interests in the MENA. And instead of the United States providing the overwhelming majority of foreign aid to allied LDCs, oil-rich countries, particularly Saudi Arabia, assumed a far larger share of financial assistance to US allies in the Third World. Such aid would, among other things, play a critical role in sustaining Egypt's shift toward the United States.

Yet petrodollar interdependence also proved to be a double-edged sword. While little appreciated by US leaders at first, the influx of American people and products produced hostility in many MENA communities, particularly when they served the repressive functions of local regimes. In becoming increasingly tied to the oil-rich Arab countries, the United States also became even further tied to the repercussions arising from the Arab-Israeli conflict. When the Lebanese Civil War threatened to ignite another full-scale Arab-Israeli war, US policymakers feared that petrodollars could be used as a financial weapon against the United States and its allies. And while petrodollar aid assisted in the US effort to reform the political and economic orientation of

Egypt, it also produced unintended social consequences that undermined Sadat's regime.

During the mid-1970s the global price of oil remained high compared with pre-1973 levels, but it did experience a small, gradual decline. The OPEC posted price of $11.25 instituted in November 1974 remained in place until October 1975, at which point it was raised to $11.51 (still lower than the nominal price at the start of 1974), where it would remain through the end of 1976. The real value of oil sales decreased from 1974 to 1976 due to inflation.[7] Saudi Arabia remained the primary restraint on oil prices, while most other members of OPEC, led by Iran, pushed for higher rates. From 1974 to 1976, Saudi Arabia constituted the largest producer of oil within OPEC, at 27 percent of total output by volume, while Iran came in second at 20 percent.[8] Each served as a counterweight to the other, and the price increase of October 1975 was an uneasy compromise between the two. The Ford administration continued to implore Riyadh and Tehran to prevent additional OPEC price hikes in the short term while endeavoring to increase their interdependence with the United States through things like development projects over the long term. The shah regularly rebuffed US requests, while the Saudis sought to extract concessions from Washington on the Arab-Israeli peace process in exchange for their price restraint.[9]

The Ford administration's fears about another OPEC oil price hike peaked in late 1976. In October, Scowcroft told Ford that any increase "would have serious and perhaps even catastrophic effects in both developed and developing countries," and was particularly concerned about the potential "strain on the economic and political stability" of Italy and the United Kingdom due to their ongoing balance-of-payments difficulties. State believed a 15 percent price increase would reduce US GDP by a full percentage point. Ford and Kissinger sought to apply pressure on Iran and Saudi Arabia, though the latter continued to doubt threatening a withholding of arms from the shah would work until the French joined such an effort. At the OPEC conference in mid-December, Iran and Saudi Arabia failed to reach a compromise, resulting in a split in the OPEC posted price starting in 1977, with Saudi Arabia and the UAE raising the posted price by 5 percent to $12.09 per barrel while Iran led the other eleven members in raising the posted price by 10 percent to $12.70 per barrel. Washington was pleased with the Saudi decision to insist on a lower price, but also knew the Saudis expected the United States to show its appreciation by helping to achieve a final Arab-Israeli peace settlement.[10]

Even with the partial decline in the real value of posted petroleum prices after 1974, however, the oil-exporting MENA countries still accrued unpre-

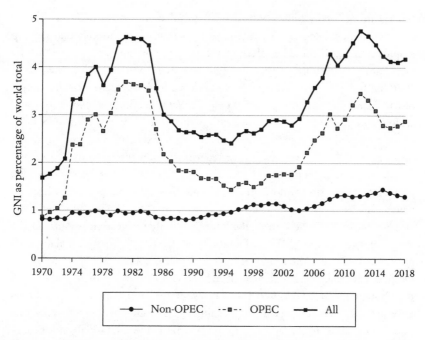

Figure 4. MENA countries as share of gross world product, 1970–2018. Source: United Nations, National Accounts Main Aggregates Database.

cedented petrodollar revenues, spurring the rapid growth of their economies. From 1970 to 1977, Saudi Arabia's ranking in largest gross national income (GNI) jumped from fifty-fifth to nineteenth, its GNI increasing by an annual average of 58 percent. For the same period, Iran's GNI ranking rose from thirty-sixth to twentieth, with an average annual increase of 26 percent.[11] Across the oil-rich MENA states, petrodollars funded rapid industrialization and urbanization. While cognizant of how petrodollar spending contributed to problems like inflation and corruption, MENA governments were generally optimistic that such issues could be contained and were minor compared with the military and developmental gains derived by the spending of their newfound wealth.

In contrast, the United States experienced the worst economic recession since the 1930s. Unemployment steadily increased from 5.4 percent in August 1974 to a high of 9 percent in May 1975. This coincided with a breakdown of the general price stability after World War II, with inflation rising from 3.4 percent in December 1972 to 12.3 percent in December 1974. The rise in unemployment and inflation derived from a variety of factors, including structural changes in the global economy and US policies, but the oil price rise significantly contributed to both as well. Simultaneous high inflation and un-employment challenged the contemporary economic orthodoxy that sagging employment levels could be solved by inflationary measures and vice versa. The Ford administration largely prioritized deflationary policies, and at the end of 1976 the inflation rate had been brought down to 4.9 percent, but the unem-ployment rate remained high at 7.8 percent. Yet while higher oil prices caused widespread economic dislocation within the United States, some US busi-nesses benefited from a surge in investments from and exports to the petrodollar states, especially in the sectors of finance, arms manufacturing, and engineering.

For most of the other OECD countries, the mid-1970s brought similar problems of recession and inflation, to a significant degree spurred by high oil prices. In 1974 and 1975 industrial output in the MDCs plummeted by 10 percent. In 1975 the United Kingdom and Italy received nearly half of the funds of the second IMF oil facility to address their massive balance-of-payments deficits; OECs now served as a major source of aid to MDCs.[12] Despite this assistance, the deficits of the two countries continued, and in 1976 they both reluctantly adopted austerity programs in exchange for traditional IMF bailouts.[13] To the alarm of Washington, the United Kingdom became hobbled by labor unrest, and communist parties made substantial gains in sev-eral European countries—above all in Italy, whose citizens cast over a third of their votes for communists in 1976, putting into question the viability of ma-jor NATO members.[14] The differing policy views and interests of Western European countries also continued to challenge the United States. Kissinger's goal of establishing an effective industrialized oil-consumers cartel never ma-terialized. Instead, to offset the higher cost of oil imports, Japan, West Ger-many, the United Kingdom, and France undertook successful trade offensives in the MENA and elsewhere, challenging US commerce and political influ-ence abroad.

While the oil price rise strained the economies of the largest capitalist states, it brought a windfall to the communist superpower. During this period, the Soviet Union had ample oil to fuel its economy and sell abroad to fund new domestic and foreign policy initiatives. In the Third World, the Soviet Union provided subsidized or free oil to support communist allies like Cuba, Ethio-pia, South Yemen, and Vietnam.[15] Moscow also provided partial protection from oil price increases to its allies in Eastern Europe, though this was not enough to prevent those countries from needing to increasingly take out loans from Western lenders to pay for their rising energy and other consumption bills.[16] The petrodollar boom of the MENA states had a more mixed impact on the USSR. The largest revenues went to the anticommunist monarchies of the region, and petrodollar aid from Saudi Arabia and others helped Egypt to increasingly leave the Soviet orbit. Nor was the USSR a significant recipient of MENA petrodollar investments. But petrodollars did strengthen Soviet-allied Iraq, and it and other Arab countries like Libya and Syria purchased large sums of Soviet arms, either with their own oil revenues or with petrodollar aid.

The oil price rise generally contributed to economic slowdowns in oil-importing LDCs. Many oil-poor LDCs additionally suffered from lower levels of exports to and aid from OECD countries because of recession there. The NIEO movement continued to press the United States but failed to obtain significant concessions. And while the common refrain in the West became that the invisible hand of private markets led Western banks to recycle petrodollar deposits to LDCs that needed to finance their higher oil bills, in actuality there was no correlation between an individual LDC increasing its oil imports and that same LDC obtaining an increase in private lending during the 1970s. Instead, Western banks extended loans to oil-rich but populous countries like Algeria, Mexico, and Venezuela and to oil-poor but newly industrialized countries like Argentina, Brazil, and South Korea or communist countries like East Germany and Poland while largely ignoring the remaining oil-poor LDCs, a selection process based on which countries seemed to be secure and remunerative places for investments, behavior that conformed to profit-driven institutions. A growing split thus emerged among the LDCs, with the oil-rich and newly industrialized LDCs obtaining the revenues and/or private lending needed for their continuing development campaigns and economic growth while the economically weakest oil-poor LDCs endured both a lack of significant private lending and in many cases a simultaneous drop in international aid. For many countries in sub-Saharan Africa and Southern Asia, the lack of inflowing capital and the rise in fuel and fertilizer prices compounded crises of drought and famine. An inability to pay fuel bills led India to shut down irrigation systems, resulting in the loss of wheat crops that could feed fifty million people for a year. In Tanzania starvation caused the infant mortality rate to rise.[17] Washington's efforts to undercut Western aid to bring down oil prices bore partial responsibility for such tragedies.

While petrodollar surpluses did not grow as fast as initially feared by Western economists, the foreign investments of the members of OPEC still grew rapidly and constituted a major new force in global finance. As Shultz and Simon had hoped, the vast majority of these petrodollars were deposited in US and Western financial institutions. From 1974 to 1976 the net increase in the OPEC members' foreign investments and loans was roughly $125 billion. Of this sum, roughly 25 percent went to domestic US banks, investments, and government obligations, 35 percent to the Euromarkets (including overseas branches of US banks), and 15 percent to investments in other MDCs.[18] These petrodollar flows constituted a large share of new deposits for private banks. For banks that reported to the Bank for International Settlements (BIS), which can be used as a rough measurement of MDC international banking (including the United States, most of Western Europe, Japan, Canada, and major offshore locations), new OPEC deposits as a percentage of the banks' new international loans were an estimated 44 percent in 1974, 19 percent in 1975, and 18 percent in 1976.[19]

MENA petrodollars provided badly needed capital to a financially tight US economy. From 1974 to 1976 the estimated net investments of the oil-rich countries of the Persian Gulf in the domestic United States were $26.6 billion. About 60 percent went to the government, equaling roughly 12 percent of the federal deficit for the corresponding fiscal years. From 1975 to 1976 about a third of the increase in foreign holdings of US Treasury securities occurred due to the net change in the oil-rich Gulf countries' possession of the US obligations, with new purchases led by Saudi Arabia. The other 40 percent of oil-rich Gulf investments went to the private sector, primarily in bank deposits and corporate stocks. Whether invested in the public or private sector,

Figure 5. Walter Wriston, Gerald Ford, and William Simon at the White House, September 23, 1975. Courtesy of Gerald R. Ford Presidential Library.

however, MENA petrodollars strengthened US spending power.[20] The oil-rich MENA countries concentrated their investments in the six largest US banks, five based in New York and one in San Francisco, contributing to an increase in their size relative to other domestic banks and to their expansion overseas. These banks included Citibank, which, headed by chairman Walter Wriston, led the charge in private lending to LDCs.[21]

The oil-rich Gulf countries rarely engaged in direct investment in the United States; from 1974 to 1976 the net increase in such investments rose by $68 million, or a quarter of a percent of their total investments in the domestic United States. Yet while relatively small, Arab direct investments did create new points of contact and cooperative networks between Americans and Arabs who might otherwise have never done so. One notable case was Democratic governor of South Carolina John West.[22] West had demonstrated no apparent interest in the Arab world before the mid-1970s; he had visited Israel and India, but nowhere in between. He was, however, an active proponent of attracting foreign investment to South Carolina, at first primarily from Western Europe and Japan. When Kuwaiti investors purchased the South Carolina island of Kiawah in early 1974 from a private individual and announced plans to develop a resort with projected costs of up to half a billion dollars, however, West quickly made the Middle East a new focus for South Carolina's foreign investment attraction efforts, and he ingratiated himself with the Kuwaitis while hosting them on a visit of their new purchase in April 1974.[23]

Such direct investment plans could raise the ire as well as the support of Americans, however. Many Americans opposed the development plan for Kiawah, either because they desired to preserve the wilderness of the island or because they harbored feelings of anti-Arab xenophobia. Rumors circulated that the Kuwaitis were stockpiling weapons on the island.[24] Sometimes preservationist and anti-Arab sentiment intertwined, as was the case for one concerned citizen from New Jersey, who wrote to West, "I feel very sorry for the people of South Carolina after reading of the planned rape of Kiawah Island. . . . For an unspoiled island—a real rarity in the U.S.—to be sold to the Arab oil mongers who have milked so much money from the American public—it is a real crime."[25] Environmentalist groups led a national campaign to cancel the deal, and the Charleston Natural History Society telegrammed Kuwaiti emir Sabah al-Salem al-Sabah with a request that he delay the development of Kiawah until the people of South Carolina can decide whether they want to establish a protected natural park there instead.[26]

Determined to obtain the petrodollar investment, West assured the Kuwaitis that the Society did not represent the views of the majority of South Carolinians and attempted to persuade the Society to cease its efforts.[27] West visited Kuwait at the end of 1974 and met with the Kuwaiti crown prince and prime minister. West assured the Kuwaitis that South Carolina desired trade with and investment from them, but also suggested that the Kuwaitis create television spots and hire a public relations firm "to guide your efforts in changing the image of Arabs . . . and Arab investments."[28] The Kuwaitis heeded West's advice, launching a media campaign to address the concerns of preservationists.[29] Development on Kiawah moved forward, and the new resort welcomed its first guests in May 1976.[30]

While West ended his term as governor in 1975, his interest in the Arab world continued. West served as one of four principal founders of Arab-American Development Services, a company that provided information, contacts, and negotiation services for US businesses seeking market opportunities in the MENA. West likewise oversaw a South Carolina State Development Board trade mission in 1976 to Saudi Arabia, Kuwait, and Jordan.[31] One participant in the trade mission, Lockwood Greene Engineers, signed a contract with Saudi Arabia to engineer a major port facility for roughly $150 million.[32] West's friendship with Jimmy Carter and early support for Carter's presidential bid enabled West to successfully lobby to become the US ambassador to Saudi Arabia.[33] West's encounter with Kuwaiti investors profoundly affected his life, and in turn he became a significant conduit for exchanges between the United States and the Arab world.

While investment opportunities initially interested West in the MENA, he soon looked to export prospects as well, a natural progression given the burgeoning demand for goods and services within the oil-rich states. From 1972 to 1978 the current value of global exports to the MENA OPEC members increased from $5.8 billion to $59.3 billion and totaled $230 billion. The United States secured the largest nominal share of this trade at 13.7 percent of the world's total, primarily through its exports to Iran and Saudi Arabia. The United States faced stiff competition from Japan, West Germany, France, the United Kingdom, and Italy, however, which combined with the United States secured 63.8 percent of the world's exports to these countries for the period. On the one hand, Western competition posed economic and political challenges to US supremacy in the region and globally. On the other hand, the economic success of the United States' more developed allies mitigated the risks of communist challenges in the region; for the same period, the Soviet Union and China garnered only 1.2 and 1.0 percent, respectively, of total exports to the region.[34] The oil-rich countries, including Soviet-allied Iraq, demonstrated a general preference for capitalist goods and services, and Western corporations and governments were eager to do

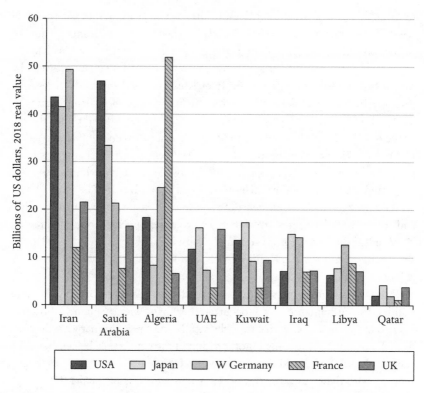

Figure 6. Exports to MENA members of OPEC, 1969–1978. Source: IMF, Direction of Trade Statistics.

business, which meant that the oil shock expanded the ties of the MENA to global capitalism.

One of the few MENA export markets that the Soviet Union did successfully compete in was the arms trade. Rising oil prices and ongoing regional tensions significantly escalated arms races in the MENA, with the Soviet Union and the United States the two unparalleled weapons dealers. Yet even leftist states like Iraq and Libya turned to France for some of their arms to reduce their dependency on Moscow, which was met with approval in Washington.[35] And while both superpowers transferred massive numbers of arms to their respective clients, US allies tended to maintain or expand their military advantages, with Iran in particular able and willing to outspend regional adversaries on arms and possessing the manpower to deploy them. Starting in 1972, Iran combined a military buildup on Iraq's border with the increased transfer of arms and aid across it to rebelling Kurds and succeeded in enlisting US contributions to this effort as well via the CIA. Unbeknownst to Washington, the shah initiated this campaign to compel Baghdad to accede to the Iranian claim to possession of half the Shatt al-Arab along the Iran-Iraq border, rather than the Iraqi claim to the entire river as agreed to in a 1937 Iran-Iraq treaty overseen by the British. Iranian support for the Iraqi Kurds enabled them to successfully resist the Iraqi army and establish autonomy from the Arab-favoring regime in Baghdad. Desperately seeking an end to the high economic and political costs of the ongoing Kurdish rebellion, Saddam Hussein met with the shah in Algiers in March 1975 and acceded to Iran's territorial demands in exchange for Iran's secret pledge to cease its support for the Kurds. The cutoff of Iranian support devastated the Kurds, whose rebellion collapsed a month later. The Ford administration was generally displeased with the Iranian abandonment of the Kurds and embarrassed when reports of the CIA's role were publicized in the press by Kurdish leaders. But the Ford administration ultimately prioritized its relationship with Tehran over the Kurdish rebels, and Iran had clearly demonstrated its ability to militarily cow Iraq.[36]

From Washington's perspective, a more harmonious use of US arms and training by the Iranian military occurred in Oman, where Sultan Qaboos remained locked in an existential struggle with Marxist revolutionaries, who controlled much of the sweeping Dhofar region of the country. In December 1973 Iran deployed 1,500 additional troops to Dhofar, who engaged in heavy fighting with the revolutionaries. In 1974 Iran sent an additional 2,900 troops as well as F-4s to Oman to fight the Marxist militias and deter any potential intervention by South Yemen on their behalf. The Omani Marxists declared their opposition to "American imperialism" and "the Arab and Iranian reactionaries," and its fighters fiercely resisted Iranian and Sultanic forces. The Iranian troops played a key role in turning the military tide against the Marxist revolt, cutting off the revolutionaries' supply lines and overwhelming them with superior numbers and arms. In early 1976 the revolutionaries were militarily defeated. Iran had fulfilled its role within the Nixon Doctrine, defeating a local Marxist threat to a Western-aligned Arab state, violently suppressing an effort to end the absolute monarchy in Muscat and bring about real political participation for Omanis as citizens rather than subjects.[37]

The increase in US arms and training not only assisted Iranian interventions abroad but also strengthened the Iranian military and police forces that cracked down on dissent and maintained the shah's dictatorship. The same held true for the United States' oil-rich monarchical Arab allies; Soviet and European goods and services developed the security forces that maintained the undemocratic governments of Algeria, Iraq, and Libya. Across the MENA and its ideological

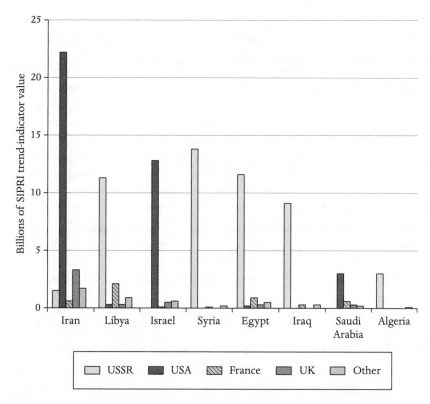

Figure 7. Arms transfers to largest MENA recipients, 1969–1978. Stockholm International Peace Research Institute (SIPRI) trend-indicator value is a common unit designed to represent actual production costs of arms rather than the variable sales price. Source: SIPRI, Arms Transfers Database.

lines, directly and through aid or interventions, the massive increase in arms spending facilitated by petrodollars increased the trend toward authoritarianism.

Yet if many individuals in the MENA lamented how arms sales reduced their political rights or participation, many US arms and military construction companies with headquarters and production plants in states such as California, Massachusetts, Michigan, Missouri, New York, Texas, Washington, and Wisconsin viewed these sales as newly vital. These businesses suffered from a significant decrease in US defense spending with the drawdown of US involvement in the Vietnam War; the real value of post–Korean War US defense spending would peak in 1968 and then rapidly decline, bottoming out at a nearly 40 percent reduction in 1976.[38] Exports to MENA countries provided arms and construction companies a significant way to recover profits. Indeed, MENA arms sales became a lifeline for some US businesses, including Grumman Corporation, whose $2 billion sale of F-14 fighters to Iran saved it from insolvency.[39] Furthermore, any weapon that a US manufacturer sold to MENA countries had already been designed for the US government. That meant the company had already invested a large sum of money into research and development, and any additional sales of the weapon would not have to figure those costs into the business's bottom line. New sales of a weapon to other countries thus significantly improved that weapon's profitability for the corporation that produced it.[40]

Both Iran and Saudi Arabia desired to significantly increase their military capabilities, and they both favored US arms and engineering services due to their technological sophistication and to the political tie they created with the United States. From fiscal year (FY) 1971 to 1977, US Foreign Military Sales (FMS) agreements totaled $9.7 billion with Iran and $6.6 billion with Saudi Arabia, 24 and 16 percent of all US FMS agreements, respectively. From FY 1973 to 1979, FMS deliveries totaled $10 billion to Iran and $4 billion to Saudi Arabia, 31 and 13 percent of the world total. In addition to the F-14 sale, major Iranian commitments included 160 General Dynamics F-16 Fighting Falcon jet fighters costing $3.2 billion, 209 McDonnell Douglas F-4s for $1 billion, and 4 Litton Industries DD-963 Spruance-class missile destroyers costing $1.5 billion. Through 1977 Saudi arms agreements with the United States did not include the most advanced fighters or destroyers and instead focused on the modernization of ground forces. To an even greater degree the Saudis worked with the United States to develop the kingdom's defenses through the extensive construction of military facilities and infrastructure. From FY 1971 to 1977, US Foreign Military Construction Sales agreements with Saudi Arabia totaled $10.3 billion, and Foreign Military Construction Sales deliveries to the Saudis from FY 1973 to 1979 totaled $4 billion; both constituted over 99 percent of the total of such agreements and deliveries for the respective periods. The surge in Saudi spending on US military construction services was the key factor in making total US FMS agreements to Iran and Saudi Arabia constitute 63 percent of its world total in FY 1976.[41]

The petrodollar economy also provided a testing ground for the privatization of services that were previously the exclusive domain of the US military. The Saudi Kingdom hired California-based Vinnell Corporation to train the twenty-six thousand members of the Saudi National Guard in modern weapons use and military tactics under the supervision of former US army officers. This deal was the first instance of the Pentagon outsourcing the training of foreign armies to a private contractor; while the US military had trained and continued to train the

Table 3. US arms and military services and construction sales agreements, FYs 1970–1986 (millions of US dollars, nominal value)

	Saudi Arabia	Israel	Iran	Egypt	Other MENA	MENA total	World total	MENA percentage of world
1970	63	151	134	—	37	385	1,067	36.1
1971	15	285	348	—	19	667	1,382	48.3
1972	300	380	427	—	29	1,136	2,822	40.3
1973	2,171	146	2,065	—	16	4,398	5,737	76.7
1974	2,037	2,344	3,231	—	118	7,730	9,443	81.9
1975	3,604	767	1,180	—	651	6,202	13,186	47.0
1976	7,114	948	1,332	80	718	10,192	13,313	76.6
1977	1,664	451	1,159	1	257	3,532	5,899	59.9
1978	1,766	1,319	241	155	141	3,622	6,931	52.3
1979	5,974	730	14	396	289	7,403	13,056	56.7
1980	4,194	507	—	1,808	690	7,199	13,600	52.9
1981	1,841	114	—	278	493	2,726	6,875	39.7
1982	3,866	550	—	1,410	597	6,423	14,654	43.8
1983	733	2,056	—	663	591	4,043	13,778	29.3
1984	2,873	93	—	768	318	4,052	12,068	33.6
1985	3,176	84	—	331	507	4,098	10,767	38.1
1986	633	165	—	489	372	1,659	5,954	27.9
Total	42,024	11,090	10,131	6,379	5,843	75,467	108,910	69.3

Source: US Department of Defense, Defense Security Cooperation Agency, *Historical Facts Book: Foreign Military Sales, Foreign Military Construction Sales and Other Security Cooperation Historical Facts as of September 30, 2016.*

Note: US FY 1976 was extended to fifteen months; all other fiscal years are twelve months in duration.

Saudi and Iranian armies, the institution of the all-volunteer US military in 1973 made the deployment of US soldiers to train foreign soldiers far more expensive, so private outsourcing was pursued as a cost-saving measure. For its part, Vinnell Corporation had primarily served as a construction company for both domestic projects like the Los Angeles Dodger Stadium and overseas projects like building military bases in East Asia. Faced with declining construction profits in the late 1960s and early 1970s, Vinnell decided to diversify its services by offering military training to foreign armies. For years the Pentagon had hired private engineering companies to develop foreign military bases; now the Pentagon had begun to outsource the training of foreign armed forces to private companies as well.[42] Private contractors were soon also training Iranian military forces.[43]

US trade with the MENA was not limited to arms sales. There was also high demand for US engineering services and consumer goods. Here, European and Japanese competition was stiffer, but US firms still fared well. Iran and Saudi Arabia, looking to rapidly develop their infrastructure and economic diversity, sought the expertise of US engineering firms. Iran commissioned General Telephone and Electronics Corporation to provide the telecommunications infrastructure for two million telephones as well as television service and increased international communication for $500 million.[44] Saudi Arabia commissioned the largest engineering contracts, however, and US corporations landed the largest of these deals. In 1975 Bechtel signed an initial $9 billion contract, which was quickly expanded, to construct over several years an industrial city for over one hundred thousand people, with a steel mill, petrochemical, fertilizer, and aluminum plants, and oil refineries, at the small fishing village of Jubail. In 1983 *The Guinness Book of Records* listed the construction project at Jubail as the largest undertaken in history. A projected $14 billion project to construct a natural-gas-gathering system was awarded to Aramco and the Texas-based Fluor Corporation.[45] US construction firms were contracted to vastly expand Saudi cities; the firms redesigned formerly small, condensed cities like Riyadh into US-style sprawling suburban metropolises of tract houses and long highways to avoid more impoverished sections of cities that housed migrant laborers.[46] US firms conducted business in other Arab countries as well. Bechtel landed deals totaling $950 million to develop gas fields and processing plants in the UAE in 1977 and a $626 million deal to develop gas fields in Algeria in 1978.[47]

Iran and Iraq pursued the construction of nuclear power plants with the assistance of Western powers during the mid-1970s. While such facilities would provide a country with energy, they also increased the risk that a country could secretly develop nuclear weapons. The Nixon and Ford administrations sought to prevent the proliferation of nuclear arms to other countries, even allies. The construction of nuclear power plants would take years, let alone the development of an atomic weapon, so the issue was not of immediate urgency. Yet the Ford administration's effort to ensure Iran's nuclear program would be limited to nonmilitary purposes was unencouraging. The Ford administration hoped to secure contracts worth billions of dollars for US companies to develop Iran's nuclear power plants, but it also sought formal agreements from Tehran that would place greater US oversight on Iran's nuclear program than required by the international Non-Proliferation Treaty. The shah balked at this stipulation and instead agreed to nuclear development contracts with France and West Germany in 1976, as neither of these countries insisted on such oversight. Ford had not found a way to persuade the European allies to agree to greater stipulations or to bring the shah on board with the US program when he left office in early 1977.[48] Given its limited ties, the United States had even less leverage in the case of Iraq, which obtained a French contract to construct a nuclear reactor, called Osiraq, to be fueled with highly enriched uranium that could be weaponized.[49] The combination of petrodollar wealth and the multiplicity of countries willing to do business with the oil-rich states had once again undermined Washington's ability to control the geopolitical order.

For US businesses, trade with the oil-rich states provided badly needed revenues in the context of domestic stagflation. Texas-based oil-services companies like Halliburton increasingly looked to the Middle East and other oil-rich regions for their revenues, and in fact enjoyed record profits in the wake of the oil shock.[50] US engineering and construction companies had been particularly hard hit by the decline in defense contracts from the US government with the drawdown from the Vietnam War and a depressed domestic housing market.[51] US business leaders pushed for greater government support in promoting US exports in the face of foreign competition. The executives at the April 1975 Economic Policy Board meeting "stressed the small scale of U.S. Government programs relative to our major competitors for export sales. . . . They stressed the important role of commercial officers abroad, especially in new market areas such as the Middle East."[52] Responding to such demands, the Treasury and Commerce Departments, sometimes in cooperation with the National Association of Manufacturers, connected US businesspeople with relevant Middle Eastern contacts, personally introduced US businesspeople and Middle Eastern delegates at federal events, and provided information on MENA projects seeking goods and services.[53]

The Nixon and Ford administrations privileged the private sector over the public in the economic development of its MENA allies, an outgrowth of their ideological commitment to reducing governmental programs in the belief that private enterprise would achieve better outcomes, both economically and politically. Regarding Saudi Arabia, Simon wrote that as a general guideline, "where both the U.S. Government and the U.S. private sector have the capability to provide assistance desired by the Saudi Arabian Government under the U.S.-Saudi Arabian Joint Economic Cooperation Commission, there should be a strong presumption in favor of utilizing the private sector. . . . This policy should result in the greatest longterm [sic] benefits to our economic relations with Saudi Arabia and will prevent the inequities and criticisms attendant on U.S. Government preemption of the U.S. private sector." The US government would play a role in securing US private commerce abroad to safeguard US economic interests and see to it that private corporations served geopolitical interests, particularly in leading development plans that would secure the political and economic strength of allied regimes, but the work of the development projects themselves would primarily be left to private US companies.[54]

The increase in MENA-US trade created new political networks where US business and governmental leaders previously uninvolved in MENA issues now became partners and advocates of Arab and Iranian officials and positions. Sometimes these new connections went against the grain of dominant US policy. When Democratic governor of Mississippi William Waller led a state trade commission to Kuwait, Iran, and Iraq in April 1975 to attract foreign investment and secure export deals of food and manufactured materials, he showed a particular interest in Iraq. Waller returned there in October and met with top Iraqi officials, including Foreign Minister Fadoon Hamadi, to further the progress toward agreements on Mississippi commodity sales to Iraq. Shortly thereafter, Waller wrote a letter to Ford in which he urged his administration to "address itself to a strong political position in favor of a just and permanent peace for all nations in the Middle East and in favor of extended trade relations with all Arab states . . . [and] immediate consideration of steps to be taken to establish formal diplomatic relations with Iraq." Waller offered his diplomatic services toward these ends, arguing that "since Mississippi's friendship and relationship with Iraq might be better than that of any state at the present time, I respectfully suggest that Mississippi be invited to participate in any discussions furthering and improving the relationship with Iraq and with other Arab states. We respectfully urge a meeting with designated officials of your office or of the State Department to advance this most important matter."[55] Starting from a desire for increased trade, Waller had become an unlikely advocate for stronger US relations with Baathist Baghdad.

It appears the Ford administration did not seriously consider Waller's offer to pursue better relations with Iraq, but other business connections would prove to have a deeper influence on US foreign policy. In the mid-1970s, Bechtel acquired four high-level former government employees from the Nixon and Ford administrations, including former secretary of health, education, and welfare Caspar Weinberger, a reputed administrator, and George Shultz, who by May 1975 had been promoted to Bechtel's president.[56] Utilizing their knowledge of US policy and law and their contacts with government and business leaders across the world, former US government officials furthered the development of commercial networks between the United States and the MENA while enriching themselves in the process. Shultz and Weinberger would later serve as top cabinet officials in the presidential administration of Ronald Reagan.

New points of contact generated by petrodollars were not limited to MENA and US elites. As on-site jobs proliferated in the MENA, thousands of new Americans arrived in the region. By 1978, an estimated twenty-eight thousand Americans were working in Saudi Arabia, and an estimated thirty thousand Americans were in Iran.[57] Americans often found it difficult to make the transition to the new culture and often rugged conditions. Many Americans chose to prematurely terminate their contracts after a few months on the job; some companies in Saudi Arabia reported a 30 percent early turnover of employees.[58] American workers also sometimes demonstrated a disregard for local Arab and Iranian values and culture. One of the most egregious examples of the latter occurred in the Iranian city of Isfahan, when bored American helicopter pilot instructors for the Iranian military passed the time by getting drunk, engaging in brawls, and even driving motorcycles through a mosque.[59]

The oil-rich states also increased their investments in the services of US higher education and subsidized the cost of attending US colleges for their citizens in an effort to modernize their workforces. US colleges, hard hit by the recession, welcomed the petrodollar-funded endowments and tuition. By 1977 Iran had an institutional connection with roughly fifty US colleges to further develop the Iranian education system, economy, state bureaucracy, and military. Over the decade of the 1970s the number of Iranian students in the United States quadrupled to nearly fifty thousand; from 1974 to 1978 the number of Saudi students in the United States quintupled to ten thousand. Paradoxically, the increases in Arab and Iranian students and funds to US universities served the purpose of strengthening the economic and developmental foundations of US empire in the MENA while also undercutting its cultural support. The increase in Arab funds and students contributed to shifts in the US field of Middle East studies that took a more critical view of US support for Israel. The experience of freedom of intellectual inquiry and speech led many Iranian students to mobilize human rights protests against the shah's authoritarian and violent rule, undermining popular US support for the Iranian government and alarming the shah.[60]

While the members of OPEC generally did not purchase a large amount of exports from or make many investments in oil-poor LDCs, the oil-rich LDCs, and particularly the sparsely populated oil-rich Arab states, did significantly increase the size of their aid to a widening number of select LDCs after 1973. The OECD tabulated the verified net disbursements of bilateral and multilateral aid (not including the IMF oil facility) from Iraq, Kuwait, Libya, Qatar, Saudi Arabia, and the UAE from 1974 to 1976 to be $17.5 billion; the true figure was likely billions of dollars higher due to limitations in record keeping and disclosure by the MENA states. Of the verified amounts, the vast majority came from Saudi Arabia, Kuwait, and the UAE, with only about 10 percent coming from Iraq and Libya. The increase in aid levels was particularly dramatic for Saudi Arabia. In 1973 official Saudi foreign aid totaled roughly $335 million; the following year it rose to $1.6 billion, the second-largest contribution of aid in the world, surpassed only by the United States. Furthermore, while prior to 1974 Saudi aid almost exclusively went to Egypt, Jordan, and Syria, in the following few years Saudi aid increasingly made its way to additional countries in Africa, the Middle East, South Asia, and even as far as South Korea and Brazil, with large sums going to Pakistan and North Yemen.[61]

On the whole, Arab and Iranian foreign aid aligned with the goals of the Nixon and Ford administrations. On a global level, this aid fit within the plan for members of OPEC to offset the current account deficits of LDCs rather than through an increase in US aid. Furthermore, LDCs often used their petrodollar aid to buy US and Western exports. Petrodollar aid flows also primarily went to countries geopolitically favored by the United States due to the dominant financial position of Saudi Arabia and Kuwait within OPEC aid flows; from 1973 to 1981, of the top ten aid recipients of bilateral OPEC aid, eight were aligned with the United States, including the top recipient, Egypt, which received $6.1 billion, and the third largest, Jordan, which received $3.9 billion. It was true that some aid from both allied and hostile Arab states went to countries like Syria or Palestinian groups that challenged US designs in the MENA and spent funds on Soviet arms. Syria would receive roughly $6 billion in bilateral OPEC aid, the second largest recipient, enabling it to purchase advanced weapons like the MiG-23 jet fighter. Yet Kissinger would actually lobby Iran and Saudi Arabia to provide aid to Syria in 1976 when Asad aligned himself with US objectives in the Lebanese Civil War, so even with Syria OPEC aid was sometimes considered useful by Washington, though such assistance would not be appreciated by Washington during later periods of Syrian-US hostilities.[62] US Arab allies likewise contributed some aid to adversaries like South Yemen through multilateral organizations, and Iraq and Libya directly funded states and groups that challenged the United States and its allies. On balance, however, far more petrodollar assistance went to US allies than US adversaries, and at a time of increasing financial difficulties and growing public opposition to foreign aid in the United States.

The final way that many LDCs acquired a large number of petrodollars was through the remittances of laborers working in oil-rich countries. The oil-rich Arab Peninsula states and Libya especially desired both menial and educated foreign laborers to augment their own sparse populations. These countries often hired employees from Arab oil-poor countries due to commonalities in language and culture, proximity, transnational ties, and the range of useful skills these laborers could provide. While poor record keeping makes estimates rough, there was a clear rise in the number of inter-Arab migrant laborers after the 1973 oil shock, rising from under 700,000 in 1973 to 1.3 million in 1975 and 2.2 million in 1977.[63] Of the 1975 total, Saudi Arabia imported roughly 54 percent of all inter-Arab migrant laborers, Libya 24 percent, and Kuwait 11 percent. Egypt exported roughly 31 percent of the total, North Yemen 22 percent, and Jordan-Palestine 20 percent (many Arab governments during this period used Jordan-Palestine as an identification for both Jordanian citizens and Palestinian refugees in their records; the majority of migrant laborers were Palestinian refugees).[64]

The value of Egyptian remittances grew at a phenomenal rate. In 1970 Egypt accrued under $10 million in official remittances; in 1978 this figure had risen to $1.76 billion. Egyptians also brought back hundreds of millions of dollars' worth of durable goods (like cars and electronics) that went unreported and remitted additional sums of money through the currency black market (which offered better rates of exchange than the government) in amounts estimated to equal 20–100 percent of reported remittances. While not all of these remittances came from work in oil-rich countries, most did.[65] Remittances, along with petrodollar aid, were major contributors to an increase in economic growth in the oil-poor Arab countries which, while not approaching the same boom as the oil-rich countries, still achieved higher rates of economic growth from 1973 to 1982 than the previous decade.[66]

Here again, the impact on US interests was mixed. Migrant labor sustained the development of an increasingly hostile Libya, while remittances to countries like Syria and South Yemen assisted these antagonistic states and funded Soviet arms purchases. The PLO and other Palestinian resistance groups relied heavily on remittances from migrant Palestinian laborers in the Gulf.[67] To an even larger degree, however, migrant labor supported the rapid development of both oil-rich and oil-poor Arab states allied with the United States. Some migrant Arab laborers also used some of their petrodollar wages to purchase US consumer goods, supporting the increase in US exports to oil-poor Arab countries. In 1972 US exports to the oil-poor Arab countries totaled $454 million; by 1976 the total had risen to $2.149 billion.[68] More broadly, the decision of most oil-poor Arab states to decontrol international movements of labor, capital, and goods in the pursuit of petrodollars matched the United States' support for global free markets.

The impact of migrant labor on the populations of countries like Egypt was mixed. Egyptians could obtain pay rates in the Gulf that were often ten times the rates in their home country, bringing migrant laborers and their families increased purchasing power. On the other hand, the lure of petrodollars created brain drains in Egypt in critical fields like education and construction, hindering domestic development. Migrants experienced an increased lack of political and social liberties in Saudi Arabia (removed from the protections of citizenship and community back home), increasingly resented the higher incomes of hiring Saudis who often did little work or had less experience, and some Saudi employers physically abused their migrant laborers and kept them in appalling conditions, controlling them by holding their passports and wages. Individuals and entire communities that voiced complaints over work conditions were routinely expelled from the country. This system of control over migrant laborers, combined with the vastly expanded government subsidies and incomes provided to citizens, drastically undercut labor movements and their political challenges to the state in Saudi Arabia and other Arab monarchies during the 1970s.[69]

While petrodollar flows reshaped the political economy of the MENA largely along lines favored by the United States, petrodollar interdependence also occasioned to seriously threaten US interests within the context of the ongoing Arab-Israeli conflict, a point driven home during the first phase of the Lebanese Civil War from 1975 to 1976. The Lebanese Right, overwhelmingly Christian, sought to preserve the confessional system of the Lebanese government that gave Lebanese Christians a majority in Parliament as well as the powerful presidency despite the minority share of Christians within the Lebanese citizenry, uphold the pro-Western and capitalistic orientation of the country, and expel the PLO from Lebanon to secure the latter's sovereignty and end the violent retaliatory attacks that Israel executed on Lebanon in response to Palestinian raids originating there. The Lebanese Left, primarily Muslim, sought to end the confessional allocation of power in the Lebanese government, reorient the country's economy toward socialism and politics toward Arab nationalism, and support the PLO's efforts against Israel. The PLO allied itself with the Lebanese Left, and the PLO's militias, well armed in part from Arab petrodollar assistance, initially helped turn the tide of the civil war against the Lebanese Right.

As the position of the Lebanese Right deteriorated, Israel warned that it would not accept a Palestinian–Lebanese Left victory and would militarily intervene if necessary. The Syrian government also considered the Lebanese

Civil War to be a threat to its stability and security, and by the beginning of 1976 it had determined that, despite the traditional alliance and ideological affinities between Baathist Syria and the PLO and Lebanese Left, the latter two needed to be reined in lest they spark a broader war with Israel that would pull in an unprepared Syria. Ironically, Israel and Syria each sought to apply military force to subdue the PLO and Lebanese Left, but each also warned that the military entry of the other in Lebanon would be cause for war. Despite sharing a common goal to end the Lebanese Civil War, Israel and Syria also feared that the other country would gain long-term military advantages if the other occupied Lebanon. Yet as the Palestinian–Lebanese Left forces ignored Damascus's entreaties to reach an accord with the Lebanese Right and instead neared total victory in March 1976, Israeli and/or Syrian intervention became increasingly likely.[70]

As Syria privately communicated to Washington its desire to intervene in Lebanon, Israel continued to maintain both publicly and privately that it would launch its own military intervention into Southern Lebanon in response. The Ford administration believed this scenario would lead to war between the two and then a wider regional conflict. "The Syrians could not stand still and face the charge of partitioning the country [Lebanon] to share it with Israel," Kissinger professed at an NSC meeting on April 6. "They would have to attack [Israel]." At that point, Kissinger predicted the Jordanians and Egyptians would be forced to join in the war against Israel. Kissinger anticipated that "Saudi Arabia would support [the Arab states] and there would be an oil embargo." Nelson Rockefeller added that there would "not only [be] an oil embargo. The Arabs own twenty billion [dollars] in American assets they could dump. The disruption would be terrible." This prompted Kissinger to note that "[Chairman of the Council of Economic Advisers Alan] Greenspan says the only way the Western Europeans can live within their means is thanks to Arab deposits. If the Saudis and Kuwaitis got out of the British pound, it would collapse."[71]

The US-Saudi petrodollar order in the Middle East was once again imperiled by local actors. While petrodollar concerns were not the sole reason for why the United States sought to prevent the outbreak of another Arab-Israeli war, they featured prominently. Petrodollar investments, the Ford administration feared, could be used to wreak havoc on the US economy and to either blackmail Western Europe into not cooperating with the United States or punish it.

The Ford administration endeavored into May to prevent either Israel or Syria from launching an overt military intervention into Lebanon; it also worked toward establishing a cease-fire between the Lebanese Left and Right. The Ford administration refused to address the key demands of the Lebanese

Left, however, and the fighting continued. Either with or without a previously agreed understanding with the United States (the Ford administration maintained there was no such understanding, a claim supported by the available documentary record), the Syrian military invaded Lebanon on the night of May 31. The Ford administration then pressed Israel not to challenge the Syrian intervention or launch its own invasion into Southern Lebanon. The Israeli government privately agreed not to take action as long as Syrian forces did not enter Southern Lebanon, an offer the Syrians readily accepted.

After initial setbacks, the Syrian army severely weakened the militias of the PLO and the Lebanese Left in September. Saudi Arabia then called for negotiations to end the conflict in Lebanon. Arab disunity, the Saudis argued, had weakened the Arab position in the Arab-Israeli conflict. A new opportunity would soon be available to advance the peace process and obtain concessions from Israel with the conclusion of the US presidential election, but only if the Arabs were united. In October, Saudi Arabia, Kuwait, Syria, Lebanon, the PLO, and Egypt convened in Riyadh and then Cairo to hammer out an agreement. The PLO and Syria agreed to a cease-fire, and the oil-rich Arab countries agreed to fund an Arab Deterrent Force of thirty thousand (mostly Syrian) troops to maintain order in Lebanon until stability held. Deprived of the military support of the PLO, the Lebanese Left was forced to accept the cease-fire for the time being as well, and the level of violence temporarily decreased.[72] Riyadh and Washington had succeeded in preserving the Saudi-US Arab bloc through the first phase of the Lebanese Civil War. The core issues of the conflict remained unresolved, however, and the war would continue for another fourteen years, with repeated intermittent escalations that would again endanger Arab-US relations.

The crisis in Lebanon reinforced the Ford administration's already strong desire to secure Egypt's allegiance and thereby mitigate the risks of a full-scale Arab-Israeli war. Petrodollars continued to play an important, if often contradictory, role in this effort. This extended to the issue of US arms transfers to Egypt, urgently desired by Sadat but at the start of 1975 not yet initiated by Washington. By April the Ford administration had determined that attempting to secretly sell arms to Egypt through Saudi Arabia would not work after all, having apparently come around to Saunders's argument that it would be both illegal and inevitably leaked to the public, creating a scandal that could set back future US arms sales to Egypt. Ambassador Eilts informed Sadat of the change in policy on April 19. Eilts noted that the United States was not opposed to Saudi funding of a public US arms sale to Egypt, but also added that the Ford administration could not guarantee any arms sales at the present. Sadat expressed disappointment but held out hope for a US arms sale to Egypt soon.[73]

As months passed without a US arms proposal, the United States received reports of growing unrest in the Egyptian military. "It is the Egyptian armed forces that Sadat must watch carefully for signs of unease or disaffection," Kissinger wrote Ford on October 24. "Egyptian military officers must be concerned that Sadat's policies have placed the Egyptian armed forces at a serious disadvantage with Israel." Hoping to ease Sadat's position, but also anticipating that Congress and the US public would need to be eased into advanced military sales to Egypt, Kissinger proposed starting with the sale of nonlethal military equipment, including the C-130 military transport plane.[74] Ford supported the idea, and after overcoming some initial congressional resistance, gained approval in April 1976 for the sale of six C-130s to Egypt. Saudi Arabia paid for the planes on Egypt's behalf. From a military standpoint, the $65 million arms deal was of marginal significance. Symbolically, however, the sale marked a turning point in Egyptian-US relations after a twenty-year US-arms embargo against Egypt.[75] It was also significant as the first instance of an oil-rich Arab country purchasing technologically advanced arms from the United States for Egypt. While not exactly an example of "triangular investment," the C-130 deal could be called the first Egyptian "triangular military sale."

On the issue of petrodollar triangular investment, little progress had been made by 1976. Visiting Egypt in March of that year, Simon commended Sadat's initial steps toward market liberalization while advocating for further deregulation to stimulate "a private sector Marshall Plan" for Egypt.[76] Nothing so grandiose occurred during Simon's tenure as Treasury secretary, however. Despite Egypt's reforms to attract foreign investment, US businesspeople felt many obstacles remained. They criticized Egyptian law that set a two-tier exchange rate for the Egyptian pound, which forced those bringing money into Egypt to accept an artificially low value for their currency while maintaining a higher value for money taken out of the country. They also complained that Egyptian investment laws remained too vague and that the Egyptian bureaucracy imposed too many requirements and delays on proposed projects. By the end of 1976, the only US businesses to open major branches in Egypt were a few banks, such as Chase and Citibank. These banks conducted a busy business in currency exchanges but little in the way of financing.[77]

The Egyptian economy grew rapidly from 1974 to 1976 in terms of GDP, in large part due to aid and remittance flows into the country. Much of the aid and remittances Egypt garnered was spent on foreign arms, consumable goods, and debt repayment rather than invested in Egyptian industry or agriculture, however, leaving Egyptian exports and import substitutes relatively stagnant. Egypt thus remained reliant on imports for basic food and security needs, while simultaneously relying on foreign assistance to pay for these imports. At the same time, the influx of foreign aid and remittances, high levels of government military and domestic spending, and rising oil prices all contributed to high rates of inflation in Egypt. To protect lower-income Egyptians from the harm of inflation and preserve popular support for Sadat's regime, the Egyptian government rapidly increased government subsidies for basic consumer goods. Since many of these goods were imported, the subsidies further harmed Egypt's balance of trade. The end result of all this was that between 1973 and 1976 Egypt's foreign debt nearly tripled while domestic subsidies increased thirteen-fold.[78] Rather than break Egypt out of the cycle of debt, petrodollar aid and remittances facilitated government policies that deepened it.

While the Ford administration had helped put together a multilateral aid package for Egypt in the spring of 1975 in order to shield Egypt from IMF and World Bank stipulations, by the fall of 1975 the administration had concluded that Egypt needed to seriously begin the process of restructuring its economy in order to improve its balance of payments. The US government sought to ease this transition and reward Egypt for warming relations by increasing US aid from $372 million in FY 1975 to $987 million in FY 1976.[79] But the Ford administration also increased pressure on the Egyptians to curb government spending. In October 1975 State drafted a briefing paper to address the issue. State noted that Cairo hoped to see a continuation of high levels of aid from foreign donors in 1976, including about $2.5 billion in non–US aid, but believed this was unlikely to occur. "The planned sharp increase in U.S. aid and the easing of Egyptian confrontation with Israel [after Sinai II] may give Arab and other countries the excuse to cut back on aid to Egypt," State wrote. "The refusal of Japan and Germany to provide the full $100 million requested of each of them in 1975 reflects, in part, their dissatisfaction with Egypt's economic mismanagement and their belief that the United States and the rich Arab countries will keep Egypt afloat." In short, "the U.S. government cannot successfully repeat in 1976 the role it played in raising emergency aid [from Western and Arab governments] for Egypt [in the summer of 1975]." Instead, State advocated that Egypt seek aid from the World Bank. "U.S. political interests in Egypt preclude unilateral U.S. pressure on Sadat for economic reforms," State noted. "Coordinated and politically anonymous approaches to these policy issues by Arab and western [sic] leaders can be achieved only under [World Bank] leadership."[80] State could have included the IMF along with the World Bank, but the point was clear: since the United States did not want to strain its relationship with Egypt by forcing it to restructure its economy, and other donor countries including Saudi Arabia were resistant to continued high levels of unconditional aid, Egypt would instead be forced to obtain aid from the World Bank and/or IMF on the condition that it would restructure its economy.

The IMF and World Bank had been eager to participate in a restructuring of Egypt's economy as early as 1974, buoyed by Sadat's declarations of an open-door policy.[81] As time passed, however, the two institutions became frustrated with Egypt's inability to make good on its stated goals. In November 1975 IMF official John Gunter privately complained that Egyptian minister of finance Ahmed Abu Ismail "showed little interest in foreign exchange policy and his draft 1976 budget makes little progress in coming to grips with the deep-seated fiscal problems" such as the ballooning cost of government subsidies of basic consumables.[82] Similarly, in April 1976 McNamara expressed to an Egyptian adviser his "concern about what [McNamara] considered two major problems affecting Egypt's economic recovery: overspending and administrative inefficiency."[83] Cairo, lacking the United States' support for gathering direct international aid without conditions as it had in 1975, went to the IMF in the spring of 1976 and agreed to reduce subsidies and lower the overvalued exchange rate of the Egyptian pound in return for IMF lending. The Egyptian government quickly reneged on the offer, however, apparently believing it could obtain additional aid from the oil-rich Arab countries instead.[84]

Saudi Arabia had become increasingly reluctant to extend aid to Egypt, however. Throughout 1976 the Ford administration encouraged Riyadh to extend generous aid to Egypt, but it also internally noted that "the Saudis have grown increasingly critical of Egypt's inability to manage its finances over the past year." A July 26 speech in which Sadat criticized the levels of Gulf Arab aid to Egypt also seriously angered the Saudi government.[85] In September, Saudi officials told the IMF that they agreed with its efforts to force Egypt to address its balance-of-payments deficit and debt. The IMF welcomed Saudi support for its position but also encouraged the Saudis to be forthcoming in pledged aid to Egypt, arguing the country would be in a tight spot even with Saudi aid.[86]

Arab petrodollar aid remained slow, and in October Sadat wrote to Ford in the hope that he could arrange a new emergency international aid package to avoid IMF conditions for lending. Sadat feared that restructuring along IMF lines could cause massive social upheaval directed against him.[87] On November 30, Ford replied to Sadat. Noncommittal about the prospects of a new emergency aid package outside of the IMF, Ford told Sadat that "only you can make the decisions as to what will best serve the interests of your country" but that "my own judgment is that the immediate problems arising from sound albeit difficult economic decisions will be more than compensated by a greater willingness on the part of potential donors to increase assistance to Egypt."[88] Egyptian and IMF officials met in Cairo in mid-December to renew discussions about lending and restructuring. IMF officials noted that while the Egyptian officials "acknowledged the need for a program to bring about a major change in the direction of economic policy . . . they [also] realized that an adequate program would result in a substantial price adjustment with consequent political problems and were under pressure from other members of the [Egyptian] Cabinet to reduce the impact of the programs." The meetings ended without an Egyptian commitment to IMF restructuring proposals.[89] In early January 1977 Foreign Minister Fahmy made a final appeal to Saudi Arabia and Kuwait for increased assistance, but they refused.[90] Cairo reluctantly concluded it had no choice but to adopt some of the IMF's recommendations. On January 18 Egyptian newspapers announced that subsidies for some thirty commodities, including essentials such as rice, sugar, butane gas, and petroleum, would be reduced.[91]

The decrease in subsidies constituted an onerous burden to millions of lower-class Egyptians. Thousands expressed their anger with two days of protests, lootings, and destruction of property in cities across the country, the worst civil disturbances in Egypt since the end of the monarchy. Leftist activists joined the protests and riots, arguing that Sadat had betrayed the legacy of Nasser. Order was restored only when Sadat promised to preserve the previous level of subsidies and deployed the army in the streets. Egyptian security forces killed at least seventy-nine people, arrested two thousand, and wounded thousands more before the unrest ended.[92] Sadat's first attempt at economic adjustment involving the reduction of subsidies had ended as soon as it had begun. The oil-rich Arab monarchies, alarmed by the threat to Sadat's regime, pledged a new $1 billion loan to Egypt two week after the riots, which would be supplemented with additional assistance in the following months.[93]

The petrodollar economy contributed to many global trends that furthered US empire. Petrodollar interdependence between the United States and the MENA advanced the political and economic aims of the Nixon and Ford administrations and many US corporations. The United States and its Western allies garnered the lion's share of the petrodollars flowing out of the OECs. Petrodollars funded the significant increase in Iran's ability to serve as a regional defender of US interests and Saudi Arabia's ability to provide aid to US allies across the Third World, both operating within the logic of the Nixon

Doctrine. And petrodollar flows often encouraged economic liberalization across much of the Third World, whether in the shift of select countries toward acquiring international loans from private rather than public sources or the increased flow of migrant laborers seeking higher wages in the oil-rich states. Yet the petrodollar economy also contributed to difficulties for US power. Petrodollars, sometimes even those of US allies, were also provided to states and organizations hostile to Washington. Petrodollar interdependence also opened the United States to additional vulnerabilities to MENA retaliation within the Arab-Israeli conflict. And petrodollar inducements to shift toward neoliberal economic policies could result in popular revolts against US allies, as made clear in the Egyptian bread riots. Given the wide range of impacts of the petrodollar economy, Americans, Arabs, and Iranians increasingly debated the cultural and political significance of this order and the role of the United States within it.

Chapter 6

Visions of Petrodollar Promise and Peril

"The city of Tacoma soon may have claim to a dubious distinction: the dung-exporting capital of the Northwest," the Associated Press reported on November 15, 1974. Pacific Northwestern cattle owners had entered into a deal with R.J.B. Sales Inc., a company headed by Richard Briggs, patent holder of a process to liquefy and deodorize cow manure, and World Wide Marine Inc., a commodity barge transport company operated by Michael Randazzo, to provide monthly shipments of fifty thousand metric tons of liquefied bovine excrement for three years to Bahrain and Dubai. Beginning early in the next month, the muck, branded "Nature's Own," was to be shipped out from Washington on barges to Louisiana, where it would be pumped aboard oil tankers destined for the Persian Gulf. Upon delivery to Bahrain and Dubai, the liquid waste would be mixed with pulverized wood chips and spread as fertilizer on the kingdoms' arid sands and seeded with grass as part of a desert reclamation project. In return, the two Arab polities would pay $1.2 billion. Briggs and Randazzo stood to make millions, and the cattle owners would have a new source of badly needed revenue. "This will save our lives," Virgil Baker of Mountain Viewing Farms declared. "The dairy business is so depressed right now we've been operating $3,000 a month in the red. Now we can make up to $4,000 a month on manure. It seems like a fairy tale."

Within a few months, however, the fairy tale proved to be a farce. In the fall of 1974 Randazzo reported to Briggs that he had reached the $1.2 billion deal with Bahraini prince Mohammed Kahlil Ebrahaim, with $10 million to be provided in advance to help cover initial costs. Briggs, Randazzo, and Ebrahaim signed a contract, and the Northwestern National Bank in Port Angeles, Washington, advanced about $400,000, roughly half of the bank's total lending capacity, to fund the project. Randazzo, despite his poor credit rating, personally received $94,000 from the bank to rent barges, but he failed to do so; he did, however, spend $20,000 on Lincoln Continentals to entertain the Bahraini prince. Meanwhile, some of the cattle owners began to purchase expensive holding tanks for the project. In December Randazzo reported receipt of the first check from Bahrain, written for $16 million. But when the check was deposited, it was returned unpaid due to the account's insufficient funds. Bahraini police then discovered the man who claimed to be a prince was actually an airline clerk and detained him. Officials in Bahrain and Dubai claimed no knowledge of the proposed fertilizer project. It was also revealed that Randazzo had been convicted in 1972 of possessing a false ship master's license. Years later it was still unclear where the fraud had begun, but the business venture was unequivocally over. The Northwestern National Bank in Port Angeles barely survived the debacle, the Federal Bureau of Investigation (FBI) and Interpol investigated the matter, and multiple lawsuits ensued.[1]

While outlandish, this story is characteristic of larger economic and cultural trends emerging from the US-led petrodollar economy. As one 1977 *Wall Street Journal* article put it, "These days, it seems, there are few limits to what would-be entrepreneurs will do to get a piece of the action in the Middle East."[2] The fertilizer export scheme emblemized the widespread optimism that anything was possible with petrodollars—that the Middle East had become a place of such wealth that even dung transported halfway across the globe could conceivably be sold for a fortune. Yet the story ultimately served as a cautionary tale, reflecting fears that the petrodollar economy could bring disastrous consequences.

During the mid-1970s, many Americans, Arabs, and Iranians experienced a new era of globalization due to petrodollar flows, and they came to impart meaning to the changes occurring within their globalizing societies through the production and consumption of competing narratives about MENA-US petrodollar interdependence. For some, the US-led petrodollar order represented the best possibility for mutual cooperation and benefit between the societies of the MENA and the United States. For others, the same order threatened the livelihoods, sovereignty, values, and even lives of their peoples and allies, facilitating foreign assaults upon them; these parties offered alternative visions for structuring petrodollar flows. In their struggle to promote popular understandings of petrodollars, differing parties sought to gain popular legitimacy, and thus power, for their particular vision for the global political

economy and responses to US empire. These debates, shaped into many different forms, surfaced throughout mass culture, news media, political and economic
analysis, and a variety of policy-setting forums. They provided justifications for
policies in various governments and the frameworks for their propaganda
campaigns.

In the 1970s Americans across the political spectrum increasingly voiced
fears that the United States was in decline geopolitically, economically, and
morally. At the start of the decade the Vietnam War played a central role in
these anxieties. On the left, Americans increasingly questioned the morality
of their government for waging what they considered an unjust war, while
those on the right increasingly feared their fellow Americans had lost the moral
resolve necessary to combat communism. Just months after the final withdrawal
of US troops from Vietnam came the oil shock. In US media, widespread narratives responding to the end of US energy independence characterized the
United States as a junkie addicted to Arab oil or a flabby consumer who could
not produce for oneself anymore. The oil crisis thus became another preva-
lent symbol of declining US geopolitical power and moral failing for many
Americans, one that would overlap with additional blows to American confidence like the revelations that emerged from the Watergate investigation in
1974 and the collapse of South Vietnam to communist forces in 1975. Furthermore, higher oil prices coincided with (and were largely understood to
drive) high rates of inflation and unemployment in the United States, which
raised American concerns about the foundations of the US economy.[3]

The Arab oil embargo and the new petrodollar wealth of the Arabs and
Iranians were particularly unsettling for many Americans because they challenged their widely held, centuries-old orientalist belief in the superiority of
Westerners and the subordinate position of Middle Easterners. In this world-
view, Americans cast Middle Eastern peoples as an inferior, irrational, immoral,
and perverse other, a group that either required Western tutelage or should be
forcefully kept away. Yet now oil-rich Arab countries and Iran were exhibit-
ing an unprecedented economic boom and geopolitical self-assertiveness while
the United States entered into a recession and energy crisis and was forced to
attend to Arab political concerns to end the oil embargo. This led many Americans to fear they had become subordinate to Middle Easterners. Yet if many
Americans believed Arabs and Iranians had reversed power relations, their negative assessment of Arab and Iranian societies remained unchanged. These
Americans believed that the oil-rich Middle Easterners would use their petrodollar power in ways harmful to US interests. Recent political disputes, par-

ticularly the Arab-Israeli conflict and the Arab oil embargo against the United States, further popularized for many Americans a sense of antagonism toward Arabs in particular. When figures such as former vice president Spiro Agnew and former Democratic senator from Arkansas J. William Fulbright voiced critiques of the United States' pro-Israel policies, they were roundly attacked in the media as agents of the "Arab lobby," characterized as promoting these views in exchange for Arab payoffs to them and corporations they had ties to rather than from conviction. Media campaigns likewise condemned Arab endowments to colleges like Georgetown University and the University of Southern California as evidence that US institutions were being corrupted by petrodollars, turning them into mouthpieces for anti-Israeli propaganda.[4]

One response within US media to the fear that Middle Easterners had achieved superiority over Americans through their petrodollar wealth was to reject this premise and instead reaffirm the cultural and economic superiority of the West. One common narrative argued that the economies of the OECs, in spite of or even because of their petrodollar windfall, remained mismanaged, corrupt, undiversified, unsustainable, and racked by cultural contradictions in comparison with Western economies.[5] Other critics maintained that Middle Easterners lacked a claim to civilizational greatness or higher petrodollar revenues because they had not independently developed their oil industries. "Arabs and Berbers," argued one December 1973 letter to the editor in the *New York Times*, "would still be sitting in the sand contemplating their navels had it not been for American and European ingenuity, risk and business acumen, which discovered, mined, processed and sold oil that nature stored under those sands—without the slightest help from the herders drifting from oasis to oasis."[6] Such arguments overlooked the important role of Middle Easterners in developing their oil industries and of sovereign resource rights, but they justified to many Americans why they should not have to pay more for foreign oil and why Arabs and Iranians did not deserve their wealth.

Many Americans also argued that higher oil prices did not constitute a fair economic exchange but was rather a form of political extortion or attack. On this basis, these Americans called for a political response by the United States to end the unjust loss of money from Americans and unearned enrichment of unscrupulous adversaries. In January 1975 the American Federation of Labor and Congress of Industrial Organizations called for a US boycott of oil from countries that had participated in the 1973–1974 boycott against the United States as a necessary measure for US economic independence. The organization's president, George Meany, condemned Kissinger for paying "tribute" to the Arab states and called for "no foreign aid, no trade, no jet fighters to these people—nothing until the blackmail stops." Meany admitted that boy-cotting Arab oil would bring some economic hardship to Americans, but ar-gued that "allocations and rationing are a small price to pay to avoid total economic collapse and to take America's economic destiny out of the hands of the Arab oil sheiks."[7] Two months later in *Harper's Magazine* Miles Ignotus, the pseudonym of neoconservative Johns Hopkins political scientist Edward Luttwak, argued that high oil prices justified a US military response. He pro-posed that the United States invade Saudi Arabia and seize its oil to break up OPEC rather than accept high petroleum prices that would turn the oil-importing world into an "authoritarian slum" with "all of us being forced to finance the executive jets of the sheiks and the fighter bombers of the dicta-tors."[8] Notably, it was not only the higher cost of oil that Meany and Ignotus found galling but also the ability of Middle Easterners to use their petrodollars to purchase expensive and modern products like jet fighters.

Narratives casting Arab petrodollars as unearned and put to nefarious use made their way into popular fiction as well. From its early days the US film industry had produced movies featuring orientalist depictions of Arab sheikhs as dimwitted, opulent, sex-crazed, tyrannical, and/or bloodthirsty villains. The petrodollar boom contributed to an uptick in the use of such characters while providing the sheikh with an updated backstory in that he had obtained his unearned wealth and power from oil profits.[9] The 1976 sexploitation and cap-tivity film *Ilsa: Harem Keeper of the Oil Sheiks* cast the Arab oil sheikh El Sharif and his Nazi SS accomplice Ilsa as the villains. The film is laden with graphic depictions of orientalist tropes: El Sharif uses his petrodollars to create a ha-rem of abducted white women, including an American heiress, who are forced into El Sharif's sexual service and brutally tortured for disobedience by harem master Ilsa; an occasional man or young boy is shown as a sex slave; and other Arab sheikhs bid for sex slaves at an auction. A US diplomat, Dr. Kaiser (who resembles Kissinger down to the German accent), and a US secret agent pos-ing as Kaiser's aide, Commander Adam Scott, fly to El Sharif's kingdom in the hope of either persuading El Sharif to increase oil production or discov-ering information they can use to blackmail him with. "That small patch of desert sits on top of a bottomless pit, an ocean of oil, and we need it!" Dr. Kaiser tells Scott. "We are being held to ransom by an unscrupulous son of a bitch who just happens to rule a few hundred acres of sand. Hell, our compa-nies helped to build this bloody country: roads, refineries, pipelines, military equipment."[10] By having Kaiser describe the situation as one of ransom, the film parallels the situation between the United States and oil producers with the captivity and abuse of the Western women in El Sharif's harem. By noting the role of US companies in developing Arab countries, the film likewise works to delegitimize Arab rights to oil revenues.

The film goes on to impart the idea, much like Miles Ignotus, that US force was justified and needed to bring the oil-rich Arabs to heel. Dr. Kaiser's attempts at diplomacy with El Sharif fail, and Kaiser departs, but Scott remains at El Sharif's palace, as he is in the process of seducing Ilsa. Scott succeeds in this when he forces Ilsa to have sex with him at knifepoint, an act that elicits Ilsa's devotion as it satisfies her desire as a woman to be dominated by a more powerful man. Scott and Ilsa then launch a successful armed revolution against El Sharif. Scott secures the allegiance of the new ruler, a young nephew of El Sharif, while Ilsa is thrown in a dungeon due to her continued cruelty and killing of innocents (love does not trump Nazi habits, apparently).[11] The film, through the failure of Kaiser and the success of Scott, suggested to Americans that a violently masculine and dominating approach, rather than impotent diplomacy, was the better approach to dealing with the petrodollar-rich Arabs.

In a very different way the 1977 comedic film *The Happy Hooker Goes to Washington* also suggested that confronting oil-rich Arabs was both necessary and doable. The heroine of the film is Xaviera Hollander, a Dutch immigrant to the United States who has become America's most famous sex advice columnist, advocate for sexual liberation, hooker, and madam. The CIA recruits Xaviera to prevent "Sheikh Ali . . . the most ruthless, egocentric, self-indulgent oil billionaire of the Middle East" from attending a conference of Arab leaders where he intends to launch "a war which would be disastrous for the economy of the free world."[12] Xaviera goes to Miami Beach and meets Ali, who speaks in an effeminate, nasally lisp. Ali brags that his harem girls "say that my mighty member is like an oil derrick, gushing a hundred barrels a day," but when Xaviera grabs Ali's crotch, she frowns and says, "It's not much of a gusher is it?" Ali sobs that "it's a mirage," but Xaviera assures him she can help fix his problem. She beds Ali and keeps him from the meeting, thus preventing the war. Xaviera then discovers, and publicly exposes, a US senator who is secretly involved with Ali in the "white slave trade."[13] In linking the senator to Ali, *The Happy Hooker* played to Americans' post-Watergate cynicism about their government leaders and fears that Arab petrodollars could be used to subvert US democracy. Despite the failings of their leaders, however, the film affirms that Americans can still defeat the oil-rich Arabs if they so choose. Indeed, the film suggests that the Arabs are in fact not nearly as powerful as they are projected to be if actually confronted. Ali, described as the most "ruthless" and "militant" of the Arab leaders, proves to be comically inept, insecure, and unmanly. The power of the Arabs and their petrodollars, just like Ali's "derrick," proves to be a mirage.

While many US narratives extolled confrontation with OECs, US foreign policy elites and internationally oriented business leaders that embraced petrodollar interdependence articulated the perceived benefits of cooperation with the Arab world and Iran. In response to the varied international challenges of the 1970s, of which the oil crisis and petrodollar surpluses counted two among many, most mainstream US policy elites embraced the idea of the United States managing an increasingly multipolar world in a cooperative fashion rather than through confrontation.[14] In US popular media, particularly those catering to the college educated, advocates of petrodollar cooperation emphasized the perceived economic and geopolitical benefits arising from the surge of US exports to and investments from the MENA. Such narratives refuted accusations that MENA petrodollars demonstrated US weakness or that they might be used to undermine US institutions and interests. Instead, petrodollar flows were held up as evidence of the benefits of globalized capitalism and the relative openness of the US economy to foreigners. The inflow of petrodollars to the United States was cited as proof that the country remained an ascending power and dynamic economy, countering those who maintained that events like the Vietnam War or stagflation had left US institutions in decline. Advocates of petrodollar interdependence also promoted US economic ties with the MENA as both a means toward and evidence of the feasibility of cooperation among Americans and Arabs and Iranians. This theme countered cultural understandings of Middle Eastern peoples as adversaries of the United States, and much of the news media showed a far greater receptivity to discussing Arabs and Iranians in respectful and even admiring terms than before the oil shock. At the same time, the narrative of cooperation also worked to reassure Americans that they retained a leadership role over the MENA; Arabs and Iranians now had wealth, but they still needed US expertise, technology, and geopolitical support. In general, these narratives advanced a positive case for petrodollar interdependence that aimed to build support for it and counter competing hostile narratives.

Time emerged as a prominent advocate for the benefits of petrodollar interdependence. A December 1974 *Time* article argued that investments from the oil-rich countries would improve the US economy by providing it with needed capital, while also noting that the United States had championed broad freedom for foreign investment as an important international principle for many years. The article also articulated the strategy of seeking petrodollar interdependence as pursued by the Nixon and Ford administrations. "The greater the OPEC share in the U.S. economy and the bigger its interest in U.S. businesses, the more the oil nations would become hostages to that economy and the less anxious they would be to impose another embargo that would damage their own investments," the article stated, and then, in an ironic allusion to Third World takeovers of Western oil companies, added that "if any company controlled by petroleum potentates got out of hand, the U.S. could always nationalize."[15]

A month later *Time* declared King Faisal the magazine's "Man of the Year" for 1974. The cover story exemplified the argument that petrodollar cooperation between the United States and the OECs was necessary. The piece struck a balanced tone on OPEC and the oil-importing countries, arguing that each side had legitimate grievances and needs. The article raised alarm about the danger of not successfully recycling petrodollars and pushed for Western countries to help the oil producers industrialize, develop their agriculture, and find useful outlets for investment in the belief that this would benefit both sides and help alleviate dangerous global economic imbalances. "In the difficult decade ahead, the best hope is that all sides will realize that they are really interdependent—for resources, technologies, goods, capital, ideas," *Time* concluded. "The old world of Western dominance is dead, but if the oil powers try to dominate the new world of interdependencies, the result will be bankruptcies and deflation in the West, and even worse poverty and hunger in the have-not developing countries. . . . In this great global clash of interests, it is time for both sides to soften their anger and seek new ways to get along with each other. If sanity is to prevail, the guiding policy must be not confrontation but cooperation."[16] In this view, only recognition of the global interdependence caused by oil and petrodollars, in conjunction with a cooperative response to this interdependence, could avoid disaster for the United States, the oil-rich countries, and the world.

Other pieces forcefully argued that the mutually beneficial economic cooperation envisioned in *Time*'s "Man of the Year" article on Faisal had indeed occurred. These articles maintained that the economic growth of MENA countries benefited the United States and challenged negative narratives about oil-rich sheikhs gauging ordinary Americans through high oil prices. "The relationship between the United States and Saudi Arabia is most often perceived in simplistic images of tankers carrying oil west and billions of precious American dollars just as surely flowing east," one 1977 *New York Times* article began. "But fortunately for the United States, those petrodollars are not resting in Saudi coffers nor are they being used to buy out Western companies, as was the popular fear a few years ago. Instead, they are, for the most part being churned back into the world economy in general and into the United States economy in particular."[17] From this view, Saudi Arabia was not an adversarial threat to the United States but rather a beneficial partner, and the increasingly interdependent global economy was not a net cost for Americans but a beneficial equilibrium. *Time* similarly opined a few months later that the Saudis had shown that they "can be expected to wield their petropower prudently" due to their interdependence with Western economies and anticommunist efforts.[18]

Some of the most dramatic arguments favoring petrodollar interdependence came from literature on US construction projects in the MENA. One 1976 *Fortune* article argued that the "immense tide of construction" in the Arabian Peninsula "is more than satisfying to American firms lucky enough to be hired by the Arabs. It may be keeping some of them in business. Fees on the [Arabian] peninsula are high, and promptly paid—not always true . . . back in Chicago or New York, where during the recent recession the building industry has been as hard hit as any." Access to growing foreign markets, in short, served to counterbalance downturns in domestic ones. Furthermore, the successes of US engineers served to reassure readers about the continued vitality of America's spirit and its enduring influence in the face of narratives of decline. The article described one meeting in Abu Dhabi between American architects and a sheikh, imparting notions of primitiveness to the latter by noting that he held the gathering in a tent in the desert since he was falconing. The Americans, by contrast, are bringing modernity, with plans for an upscale 450-room hotel, and in return are obtaining a petrodollar windfall from the sheikh, who is financing the project; indeed, on a whim the sheikh asks for 300 more rooms, to which the Americans happily oblige. *Fortune* presented the Middle East as the latest frontier in US history, a "Klondike without ice" where Americans yet again achieved wealth and established civilization.[19]

The ability of US engineers to construct unprecedented marvels under difficult conditions likewise projected American pride, even if those marvels were not in the United States. "Everything is or will be the biggest in the world: the biggest sea-water in-take and treatment plant, the biggest natural-gas liquid plants, the biggest crude oil terminal and loading facility and tank farm, the biggest oil refinery," one 1977 *New York Times* article read, describing US-led construction projects under way in Saudi Arabia. "Jubail, a desert today, will be a city of 500,000 in five years."[20] While these projects benefited Saudi Arabia, they also represented striking proof of enduring American greatness and global appeal. US literature championing petrodollar interdependence celebrated Americans selling other exports to the MENA as well. A 1975

New York Times article argued that "despite anti-Americanism in much of the region through the past decade and sharp Japanese and European competition, there is a marked preference for American products, American businessmen returning from the Middle East report."[21] The strength of US exports to the petrodollar-rich MENA provided assurances that the United States was succeeding in an increasingly global economy, even in the face of ongoing political disputes with segments of the Arab world and rising trade competition from Europe and Japan.

US advocates and opponents of petrodollar interdependence clashed on a number of specific issues. One of the most prominent was the investment of petrodollars in US corporations. Proponents of petrodollar investments argued that they strengthened the US economy by supplying needed capital and demonstrated the continued strength of the US economy in that it remained an attractive location for deploying assets. Opponents charged that foreign investors, with the complicity of greedy US corporations and politicians, could use their financial influence to manipulate public opinion, undermine democratic institutions, and harm US national interests, and they saw the specter of Arabs buying up US businesses and properties as evidence of a decline in the strength and independence of the US economy. Arab investments thereby became a central focus in early US debates over how to understand and respond to the rise of global capital flows that increasingly involved foreign investments flowing into the United States rather than the reverse, as had been the dominant trend since World War I. Such debates would parallel legislative struggles between those who sought to place greater oversight and restrictions on petrodollar flows and those seeking to encourage petrodollar investments.

Notably, while US media focused on the issue of Arab and Iranian direct investments, where they would have a controlling interest over a company, the vast majority of Arab and Iranian investments in the United States were actually portfolio investments, where their shares in a company were too small to affect its governance. Indeed, the bulk of foreign direct investments in the United States came from Western Europe and Canada during the 1970s; in 1976 they constituted 85 percent of the total.[22] Yet even Arab-friendly US media repeatedly described the size of the OECs' revenues in terms of how many US corporations they could buy out as a way to dramatically describe the size of OPEC's windfall, reinforcing the notion that Arab and Iranian control of the US economy was a real possibility. *Time*'s article naming Faisal its 1974 man of the year, for example, stated without explication that OPEC's price hikes in the early 1970s had resulted in "the greatest and swiftest transfer of wealth in all history" and that at its current rate of accumulation, OPEC could buy out "all IBM stock in 143 days, all Exxon stock in 79 days, the Rockefeller family's wealth in six days."[23] Such figures were highly misleading, since the countries in OPEC were not a singular unit and they had to spend much of their revenues for domestic purposes, but they gave the erroneous impression that OPEC's financial power was eclipsing that of the far larger US economy and that Arabs and Iranians were poised to buy up major US businesses.

The prominence of hypothetical Arab direct investments in media attacking petrodollar ties as a threat to US sovereignty reflected a convergence of the popularized ideas that the Arab states had near-limitless funds at their disposal and that Arabs were either insensitive or hostile to US society. Even though other countries held far larger direct investments in the United States, US media during the 1970s often focused on the Arab countries as the primary example of the threat posed by foreign direct investment, in part due to the preexisting prevalence of negative stereotypes of Arabs and opposition to Arab foreign policies in US culture. A range of media popularized the idea that Arab investors would buy up cherished US businesses and properties. *The Sonny and Cher Comedy Hour* ran a skit in which Arabs took states off a map of the United States while singing "This Land Is Your Land, This Land Is My Land."[24] The comic strip *Tank McNamara* featured a weeklong series where oil-rich Arabs purchase the Boston Bruins hockey team and relocate them to Beirut as the renamed Petrodollar Penguins, despite the nouveau riche Arabs lacking a basic knowledge of the sport, such as the fact that it requires ice.[25] The 1975 novel *The Forty-First Thief*, by Edward Pollitz Jr., presents a fictitious oil-rich Arab nation utilizing a combination of bribery and blackmail over US financial leaders indebted to it to launch an attempt at a hostile takeover of General Motors in order to prevent the company from developing a solar-powered car that can free Americans from dependence on foreign oil.[26]

In the 1976 dark comedy and Academy Award–winning film *Network*, popular news anchor Howard Beale informs his audience that a Saudi conglomerate is secretly moving to purchase his television station with petrodollars washed through Western banks. This purchase, Beale makes clear, is part of a larger trend. "Right now the Arabs have screwed us out of enough American dollars to come right back and with our own money buy General Motors, IBM, ITT, AT&T, DuPont, US Steel, and twenty other American companies," Beale shouts. "The Arabs are simply buying us. There's only one thing that can stop them: you!" Beale calls on the American people to flood the White House with telegrams declaring "I don't want the banks selling my country to the Arabs!" The film both assumed and promoted a widespread

Figure 8. Even beloved US sports teams are not safe from petrodollar takeovers in the comic strip *Tank McNamara*. Published in the *Washington Post* on January 20, 1975. TANK MCNAMARA © 1975 Millar/Hinds. Reprinted with permission of ANDREWS MCMEEL SYNDICATION. All rights reserved.

populist demonization of Arabs among US filmgoers, a demonization anchored in the assumptions that Arabs had undeservedly taken money from Americans, that Arabs were inherently inimical to US values, and that Arabs sought to control the United States. The film implied that US power and sovereignty could be reasserted only if Americans reengaged themselves in politics for the purpose of preventing foreign economic takeovers.[27]

The chairman of the company that owns Beale's station, Arthur Jensen, then meets with Beale in private, whereupon Jensen launches his own tirade against Beale's actions. "The Arabs have taken billions of dollars out of this country, and now they must put it back!" Jensen declares, but not for America's sake— rather, for the sake of international finance. "You are an old man who thinks in terms of nations and peoples," Jensen continues. "There are no nations, there are no peoples . . . there are no Arabs, there are no Third Worlds, there is no West. There is only one holistic system of systems . . . the international system of currency which determines the totality of life on this planet." The film thereby casts multinational corporations as coconspirators with the Arabs in undermining US sovereignty. The pursuit of money had led corporate executives to sell out the United States to the Arabs; indeed, some of these executives had become so consumed by the pursuit of wealth that they no longer recognized a difference between the two. For businesspeople like Jensen, the new globalized economy, of which petrodollar recycling was a key part, erased all identities and values other than money.[28]

Yet whereas *Network* presents capitalism's erasure of national divisions as a threat, many conservatives embracing neoliberal economics celebrated the idea that an increasingly global free market would break down excessive state barriers to exchanges between peoples. These conservatives sharply disputed assertions that Arab investments posed a threat to the United States. Citibank's Walter Wriston publicly argued that Arab investors could be expected to behave like economically rational actors just like anyone else, as "the purchase of equity control of a company does not remove market forces and does not remove the law."[29] If an Arab-controlled firm in the United States took hostile action against Americans, it would be disciplined either by consumer choice or by the US government.

Some conservatives accused opponents of Arab investment in the United States of being bigots. In 1975 the *National Review* maintained that efforts to limit the flow of petrodollars into the United States were driven by unreasonable antipathy toward Arabs, and ascribed these efforts to Americans on the left, sardonically claiming that "the Arabs have managed to make the ethnic slur respectable in liberal circles." The magazine insisted that "shrinking the area in which resources flow freely is never desirable from the point of view of economic efficiency. . . . We need to encourage an inflow of foreign capital to balance the outflow of dollars for oil imports, and also to provide funds for our domestic capital markets."[30] The *National Review* thus combined a call for global free trade with the ideal that Arabs should be treated as respected partners of the United States, part of a larger trend in US culture during the 1970s wherein free market values increasingly converged with a cultural ethos of inclusiveness toward all races and nationalities.[31]

Works of fiction also defended Arab investments in the United States and pushed back against economic nationalism. The 1975 novel *The Petrodollar Takeover*, authored by Peter Tanous and Paul Rubinstein, presents a fictional effort by Saudi Arabia to obtain a controlling share of the stock of General Motors in a positive light. In the novel the Saudis' motivation to control General Motors is cast as a reasonable act of self-defense, rooted in an effort to derail an armor sale to Iran, whose young new shah has engaged in belligerent border attacks against Saudi Arabia. The Saudi acquisition effort serves as a vehicle in the book to champion the freedom of international commerce generally. As one of the protagonists, the Syrian American investment banker John Haddad, puts it to the reader, "The world had become much too small and nations too interdependent to allow the petty nationalistic obstacles of small minds to stop the natural functioning of trade and commerce."[32] The book presents Saudi investments as bringing higher earnings to US bankers, executives, and auto workers alike. At the same time the book also argues that if the United States restricted foreign investment in its own domestic economy, other countries would retaliate by restricting or nationalizing US investments abroad, crippling the US economy. Interdependence, petrodollar or otherwise, was a net good for everyone who sought peace and economic growth.

In real life, Arabs seeking to make direct investments in the United States found a very hostile environment, with many Americans espousing the negative media narratives about petrodollars. During two unrelated attempts by Arabs (a Saudi and a Lebanese national, respectively) to obtain controlling shares of two modest-sized banks (assets in the $300 million range) in San Jose, California, and Pontiac, Michigan, in early 1975, local resistance included a contemplated boycott by Jewish merchants, the withdrawal of deposits by bank patrons, bank directors guiding opposition campaigns for stockholders, and pursuit of a court injunction. One liquor store owner in San Jose summarized popular local sentiment by saying, "It worries me that with all those petrodollars, the Arabs will come in and buy us all up." In both cases, the popular backlash prevented the Arab investors from obtaining controlling shares of the banks.[33] During the same period the Treasury Department was so concerned about the possibility of the Arabs and Iranians inciting popular American anger over foreign investments that it directed George Shultz, now at Bechtel but serving as an unofficial government envoy to the Gulf states, to stress to the Arabs and Iranians "the benefit to the investing oil-producing countries in carefully and publicly putting emphasis . . . [on] longer term investments in industries not closely related to national defense, public opinion formation, or negotiations with the producing countries themselves . . . [as these] would be likely to generate disruptive public debate and overlie restrictive regulations."[34] Popular backlash, in short, undercut Middle East investment in the United States.

Foreign investors also faced increased scrutiny by some members of Congress. Whereas the Nixon and Ford administrations promoted petrodollar investments, the more numerous elected officials in Congress represented a broader range of ideologies and electoral concerns. While some congresspeople encouraged foreign direct investment and argued that existing law provided sufficient safeguards to national security interests, other representatives, whose motivations ranged from support of Israel to economic nationalism, called for greater restrictions and oversight. Congressional concern had already increased during the period of 1969 to 1973, when foreign direct investments in the United States, largely from Western Europe and Japan, increased more than 50 percent, and some Americans expressed concern about European and Japanese competition in the US domestic economy. The projected gigantic surpluses of the OECs after the 1973 oil shock brought a new sense of urgency to the US debate on the issue, however. In January 1974 Democratic representative from

California John Moss submitted a bill that would limit foreign ownership of US energy and defense companies to 10 percent in order to protect national security interests, while Democratic representative from Pennsylvania John Dent submitted a bill that would prohibit foreign ownership of more than 5 percent of any US corporation's voting stock.[35] In February 1975 Democratic senator from New Jersey Harrison Williams Jr. sponsored a bill that would grant the president discretionary power to prevent any foreign investment totaling more than 5 percent of the stock of any US company with assets of $1 million or more and would require domestic companies to fully disclose all foreign and domestic ownership, in part due to reports that Arabs had used their petrodollars to harm Jewish banks in the United States. "[We should be] leery of claims that economic power will never be used to win political objectives," Williams declared. "The dangers inherent in our traditional open-door policy toward foreign investment can no longer be ignored."[36]

The Nixon and Ford administrations resisted these congressional efforts to increase the regulation of foreign investments, as they sought to preserve petrodollar flows into the United States, good relations with allied MENA countries, and the broader US commitment to minimally restricted foreign investment as a global norm.[37] Treasury spearheaded the effort to dissuade Congress from limiting foreign direct investment in the United States, insisting that it helped the US economy and that there were already adequate protections for national security interests. Treasury under secretary Edwin Yeo testified before Congress, arguing that "to the degree we are successful in attracting additional capital we facilitate to that degree economic recovery."[38] The Ford administration as well as corporations such as General Electric, BFGoodrich, Rockwell International, Carrier Corporation, and Hewlett-Packard also raised the danger of retaliation against US direct investment in other countries, which was six times larger than the total of foreign direct investment in the United States, if the United States increased restrictions.[39] The Ford administration succeeded on the legislative front; Congress did not pass new legislation increasing restrictions on foreign direct investment.[40] Opponents did, however, succeed in creating a discouraging environment for Arab and Iranian direct investment in the United States. From 1974 to 1976 the net total of direct investments in the United States by the oil-exporting MENA countries constituted a mere $68 million.[41]

The Ford administration had even greater difficulty dealing with Congress on the issue of the Arab boycott against Israel. The member states of the Arab League implemented a boycott against Israel in 1948, and over time extended the boycott to many companies that engaged in business with Israel; enforcement varied at the secondary level, with numerous companies receiving exemptions if their services were needed by the Arab countries. By 1972 the Arab countries had blacklisted an estimated fifteen hundred US companies due to their business ties with Israel.[42]

Before 1973 most companies had ignored or were unaware of the Arab blacklist, but after the oil shock many corporations reportedly avoided business with Israel for fear of losing access to Arab petrodollars.[43] In February 1975 the Arab boycott garnered headlines when the Kuwait International Investment Company dropped out of two lending syndicates because the deals involved the blacklisted banking firm Lazard Frères as an underwriter.[44] Senator Harrison Williams publicly called on the Ford administration to investigate the matter and determine whether the Arab boycott illegally discriminated against Jewish or other Americans.[45] Shortly thereafter the Anti-Defamation League of B'nai B'rith charged that the Army Corps of Engineers, the Overseas Private Investment Corporation, and six private US companies were illegally discriminating against the hiring of Jewish employees in onsite jobs in Arab countries. The Senate Foreign Relations Subcommittee on Multinational Corporations, chaired by Democratic senator from Idaho Frank Church, held hearings on the Arab boycott in late February and early March, where the Anti-Defamation League called for a ban on Arab investment in the United States until the Arab boycott issue was addressed.[46]

The Ford administration investigated for any violations of US law committed by Arab states, but it did not push for legislative action on the Arab boycott, arguing the issue was "best dealt with through quiet diplomacy and persuasion."[47] Many congresspeople disagreed and submitted new laws to criminalize participation in the Arab boycott.[48] This angered Saudi leaders, who told the Ford administration that "there is room for quiet, practical improvement in the application of visa and business policies related to the Arab boycott but that they will react very strongly against any attempt to force their hand by public pressure and U.S. legislation."[49] Hoping to appease both Congress and Riyadh, in November Ford proposed legislation to prohibit US businesses from discriminating on the basis of race, religion, nationality, or sex but not for adhering to the Arab boycott against Israel.[50] In 1976, however, Congress continued to propose bills against the Arab boycott in spite of the Ford administration lobbying against them. One measure that denied certain tax breaks to companies that participated in the Arab boycott was attached as an amendment to a tax revision bill that Ford was unwilling to veto, and in October 1976 Ford reluctantly signed it into law.[51] Riyadh then warned the US government and major US corporations that any additional antiboycott legislation might force Saudi Arabia to stop holding the price of oil down since they would not have any examples of US reciprocity for Saudi help.[52]

Another important area of petrodollar contention was the massive quantity and technological capability of US arms sold to oil-exporting MENA countries. Many Americans contended that US arms sales to the MENA were a potential danger to peace, human rights, and US strategic interests. For supporters of Israel, US arms sales to Arab countries were considered particularly ominous.

Many commentators raised the possibility that US arms sales to Middle East allies might be used against US interests or fall into different hands. A 1975 *Time* cover article on US arms exports argued that weapons sales had reached "insane" levels and warned that "today's favored arms customer may become tomorrow's Frankenstein monster. Governments can change abruptly; a coup in Iran or Saudi Arabia might bring to power a regime as radical as that of Libya's Colonel Muammar Gaddafi. The new leader would inherit a cache of the latest military hardware, which he would almost surely use against the interest of the Western states that originally provided it."[53] In 1976 the *New York Times* opined that foreign arms sales had become "mindless" and "excessive" and argued that the sophistication of weapons sold to countries like Iran required thousands of on-the-ground US personnel that could draw the United States into a regional conflict, raising the memory of the deployment of US military advisers to Saigon at the start of US involvement in the Vietnam War.[54]

The Crash of '79, a 1976 novel by Paul E. Erdman that made the *New York Times* Best Seller List and the bookshelf of Saudi intelligence chief Prince Turki bin Faisal, dramatizes concerns that the arms-petrodollar trade could lead to an apocalyptic near future.[55] The real-life shah of Iran is cast as the main villain, depicted as a megalomaniac tyrant and sadistic rapist who maintains a murderous, authoritarian regime. The shah plays on the United States' myopic pursuit of petrodollars to purchase a massive arsenal of US weapons, even including two rented aircraft carriers, with the intention of conquering his oil-rich Arab neighbors and Israel to establish Iran as a third superpower. The fact that Iran was in reality buying advanced US weapons lent an air of possibility to the scenario presented in the novel. When the shah launches his invasion, Erdman describes his command bunker as "a marvel of modern technology . . . constructed by Bechtel Corporation of San Francisco and equipped by Raytheon, Westinghouse, Litton Industries, and Texas Instruments with the very best in communications equipment. Nothing in either the Pentagon or the White House in Washington even came close."[56] The admiring prose

"It Helps Maintain A Better Balance"

Figure 9. The cartoonist Herblock satirizes the Ford administration's argument that selling arms to the Persian Gulf countries will promote peace. Published in the *Washington Post* on January 28, 1975. A 1975 Herblock Cartoon, © The Herb Block Foundation.

used by so many real newspaper and magazine articles to describe US engineering projects in the MENA is parodied by Erdman to sardonic effect. The shah fails in his effort to establish a new Persian empire, but his war does lead to the destruction of the Persian Gulf's oil supplies and a global financial collapse, bringing the world to a preindustrial state. Erdman's novel suggested to Americans, in a sensational fashion, that the United States' growing arms trade with Middle East tyrants was both immoral and strategically unwise.[57]

Many members of Congress either shared the growing concerns about US arms sales to the Middle East or felt political pressure to act on them. A coalition of congresspeople that included defenders of Israel, antiwar advocates, human rights supporters, and those concerned about US military technology falling into hostile hands increasingly organized as the arms-petrodollar trade accelerated. Citing concern that ballooning US arms sales to conflict-ridden regions like the Middle East (and often to countries on both sides of disputes) potentially endangered US security interests, members of Congress championed greater legislative control over the executive branch's foreign arms transfers, which up to 1974 had not been subject to congressional oversight.[58] The petrodollar-rich states were particularly unregulated by Congress, for while legislators determined US funding for military aid, they had no control over arms sales that were fully paid by the receiving nation, as was now the case for countries like Iran and Saudi Arabia. In late 1974 Congress therefore passed legislation requiring that it be notified of any proposed foreign arms sale exceeding $25 million and empowered it to veto the sale with a majority vote in both chambers.

The Ford administration faced the greatest amount of resistance to MENA arms sales from Congress in 1976. The year began with the release of a report prepared by Republican representative from Delaware Pierre du Pont IV charging that the United States could not prevent weapons sold to the Gulf states from being transferred to Arab states bordering Israel in the case of renewed conflict, and that the US government lacked a coherent policy on foreign arms sales.[59] Members of Congress proposed and drafted new regulations on the arms trade, including setting a cap on the value of US arms exports that could be approved in a year.[60] Democratic senator from Wisconsin William Proxmire charged that massive arms sales to countries like Iran had diverted critical manpower and weapons needed by the US military, and urged that American needs be reprioritized.[61] Outside Congress, popular activism against Iran's mass imprisonment and torture of political prisoners was also growing as part of a larger American embrace of human rights activism during the 1970s.[62] At a February meeting at Columbia University, attendees listened to Iranian poet

Reza Baraheni describe how Iranian agents of the internal police force SAVAK struck him seventy-five times with a wire whip and to former US attorney general Ramsey Clark declare that "we are supporting tyranny abroad. . . . All that wealth and all that oil should not mean more to us than human dignity. We must form a policy based on human rights."[63]

Proposals to curb arms sales alarmed the shah. "If you try to take an unfriendly attitude toward my country, we can hurt you as badly if not more so than you can hurt us," the shah warned the United States in an interview with *U.S. News & World Report* in March. "Not just through oil; we can create trouble for you in the region. If you force us to change our friendly attitude, the repercussions will be immeasurable."[64] Despite the shah's strong words, in April Congress passed a bill that capped total US foreign arms sales at $9 billion per fiscal year starting in 1977 and allowed Congress to bar sales to countries with human rights violations. Ford vetoed the bill, arguing that these measures limited the United States' ability to help allied countries and "obstructs U.S. industry from competing fairly with foreign suppliers."[65] Still, the ability of congressional protests to strain Iran-US relations had been made clear.

Even more congresspeople objected in July 1976 when the Ford administration requested the sale of 2,000 Sidewinder air-to-air missiles and 1,800 Maverick air-to-surface missiles, manufactured by Raytheon, to Saudi Arabia. Seeking to assuage congressional concern over Israel's security and the general surge of US foreign arms sales, the Ford administration reduced its request to 850 Sidewinder and 650 Maverick missiles.[66] Even then, Congress allowed the sale to go forward only after Kissinger met with Senate leaders to impress on them the damage that could result to Saudi-US relations if the deal was scuttled.[67]

Jimmy Carter, former Democratic governor of Georgia and Democratic nominee for president in 1976, campaigned on restoring human rights and idealism as guiding principles for US foreign policy, rebuking the realpolitik of Ford and Kissinger. Carter courted Americans who supported Israel, opposed US support for countries with routine human rights violations, or were concerned about arms races, by seizing upon the recent controversies over the Arab boycott and US arms sales in his campaign against Ford. On September 30 Carter condemned the Ford administration for "bowing down to foreign blackmail" by blocking legislation against the Arab boycott and selling Sidewinder and Maverick missiles to Saudi Arabia.[68] Six days later Ford attempted to counter Carter's charges by announcing that his administration would disclose the names of companies that participated in the Arab boycott.[69] Yet when Ford visited New York City on October 12, protesters opposed to his administration's arms sales to Arab countries and leniency on the Arab boycott greeted him with jeers and effigies of him and Kissinger.[70] While strategic and economic imperatives had driven Ford to encourage petrodollar interdependence between the United States and the MENA, this course proved to be a political liability. In November, Ford narrowly lost his bid for reelection against Carter; and while his loss was tied to a variety of factors, mounting public opposition to Ford's petrodollar policies hurt his campaign.

In contrast to the United States, media in the Arab world in the mid-1970s rarely disputed that the rise in Arab petrodollar profits was justified. Oil rich or oil poor, radical or conservative, Islamist or secular, Arab media regularly expressed the understanding that the Arab world deserved and needed the increased infusion of petrodollars on the basis of sovereign rights and the less-developed state of their economies compared with the West. Debates in Arab media instead centered on the best way to maintain high oil profits and use the accrued funds. The state-backed media of Egypt, Iraq, and Saudi Arabia, three of the largest channels of Arab discourse during the 1970s, evinced the largest degree of narrative cohesion during the period of the oil embargo against the United States, united in opposition to US support for Israel and sizable reductions in petroleum prices.

Even before the 1973 war, the media of Baathist Iraq promoted narratives of struggle against the United States and its European allies. After 1972, much of this focused on Baghdad's nationalization of the IPC. On June 1, 1973, Saddam Hussein gave an interview with the Baghdad-based Baathist newspaper *al-Thawra* to discuss the reasons for and impacts of the decision to nationalize the IPC at its one-year anniversary. "The position and behavior of the monopolizing companies [the IPC] conflicted with the interests of the country," Saddam argued. "Therefore, it was imperative to resolve this contradiction in favor of exercising our sovereignty over our own wealth."[71]

In the aftermath of the 1973 oil shock, *al-Thawra* regularly published articles and cartoons that credited rising Iraqi petrodollar revenues to the Baath Party's decision to nationalize the IPC and called on the Arab and Third worlds to join Iraq in opposing US economic imperialism. When Nixon announced his desire for an oil consumer-producer dialogue in January 1974, President al-Bakr publicly denounced the proposal. *Al-Thawra* described al-Bakr as characterizing Nixon's offer as part of an "American imperialist strategy" and a scheme that sought "the detriment of the positions of the oil-producing countries and their legitimate rights." The newspaper called on the world to "reject the American mandate on global power and lift up just relations and equality between the [oil] producing and consuming countries."[72] *Al-Thawra* likewise

Figure 10. "Nationalization" smashing "the monopolies." Published in *al-Thawra* on February 12, 1974. Artist: Amer Rashad al-Jalili.

ran articles celebrating the new oil economy for bringing unprecedented development to and rising living standards for Iraq.[73] These were accompanied by political cartoons that depicted the Western oil companies, represented as a wealthy man with a top hat, being punched by the fist of nationalization. One such cartoon illustrated a simple equation: the fist of nationalization smashing the head of a man labeled "the monopolies" plus an Iraqi worker inscribed with the words "resilience and increase of production" equals joy and prosperity for Iraqi children.[74] Through its regular commentary on the nationalization of the Iraqi oil industry and opposition to Washington, the Baathist government promoted its domestic and international legitimacy in narratives that presented its policies as simultaneously challenging US empire and establishing rapid economic development in Iraq.

The eponymous newspaper of the Saudi capital, *al-Riyadh*, likewise adopted an antagonistic stance toward the United States during the period of the Arab oil embargo. A cartoon at the start of the embargo in October depicted Faisal as a tall, rifle-wielding soldier who informed a diminutive Nixon, drawn as a cowboy holding a gas canister, that oil is "for friends only."[75] Similarly, the following month a cartoon depicted Santa Claus with bottles of gasoline, who stated that he was "only going to give [them] to the good people of the West."[76] In early February 1974, *al-Riyadh* blasted the "shallow hopes of Washington" to create an MDC oil consumer bloc to challenge OPEC and the new price of petroleum at its upcoming energy conference.[77] Later that month the newspaper ran an editorial declaring that "justice is more valuable than oil . . [*sic*] and the law is greater than the Jews."[78] While tensions with the United States remained high, *al-Riyadh* evinced a willingness to vocally challenge the United States on the issues of the pricing of oil and the Arab-Israeli conflict, demonstrating a rhetorical militancy that aligned with Baathist Iraq.

Media in oil-poor Arab countries also joined in celebrating the oil weapon and the new petrodollar profits of the oil-rich states. On March 14, 1974, for example, *al-Ahram*, the newspaper of record for Cairo, ran a cartoon with the caption "the philosophy of petroleum" that showed a happy Arab standing with his hand on the spigot of an oil barrel and telling an eager-to-please Uncle Sam that "as long as the hands are mine . . [*sic*] that are on the spigot . . [*sic*] I am able to open [it] and I am able to close [it]!"[79] Two days later another cartoon depicted Uncle Sam in a prison labeled "petroleum embargo." A jovial Arab jailor tells Uncle Sam that the Arab petroleum ministers might release him early "if you are on good behavior."[80] In early 1974 one of the leading newspapers of Lebanon, *al-Nahar*, reveled in the fact that "'the oil revolution' turned the gaze of the West toward the Arab world," and the paper's weekly economic special boasted that "Washington and Bonn [were] covetous of Arab money."[81] During the period of the oil embargo, Arab media displayed a widespread sense of pride in rising oil revenues and united opposition against Washington, encouraging a sense of antagonism among Arabs against the United States.

After the end of the oil embargo and the rapprochement between Riyadh and Washington, latent divisions over the proper uses of oil wealth reemerged in the state-backed media of Iraq and Saudi Arabia, as well as in Arab Islamist literature. Much of these debates centered on whether the Arabs should pursue petrodollar interdependence with the United States. Baathist Iraq increasingly criticized Iran directly and Saudi Arabia indirectly for their petrodollar ties with the United States as a threat to Arab interests. From a different ideological starting point, many Arab Islamists expressed concern that petrodollar ties with the United States were corrupting and weakening the Islamic world. The Saudi monarchy, in contrast, endeavored in its media to justify Saudi-US petrodollar ties in the face of widespread Arab and Muslim anger over US policies on matters like the Arab-Israeli conflict.

The Iraqi government narrated itself as leading the Arab and Third worlds in the struggle to end the economic and political exploitation of US imperialism, while condemning "reactionary regimes" for their high levels of investments in and trade with the United States. The Baathists thereby capitalized on anti-US sentiment and the vastly different levels of Iraqi and Saudi economic ties with the United States to affirm their anti-imperialist credentials and shore up political support at home and abroad. State-supported media in Iraq argued that petrodollar flows to the United States harmed the Arab cause. In a representative 1974 article in *al-Thawra*, the Iraqi press charged the United

States with launching an "invasion of American exports to the Arab region [to] plunder and impoverish its economy" by selling overpriced and worthless goods to the Arabs in order to recoup the petrodollars the United States paid for Arab oil. The newspaper called for all Arab countries to avoid commerce with the United States in order to avoid this imperialist trap.[82] *Al-Thawra* also routinely celebrated Iraq's nationalization of the IPC through the rest of the decade, exulting that this established the basis for a prosperous future for the Iraqi people, in sharp contrast to US descriptions of Arab sheikhs and dictators living lives of opulence while their subjects lived in squalor. In 1977 a typical cartoon argued that when "Arab oil [was] for the Arabs," rather than Western oil companies, the result was large sums of money for national development.[83] In this way, the Baath Party worked to bolster its popularity and legitimacy by reminding Iraqis of the party's stand against Western imperialism and that oil-funded government projects and jobs were boosting the country's living standards.

Iraq also faced the reality that Iran spent billions of petrodollars on US arms. Some of these US arms fired upon and killed Iraqi soldiers, either in combat with Kurdish resistance forces armed by Iran or in border skirmishes with the Iranian army. Speaking to international reporters in 1974, Saddam condemned the shah's petrodollar ties with the United States while arguing that Iran's purchases of US arms did not threaten Baathist Iraq. Saddam argued that "progressive noble patriots" should not fear for the ongoing Iraqi revolution, despite Iran possessing the "effective weapons of America," for while the shah was "continually buying [US] arms and stockpiling them," they did him little good since he lacked the genuine support of the Iranian people, unlike the Iraqi Baathists, who enjoyed popular support among Arabs across the region. "The authorities in Iran can buy the conventional arms in the markets of the West, but they cannot pay a nation to believe in them or their policies," Saddam opined. "America can give arms [to the shah], but there will be few who will carry them. These weapons do not frighten us." Furthermore, Saddam warned the shah that "there is no honor in talking about stockpiling armaments at a time when [one's] people sleep naked on the pavement, walk barefoot and find little food to eat. . . . What serves the people of Iran is the search for a way to build a society free from hunger . . . a society with no individuals gorging themselves and others with empty stomachs."[84] Saddam thereby attacked the legitimacy of the shah's regime by claiming it kept the Iranian people in poverty as a result of its profligate yet futile purchases of US arms.

Saddam then claimed that "we are not annoyed by the expansion of the armies and abundance of weapons in service of the reactionary regimes," because this brought more of the peasants and workers into military positions, increasing the opportunities for ordinary people to seize power in a revolution like the one that overthrew the Iraqi monarchy in 1958. Notably, by transitioning from a discussion of Iran specifically to one of reactionary regimes generally, as well as his reference to the overthrow of the Iraqi monarchy aligned with the United States, Saddam implicitly suggested that the remaining Arab monarchs as well as the shah were setting the stage for the overthrow of their regimes by relying on US arms for repressive military buildups rather than responding to the progressive will of their peoples. Such outcomes, Saddam suggested, were both welcome and inevitable, as Arab and Third world peoples joined the Iraqis in the winning causes of revolutionary nationalism, socialism, and anti-imperialism.[85]

Al-Thawra likewise regularly reminded its readers that Iraq's adversaries used their petrodollars to purchase US weapons. In one cartoon addressing Iraq's border tensions with Iran in 1974, a banner reading "preparation for popular Arab conference in Baghdad to denounce Iranian aggression" causes a trampled and bruised Iranian soldier to flee in terror and drop his gun, which has a "USA" label.[86] *Al-Thawra* regularly labeled Iranian arms as made in the USA in its cartoons, a way of regularly reminding readers that the United States supported Iraq's enemies and thereby reinforcing narratives about the perfidy of Washington and the anti-imperialist credentials of the Baathists. The cartoons also reiterated Saddam's theme that US arms to the Iranian army posed no significant threat to Iraq since popular pan-Arab support for Baghdad easily countered the uninspired soldiers of the shah, no matter what advanced US weapons they possessed.

Arab Islamists also criticized Arab governments' uses of petrodollars, arguing that they were being used in ways that undermined Islamic principles and served the interests of the West rather than ordinary Muslims. Popular media personality and Egyptian Islamist Mustafa Mahmoud published the book *Marxism and Islam* in 1975, condemning both communism and capitalism as foreign and inferior to Islam and castigating Arab petrodollar ties with either the communist East or capitalist West. Mahmoud condemned both sides as "colonial powers . . . they invade us either ideologically or economically. They sell us weapons then make us attack one another, thus killing many birds with one stone. They get back the money they pay for our oil in hard currencies, build factories, provide work for their unemployed, disrupt our unity, ensure that the zealous Arab elite are killed by the hands of an equally zealous Arab elite, then sit down to toast their victories over a world of asses—an Arab world kept backward by its so-called 'progressive vanguard'!"[87] Mahmoud's economic critiques and call for the implementation of truly Islamic governance in the Arab world as the solution to the region's backwardness challenged both the secular regime in Baghdad and the theocratic monarchy in Riyadh. The Muslim Brotherhood magazine *al-Da'wa* regularly condemned the widespread practice of charging interest on loans (which they defined as usury [*riba*], an act forbidden in the Qur'an) in Muslim-majority countries, implicitly critiquing Arab republics and monarchies for allowing petrodollar deposits to be used in such a fashion.[88] Indeed, while Riyadh promoted the development of international Islamic banks that eschewed charging interest abroad, it virtually never granted licenses to Islamic banks to operate within Saudi Arabia, presumably because Saudi leaders did not want to suggest that the conventional banks within the kingdom, which the Saudi elite used for the bulk of their petrodollars, were un-Islamic.[89] In 1974 Saudi Arabia also insisted that the US government not publish country data on Saudi investments in the United States, as it did for most countries, but instead publish aggregate figures on oil-rich MENA investments, something Treasury agreed to and then defended for decades to ensure that Saudi petrodollars flowed into US institutions.[90] Riyadh's demand for confidentiality likely stemmed from a desire to minimize leftist and Islamist accusations that the Saudis financially supported the United States and partook in usury.

Militant Islamists were often more direct in their condemnations of the Saudi Kingdom. When sociologists interviewed violent Islamists arrested in Egypt from 1974 to 1977, the militants widely expressed the belief that oil wealth had been squandered on the decadent lifestyles of Arab elites rather than used to strengthen Islamic polities against foreign threats and eliminate poverty. The researchers summarized the Islamists' belief "that no true Muslim rulers would allow Muslims to enjoy too much wealth while fellow Muslims elsewhere were starving (as in Saudi Arabia as opposed to Bangladesh)."[91]

Unable to completely deny the large number of petrodollars flowing from Saudi Arabia to the United States and facing both secular leftist and Islamist challenges, the Saudi state directed its media to emphasize arguments on how Saudi-US petrodollar interdependence enabled Riyadh to extract economic and political benefits from the United States for Saudi Arabia and the wider Arab, Third, and Islamic worlds. For example, when *al-Riyadh* announced in April 1974 that the Saudi government planned to join two joint economic and military commissions with the United States, the newspaper emphasized that the Saudis stood to gain US assistance "in the areas of economics, technology, manufacturing, and supplying the Kingdom what it needs for defensive purposes." Furthermore, the Saudi government insisted that Saudi-US economic collaboration would be predicated on the US government reaffirming its commitment to "achieving a just and lasting peace in the region of the Middle East to be enjoyed by its entire people in stability, and to work toward the development of the region and its prosperity."[92]

Three days later al-Riyadh ran as its headline story the announcement that Saudi Arabia would spend a billion riyals on US air and ground missiles to develop a defensive network across the kingdom, emphasizing the military advantages of a close relationship with Washington.[93] Al-Riyadh thus justified Saudi-US collaboration on petrodollars as a means of extracting benefits from the United States and preempted oppositional critiques by ensuring that the Saudi government would cooperate with the United States only if it advanced Arab, Third World, and Islamic causes. The Saudi leadership placed so much importance on the US government approving arms sales in part for propaganda purposes; approval of a sale could be used by the kingdom to validate its collaboration with the United States, while disapproval of a sale could be used by detractors to attack the legitimacy of the Saudi monarchy's rule.

Arab media also focused on the issue of how petrodollars might impact the oil-poor Third World. On this issue, Iraqi state media held up Iraq's oil-fueled economic and political development under socialist and anti-imperialist principles as a model for other Third World countries in how to successfully resist the United States. As Saddam Hussein put it in a 1978 May Day speech at an international trade union conference in Baghdad, Iraq's progress in developing revolutionary and scientific socialism at home "continue[s] the march . . . not only towards liberating our Arab people in the whole Arab homeland, but also towards placing the potentials, achievements and experience of the revolution at the service of humanity as a whole," which is "why the Iraqi Revolution has been fought by imperialism since 1968."[94] Iraqi media regularly featured articles in which visiting leaders from other Third World countries commented favorably about the Baathist government and cited its policies as a paradigm that they sought to emulate in their own efforts at achieving political and economic independence from US neo-imperialism.

A notable example of this occurred in a series of February 1974 articles in al-Thawra when Stokely Carmichael visited Iraq. Carmichael, a Trinidad American, had been a prominent black civil rights activist in the United States during the 1960s who increasingly came to view the US government as the opponent of colored peoples globally. In the late 1960s he obtained asylum in Guinea, where he developed close ties with Guinean president Sékou Touré and the exiled Ghanaian president Kwame Nkrumah, both celebrated leaders of the movement for anti-imperialism, socialism, and Pan-Africanism. Nkrumah placed Carmichael in a leadership position in his All-African People's Revolutionary Party, and it was in this capacity that Carmichael headed a delegation to Iraq. *Al-Thawra* emphasized that Carmichael described Baathist-ruled Iraq as a model for and ally to the All-African People's Revolutionary Party and Guinea. At a university symposium, *al-Thawra* reported, "freedom fighter Stokely Carmichael, one of the leaders of the African Revolutionary Party, who is currently visiting the country and its facilities, said it benefited them a lot and they gained a lot of experience from the struggle of the Socialist Arab Baath Party against Zionism and colonialism, and he said: we have embraced a lot of the ideology of the Baath through our stay in Iraq. . . . He said that the Arab and African people share common ambitions and a common struggle against one enemy, imperialism and Zionism," and supported Iraq's use of oil as a weapon against these enemies.[95] Two days later *al-Thawra* reported Carmichael as saying, "The progressive world continues today to admire and appreciate the experience of the Iraqi people and its continuing triumphs."[96] Stokely's stature in Third World politics made him an ideal source of validation for the Baath Party. Through Stokely's words, *al-Thawra* narrated to its readers that Baathist Iraq was a leader in the Third World, a successful model of socialist governance and resistance to US imperialism that other freedom fighters from around the world studied as a model for their own peoples.

The ruling Saudi royals could not cast themselves as leaders of revolutionary socialism, but they did have a far larger petrodollar surplus to use for foreign aid to Third World countries. Such aid was a useful tool in gaining other countries' support, but it was also used to reaffirm the benevolence of the Saudi monarchy to its domestic subjects. Saudi newspapers regularly ran articles highlighting the large sums of aid that Riyadh provided to Third World countries.[97] Similar narratives were deployed in these newspapers' cartoons. On World Health Day in 1974, for example, *al-Riyadh* published a cartoon noting that Saudi Arabia had pledged $50 million to aid programs aimed at combating world hunger; the cartoon depicts a towering Saudi King Faisal holding out a copious bundle of grain to the world, personified as a hunched-over, struggling farmer, whose mouth gapes in astonishment at Faisal's generosity.[98] Such representations reaffirmed to readers both the power and the benevolence of the Saudi monarchy and implicitly countered criticisms that high oil prices were harming the economies of oil-poor Third World countries. The cartoon also implicitly cast Faisal as a model of Islamic charity, a characterization that sought to elicit the approval of both Islamists and Muslims generally.

In the immediate aftermath of the 1973 war, Egyptian media expressed renewed optimism about Arab unity and faith that Egypt's economy would soon rapidly develop with the infusion of large sums of petrodollar aid and investments.[99] The Egyptian press made a point of not characterizing such grants or loans as charity; rather, such financial transfers were earned by Egypt for the sacrifices of blood and treasure it had endured in defending the entire Arab nation from Israel. When King Faisal visited Egypt in August 1974 and announced a Saudi contribution of $1 billion to the country, al-Ahram made the donation its lead story and emphasized that Saudi Arabia had provided the money "to the fighting people of Egypt."[100] Later during Faisal's visit, al-Ahram ran as its lead story Faisal's declaration that "the sacrifices of Egypt [have] lifted the heads of the Arabs and returned to them their honor."[101] Implicit in these narratives was that Egypt had a right to a share of its Arab brethren's petrodollars.

Egyptian media also defended the Arab oil states from US rhetorical attacks, supporting the Arab world's claim to a greater degree of compensation for the sale of its resources while downplaying the impact of higher commodity prices on the West. In January 1975, when Ford approvingly reiterated Kissinger's *Business Week* statement about the hypothetical need of the United States to militarily respond if facing "strangulation" by exorbitantly high oil prices, al-Ahram responded with a cartoon. Playing on Ford's use of the word "strangulation," the cartoon depicts a man labeled "the West" being strangled not by the Arab oil producers but by a giant brute labeled "inflation." Arab readers would readily understand that this inflation was due to US economic policies rather than rising oil prices, as this view was constantly repeated by Arab leaders. In the cartoon, however, Ford threatens to use force against the Arab oil producers to save the West, despite the obvious fact that the giant "inflation" stands before Ford strangling the West while the Arabs innocently mind their own business in the background.[102]

As time passed, however, the state-backed Egyptian press became increasingly critical of the disproportionate rate of Gulf investment in the West rather than Egypt. A November 1974 editorial in al-Ahram casting Egypt as the base of the Arab struggle rhetorically asked the Gulf Arabs, "Why do they delay the development of Arab power? And where are they investing those millions and billions [of dollars]?" An al-Ahram piece the following January by Lutfi al-Khuli advanced the theory of "petro-blood and petro-dollars," claiming that the increase in petrodollars enjoyed by the oil-rich Arab states was directly caused by the sacrifices of blood made by the oil-poor Arab states that had undertaken the actual fighting against Israel. Al-Khuli condemned the Arab oil countries for having "attained enormous wealth" while allowing "the Arab states fighting the Zionist, imperialist enemy [to fall] into an abyss of poverty and misery." Another round of attacks on the oil-rich Arab states emerged in

the Egyptian press after the January 1977 food riots. The weekly Egyptian paper *Ruz al-Yusuf* suggested that Egyptians would abandon Arab nationalism if
the other Arabs did not accept their responsibilities to Egypt. The economic
newspaper *al-Ahram al-Iqtisadi* evoked South Africa in describing Egypt as being subjected to an "economic apartheid" in the Arab world and condemned
the behavior of oil-rich Arab tourists "visiting Egypt with great purchasing
power, dividing and ruining Egyptian society from within."[103] The triangle of
petrodollar flows that Sadat and Simon had promoted was proving increasingly
unsatisfactory to many Egyptians, generating Arab divisions.

Arab Islamists had their own critiques of the economic and cultural changes
being wrought in the oil-poor Arab countries by the spread of Western capitalism and consumerism, trends facilitated by the flow of petrodollars to these
societies. In *Marxism and Islam*, Mahmoud uses Fez, Morocco, an ancient center of Islamic learning and culture, as an example of the transformations generated by Western consumerism. "Now the children of these good and
godfearing people wear mini-skirts and modern shirts with floral designs,"
Mahmoud wrote. "Outside old Fez a new, western-styled city is rising, with
wide streets, modern cafes and huge recreation centers. Modern American cars
whiz past you. . . . Unless these people realize the impending danger, and do
something to avert it . . . this city will end up a spiritually starved place. . . .
The young will end up in mental asylums or commit suicide; luxury and afflu-
ence will spell out the end as sensuous pleasures stifle the life of the heart!" Furthermore, Mahmoud warns that "what seems about to happen in Fez can, in
fact, happen to any Arab city" and that this trend constituted "a great victory
for the West" as Muslims' "homes, even our minds and hearts have been conquered."[104] For Islamists like Mahmoud, the new oil wealth of the Arab world
was not being used to construct a better society; instead, it was being used to
build a corrupt, Westernized one focused on consumerism rather than prin-
cipled spiritualism.

Yet Mahmoud also held out hope that a different petrodollar order, one that
combined the labor force of the oil-poor Arab countries with the wealth of
the oil-rich Arab states under Islamist precepts, could achieve a spiritual and
military repulsion of the West's assaults. "If we start to carry out our economic
plan in [a] religious spirit we shall work wonders and catch up in no time with
the rest of the world," Mahmoud stated. "Economically integrated, the Arab
states make up a nation richer and potentially stronger than the USA. . . . Just
consider the combined economic potential of Saudi Arabia, Kuwait, and the
Gulf States on the one hand, and that of Egypt, Sudan and Arab North Africa
on the other!"[105] In the writings of Mahmoud and other Arab Islamists, a

different petrodollar order was being articulated, one that challenged the legitimacy of existing Arab regimes in both the oil-rich and oil-poor countries.

Like the leadership of the Arab oil-rich countries, the shah argued that the Iranian people enjoyed significant material and cultural gains due to his acquisition and use of higher petrodollar revenues. In his book *Toward the Great Civilization*, published in 1978, the shah summarizes themes he had been expounding on in speeches to the Iranian people and world media for the past decade. Iran had often been at the forefront of civilizational advancement, the shah explains, but it had also experienced disasters, most recently the deterioration of Iranian power under decadent leaders during the nineteenth and early twentieth centuries. This had left Iran open to European exploitation, including "oil imperialism . . . one of the most inhumane imperialisms of the modern world." Through the successful efforts of the shah to regain for Iran the "full and definite ownership and sovereignty over its oil industry," however, the income from petroleum was now being used for "the reconstruction of the country." Now Iran was on the path to auger in the third millennium with a "'Great Civilization'. . . . in which the best elements of human knowledge and vision shall have been employed to ensure the highest standard of living and spiritual living for every citizen."[106]

In *Toward the Great Civilization*, the shah attributes none of Iran's progress to relations with the United States but rather darkly hints that US oil companies and Washington had conspired against him and Iran. After the 1973 oil shock, "the intelligence and propaganda agencies of the industrial world . . . immediately mobilized in the most violent manner against the oil exporting countries," the shah states. "Their goal was to convince the people of the Western world (and of the Third World) that OPEC had set out to destroy the world economy and to destabilize the human civilization. . . . I do not wish to introduce in this brief history an account of the personal risks I have taken facing the oil 'empires' and 'giants' and the political powers that support them . . . [but] these developments have been accompanied . . . by the most dangerous struggles imaginable."[107] The shah had launched a larger media campaign against the United States in earnest two years earlier in 1976, when he determined the best way to address rising anti-Americanism in Iran was to co-opt it. The shah encouraged the state-controlled presses to publish severe criticism of the United States, blaming it for Iranian domestic problems, and he lent his name to broad, public charges questioning the reliability of dealing with Washington. Yet while this campaign failed to deflect popular anger against the shah, as he was already too closely tied to the United States in the minds of most Iranians, it did facilitate the deepening of anti-American views among Iranians.[108]

One of the most popular and articulate Iranians to attack both the United States and the shah was Ali Shariati. An academic philologist, Shariati synthesized leftist Third Worldism with Islamist spiritualism in his veiled critiques of the shah's regime and its ties to the West. Repeatedly arrested by the Iranian police for his university lectures, Shariati left Iran for London in the spring of 1977, only to die there weeks later. Many Iranians suspected SAVAK had murdered him, making him a martyr. His death turned him into a mythical figure and further increased the popularity of his lectures, which were mimeographed and sold in collections by the hundreds of thousands by Iranian bookstores and sidewalk vendors. Shariati proved especially popular with students and young Muslims.[109]

In one of his highly published lectures, Shariati argued, much like Mustafa Mahmoud, that the "Muslim nations . . . have been victimized by economic and, still more tragic, intellectual and moral colonization" by the capitalist states, which used "every possible trick and inhumane plan to transform countries into market places for goods and products. To that end, all human beings must become 'consumer animals' and all nations must be stripped of their authenticity." The West purposefully worked to destroy the intellectual traditions of other lands, recognizing that this led to the decline of their economic productivity. Furthermore, "the colonialists have identified religion as the biggest barrier in the way of their cultural and political penetration among other nations . . . fighting the rapid transformation of the society into a new consumer market . . . preventing people from changing drastically into creatures whose only function is to be helpless and greedy mouths dependent upon Western production."[110] In the context of the US-led petrodollar economy, Shariati offered an explanation for both the economic inequalities and social dissatisfaction that so many Iranians experienced in spite of the petrodollar wealth being accrued by their country: the shah and his subordinates had allowed Iran to be colonized, economically and intellectually, by the West. Shariati argued that Iranians would liberate themselves only when they returned to their authentic culture, revolutionary Shia Islam. In a different lecture, Shariati expounded on how the early Muslims, through their faith, defeated the Byzantine and Persian empires, "who were even more oppressive and colonialist than the contemporary superpowers." Shariati maintained that "the present generation of Muslims can rule the world if they know Allah."[111] Shariati thus provided an Islamist solution to the subordination of Iran within the US empire.

Operating in Iraq, Khomeini issued more direct criticisms of the shah's role within the US-led petrodollar order via published speeches and letters. During the 1973 war, Khomeini addressed the world's Muslims, condemning the shah for his "increasing servility to America" and support for Israel by undercutting the Arab oil weapon with an increase in Iranian oil production. Khomeini expressed fear "that the billions of dollars of weapons that [the shah] has acquired from his world-devouring masters—taking Iran to the brink of bankruptcy in the bargain—will now be sent to Israel" or used by the Iranian army directly "to target the warm-hearted, sympathetic crusaders of Islam." In a March 1975 message to the Iranian people, Khomeini offered an extended attack on the shah's use of petrodollars. "Instead of using the [oil exports] income for the benefit of this poor, hungry nation, he loans it to his imperialist masters, or purchases weapons of destruction . . . to continue the massacre of people and the suppression of anti-imperialist movements," Khomeini argued. Because of his lending to and spending in the West, the shah had neglected Iran's agriculture and industry, allowing them to decay. This had left Iran dependent on imports for food and foreign managers for the operation of industry. In Khomeini's telling, the shah had wasted Iran's oil wealth and allowed the country to become increasingly dependent on foreigners. "By exhausting the oil reserves, this regime has so impoverished the people that it will result in their enslavement," Khomeini warned. "The noble nation of Iran . . . will have to grapple with poverty and adversity, or labor for the capitalists."[112] In this way, Khomeini provided a populist framing of US-led globalization as impoverishing and weakening Iran, one that resonated with many struggling or displaced Iranian farmers, laborers, and merchants who were not included in or harmed by the shah's petrodollar dealings with the West.

Khomeini also addressed American Muslims through correspondence with the Islamic Association of Students in America and Canada. In 1975 he issued a message to the association's Seventh Congress, raising the theme of US economic exploitation in Iran. "We have been witnessing the squandering of money from the treasury of the Muslims, and spending the hungry nation's reserves on meeting the demands of the foreign powers," Khomeini declared. "We have been witnessing the massive purchases of armaments worth billions of dollars for the protection of the foreigners' bases." Through the address, Khomeini worked to develop transnational Muslim allies who might challenge the US government's support for the shah.[113]

Khomeini's hope that American Muslims would find a US president willing to listen to opponents of the shah may have risen with the election of Jimmy Carter. Six months into the Carter administration, Khomeini again wrote to the Islamic Association of Students in America and Canada, imploring its members to "let their voice be heard by the international community and make the US president understand that the Islamic nations attribute the crimes of this [Pahlavi] dynasty, especially in recent years, to the American leadership." Alluding to Carter's rhetoric on the promotion of human rights as a pillar of his US foreign policy program, Khomeini argued that "it is essential that the incumbent president, in keeping with his promises, refrain from the criminal acts of previous administrations. We are now waiting to see whether the present American administration will sacrifice its honor and that of its people for the sake of material gain and use the oil of a poor, noble nation to wash away its own prestige, or whether, by eschewing its support for these evil elements, it will restore its reputation and honor."[114]

Chapter 7

Reform and Revolt

On October 6, 1976, an estimated one hundred million American television viewers tuned in to watch a live presidential debate between Carter and Ford. Carter opened with a broad critique of the Ford administration's foreign policy. One of the issues Carter raised was US foreign arms sales. Under Ford, "we've had a chance to become now—contrary to our longstanding beliefs and principles—the arms merchant of the whole world," Carter charged. "We've tried to buy success from our enemies, and at the same time we've excluded from the process the normal friendship of our allies." Carter returned to the theme later in the debate. "When this Republican administration came into office we were shipping about $1 billion dollars worth of arms overseas, now $10 to $12 billion dollars worth of arms overseas to countries that quite often use these weapons to fight each other," Carter stated. He then added that "under the last Democratic administration 60 percent of all weapons that went into the Middle East were for Israel. Now 60 percent goes to the Arab countries and . . . only 20 percent goes to Israel. This is a deviation from idealism; it's a deviation from a commitment to our major ally in the Middle East, which is Israel; it's a yielding to economic pressure on the part of the Arabs on the oil issue."[1]

Once in office, the Carter administration consciously pursued continuity with the Ford and Nixon administrations on many issues pertaining to the US-petrodollar order. In the strategy of the new administration, the system of cooperative empire with Iran and Saudi Arabia would continue. The Carter administration expected petrodollars would continue to be utilized to protect

US interests in the MENA and beyond. Petrodollar-funded investments in and export purchases from the United States by the MENA states would continue to be welcomed. Petrodollar triangular trade and aid would continue to serve as a key component in drawing Egypt into the US empire.

But on the issue of arms exports, the Carter administration would during its first two years pursue a serious reform of this part of the petrodollar economy. Here, Carter actively worked to reduce not only US arms transfers to the MENA but also the global trade of weapons to the MENA and the broader Third World, for both strategic and moral reasons. This effort constituted the most powerful challenge yet mounted to the petrodollars-arms complex, one largely underappreciated for the reduction in US arms exports it initially achieved. Persuading the other major arms-exporting countries to restrain their sales or the MENA importers to restrain their purchases proved more difficult, but the Carter administration had not given up on achieving a global framework for reform at the end of 1978.

Yet even as the Carter administration worked to reform one key aspect of the US-led petrodollar order, others in the MENA endeavored to achieve a revolution that would overthrow the entire system of US cooperative empire. In Iran, such revolutionaries were on the cusp of a historic victory. There, the tensions and dislocations generated by the shah's petrodollar policies fueled broad-based dissent and, by early 1978, popular uprisings, the beginning of the Iranian Revolution. And while the Iranian revolutionaries came from across the ideological spectrum, the revolution quickly came under the guidance of Khomeini, who provided a regular flow of powerful speeches condemning US imperialism and promising a new petrodollar order for Iran once the shah was removed from power.

Guided by his evangelical Christian morality and understanding that the United States must guide international affairs, Jimmy Carter sought to transcend the wasteful costs of the Cold War and achieve greater action on North-South issues, global economic growth, and human rights.[2] This outlook drove Carter's desire to reduce the expensive and dangerous arms races of the MENA. A savvy politician, Carter also realized curbing the global arms trade resonated with sizable constituencies within the US electorate and ran on the issue at Ford's expense. On the campaign trail Carter's vice presidential running mate, Democratic senator from Minnesota Walter Mondale, also criticized Ford for "selling arms to all comers, no matter how repressive or tyrannical the government" and argued that the arms race in the Middle East ultimately took money away from US taxpayers since "if we sell a half-billion dollars in arms to Saudi Arabia, we then will need to give more economic and military aid to Israel to preserve the balance."[3]

Like the Nixon and Ford administrations, the Carter administration affirmed the view that the Middle East was a vital US interest as a source of Western oil, bulwark against Soviet expansion, and center of global financial power, and that Washington would continue to transfer arms to and cooperate closely with traditional allies in the region.[4] But Carter also implemented policies to decrease US arms transfers to the MENA and other LDCs. Carter's interest in this topic was shared by his trusted secretary of state, Cyrus Vance, a former lawyer and under secretary of defense who in 1976 publicly supported proposals for an immediate US moratorium on the transfer of advanced weapons to Third World countries; Soviet-US negotiations to turn the Indian Ocean into a demilitarized zone; and multilateral cooperation among the United States, Soviet Union, United Kingdom, and France to curb global arms exports.[5] Neither Carter nor Vance anticipated a total cutoff of US arms to the MENA as realistic in the near term, but both believed they could balance the seemingly contradictory impulses of strengthening regional allies in the MENA and curbing arms sales to them by making such reductions gradual and by instilling greater stability in the region, particularly by negotiating an end to the Arab-Israeli conflict and securing agreements from the other major arms-dealing countries to reduce their own transfers to the region.

Following Vance's blueprint, the new Carter administration implemented an undeclared moratorium on arms sales at its outset, sending no new arms sale proposals to Congress and freezing $6 billion worth of arms sales approved by the Ford administration, including major packages for MENA countries, until they could be reviewed by Carter officials. After review, in February they canceled the sale of certain kinds of percussion bombs to Israel, a decision likely made to convey that the Carter administration was serious about arms restraint and to reassure Arab allies that Carter would treat Middle East states evenhandedly after his pro-Israeli campaign rhetoric.[6]

The Carter administration also reached out to the major arms-dealing countries. In March, Vance visited Moscow and secured an agreement from the Soviets to form a working group to study the issue of mutual arms transfer reductions.[7] Carter took the lead with European allies, telling the British in January that he would pursue arms restraint in the Middle East and that while "he did not expect early results, and recognized the difficulties," conventional arms control "meant a lot to him and he would be persistent."[8] Meeting with British prime minister James Callaghan, French president Valéry Giscard d'Estaing, and West German chancellor Helmut Schmidt in London on May 8,

Carter encouraged them to curb the global arms trade. Carter shared with them an internal memorandum that directed his administration to "reduce the thrust of arms sales." He assured them that this would not apply to NATO allies and instead listed Iran and Israel as countries to which he aimed to reduce arms transfers. Carter stated this was "a unilateral decision on his part" but left open the possibility that the European leaders could join his efforts. To offset European fears that a reduction in arms sales to LDCs could harm their defense industries and economies, Carter offered the carrot of increased US purchases of European arms for its own military at the expense of US arms manufacturers, stating that on NATO arms transfers he "genuinely wanted more two way traffic" and that he "had no obligations to the military complex in the United States."[9]

On May 19 Carter issued a statement arguing that as the world's largest arms supplier, the United States bore "special responsibilities" to reduce the global sale of weapons. To that end, he declared, "the United States will henceforth view arms transfers as an exceptional foreign policy implement, to be used only in instances where it can be clearly demonstrated that the transfer contributes to our national security interests. We will continue to utilize arms transfers to promote our security and the security of our close friends. But in the future, the burden of persuasion will be on those who favor a particular arms sale rather than those who oppose it." Carter also announced the implementation of several new policies: that the United States would not be the first to supply advanced weapons to a region that previously did not have such capabilities, stricter limits on the coproduction of advanced weapons systems, the prohibition of developing or significantly redesigning weapons for the sole purpose of foreign sale, and the requirement of State authorization for any governmental or private efforts to promote foreign arms sales. Finally, Carter pledged that the value of US foreign arms transfers in FY 1978 would be reduced from FY 1977.[10]

There were important caveats to the new arms policy. Carter exempted all NATO member countries, Japan, Australia, and New Zealand from its provisions. The backlog of previously approved arms sales, valued at $32 billion, would remain largely untouched.[11] Cases the president determined to involve either "extraordinary circumstances" or friendly countries that depended on arms "to maintain regional balance" could also receive exemptions from the new provisions. As the *Washington Post* put it, "How well the new policy works in practice is likely to depend largely on the extent to which Carter exercises his authority to grant exceptions to it."[12]

Despite these caveats, the new policy represented an important shift in the executive branch's attitude toward arms transfers. Americans endeavoring to curb the international weapons trade could cite the provisions of the policy, particularly the pledge to reduce the value of arms transfers in the upcoming fiscal year, to hold the Carter administration accountable. The Carter administration could likewise cite the policy to allies to justify reductions in arms transfers. This new policy, coupled with the efforts to negotiate joint arms transfer reductions with the Soviet Union, France, United Kingdom, and West Germany, constituted a distinctly different strategy from the efforts of the Nixon and Ford administrations to encourage US arms sales to the MENA with few restrictions. Such a shift in US policy would not go unchallenged, however, by the MENA countries themselves.

Carter's new arms policies, coupled with his rhetoric on promoting human rights, worried the shah, who remained determined to acquire more advanced US arms and prevent foreign oversight of his governance. Periodically the shah even worried that Carter's positions were evidence of the new president's desire to do away with him. Discussing one of Carter's speeches in May with Alam, the shah noted that Iran had not been mentioned as a country the United States would supply weapons to without strings attached. "Does [Carter] suppose that, strategically speaking, Iran is less significant than a country like New Zealand?" the shah wondered aloud. "Perhaps the Americans and the Soviets have devised some scheme to divide the world between themselves." Alam attempted to reassure the shah that "the Americans will never abandon us."[13] The Carter administration also sought to allay the shah's evident concerns. The new administration considered Iran critical to bringing down oil prices and maintaining security in the Gulf; it worked to avoid confrontation with the shah while gingerly setting a course for gradual change. On the issue of human rights, the Carter administration generally avoided public condemnation of Iran and privately supported the modest reforms enacted by the shah since mid-1976. In the realm of arms, Carter would seek only a modest reduction of US exports to Iran in the near term.[14]

The Carter administration chose the sale of seven Boeing Airborne Warning and Control System (AWACS) aircraft to Iran as its first major step in establishing a good relationship with the shah while gradually reducing arms exports. AWACS were among the most advanced and expensive planes in the US fleet, designed to provide surveillance and direction of battle commands over a large area using state-of-the-art radar and communications equipment. Despite their high cost at $170 million per plane, the Carter administration considered the sale an arms reduction measure, as the Iranian acquisition of seven AWACS would enable a 60 or 70 percent reduction of a proposed ground radar system for Iran projected to cost $32 billion. The Carter administration also hoped the reconnaissance and coordination capabilities provided by the AWACS would reduce the number of Iranian combat planes needed to defend the country through better lead time and logistics. For Tehran, the AWACS deal appealed as a cost-saving measure, an acquisition of new US military technology, a quicker augmentation of its surveillance capability compared with the ground radar plan, and a demonstration of the new administration's commitment to the Iranian armed forces.[15]

The Carter administration announced its intention to propose the AWACS sale on April 26 and formally notified Congress on July 7. It was the first major weapons sale proposed since the declaration of the administration's new arms transfer policy.[16] To Carter's chagrin, seven bipartisan senators sponsored a resolution to block the sale, citing his administration's policies as justification.[17] "This program goes contrary to President Carter's own stated policy on arms sales, which declares that sales are exceptions, to be used only when it can be clearly demonstrated that the sale contributes to our own national security interest," Democratic senator from Iowa John Culver declared. "The President also has stipulated that the United States will not be the first supplier to introduce advanced weapons into a region that gives greater combat capability."[18] Democratic senator from Missouri Thomas Eagleton and Senator Culver raised the possibility that a single Iranian defection could lead to secret US technology falling into the hands of the Soviets, endangering the US air force and Western European defenses. "Iran's governmental status, centered on a mortal leader, is fragile and subject to radical change," Eagleton also warned a Senate subcommittee. "To endorse this sale is to take an imprudent risk to American national security."[19]

On July 21 CIA director Stansfield Turner testified to the House that he stood by a statement he had made in a letter to the Government Accountability Office, since leaked by Senate opponents of the AWACS sale, that the transfer of AWACS to Iran could result in the United States losing technological secrets to the detriment of its military advantage.[20] The next day Senate Majority Leader and Democratic senator from West Virginia Robert Byrd wrote to Carter asking him to delay his request for the AWACS sale until the next year in order for the Senate to properly study the possible security risks.[21] In response to Byrd's letter, the US embassy in Iran reported that "Senate approval of the [AWACS] sale *at this time* is vital . . . as the President has already written the Shah informing him that AWACS would be available, the President's personal prestige would suffer a serious blow in Tehran if the sale were now cancelled . . . [and] Brezhnev can have a field day during his upcoming visit to Iran."[22] The Carter administration informed the Senate on July 25 that it would not grant Byrd's requested delay.[23]

Despite the White House's stance, House Speaker and Democratic representative from Massachusetts Thomas "Tip" O'Neill Jr. then publicly declared that the AWACS sale "ought to be held up for a while" since the airplanes contained "highly sophisticated equipment that might fall into the hands of the Soviet Union."[24] The Democratic, majority leadership in both houses of Congress was now openly calling for a delay in the sale. On the morning of July 28 the House International Relations Committee voted nineteen to seventeen to block the sale, moving the House closer to passing a resolution against the deal. At this point the Carter administration beat a tactical retreat, agreeing to resubmit the sale to Congress in September after it returned from recess to allow further congressional study.[25] In response, on July 31 Iranian newspapers suggested that the Iranian government might refuse to purchase the AWACS due to anger over Congress's treatment of the issue.[26]

When Carter resubmitted the AWACS sale to Congress in September, he stipulated that the AWACS sold to Iran would not include some sensitive cryptographic equipment, obtained an Iranian guarantee to use the aircraft only for defensive purposes, and guaranteed that US air crews would not fly the planes in operational missions for the Iranians. The new conditions won over key legislators and, despite a last-ditch effort by twenty-one senators, the AWACS deal passed the deadline for congressional disapproval on October 7 without incident.[27]

Yet while the AWACS sale to Iran was ultimately approved, Congress had demonstrated a new willingness to challenge the petrodollars-arms complex between the United States and the MENA and had succeeded in imposing stipulations on the original package proposed by the executive branch. Evincing this shift in mentality, Senator Byrd declared that after the AWACS deal the US government should impose a moratorium on arms sales to Iran until it could be determined whether the Iranians could use advanced US weapons without US personnel.[28] Senator Culver boasted that by delaying the AWACS sale into FY 1978, Congress had kept the FY 1977 value of arms transfers over $1 billion lower, meaning the Carter administration's self-imposed ceiling of a lower value of arms transfers in FY 1978 would have to correspondingly drop.[29]

Yet while the Carter administration believed the AWACS sale had been necessary to maintain the US alliance with Iran, it also continued to believe that it could reduce US arms transfers to the less developed world, particularly to

Figure 11. Jimmy Carter and the shah inspect US troops on the White House South Lawn, November 15, 1977. Courtesy of Jimmy Carter Presidential Library.

the MENA, and desired to do so. Carter's trusted national security advisor, Zbigniew Brzezinski, a Polish refugee of fascism and communism and political scientist preoccupied with opposing the Soviet Union and developing techno-cratic global governance to address OECD and North-South issues, suggested to Carter that clearly explaining to the shah "the political realities (as evi-denced by the AWACS case)" might help induce the monarch to pursue a "moderating and stretching out of his arms requests" to avoid a congressional struggle that "could damage the Administration's credibility and undermine the basis of our [Iranian-US] continued cooperation."[30] The Carter adminis-tration continued to pursue its gradual reduction in US arms sales to Iran while maintaining the Iranian-US alliance.

Carter also continued to resist economic incentives to sell arms to coun-tries like Iran. Concerned about the declining value of the dollar and widen-ing US trade deficits, in late 1977 Carter solicited policies from his cabinet to address these issues. One of Treasury secretary Michael Blumenthal's recom-mendations was to pursue a "moderate expansion of [foreign] military sales" of roughly $500 million per year, stressing that this not be publicly linked with balance of payments. Vance opposed Blumenthal's proposal, arguing that "the low level of temporary impact is not significant enough to warrant contradiction of your [Carter's] present arms sales policy." Carter sided with Vance.[31]

As the Carter administration began its new arms sale policy, Iran and Saudi Arabia battled over OPEC's pricing of oil. After the split at the December 1976 OPEC meeting, Iran led most members in selling oil at a 10 percent increase, whereas Saudi Arabia, joined only by the UAE, increased the posted price by only 5 percent. To bring the rest of OPEC to heel, the Saudis also increased their oil production to undercut the exports of other members. Privately, the shah railed to Alam that "the blasted Saudis have betrayed both us and themselves" while lamenting that "we're broke. . . . Many of the programmes we had planned must be postponed." Publicly, Iran, Iraq, and others stridently denounced the Saudi decision, charging the Saudis as reactionaries who had betrayed the Arab and Third worlds for their Western masters. Riyadh continued to flood the market with cheaper oil, however. While most of the members of OPEC lost market share because of the Saudi actions, Iran was especially poorly situated to weather a shortfall in petrodollars as its economic planning had left no hedging for a possible decrease in revenue. The shah was forced to implement painful and chaotic cuts to development programs; across Iran economic dislocations resulted in a surge in shortages of electricity, food, and water, a sharp drop in industrial productivity and construction, and a rise in the ranks of the under- and unemployed. In June the shah buckled; to obtain relief from the Saudi undercutting of Iranian exports, he agreed to drop his demands for higher prices for the foreseeable future in return for Saudi Arabia and the UAE raising their price 5 percent, back to parity with the rest of OPEC. On the decision, Alam wrote in his diary that "we've surrendered to the Saudis, which means in effect Carter."[32]

Like its predecessors, the Carter administration considered Saudi Arabia, not Iran, as the key to holding down oil prices.[33] When Saudi Arabia publicly announced in July that it favored a price freeze through 1978, State appeared surprised that "Iran, atypically, did not rule one out."[34] Even so, as Blumenthal prepared to visit the shah in October and discuss US support for a continued price freeze, Vance encouraged him to "raise the issue but not to press it."[35] When Blumenthal met with the shah, the monarch uncharacteristically "volunteered that it had been decided that Iran should not take a strong position [on raising the oil price] in OPEC at this time."[36] When visiting Carter in Washington the following month, the shah confirmed that Iran would not seek a price increase; the shah only asked vaguely for "something concrete to show for this" in the face of Iraqi and Libyan criticisms.[37] With Iran reluctantly joining Saudi Arabia as a price dove, the hawks were forced to accept no increase in price for 1978 at the December OPEC meeting.[38]

From 1977 to 1978 the stabilization of oil prices, coupled with the continued rise in the OECs' consumption of foreign goods and services, caused a relative shift in petrodollar flows away from US financial institutions and toward export industries. In May 1977 the Carter administration passed legislation targeting the Arab boycott of Israel, making it illegal for US corporations to enforce foreign boycotts or to enter into any agreement that stipulated boycotting a third country as a condition of conducting business. The law caused US companies to lose some new business opportunities in the Arab world, particularly Saudi Arabia, to other countries like Japan.[39] Still, the curtailment of Arab-US trade was relatively minor, and the value of US exports to the oil-rich MENA countries rose to $8.7 billion in 1977 and $10.6 billion in 1978. Net investments by the Middle East oil exporters within the United States rose $7.7 billion in 1977 and then reversed into an outflow of $1.4 billion in 1978, the decline primarily coming from withdrawals from Treasury securities and commercial bank liabilities. This trend replicated itself on an international scale, with the size of new OPEC deposits to the net sum of international lending by BIS reporting banks dropping from 16.7 percent in 1977 to 3.6 percent in 1978.[40] This shift ended most voicings of concern by mainstream capitalist economists about the feasibility of recycling petrodollars back into the global economy.

The bifurcated structure of private lending, or lack thereof, to oil-poor LDCs continued during these years. The Carter administration shared its predecessors' wariness of the NIEO's economic and political platform, but it also sought to replace it with a genuine prioritization of development aid as a path toward greater North-South equality. Carter faced a bipartisan majority in Congress that continued to view foreign aid as ineffective or too costly for a still-weak US economy, however. Faced with strong congressional opposition on many foreign policy issues, the Carter administration ultimately prioritized other contentious issues, such as the Panama Canal Treaty and the Arab-Israeli peace process. Under Carter, US foreign aid levels would decline as a share of GDP.[41]

The top priority for the incoming Carter administration was combating unemployment, which at the start of its term hovered at the rate of 7.5 percent. In 1977 Carter passed a major stimulus package to bring unemployment down. His administration also hoped that lower foreign oil prices would free up domestic consumer spending and generate new jobs.[42] At the same time, the White House also sought to prevent another spike in inflation, which stood at a rate of 5.2 percent in January 1977, and lower oil prices served this end, too. Yet as of June 1978 Carter's expansionist fiscal policies, coupled with flatlined but still high oil prices, had produced mixed results: the US unemployment rate had dropped to 5.9 percent, but inflation had risen to 7.4 percent.

Inflationary US policies contributed to a steady decline in the value of the dollar, reversing the relative stability it had enjoyed in the mid-1970s and once again disquieting the oil exporters. In December 1977 Fahd told Vance that the dollar's decline "greatly concerns Saudi Arabia." Fahd noted "the opponents of an oil price freeze will argue that since the dollar is going down the price of oil must be raised," making it harder for Riyadh to counsel price moderation. He also expressed apprehension "about the drop in the value of the dollar because it affects the value of Saudi holdings in the United States." Fahd stressed that it was important for "the US Government [to] respond seriously to this problem."[43] The Carter administration pursued some steps to address the issue, including a modest increase in Federal Reserve interest rates that month, but the value of the dollar continued to decline in 1978.[44]

With Iran demonstrating a new moderation on oil prices and a continued commitment to providing security for US interests in the Gulf, it is little wonder that when Carter visited Tehran on New Year's Eve in 1977, he effusively praised the shah for his "great leadership" in establishing Iran as "an island of stability in one of the more troubled areas of the world."[45] In truth, however, the shah's regime faced mounting crises. Iran's oil revenues had stagnated since 1976 owing to the OPEC price battles, but existing petrodollar expenditures caused inflation to persist. In August 1977 the shah appointed the economist Jamshid Amuzegar as prime minister to address mounting financial concerns. Amuzegar pursued a deflationary campaign, but the shah largely prevented him from reducing government spending on the military and long-term industrial projects. Amuzegar therefore made cuts to other economic sectors, particularly urban construction, which rapidly increased the number of unemployed. Workers strikes increased in frequency despite being confronted by the threat of violence from security forces. Government price controls and antiprofiteering arrests of Iranian businesspeople meant to stifle inflation outraged the bazaar merchants and small industrialists. The marked economic disparity between well-connected Iranian elites, who continued their binge of hyperconsumerism, and average Iranians, who increasingly feared for their livelihoods, magnified popular discontent. Amuzegar also imposed severe cuts in government subsidies to the ulama, further alienating the Shia leadership and their followers. Despite these measures, the continuation of government purchases of arms and capital-intensive industrial projects ensured that high rates of inflation persisted even as unemployment swiftly rose. Largely due to its choices in where to allocate its petrodollars, Iran was now experiencing its own painful version of stagflation.[46]

By 1977 the shah had managed to alienate every major segment of Iranian society: rural peasants, urban laborers, bazaar and small-factory owners, the ulama, middle-class professionals, and college students. Only military officers, senior civil servants, and royal courtiers remained widely loyal to the Pahlavi dynasty. Peaceful protests and the dissemination of open letters condemning the shah's rule increased in frequency, circulated from across the Iranian ideological spectrum. Increasingly, however, Khomeini became the symbol of opposition to the shah, and his network of religious students increasingly led the Iranian resistance.

Then, on January 7, 1978, in an effort to undermine Khomeini's growing popularity, the Iranian state-backed newspaper *Ettelaat* ran an article claiming Khomeini was a paid British agent of Indian descent working to recolonize Iran and a faithless man who had lived a licentious life of writing love poetry and drinking wine. The clumsy effort to discredit Khomeini backfired spectacularly. Over the next two days, Shia seminary students in the holy city of Qom organized protests and shutdowns in the larger community. Iranian security forces responded with force, killing some of the protesters. The massacre in Qom marked the start of the Iranian Revolution, triggering a yearlong cycle of popular Iranian protests and securing the position of Khomeini and his followers as the leaders of the revolution.[47]

From Najaf, Khomeini guided the revolutionaries through speeches that were smuggled into Iran in pamphlets and cassette tapes. In his speeches, Khomeini regularly imparted to his listeners that Iran's problems were ultimately caused by US control over Iran's oil wealth. In a speech given forty days after the massacre at Qom, the fortieth day after a death a day of public memorial for the deceased in Shia tradition, Khomeini framed the deaths of the martyrs as part of an antiimperialist struggle against the United States. "America . . . imposed this Shah upon us," Khomeini declared. "He has turned Iran into an official colony of the US." Reflecting on the poverty in Iran despite its oil revenues, Khomeini rhetorically asked: "What happens to all [Iran's] money?" He answered his own question by explaining that the Americans, through their puppet the shah, had fleeced the Iranian people of its oil wealth. "How many American officials there are in Iran now and what huge salaries they receive!" Khomeini marveled. "That is our problem—everything in our treasury has to be emptied into the pockets of America, and if there is any meager amount to spare, it has to go into the pockets of the Shah and his gang." Khomeini contrasted the luxurious lifestyles of the Americans and the shah's retinue with descriptions of the slums of Tehran, where the poor did not even have drinking water, and of the countryside, where destitute villagers resorted to using urine to open the trachoma-infected eyes of their children. Khomeini likewise condemned the United States for enabling the shah to militarily repress the Iranian people. He lambasted Carter for campaigning on human rights but then supporting the shah once in office, even as he massacred his own people. Carter, Khomeini claimed, now said, "'We have military bases in Iran; we can't talk about human rights there. Respect for human rights is feasible only in countries where we have no military bases.'"[48] In this way, Khomeini addressed key parts of the US-led petrodollar order, such as US military trainers and catering to elite consumerism, and linked them to the populist grievances of the Iranian people, thus mobilizing a revolutionary movement to overturn the US-led petrodollar order.

Through their actions, Iranian protesters likewise signaled their opposition to Iranian-US petrodollar interdependence. The protesters overwhelmingly eschewed violence against people, including Americans. Rare acts of terror did occur, however, including the murder of a US contractor in Kerman in January 1979; his body was left on the street beside a wall spray painted with the message "go home." Protesters regularly destroyed banks that serviced foreign transactions, liquor stores that catered to Western tastes, and cinemas that played sexually explicit Hollywood films. Revolutionaries sent letters to the Grumman Corporation office in Tehran, charging the company with forcing the Iranian government to purchase unnecessary arms and threatening to sabotage its operations in Iran.[49] In targeting US commercial and military links with Iran, Iranians symbolically and materially broke down US imperialism and its petrodollar order.

Over the course of 1978 the shah's police and military, armed with US weapons, would frequently respond to both peaceful and violent protests with indiscriminate force. The revolutionaries would ultimately claim that sixty thousand Iranians were martyred by the shah's forces from January 1978 to February 1979; scholars have put forth figures ranging from around three thousand to twelve thousand.[50] Even the low estimates constituted unprecedented casualties from a domestic crisis in modern Iranian history. Yet rather than silencing dissent, the Iranian state's violence only served to produce a new set of martyrs that generated new opponents of the regime and larger memorial protests.

As Iranian protests grew in 1978, they increasingly threatened to topple the shah's regime, and with it a pillar of the US-led petrodollar order. For most of the year, however, the top officials of the Carter administration were oblivious to this threat. In part, they sensed no reason to distrust US intelligence reports, which largely relied on rosy assessments from SAVAK, that claimed the shah faced no significant threat to his rule. Furthermore, the White House was busy with several major foreign policy initiatives, including the Panama Canal Treaty, normalization of relations with China, and the Strategic Arms Limitation Talks with the Soviet Union. In the Middle East, the Carter administration focused most of its attention on achieving progress in the Arab-Israeli peace process and passing a major arms sale package for Egypt, Israel, and Saudi Arabia.[51]

Like the shah, the Saudi royals worried about Carter's campaign rhetoric on arms sales. Their highest priority was reaffirmation of Ford's pledge to sell them F-15 fighters, something Prince Sultan, the Saudi defense minister, pressed the Carter administration on from its first weeks onward.[52] Meeting with Vance in February 1977, Fahd argued Saudi Arabia needed advanced fighters to defend itself and the smaller Gulf kingdoms against "other regional states that are armed most strongly by the Soviets," an allusion to Ethiopia, Iraq, Libya, and South Yemen.[53] In a different discussion with Brzezinski, Fahd claimed he needed the arms to maintain his support within the military. "Unless we have modern equipment, the Saudi Arabian armed forces will be demoralized," Fahd said. "The officers of the Saudi Arabian armed forces question why they don't obtain the arms they need when our neighbors are getting large quantities from the Soviet Union. It has been difficult for me to answer our officers, except to say that we are obtaining such weapons from the U.S."[54] The Carter administration did not immediately agree to honor the F-15 deal, but it soon determined the deal was important to preserving strong relations with the Saudis and their support for the US-led Arab-Israeli peace process. "Fahd will be looking for a reaffirmation of the U.S.-Saudi security relationship as tangible evidence of our attitude toward the Arabs," Brzezinski argued. "Any evidence that we are backing away from previous commitments at this point could have a significant influence on the message he takes back to Asad and Sadat."[55] The Carter administration thus once again pursued an exception to its arms limitation goals and in May reaffirmed to Fahd its commitment to the F-15 deal.[56]

Like Fahd, Sadat persisted in his desire to acquire more advanced US arms, and to have Saudi petrodollars pay for them. In February 1977 Sadat requested forty Northrop F-5E Tiger jet fighters. Vance supported Sadat's request, arguing that some Egyptian officers "have expressed opposition to Sadat's turning to the West precisely because it has resulted in curtailment of the Soviet arms supply. Should there be no progress in negotiations [with Israel] within a reasonable time frame and, at the same time, there is a further erosion of the combat capabilities of the [Egyptian] armed forces, the pressure on Sadat to change his policies or leave office will become inexorable," which would "probably begin the unravelling of all that has been accomplished since the end of the October 1973 war."[57] The Carter administration thus supported an exception to arms sale restraint for Egypt as well.

Anticipating that they would be difficult to pass, the Carter administration sought to delay submitting the Egyptian and Saudi fighter sales for congressional approval until after the conclusion of the AWACS sale to Iran and significant progress had been made on a comprehensive peace agreement between Israel and its Arab neighbors. The peace process bogged down in late 1977, however, in part due to the negotiating stance of Menachem Begin, the new Israeli prime minister hailing from the conservative Likud party, who adamantly sought to permanently incorporate the West Bank and Gaza into Israel. In November Sadat visited Jerusalem in an attempt to revive peace talks, but in doing so he violated the pan-Arab pledge not to directly engage with Israel on diplomatic matters while it held Arab lands. Algeria, Libya, the PLO, South Yemen, and Syria held a conference the following month condemning Egyptian unilateralism and calling for retaliatory action. Egypt responded by severing relations with all the conferees except the PLO. Yet despite Sadat's bold gambit, Begin remained intransigent on Israeli retention of Gaza and the West Bank, and the peace process remained in a morass in early 1978.[58]

Meanwhile, events in the Horn of Africa increasingly worried the Saudis. In July 1977 Somalia invaded Ethiopia in the hopes of annexing the Ogaden, an Ethiopian region largely populated by ethnic Somalis. While both Ethiopia and Somalia were Marxist states and Moscow desired good relations with both, the USSR decided to back Ethiopia when its mediation efforts failed, sending in aid and thousands of Soviet and Cuban troops to assist the faltering Ethiopian army by late 1977. The Soviets increasingly depended on Aden as an air and naval base to resupply its forces in Ethiopia, leading to an upsurge in its presence in and aid to South Yemen. The Saudis were alarmed by the increased Soviet presence on their southern flank, as well as by the increasingly bellicose rhetoric of South Yemen toward Oman. In response, Riyadh ended a years-long aid program to South Yemen aimed at moderating its behavior, and instead massed troops along the Saudi–South Yemeni border.[59] The Saudis also cited the escalating hostilities with South Yemen as a reason why they needed the prompt delivery of US arms. "The states of the Gulf look up to Saudi Arabia and consider themselves dependent on it for their protection," Fahd told Vance in December. "Suppose that South Yemen attacks one of the Gulf states and that Iraq came to the support of South Yemen. . . . [Iraqi] forces are stronger than those of Saudi Arabia. If such a thing were to happen at a time when the US was incapable of helping Saudi Arabia, the outcome would be terrible."[60]

By January 1978 Fahd had run out of patience waiting for the F-15 deal to be submitted. "The Soviet Union is giving unlimited aid to Saudi opponents in the area . . . sophisticated weapons like MiG-23s and MiG-25s," Fahd complained to US secretary of energy James Schlesinger when he visited the kingdom that month. "Saudi Arabia now desperately needs some high-performance aircraft to defend itself."[61] When, in response, Vance had Ambassador John West ask Fahd to "consider the tactical advantages of delaying [the sale] until the [Arab-Israeli] peacemaking effort regains momentum to provide a more propitious atmosphere for congressional consideration of our request," Fahd balked. Fahd told West "that the F-15 issue was a basic, crucial test of our relationship . . . that he was personally embarrassed by the delays thus far and could not willingly submit to any further such embarrassment."[62] Determining that any further delay would cause serious harm to relations with the Saudis and in turn the Arab-Israeli peace process, in early February the Carter administration decided to put forward to Congress the F-15 sale to Saudi Arabia and F-5 sale to Egypt, with Vance arguing internally that the sale would both serve their legitimate defensive needs and instill confidence in Egypt to negotiate with Israel due to the assurance of US support.[63]

Brzezinski and Vance believed there was a high chance Congress would not approve the Saudi sale, however, given the F-15's reputation as perhaps the most advanced fighter in the world and the perceived risk it could pose to Israel in Saudi hands. To improve their odds, the Carter administration presented Congress with a package deal, in which Saudi Arabia would be sold sixty F-15s for $2.5 billion, Israel granted fifteen F-15s and seventy-five F-16s worth $1.9 billion, and Egypt would acquire fifty F-5s priced at $400 million and paid for by the Saudis. Congress would have to either accept or reject the entire proposal, lest it upset the strategic balancing act envisioned by the administration. Ironically, in this way the Carter administration sought to use a transfer of arms coveted by Israel as a tool in helping secure a petrodollar-funded US arms sale to the Arab world.[64]

In addition to presenting the arms transfers as a package deal, White House officials attempted to preempt opposition from pro-Israeli advocates by stressing that the package was designed to further the cause of peace in the Middle East, maintain a military balance in the region, and deter aggression from countries like Libya; Israel's security, they insisted, would not be threatened by the deal.[65] But as expected, the announcement of the arms transfer proposal prompted an immediate outcry from pro-Israeli voices. The National Jewish Community Relations Advisory Council, which had spearheaded the campaign against Ford's 1976 reassessment of Israeli–US relations, launched a public relations campaign against the F-15 sale to Saudi Arabia. The American Israel Public Affairs Committee, whose previously modest budget would triple in size from 1974 to 1980 in part due to growing concerns about the rising oil power of Arab states, also lobbied Congress to oppose the deal.[66]

What followed was the most visible and sustained public debate over the petrodollars-arms complex in US history to date, with pro-Israeli advocates and general opponents of the foreign arms trade joining in opposition to the sale. Many critics emphasized support for Israel. "Selling Arabs the means to destroy Israel is a moral disaster for America," the conservative columnist William Safire wrote in the *New York Times*. "As long as the Saudis refuse to negotiate directly [with Israel] and as long as they are the financial backers of the P.L.O., it ought to be repugnant for any congressman to sell them American weapons."[67] General anti-proliferation concerns were also raised. The *New Republic* rhetorically asked who "will wager that Saudi Arabia, once superbly armed by the US, will not, through an assassination or a[n up]rising, be found in the vanguard of the revolutionary left, like Algeria or Libya?"[68] Democratic representative from Maryland Clarence Long argued that arms should not go to any of the three countries as it would not help the peace process or their general welfare. Long stated he was "profoundly disgusted" by the proposal and said the United States was "the salesman of slaughter."[69] In short, the many different narratives that demonized petrodollar purchases of arms were all present in the debates over the latest Middle East arms package. Furthermore, they appeared to be effective. In an early House International Relations Committee vote on May 2, twenty-two of the thirty-seven members disapproved the sale.[70]

A visibly tired Fahd, fearful that the F-15 sale would not be approved by Congress, met with West on April 26 to impress upon the Carter administration the repercussions of such a failure. Some of these were by-now standard fare of petrodollar interdependence. Fahd noted the damage such a failure would have on Riyadh's credibility domestically and in inter-Arab affairs, arguing that "should [the] plane sale fail and Egypt turn back to Soviet Union, what do Saudi leaders say to the people? Egypt, Iraq, Syria, and others will pour abuse on [the Saudi government] using all types of media." Fahd also cited the economic and geopolitical losses for the United States, stating that "U.S. factories will lose billions of dollars that could add to U.S. prosperity" and that "our only alternative is to turn toward England, France and Soviet Union to buy what we need." Yet Fahd also presented arguments that went far beyond those regularly presented within the context of petrodollar interdependence. The inclusion of the Soviets as a potential arms provider was unusual for the Saudis, and alarming for the United States. Even more shocking, however, was Fahd's very pessimistic appraisal of trends in the region due to a lack of US leadership, which he extrapolated on for over an hour: Ethiopia's victory over Somalia in the Ogaden in March demonstrated the Soviets were on the advance in Africa; Libya, Iraq, Syria, and South Yemen already followed Moscow's lead, and Egypt would have to turn back to the USSR if its people determined Sadat had failed in turning to Washington; and the Soviets were watching or perhaps abetting unrest in Iran to bring communists to power and seize the shah's arms stockpile. The "whole plan is to encircle Saudi Arabia," Fahd argued. "When completely surrounded, Saudi Arabia will have no alternative but to greet [the] Soviets with rose petals." Fahd clearly employed this tour d'horizon to garner US support for the F-15 sale. But the fears expressed were also likely genuine given their consistency with Saudi actions before and afterward, and demonstrated an increase in Saudi concerns about their security, unmatched since the 1973–74 oil embargo. In any case, West reaffirmed to Fahd that on the F-15 deal, Carter's "support is unwavering."[71]

The Saudis did not limit their pitch to the White House, however. The petrodollar boom had increased Saudi connections with Americans and their understanding of how to lobby the US Congress and public while also providing them with massive funds to do so. The Saudi government hired US advertising companies to direct a media campaign to build public support for the F-15 sale and US law firms to lobby congresspeople. One such lobbyist was Fred Dutton. A lawyer and prominent figure in Democratic politics for over a decade and a half when he accepted the lucrative position of chief legal representative for the Saudi Kingdom in 1975, Dutton used his knowledge of and connections in Washington to apply the Saudi lobby campaign to full effect.[72] An important element of the campaign involved drafting US corporations to petition on the Saudis' behalf. Companies such as Bechtel and Computer Sciences Corporation promptly lobbied members of Congress to support the sale, not because they were directly tied to the F-15 deal but because they feared the failure of the sale could strain Saudi–US relations and thus endanger their companies' present and future business activities in Saudi Arabia.[73] The urgency felt by Bechtel was enhanced by the fact that Dutton held a position in the Saudi Industry Ministry, where he negotiated contracts with Bechtel on projects like the construction of the industrial city of Jubail.[74]

Whether lobbying individual members of Congress or the general public, the theme of the pro–Saudi campaign was the same: interdependence between the Arab world and the United States. In advertisements published in *Time* and *Newsweek*, and then mailed to members of Congress, glossy color images celebrated the "special relationship" between Riyadh and Washington.[75] Aware of the broad sensitivity of Americans to the idea of oil money being used to subvert US institutions, the pro-Saudi campaign emphasized a soft sell that argued that the Americans and Arabs needed each other and that they could positively work together on issues like trade, defense, and stability in the MENA. The campaign also presented a harsher subtext, however, that a failure to cooperate could damage US interests like lower oil prices and continued Saudi support for the dollar.[76] Other voices in the media joined the hired lobbyists in arguing that interdependence was in the best interests of both the Arabs and the United States. The *New York Times* editorialized that since the Saudis could easily purchase French fighters (which France was aggressively marketing), it made sense for the United States to sell the F-15 to the Saudis to more easily control how Saudi planes were used. Noting that whoever made the sale would also train the pilots and provide ground crews, the *New York Times* concluded that "it seems inconceivable that either Americans or Israelis would wish that monitoring potential to slip out of Americans hands."[77]

As the pro-Israeli and pro-Saudi lobbies battled in early May, it appeared the Senate might vote to block the sale, which could in turn lead the House to do likewise and scuttle the entire deal. As a concession to pro-Israeli forces, on May 9 the Carter administration offered to give twenty additional F-15s to Israel; combined with previous sales, passage of the arms package would leave the Israelis and the Saudis with sixty F-15s each. The Carter administration also provided written assurances that the Saudis would not be provided certain missile capabilities for the F-15s and that the Saudis would not base the planes near Israel.[78] Despite these concessions, the Carter administration failed to dissuade the Senate from holding a floor debate and vote on the sale.[79] At that point Carter sent a letter defending the arms package to every single senator. "The long-term interests of Israel are served by the proposed sales to Egypt and Saudi Arabia," Carter wrote. "It is in Israel's interest to encourage the forces of moderation in the Middle East and to promote their close relationship with the United States." The question for the Senate, Carter maintained, was "shall we support and give confidence to those in the Middle East who work for moderation and peace? Or shall we turn them aside, shattering their confidence in us and serving the cause of the radicals?"[80] On May 15, the Senate sided with Carter, upholding the arms package fifty-four to forty-four.[81]

The Carter administration celebrated its success but also endured a final barrage of criticism toward it and Saudi Arabia. "What do we want to do with the

Israelis?" Republican senator from New York Jacob Javits asked before the Senate vote. "Sap their vitality? Sap their morale? Cut the legs out from under them?" After the bill was passed, Democratic senator from New York Daniel Patrick Moynihan lamented that "the bond of trust [between America and Israel] has been broken." More than a thousand Jewish students from New York demonstrated outside the White House, some carrying coffins symbolizing "the death of American morality."[82] Commentators noted that many Jewish Americans, a significant demographic for the Democratic Party, were ceasing to support Carter because they felt that "Carter's Mideast policy [was] strongly influenced by the dependence of the U.S. and world economies on Arab oil and petrodollars" and opposed policies like the Saudi F-15 deal.[83] While candidate Carter had attacked Ford for tilting too much toward the Arabs, President Carter found himself attacked for the same reason as he attempted to balance foreign policy concerns.

Yet while the pro-Israeli lobby in the United States remained strong, the arms package sale also portended a shift in US politics. The interdependence between Saudi Arabia and the United States, born of petrodollars, had given the Saudis far greater influence in Washington than they had before. The Saudis could now call on the large number of corporations working in Saudi Arabia to lobby on its behalf, hire the slickest and best-connected US public relations firms, and remind the US government and public alike of the ways Saudi Arabia could either help or harm the US economy through oil prices and petrodollar investments. These tactics had translated into a major legislative victory that provided the Saudis with one of the most advanced weapons in the world, a weapon the United States had never offered to an Arab country before, over the concerted objections of the pro-Israeli lobby. Additionally, while the F-5 was far less sophisticated than the F-15 or F-16, the deal still constituted the first time the United States had ever offered a fighter of any kind to Egypt, and marked a significant step in establishing a military relationship between the two countries, all while being funded by Saudi petrodollars, expanding the triangular petrodollar arms trade. While the pro-Israeli lobby in the United States remained a more influential power in the United States than any Arab lobby, pro-Israeli advocates were shaken by the vote. The extreme imagery used by Israel's supporters was evidence of their fear that Arab supporters, funded by petrodollars, were gaining serious ground in the battle over governmental opinion. "There was a time when members of Congress didn't care what Arabs thought about them," one pro-Israeli lobbyist conceded. "Now there's been a general softening in that attitude. They worry that the Arabs won't like us."[84] Whether pro-Arab groups could continue to increase their influence remained to be seen, but Israel's supporters were worried.

The sale also reverberated in Arab media debates. The Iraqi press used the arms sale to attack the Saudi-US alliance within the context of the Arab-Israeli conflict, seizing on the Carter administration's assurances to Congress that the Saudis would not be provided certain missile capabilities for the F-15s and that the Saudis would not base the fighters near Israel. A series of articles in *al-Thawra* criticized the deal as providing inferior, strictly defensive arms to Egypt and Saudi Arabia while providing offensive weapons to Israel, thus ensuring that the Egyptians and Saudis could not help reclaim lost Arab lands while enabling the Israelis to prepare for future aggressions. The deal, one article declared, provided "offensive American planes for the enemy [Israel] and defensive, outdated ones for Egypt and Saudi Arabia."[85] Another article critically cited a Saudi source who stated that the "American airplanes deal is for defensive purposes only."[86]

Saudi media, in contrast, played up the significance of the advanced technology it would soon be obtaining as evidence of the advantages of its petrodollar ties with the United States. For example, shortly after the F-15 sale to Riyadh was upheld in the US Senate, the Saudi newspaper *al-Medina* ran an article dedicated to the fact that *Time* magazine's cover story was "a special on the Kingdom [of Saudi Arabia], the country of the great desert entering into the jet age." By noting that the United States' premiere magazine had recognized the F-15 sale as evidence of Saudi Arabia's rapid technological and military advances in recent years, *al-Medina* could demonstrate that the value of the deal, as well as others made with the United States, was not merely an assertion of the House of Saud but rather a widely reported fact.[87] The Saudi leadership's professed excitement over the deal appears to have been genuine. Based on contacts with high Saudi officials, West reported that he was "convinced that the Saudis are deeply grateful and consider themselves in [Carter's] debt. . . . The Saudi monarchy had committed its full prestige to the sale, and the favorable vote vindicated their pro-Western policy approach."[88]

Having used sweeping language about the need to limit US arms transfers as a presidential candidate and in his May 1977 arms sale policy proclamation, Carter found himself the subject of disappointment for many advocates of conventional arms control and supporters of Israel. His critics had some valid points. Carter had pushed the sale of some of the most expensive and advanced weapons in the world to new countries, notably the AWACS for Iran and the F-15 for Saudi Arabia. Carter had also made significant steps in establishing a new military supply relationship between the United States and Egypt.

Internally, the Carter administration also found reason to be disappointed in its effort to curb the global arms trade. A confidential CIA report issued in July 1978 reported that while in 1977 US foreign arms sales decreased by 6 percent, global arms export sales had increased by 12 percent, in large part due to increases in European and Soviet deals. "Even though Western governments and the USSR are paying lipservice to cooperation in [arms] sales restraint, none has yet seriously entertained sales restrictions," the report stated. "Instead, they continue to pursue arms sales vigorously in their traditional markets and to look for new sales opportunities." It was expected that if Washington continued its unilateral arms sale restraint, LDCs oriented toward the United States would increasingly acquire weapons from Western Europe instead, while LDCs aligned with the Soviet Union would continue to acquire weapons from the Warsaw Pact countries. Western Europe was not expected to decrease its arms exports, because they provided jobs, generated export earnings, and lowered unit costs. Nor was the Soviet Union expected to decrease its arms exports, because they provided the Soviets with badly needed hard currency and helped the Soviets influence client states.[89]

Yet the Carter administration could also point to successes in reducing US arms sales. It had met its goal of reducing the value of military transfers (arms and construction of military facilities) to "ceiling countries" (countries other than NATO members, Japan, Australia, and New Zealand) in FY 1978 from the year prior by 8 percent, reversing the trend of escalating US arms sales.[90] Furthermore, for the period of FYs 1973 (when oil prices began to soar) to 1976, total US military transfers had averaged $9.81 billion a year, while the annual average for FYs 1977 and 1978 came to $6.42 billion, a decrease of 35 percent. New military sales agreements with the MENA were decreased by an even greater magnitude during the same two periods, dropping from an annual average of $6.71 billion to $3.58 billion, a decrease of 47 percent.[91] The emphasis on arms transfer restraint by the Carter administration, bolstered by an even more activist Congress, significantly contributed to the decline in US military sales abroad.

After September 1978 Carter could also cite the signing of the Camp David Accords between Egypt and Israel as evidence of the wisdom of his chosen exceptions to arms restraint. Despairing of reaching an immediate agreement with all Arab parties but fearing a collapse of the peace process, Carter brought Begin and Sadat to the United States for negotiations that lasted thirteen demanding days and resulted in an agreed framework in which Egypt would soon normalize relations with Israel in return for an Israeli withdrawal from the Sinai occurring over three years as well as nonbinding recommendations for future talks among Israel, its neighboring Arab states, and the Palestinians. At several points the negotiations approached the brink of failure, but Carter's mediation and ability to use superpower carrots or sticks were critical to keeping the talks going. Indeed, when at one point Sadat had packed his bags and prepared to leave in response to Begin's insistence on Israel retaining part of the Sinai, Carter implored Sadat to trust that he could change Begin's mind but also warned that the developing special relationship between Egypt and the United States would end if Sadat left now. Sadat, surely in part considering the possible loss of the newly acquired access to US arms he had spent years fighting for, stayed put.[92] Ambassador West also attributed US arms sales to Saudi Arabia as critical to gaining Saudi support for the Camp David meeting. "I think it a fair assessment to say that had it not been for the favorable action on the F–15 sale, there would have been no Camp David," West reported. Because of Carter's personal involvement in the passage of the deal, "Sadat felt he could trust the President and the Saudis felt they could support both Sadat and the U.S. in this endeavor."[93]

By the fall of 1978, then, the Carter administration had a mix of successes and failures on the issue of global arms transfers. Benefiting from a Congress and US public that broadly supported conventional arms control, at times to an even greater degree than the executive branch, the Carter administration achieved meaningful reductions in US arms transfers to the MENA and the rest of the world during its first two years in office. Furthermore, the Carter administration achieved these reductions while maintaining the United States' strategic alliances. In the cases where it had pushed for major arms packages, the Carter administration could point to geopolitical successes aimed at long-term peace to support them, most notably the Camp David Accords. In its efforts to achieve a global reduction in arms sales through bilateral or multilateral arms reduction agreements with the Soviet Union or Western Europe, however, the Carter administration had thus far failed. Carter still held out hope that agreements could be reached, but the other major arms-exporting countries had more than made up the difference in the unilateral cuts in US arms sales, frustrating the United States' primary objectives.

Yet even in the most optimistic appraisal, the fact remained that the Carter administration had transferred arms to oil-rich dictatorships like Iran and Saudi Arabia, to dictatorships receiving petrodollar aid like Egypt, and to Israel in spite of its growing settlements in occupied territories. In doing so, the United States continued to support governments that regularly trampled on human rights and denied millions of people democratic self-rule. This was a moral issue, but also a strategic one, as the United States lost popular goodwill from the peoples on the receiving end of US arms deployed by allied regimes, peoples that might take action against the United States or eventually seize power themselves. On October 5, 1978, during a House hearing on arms transfer reductions, Democratic representative from New York Stephen Solarz raised this possibility with Under Secretary of State for Arms Control and International Security Affairs Lucy Benston while referencing the growing unrest in Iran, sarcastically asking Benston if her department had made arrangements "if and when the shah should feel obliged to go into exile for him to fly out on one of the AWACS we sold him." Benston replied that no such arrangements had been made and attributed the unrest in Iran to the shah's human rights reforms.[94]

Yet one more issue in the fall of 1978 diverted the Carter administration's attention from the seriousness of unrest in Iran: the continuing fall in the value of the dollar. In addition to the Saudis, European allies increasingly pressed Carter to lower US inflation, strengthen the dollar, and raise the US oil price to global levels to reduce pressures on global supply and improve the balance of US trade. US oil imports had risen from $8 billion in 1973 to $47 billion in 1977, putting greater demand on OPEC oil and thus driving up global oil prices. The oil imports also served as the largest single force in the growing US trade deficit; in 1977 oil imports accounted for nearly half the US trade deficit. The growing trade deficit in turn contributed to the weakening of the dollar, raising the risk of OPEC deciding on a price increase. Seeking to reverse these trends, in July Carter pledged to eliminate US controls on domestic oil prices and allow them to rise to global market levels by the end of 1980. But this would take time, and in the meantime the dollar continued to depreciate. In August Blumenthal expressed concern that the continued depreciation of the dollar could set off an international financial crisis.[95]

The Carter administration was also alarmed by rising talk within OPEC of changing the pricing of oil to a basket of currencies rather than the dollar due to the latter's increasing depreciation undercutting its real revenues. Such a move had been resisted by Iran and Saudi Arabia thus far, but other members of OPEC had pushed the idea in recent months and were hoping to prevail.[96] Treasury believed currency exchange markets would react badly to such a move; OPEC was already nervous about US monetary policies, and its adoption of the basket would be taken as further evidence of the dollar's decline and cause a run on the currency. This possibility so concerned the Carter administration that in September it determined "the US should make a maximum effort to persuade OPEC not to price its oil on the basis of the value of a basket of currencies" and that this goal had an even higher priority than avoiding an OPEC oil price increase.[97]

The value of the dollar then dropped precipitously in October. Fearing a crisis, on November 1 the Carter administration announced a tighter monetary policy with significantly higher Federal Reserve interest rates to appreciate the value of the dollar by suppressing domestic inflation and attracting foreign investors. This was an important shift away from the Carter administration's previous prioritization of economic stimulus; the new approach successfully arrested the depreciation of the dollar but threatened to induce higher rates of unemployment.[98] While the Carter administration took this step for a variety of economic reasons, concerns about oil prices and petrodollars featured prominently. "One reason for the painful steps that we took on the dollar," one White House official explained, "was to give ourselves more leverage with regard to oil prices."[99] Yet even as the Carter administration reached a viable policy for the dollar crisis, the crisis in Iran was reaching a boiling point that would finally seize the attention of US leadership.

Chapter 8

Revolution and Invasions

On February 1, 1979, Khomeini returned to Iran, ending fourteen years of exile. The shah had fled the country sixteen days prior. As the ayatollah departed his chartered plane at Tehran's Mehrabad Airport, journalists and supporters greeted him.[1] Khomeini briefly addressed the gathered, thanking "all the ranks of the nation" for their extraordinary efforts and sacrifices to overthrow the shah. He then reiterated why deposing this "traitor" had been necessary. "He has transformed our country's culture into a culture of colonialism," Khomeini declared. "He has exhausted the Treasury; he has devastated the country and has made his army and the military dependent upon the foreign military and advisers. . . . Our victory will dawn when the hands of the foreigners are severed from our country and all the roots of the monarchial regime are pulled out of our native land."[2] After Khomeini concluded his speech, a motorcade slowly drove him through the streets of Tehran, where millions of Iranians jubilantly greeted him with chants of support and tears of joy.[3]

In that day's speech, Khomeini did not refer to the United States by name, but he did not have to; Iranians knew Washington was the foremost foreign supporter of the shah. In securing both the revolution and the government that followed, the ayatollah regularly returned to Iranian grievances about the US petrodollar economy, US-led globalization, and US imperialism to inspire his political base. Khomeini would make quick strides in delivering on his promises to undo the systems of US empire, achieving Iran's political and economic break with the United States and launching serious challenges against US allies in the larger MENA. The Iranian Revolution and subsequent Iranian tensions with the United States also spurred a second oil shock from 1979 to 1981, eventually tripling the cost of oil, undermining US economic policy while bringing a new windfall of petrodollars to the OECs. The Carter administration watched in horror as one of the key pillars of the US-led petrodollar order in the MENA collapsed in a torrent of anti-Americanism and revolutionary Islamism. The Iranian Revolution would prove to be the greatest reversal against the United States' petrodollar order, the transformation of a major US ally into a major US adversary. Additional crises in the MENA during 1979 and 1980—many influenced by the Iranian Revolution (as well as one outside of it, the Soviet invasion of Afghanistan)—further challenged the US petrodollar order, bringing into question the viability of the entire structure.

Yet while the Iranian Revolution constituted the greatest challenge to the US petrodollar order in the MENA to date, Khomeinism inadvertently reinforced and expanded petrodollar interdependence between the United States and the remaining Gulf monarchies. Despite concerns about the viability of its regime, the Carter administration determined the loss of an allied Saudi Arabia had to be prevented at all costs, or else the vital interests of the United States would be imperiled. To preserve this and other Arab alliances, the United States doubled down on petrodollar interdependence, particularly in the realm of arms, as the Carter administration abandoned the goal of arms transfer restraint and instead embarked on a surge of weapons sales to the MENA to improve the security of allied governments and reassure client regimes of the United States' commitment to them. US allied regimes, and particularly the Saudi royals, fearful that a rising wave of radicalism and Soviet activism might overthrow their rule, encouraged the Carter administration's strategy and even pushed it further. The second oil shock, meanwhile, ensured that the Arab monarchs had plenty of petrodollars to spend and invest in shoring up the US empire and their position within it.

During the summer of 1978 the shah attempted to quell dissent by offering superficial reforms and cabinet reshufflings while simultaneously imposing periods of martial law and moving even more violently against open displays of resistance. This neither won over nor cowed the opposition. On September 8, the shah's forces fired indiscriminately on a massive peaceful protest in Tehran; midrange estimates put the number killed at between five hundred and nine hundred. In response, Iranians across the economy launched massive, sustained work strikes, including in oil refineries, petrochemical factories, and civil service agencies. By October the Iranian economy had become paralyzed and oil production reduced to 28 percent of its normal level. That same month, in an apparent effort to stifle his influence, Iran persuaded Iraq to expel Khomeini, but the ayatollah rebased in Paris, where it proved easier for him to network with Iranian dissidents and garner international media coverage.[4]

As late as October, Carter and most high-level US officials were ignorant of the seriousness of the situation in Iran. On November 2 US ambassador William Sullivan finally spurred a top-level meeting on Iran by sending a cable giving his estimation that the shah may soon abdicate due to the deteriorating situation. At Brzezinski's urging, Carter messaged the shah his unconditional support, but the president declined to provide unsolicited advice to the shah on how to proceed. On November 9, Sullivan, growing more concerned by the day, issued another high-level cable, titled "Thinking the Unthinkable," in which he argued that the United States needed to immediately start designing and implementing contingency plans in the event that the shah fell. Vance increasingly argued the shah needed to institute more democratic reforms to expand his political base. Brzezinski countered that the shah or someone else of the United States' choosing needed to implement a sufficient show of force to bring the protesters to heel. Carter, appalled by the poor intelligence he had received thus far, avoided encouraging either option and instead ordered new studies of the situation.[5] On December 2 Brzezinski wrote a memorandum to Carter outlining his belief that an "arc of crisis" in the greater Middle East now posed the "greatest vulnerability" for the United States. "All at once, difficulties are surfacing in Iran and Pakistan . . . and there is reason to believe that the political structure of Saudi Arabia is beginning to creak," Brzezinski stated. "Fragile social and political structures" in key countries threatened to collapse and create openings for pro-Soviet forces to seize power, especially "since there is a pervasive feeling in the area that the U.S. is no longer in a position to offer effective political and military protection." Brzezinski argued that a "shift in Iranian/Saudi orientation" would be an unprecedented threat to the cohesion of the Western alliance, inducing "more 'neutralist' attitudes on the part of some of our key allies. In a sentence, it would mean a fundamental shift in the global structure of power."[6] Brzezinski had concluded that the US-led petrodollar order, and the global US empire more generally, was in danger.

Meanwhile, the shah's opposition demonstrated ever increasing power. On December 11 protesters organized a massive rally in Tehran; the estimated number of participants exceeded two million. The assembled Iranians ratified by acclamation the establishment of an Islamic Republic led by Khomeini and called for the implementation of social justice and the expulsion of imperialists.[7] Meanwhile, oil worker strikes kept Iran's petroleum industry crippled.

The resultant decrease in the global oil supply and the atmosphere of uncertainty drove up petroleum prices on the spot market, and at OPEC's December 16–17 conference, its ministers agreed to a staggered rise in the base oil price over the course of 1980 from $12.70 to $14.54, ultimately a 14.5 percent increase.[8]

For most of 1978 the shah had persisted in believing that some combination of state violence and minor concessions could preserve the Pahlavi dynasty. Toward the end of the year, however, facing outright revolt, he acted unsure and indecisive. Using greater force seemed unrealistic, as many conscripts were already refusing orders to fire and even openly voicing support for Khomeini. Pledges of political liberalization or economic justice rang hollow after decades of unfulfilled promises. At the start of 1979 the shah, bowing to the strength of the opposition, appointed one last prime minister, Shapour Bakhtiar, a left-leaning liberal and long-standing advocate of turning the monarchy into a titular role. Bakhtiar obtained an agreement from the shah for the monarch to go on an indefinite trip out of the country, which he did on January 16. Bakhtiar then endeavored to establish popular legitimacy for his own rule, ordering the release of all political prisoners and the abolishment of SAVAK, beginning a review of major foreign business deals, canceling oil sales to Israel and South Africa, and pledging a reduction in military spending. Much of the opposition denounced him as a traitor for even briefly working under the shah, however. Rightfully fearing that Khomeini intended to take power, Bakhtiar first attempted to prevent his return to Iran.[9] When this proved unfeasible, Bakhtiar announced that if Khomeini declared an Islamic Republic, he would take "strong action" against him.[10] The Carter administration, preferring Bakhtiar's relative moderation, privately voiced to him its support for arresting Khomeini should he return to Iran.[11] On February 1, the ayatollah landed in Tehran, intent on a showdown with the prime minister.

During part of his procession through the capital, Khomeini delivered another speech at a Tehran cemetery where many martyrs of the revolution were interred, rallying Iranians to his movement by channeling populist anger with an address that distilled his many attacks on US imperialism and its petrodollar order in Iran. The ayatollah again condemned the shah as a "wicked traitor" who had destroyed the Iranian economy while having "expanded our graveyards." He charged that the shah had intentionally weakened the Iranian economy to make Iran dependent on the United States, and that the shah and his ministers had

given away all our oil to foreigners: to America and other countries. . . . In return, they received arms to be used in installing bases for America! We gave away our oil to America and constructed a military base for it. . . . America has brought weapons into the country that our own army cannot use without American military advisers and experts around. This is the (real) issue regarding our oil, which, God forbid, would have been exhausted if this person had endured. If his rule had continued, our oil reserves would have been exhausted and since our agriculture has already been destroyed then this nation would have been completely impoverished and would have had to work as coolies for the foreigners. We are crying out because of this man (the Shah) and for this reason. The blood of our youth has been shed for this reason; because we want freedom.

The ayatollah charged that Bakhtiar had only the support of the Americans and the British; with the Iranian people's support, Khomeini would appoint a legitimate government. He warned the Iranian people that the United States wanted "us all to revert to that same situation . . . [and] let America devour all of our existence. We will not allow this." Khomeini concluded his speech with words directed at the members of the Iranian army. He thanked the Iranian soldiers that had joined the revolution and advised Iran's top military officials that "the nation is saying the army should be independent and should not be under the command of American and foreign military advisers; come and join us."[12]

On February 5 Khomeini declared the establishment of a government with Mehdi Bazargan, a liberal academic, as provisional prime minister. After a four-day standoff, the elite Imperial Guard, the last significant armed forces loyal to Bakhtiar, attempted to suppress several units of air force cadets and technicians in Tehran that declared their loyalty to Khomeini. Revolutionary guerilla groups and average citizens quickly joined pro-Khomeini soldiers, and after a two-day battle that left hundreds dead, the Imperial Guard had been routed and the Iranian army recognized Bazargan's government. Khomeini had achieved control of Iran. On February 21 Washington reluctantly recognized Bazargan's government, hoping to salvage Iranian-US ties.[13]

Starting with Nixon, the US government had pursued petrodollar interdependence between the United States and the MENA in the belief that this would provide both carrots and sticks to ensure friendly behavior from key countries like Iran and Saudi Arabia. The Iranian Revolution proved to be the greatest failure of this policy to date. The Nixon, Ford, and Carter administrations had expected US trade and cooperation with Iran and the Arab world in development programs and military and security buildups to strengthen the stability of allied regimes and tie them to the United States. Iran defied these predictions, as the shah's petrodollar projects and heightened US presence, held in place by increasingly repressive security forces, generated widespread anger that swept away his regime. The Carter administration had taken modest steps to try to reform the shah's rule in regard to human rights and arms sales, but it had not moved away from strongly supporting his dictatorship. Many later argued that Carter and/or the shah could have prevented the revolution with a stronger show of force, but a year of state violence in 1978 only galvanized the Iranian opposition. Only by pursuing a very different petrodollar order in Iran in the mid-1970s, one anathema to the shah, could Iran have avoided a violent revolution. Similarly, barring a radical change in the shah's governance, the only way the United States could have avoided being villainized in the minds of the Iranian people would have been to end its petrodollar alliance with the shah and instead uncompromisingly oppose his tyranny.

For the Saudis, the Iranian Revolution was just the latest and greatest event that convinced them that hostile forces were surrounding Saudi Arabia. The Saudis had been disappointed that the United States had not prevented the influx of Soviet and Cuban personnel in Ethiopia and South Yemen. When Afghan communists successfully seized power in Kabul in a violent coup in April 1978, Riyadh was further convinced that the Soviets were working to encircle the Gulf. In June the heads of state of both North Yemen and South Yemen were assassinated, apparently as part of a successful effort by an even more radical Marxist faction to take power in Aden. In September Khalid and Fahd expressed to Ambassador West their concerns that South Yemen was actively working to overthrow the government of North Yemen and unite the Yemens under its rule, telling West that the urgency of the North Yemen situation was equal to, if not greater than, that of the Arab-Israeli conflict. Khalid expressed alarm at "the circle of fire closing in on us" due to communist schemes and argued that "what has happened in Ethiopia, Afghanistan and what is now happening in Iran, should have sounded a shrill alarm into the consciousness of our great American friends just as it has to us. The situation in Southern Arabia, if not remedied, would be disastrous to all, to you as well as us." Fahd stated, "It is very, very important for us to know, directly and clearly what will you do in this case to save the situation? Will you rush to our rescue, as you have done towards certain friends or will you dally until dust settles on corpses and charred remains?"[14] At the end of 1978 West reported to Vance that "in the Saudi mind, the events of the past year in the Yemen and Iran have provided all the additional proof, if any were needed, that the Soviets are after their oil" and that with "nearly a million Yemenis mostly from North Yemen" working in Saudi Arabia, the Saudis believed "in the event of a Soviet dominated regime in North Yemen, the possibility of Fifth Column activities via the Yemen work force here is very real."[15]

The collapse of the shah's regime led the House of Saud to determine they needed to test and see whether the United States was truly willing and able to support their own monarchy in this period of crisis. On January 13 Prince Saud bin Faisal, appointed foreign minister in 1975, met with West and asked for a US defense commitment against the growing Soviet threat, arguing that Soviet adventurism in the greater Middle East "has been encouraged by a lack of U.S. response to their initiatives." West believed that "the Saudi request for a defense commitment is even more than what it says. It is a test. Refusal to engage in contingency planning will be interpreted as U.S. impotence or disinterest in Saudi Arabia."[16] Ten days later West reiterated his belief about the importance that Saudi Arabia attached to US responsiveness to its security concerns, stating that "as unpleasant as the notion of an accommodation with the USSR is to the Saudis, we do not believe they regard it as unthinkable. If they do not like the results of their probing and testing, they may reluctantly come to the conclusion that they have no choice but to come to terms with realities as they see them."[17] The CIA shared West's assessment, reporting on January 26 that "the Saudis' requests for a US defense commitment . . . to plan security contingencies is designed to test US intentions. . . . If the Saudis consider the US response to their security concerns inadequate, they probably will move toward a more non-aligned political posture, and show less willingness to accommodate US interests in the energy field or to support US-sponsored Middle East peace efforts. The heretofore unthinkable—reaching some kind of accommodation with the USSR—also appears to be a possibility." The CIA noted that "top Saudi leadership is 'bitterly unhappy' over what it sees as a very inadequate US response to the Iranian crisis. The Saudis now are deeply worried about how the US would react to a crisis of similar proportions in Saudi Arabia."[18]

Frightened for its existence, the Saudi government sought tangible reassurance from the United States in the form of increased arms sales and joint planning of coordinated responses to potential threats in the region. West summarized the Saudis' position by quoting a knowledgeable Saudi official who stated that they were looking for a commitment from the United States "such as you have with the Israelis. . . . There is no treaty, but you always respond to Israeli needs. . . . That is the kind of understanding we want and need here in Saudi Arabia."[19] The House of Saud, in effect, was doubling down on the US petrodollar order in a bid for its survival.

The Iranian Revolution increased the Carter administration's concern about the stability of Saudi Arabia. On January 23, a week after the shah fled Iran, many top Carter officials met to discuss the subject of Southwest Asia and Saudi Arabia. The concern that other MENA allies might share the conditions for revolution was widely aired. The countries of Southwest Asia, Brzezinski argued, "face a cumulative burden of social change for which their structures are not suited" and were thus vulnerable to Soviet expansionism. Blumenthal lamented that "we face a paradox: additional economic resources do not necessarily improve the situation. Indeed they can worsen it by accelerating the disintegration of social structures. For instance in Saudi Arabia if we urge too rapid exploitation of oil we will cause instability."[20] At a later meeting on February 1, Secretary of Defense Harold Brown admitted he did not know if the Saudi monarchy was any closer to its people than the shah was to the Iranians and argued that US military assistance could not solve serious internal problems in an allied country.[21]

Despite the concerns about social unrest, top Carter officials rarely, if ever, considered whether the United States should end the petrodollar order or withdraw its empire from the region. The United States, they felt, needed to address social unrest in the region rather than run from it. Furthermore, they did not see a US presence or ties to the region as inherently destabilizing, but usually the opposite. Much of the talk after the Iranian Revolution focused on reassuring worried allies in the Middle East. "The Saudis and others [in Southwest Asia] are unsure of our commitment [to them]," chairman of the Joint Chiefs of Staff General David Jones argued at the January 23 meeting. "We need to develop a clear and coherent policy, something like a 'Carter doctrine.' It is not clear to me what this would contain but we need to reestablish confidence. Perhaps we need a small US military presence at Masirah [Oman] or elsewhere and maybe joint planning with the Saudis."[22] Brzezinski agreed. "The word there [in the Arab region] is 'reassurance,'" he declared. Brown added, to Brzezinski's approval, that the Saudis "need to see results, not just to have consultations."[23]

In addition to security concerns, the Carter administration strongly desired to bring down the skyrocketing price of oil, and Saudi Arabia was understood to be the key to achieving this. Blumenthal argued at the January 23 meeting that the United States had little economic leverage to persuade Saudi Arabia to moderate its pricing and increase its oil production levels; Saudi Arabia thus had a great deal of economic leverage over the United States. The Saudis, however, looked to the United States for its security, both purchasing US arms and training for its forces and relying on the US military to deter external threats; the United States thus had a great deal of security leverage over Saudi Arabia. "We need to face the issue," Blumenthal concluded, "of how we can use our security relationship to get what we want from them on the economic side."[24] The key officials of the Carter administration agreed that Saudi help on oil prices would be a quid pro quo for US security assistance—the only debate was over how explicit this linkage should be made to the Saudis. When Deputy Secretary of State Warren Christopher argued that the Saudis would likely react poorly to an explicit linkage of US security for Saudi oil price moderation, Brown retorted that the Saudis "must know that we only love them for their oil." Brzezinski argued the linkage should not be made explicit but could be discussed within the framework of mutual security concerns.[25]

In mid-February Carter sent Brown to the Middle East to consult with allied governments, including Cairo and Riyadh, "to restore and reinforce confidence in the United States among our friends in the region" and to "discuss with the Saudis the nature of the 'special' relationship they say they desire."[26] During his visits, Brown "sought to convey the idea that . . . forms of defense cooperation are far more important to regional security and well-being than additional arms" but found that while the Egyptians and Saudis welcomed "offers of consultations and joint planning and intelligence exchange," they were not considered enough on their own. Instead, they primarily judged the United States "by how favorably we responded to arms requests." The Saudis renewed requests for advanced arms like the Chrysler M1 Abrams tank, while the Egyptians "listed equipment which would total $15–20 billion, in effect an 'Americanization' of Egyptian forces."[27] Arms sales remained the primary criteria for Egypt and Saudi Arabia in assessing the strength of US support for them.

Then, on February 24, fighting broke out between the two Yemens along their border. South Yemeni forces quickly gained the upper hand and seized a number of North Yemen border towns. On February 28 Saud bin Faisal informed West that if the situation in North Yemen continued to deteriorate, the Saudis would militarily intervene; the following day Saud asked the United States to supply arms and military planning assistance if the Saudis intervened.[28] The US Military Training Mission in Dhahran responded to the request with fear, however, for it believed "the Saudi military effort [would] almost surely fail, either because of Saudi incompetence or because of Soviet-Cuban intervention," and the delegitimizing effects of such a defeat "could lead to the eclipse of the Saudi royal family's leadership, and a political unravelling in the Peninsula."[29] Brown shared the negative assessment of the Saudi armed forces; two weeks earlier he had told Carter that "the Saudis, though they are moving ahead toward a professional air force, seem to me a military zero at this time."[30] Despite this, at a cabinet meeting on March 5, Carter "indicated that we should do what we can to assist in defense of [North Yemen], short of direct U.S. military involvement," and that the United States would provide the Saudis with arms and planning if they intervened, though remaining classifications leave it unclear whether Carter encouraged or discouraged the Saudis from taking such a course and under what circumstances.[31] Carter also sent arms to North Yemen and deployed a US aircraft carrier off the southern coast of the Arabian Peninsula as a show of US resolve. The conflict ended in mid-March through an Iraqi diplomatic initiative that restored the territorial status quo.[32] The brief war had served as an opportunity for Washington to demonstrate its commitment to Saudi security concerns, but it also highlighted the strategic impact of the loss of Iran as a US military proxy and the current inability of the Saudi military to fill that role despite the purchase of billions of dollars of US arms.

Even as the Carter administration worked to reaffirm Saudi Arabia's role within the system of US cooperative empire, the Camp David Accords were undermining another part of the US-led petrodollar order: triangular aid and investment to Egypt. When the terms of the Camp David Accords were announced, many moderate and radical Arab leaders balked, as the agreement left the Israeli occupation of Palestinian and Syrian lands in place while establishing an Egyptian-Israeli peace that would end the united Arab front. Seeking to preserve the deal, the United States looked to Saudi Arabia to shore up Arab support. In private conversations with US officials, Fahd vacillated. At times, he insisted he could not press other Arab leaders to accept a deal that did not provide solid US assurances on Palestinian self-determination; other times, he assured US officials that Saudi petrodollar aid to Egypt would continue and his diplomatic efforts would mute Arab criticisms of Egypt.[33] Yet when the Arab League members minus Egypt met in Baghdad on November 2, the Saudis joined the league's resolutions that the Arab states would break relations with and impose economic sanctions on Egypt if it signed a separate peace treaty with Israel. The league also signaled, however, that Egypt would receive billions of petrodollars in new aid if it repudiated the accords.[34]

Neither Carter nor Sadat intended to abandon the Camp David agreement, however, and the Saudi royals increasingly showed less desire to confront popular Arab opinion on the matter. When Brown met with Saud bin Faisal in February, the latter "made it clear that the US should not insist that Saudi Arabia support positions that would jeopardize the kind of relations it wishes to maintain with the other Arab states."[35] Fearing for the stability of the Saudi regime and its trust in the United States after the Iranian Revolution, the Carter administration decided not to press the issue. When Brzezinski visited Saudi

Arabia in mid-March, he told Saud that "actions to hurt Sadat would only help the radical forces in the region" but also acknowledged that he understood Saudi issues with the Egyptian-Israeli agreement and merely asked that they "understand the strategic thinking which underlies our own position."[36] Afterward West reported that the Saudis were relieved that they were not presented with an ultimatum to publicly support the treaty or else face serious repercussions like the cancellation of the F-15 sale or other indications of a decline in US security commitments for Saudi Arabia. The Saudis privately pledged to continue to work to minimize any hostile rhetoric or sanctions toward Egypt by the other Arab League states.[37]

Simultaneously, the Carter administration pledged a massive infusion of direct US aid and arms to Sadat if he followed through on the accords. In addition to securing Cairo's follow-through with its agreement with Israel, Brown believed "Egypt came the closest" to replacing Iran's role as the primary military defender of US interests in the Middle East. Sadat, in turn, told Brown that Egypt could assume the previous role of Iran "on an even grander scale than had been assumed by that country under the shah." Turner raised concern that Sadat's obsession with policing the Middle East could lead him to ignore domestic problems and generate the same problems that ousted the shah, but Brzezinski maintained Sadat needed US arms to appease the demand of Egyptian military officers for equipment. On March 19 Brown concluded the details of US military and economic assistance to Egypt and Israel, with the former receiving $1.8 billion in aid and the latter $2.2 billion through FY 1982.[38] On March 26 Begin and Sadat signed the Egyptian-Israeli peace treaty.

The Arab League reconvened in Baghdad the next day. The Saudis reportedly endeavored for a restrained response but were overwhelmed by the anger of the other delegations. Yasser Arafat called for tough sanctions against not only Egypt but the United States as well, including a resumption of the oil embargo. Libya and Syria vocally supported the PLO's position on the United States, but the other Arab countries demurred.[39] Regarding Egypt, however, there was far more support for the PLO's position, and on March 31 all members of the Arab League other than Oman and Sudan declared their support for breaking off all diplomatic ties with and aid to Egypt, as well as Egypt's expulsion from all inter-Arab organizations.[40]

While Washington was relieved to avoid another oil embargo, it was dismayed that Arab triangular petrodollar aid to Egypt had been lost for the foreseeable future. US corporations had continued to pursue triangular investments during the Carter administration, and some successes had finally materialized. In 1978, for example, American Motors opened a factory in Cairo and produced military jeeps for the Arab Organization for Industrialization, a consortium that utilized Egyptian labor and Emirati, Qatari, and Saudi financing of $1.4 billion. This collaboration ended in May 1979 when the Gulf Arabs withdrew their petrodollars.[41] The Saudis reneged on their previous pledge to pay for the purchase of Egypt's F-5s, leading the Carter administration to postpone the sale.[42] Government-friendly Egyptian media lambasted the Saudis in response. One *al-Ahram* cartoon mocked Riyadh's decision on the F-5s by depicting a Saudi royal explaining he rejected the plane, not because of the Egyptian-Israeli peace agreement but because it had "no plush seats . . . and not even a bar!"[43] Stung by the loss of Saudi aid and investments, pro-Sadat Egyptians sought consolation by disparaging the Saudis as spoiled, depraved, and nonsensical nouveau riche.

Yet, while Cairo and Washington were disappointed in the collapse of triangular aid and investments, these instruments had already achieved a core political purpose. From 1973 to 1978, billions in petrodollar aid had materially sustained Sadat's regime during the riskiest period of his rapprochement with Washington and acceptance of the US-led peace process, and at a time when the US Congress resisted providing assistance to Cairo and US businesses largely considered Egypt too risky to invest in. And while triangular investment proved to be small, the hope that these petrodollar dreams provided to the Egyptian leadership played a significant psychological role in sustaining their shift toward the United States. Petrodollars ultimately served as the bridge that brought Sadat from the 1973 war to Camp David, an outcome that might not otherwise have occurred in the fragile period of the mid-1970s.

Furthermore, in three key ways the fallout from Egypt's peace with Israel did not deprive it of MENA petrodollars. First, in regaining the Sinai and its oil fields, Egypt could generate modest petrodollar revenues directly. Second, oil-rich Arab private investment, trade, and tourism continued.[44] Third, Egyptian workers continued to labor in ever-growing numbers in petrodollar-rich MENA countries with the permission of both the Egyptian and host governments. Despite the breaking of political ties, the Arab Gulf countries and Libya could ill afford to lose their extensive Egyptian workforce, and Egypt could ill afford to lose the remittances of Egyptians laboring in the oil-rich states.[45]

Still, Arab and Iranian aid had been a significant part of the Egyptian government's income. Now the United States would offset the loss of Arab aid with its own, which Egypt used that summer to purchase US arms: hundreds of missiles, five hundred-fifty armored personnel carriers, and thirty-five F-4s (which were superior to the F-5s the Saudis now refused to fund).[46] The Carter administration had completed the long-standing US goal of integrating Egypt into the US empire. The achievement was marred, however, by the breakdown in relations between Egypt and the Arab monarchies, which collectively diminished their effectiveness as US proxies. Sadat's decisions also generated an upsurge in popular Arab anger toward his regime and the United States that US officials would only slowly come to appreciate.

For the United States, a primary aim of petrodollar interdependence was to prevent higher oil prices. Yet the US-led petrodollar order had unintentionally contributed to the trends that led to the overthrow of the shah, and the atmosphere of uncertainty created by revolutionary Iran led to global panic buying of oil by Western oil companies and automobilists, even after Iranian production returned to significant levels, driving up prices. Petrodollar interdependence arguably encouraged the Saudis to sell its oil at "official prices" well below the actual market rate; but for the rest of the oil-rich Arab states, petrodollar interdependence demonstrated little impact, as they steadily pushed up their petroleum prices in response to consumer demand. The Saudis proved either unable or unwilling to boost their own production high enough to dampen frantic global demand, and OPEC quickly abandoned its 1978 pricing schedule, and indeed proved unable to provide a credible price structure at all. Instead, members of OPEC continually escalated what they charged for their oil by adding surcharges or selling on the unregulated spot market. By mid-1979, oil on the spot market regularly sold for more than thirty dollars a barrel, a threefold increase from the start of the year.[47]

For the United States, like the rest of the oil-importing MDCs, the second oil shock brought a petrodollar windfall to certain businesses, but the economy as a whole suffered. The United States experienced gas shortages in the summer of 1979, once again sparking American outrage and occasional violence at the pump. The US inflation rate, to a large degree spurred by oil prices, rose from 8.3 percent in September 1978 to 12.2 percent in September 1979. The rising cost of imported oil compounded the pain of Carter's phased decontrol of US oil prices, which began in June 1979 and was set to be completed in October 1981. While good for rationalizing market behavior and reducing consumption in the long term, it had an inflationary impact in the short term. Alarmed by the surge in inflation, Carter appointed Paul Volcker as chairman of the Federal Reserve in August 1979. Starting in October, Volcker aggressively targeted inflation by severely tightening the monetary supply. Volcker's plan would have far-reaching ramifications in the long term, but in the short term inflation continued apace.[48]

While the Carter administration sought to end the second oil shock, the surge in petrodollars made it all the easier for the Saudis to purchase US arms.

Seeking to bolster its regional alliances, the Carter administration completely abandoned its policy of arms sales restraint and instead lavished Saudi Arabia with weapons. During FY 1979, the United States authorized $7.4 billion worth of military sales agreements to the MENA, a sum exceeding the previous two years combined. The largest share of FY 1979 sales went to Saudi Arabia, which totaled $5.97 billion. This was the highest sum yet for Saudi Arabia in a single year.[49] Furthermore, in contrast to sales agreement totals in the early and mid-1970s that were heavily weighted toward costs of constructing military infra-structure, the FY 1979 total was almost entirely for armaments and military training.[50] One package included $1.2 billion worth of arms and training to modernize the Saudi National Guard, which was charged with internal security. The notification of the sale was made to Congress in July 1979, shortly after the Saudis announced they would increase oil production by a million barrels a day.[51]

For Saudis, the second petrodollar boom elicited both bravado and con-cern. A June 1979 cartoon in the London-based Saudi-owned newspaper *al-Sharq al-Awsat* exemplified the sense among some Saudis of waxing Arab and waning Western power as oil prices reached record highs. In the cartoon, a happy Arab couple with eight children and another baby on the way stand across from a dour British couple and their single child. Using human repro-duction as an allegory for economic productivity, the Arab husband/prodi-gious father wryly tells his wife that the British "have an energy problem."[52] A cartoon published seven months prior in *al-Riyadh* captured a more tem-pered reaction to how petrodollars were impacting Saudi society. In the car-toon, two Saudis dressed in traditional thawbs discuss a man dressed in disco garb standing by a Rolls-Royce. "Truly (believe me)," says one of the cus-tomarily dressed Saudis to the other, "he is a (Saudi) national, a BS manage-ment specialist of major national companies."[53] While framed in the context of humor, the image captured a sense among Saudis that the rapid pace of foreign business and development in their country was westernizing their cul-ture, a process of which many Saudis had varying degrees of misgivings. Fur-thermore, narratives about the shah allowing the West to corrupt the culture and institutions of Iran had played a significant role in his overthrow and the rise to power of the antimonarchical Khomeini. This heightened the Saudi monarchy's sensitivity to Khomeinist and other Islamist attacks on its Islamic legitimacy due to Saudi Arabia's petrodollar ties with the West, and particu-larly the United States.

While recognizing that for the foreseeable future, US relations with Iran would be considerably weaker than they had been under the shah, the Carter administration still believed that engagement with the new Iranian government was both possible and desirable. US foreign policy leaders discounted the idea that the Iranian clerics and their supporters could actually govern, and believed moderates would control Iranian affairs of state. These Iranian moderates, the logic went, would recognize that they would need resupplies of US arms and parts to maintain the strength of their overwhelmingly US-armed military to counter threats from internal revolts and the Soviet Union.[54] Iran would thus continue its petrodollar interdependence with the United States in the arena of arms sales, albeit at a likely reduced scale, in a mutually beneficial arrangement that blocked the expansion of Soviet influence.

Khomeini, however, was determined to secure his power over Iran and free it of any US influence. Cleric-run courts executed hundreds of members of the old regime.[55] Upon the formal declaration of the Islamic Republic of Iran on April 1, 1979, Khomeini called for ongoing determination in the struggle against "supporters of international thieves and oil spongers" and declared the new Iranian government would "transform the country's education, justice administration and other departments and offices, which have been set up based on Western concepts and westernization, into a system of an Islamic nature, and demonstrate to the world social justice, educational, economic and political independence."[56] Iran quickly moved to cancel $7.7 billion worth of US arms agreements, including those for F-16s, AWACS, and Spruance destroyers, dismantling a core piece of US petrodollar interdependence with the MENA. The Iranians retained a large cache of already delivered US arms, however, including F-14s and F-4s.[57] Additionally, hundreds of millions of dollars' worth of orders of spare parts already purchased by the shah remained in the United States but not canceled, and some moderate Iranians in the Bazargan government pressed for their speedy transfer to Iran in order to better violently suppress active ethnic-minority revolts across the country and their demands for autonomy. The US embassy in Tehran pressed for the quick delivery of these spare parts to boost the Iranian moderate's standing, but the larger US bureaucracy proved slow to move on the arms issue, frustrating the Iranian moderates and US embassy personnel.[58]

In the fall of 1979 an escalating struggle in Iran between Khomeinists and more republican-minded Iranians centered on the drafting of a new constitution, with Khomeini pushing for the establishment of the Islamist *velayat-e faqeh* and Bazargan pressing for a system more similar to France's Fifth Republic. The outcome of this contest was unclear when, on October 22, Carter reluctantly allowed the shah to come to New York to receive medical treatment for his worsening cancer. Rumors in Iran that the United States and the shah were planning a counterrevolution intensified. On November 4, Iranian students loyal to Khomeini stormed the US embassy in Tehran and held its American staff captive in order to prevent them from organizing a coup. Khomeini capitalized on the crisis by supporting the detention of the Americans and the charges of a US conspiracy against the revolution. The ayatollah then submitted his preferred constitution to a referendum, declaring that those who abstained or voted against it would be abetting US imperialism and betraying the revolution's martyrs. Outmaneuvered, Bazargan first resigned from the premiership and then urged his supporters to vote for the constitution to avoid anarchy. With this, the constitution's passage on December 2 became a foregone conclusion, though some leftist parties boycotted the vote.[59]

From November 8 to 12, the Carter administration applied pressure on the Iranian government to secure the release of the hostages by barring the transfer of all undelivered military spare parts already paid for by Iran, ordering the deportation of any Iranian students in the United States found to be in violation of their visas, and announcing a ban on Iranian oil imports. On November 13, Abol Hassan Bani-Sadr, acting Iranian foreign and finance minister, stated in a press conference that the United States was waging economic war on Iran, and threatened that Tehran might pull Iran's investments out of US financial institutions in response. The petrodollar weapon, long assumed in the United States to be an Arab concern, had been brandished by Iran. Lacking readily available records, the US Treasury initially estimated Iranian investments in US institutions to be around $6 billion; a final accounting in April 1980 would in fact find over $11 billion. But even the smaller initial estimate immediately raised fears that a sudden withdrawal by the Iranians had a realistic chance of triggering a speculative assault on the value of the still shaky dollar and would remove the only security the United States held if Tehran repudiated the $3 billion in debts it owed to US claimants. For these reasons, on the morning of November 14, Carter, invoking powers granted in the International Emergency Economic Powers Act (IEEPA), issued an executive order freezing all Iranian government assets in the United States and all dollar-denominated assets of the Iranian government and Iranian nationals held abroad by US institutions and individuals, in one stroke neutralizing the Iranian petrodollar weapon.[60]

Tehran responded by demanding the return of not only the frozen assets but also funds it alleged the shah had stolen from the Iranian government and invested abroad in the West for his personal aggrandizement, investments it estimated to be worth anywhere from $17 to $32 billion.[61] Within Iran, media suggested the asset freeze proved the Carter administration valued the shah's ill-begotten wealth over the well-being of the hostages. The day after the freeze, the Tehran-based newspaper *Kayhan* ran a cartoon showing Carter holding a scale, weighing the hostages against the shah and bags of money; the president determines the latter is weightier.[62] The exact sum, sources, and locations of the shah's investments abroad were shrouded in secrecy, and it was unclear how much of it fell under US jurisdiction, but Western reporting did find that the shah had skimmed from government funds for his personal use and funneled them through banks like Chase and Citibank.[63]

As the Iranian hostage crisis continued, a wave of violent uprisings challenged Saudi Arabia and the United States at the end of 1979. On November 20, 1979, hundreds of armed Sunni militants seized control of the Sacred Mosque in Mecca, the holiest site in Islam. The leader of the insurgents, Juhayman al-Utaybi, a Saudi preacher and veteran of the Saudi National Guard, called for a mass uprising against the Saudi monarchy, to be replaced by a mahdi, a millennial religious leader. The motivations of the insurgents were rooted in anger at the US-led petrodollar order. Utaybi had developed his following by arguing that the "present Muslim rulers are co-operating with infidels" and that "the royal family is corrupt. It worships money and spends it on palaces not mosques." This rhetoric resonated with Saudis and immigrant Arabs angered by US dominance over and policies toward the Arab and Islamic worlds, the vast economic inequality that had developed in Saudi Arabia as it integrated into the global capitalist system, and the stories of Saudi royals partaking in extravagant travels to the West to engage in activities forbidden within Islam, like extramarital sex and the consumption of alcohol. Using the mosque's public address system, Utaybi declared that, in addition to the overthrow of the monarchy, an accounting of the wealth it owed to the Saudi people would be taken, oil exports to the United States would cease, and all foreign governmental advisers would be expelled.[64] The militants' call for rebellion did not spread across Saudi Arabia, but they did take numerous pilgrims hostage and repulsed attempts by Saudi security forces to dislodge them from the mosque, and both sides settled into a siege.

In Pakistan the next day, thousands of Muslims, responding to rumors that the Mecca mosque siege had been initiated by Americans and Jews, attacked the US embassy in Islamabad, US cultural centers in Lahore and Rawalpindi, and the US consulate in Lahore; two Americans and four Pakistanis were killed before the Pakistani army restored order.[65] On December 2, about two thousand protesters in Libya who chanted their support for Khomeini and their opposition to the United States set fire to the US embassy in Tripoli; all embassy personnel managed to escape unharmed.[66] The following day Saudi forces retook control of the Sacred Mosque and captured the remaining insurgents, including Utaybi, but the monarchy was shaken by the fact that its Islamic legitimacy had been so boldly challenged by a domestic Islamist group. Reports of the death toll ranged from over a hundred to over four thousand.[67] On December 15 the shah left the United States for Panama, but Iran retained its American hostages. The accumulated crises created market fears over a possible cutoff of Gulf oil that pushed petroleum prices even higher; at the December 17–19 OPEC meeting, the new official price of Gulf producers ranged from twenty-four to thirty dollars a barrel, roughly a doubling of the price from a year ago.[68]

Islamism was also on the rise in Afghanistan. The new Marxist regime in Kabul quickly jailed thousands of political prisoners, executed others, and systematically worked to replace Islamic institutions with secular ones. In March 1979, Afghan Islamists, outraged by the actions of the communists and inspired by Khomeini's seizure of power in Iran, began an insurgency. The Afghan government, with assistance from the Soviets, waged a brutal military campaign to suppress the revolt, but the Islamist opposition only grew, with many Afghan soldiers defecting to the insurgents. In July, Carter, acting on the recommendation of the CIA, which saw in Afghanistan an opportunity to counter Soviet capabilities in the region, authorized the covert delivery of a modest $500,000 worth of nonmilitary aid to Afghan rebels. Meanwhile, by autumn Moscow increasingly believed that Afghan president Hafizullah Amin was either incompetent or a US agent. The communist government was nearing the point of collapse. The Kremlin had hoped to avoid a direct Soviet military intervention, but by December Moscow reluctantly determined a brief military intervention to put in place a more effective government was the only way to arrest the Islamist insurgency that threatened not only Afghanistan but potentially the Muslim-majority Central Eurasian territories of the USSR as well. On December 25, the Soviet army entered Afghanistan. Two days later, hundreds of Soviet special forces soldiers stormed the Afghan presidential palace and killed Amin. The Soviets concurrently flew Babrak Karmal, a Marxist rival of Amin's, back into his country and installed him as the new leader of Afghanistan.[69]

Brezhnev hoped that Carter would understand and tolerate the Soviet move as one limited to Afghanistan and defensive in nature.[70] Instead, the Soviet invasion caused Carter to quickly and profoundly reevaluate his understanding of Soviet intentions and actions. Carter wrote in his private diary on December 28 that the invasion constituted a "radical departure" in Soviet behavior and that he was "determined to make this action as politically costly as possible." Carter felt compelled to take such a stance because he believed, as he wrote in his diary on January 3, 1980, that "unless the Soviets recognize [the invasion] is counterproductive for them, we will face additional invasions or subversion in the future."[71]

Brzezinski led the way in providing such a framework. "We have to move deliberately to fashion a wider security arrangement for the region, lest Soviet influence spread rapidly from Afghanistan to Pakistan and Iran," Brzezinski wrote Carter on January 3. "I cannot emphasize strongly enough the strategic consequences of such a development. It would place in direct jeopardy our most vital interests in the Middle East."[72]

On January 23 Carter declared before Congress and the world that "an attempt by any outside force to gain control of the Persian Gulf region will be regarded as an assault on the vital interests of the United States. It will be repelled by the use of any means necessary, including military force."[73] This statement constituted a profound shift in the US diplomatic posture. No longer would the security of the Persian Gulf be primarily left to regional allies, as under the Nixon Doctrine; now, the United States had assumed for itself that role, pledging a US military commitment to the defense of the region under the Carter Doctrine. To credibly implement the Carter Doctrine, Washington pursued three main strategies: (1) increase the size of the US military presence and number of bases in and near the region, (2) increase and strengthen regional alliances while enhancing the military capabilities and political stability of these allies, (3) support and arm insurgencies in communist-ruled countries in the region.[74]

The Carter Doctrine reversed the core premise of the Nixon Doctrine, and the Nixon Doctrine had been a key part of the US-led petrodollar order. But the Carter Doctrine did not signal the end of the US-led petrodollar order, only its evolution. First, a credible US military force in the region would take time to develop; in the near term, the United States would have no choice but to continue to largely rely on the military forces of its allies. Second, even in the long term, Washington expected petrodollars to play an important role in the three key strategies of the Carter Doctrine, a role similar to the one they had performed thus far. The Carter administration expected Saudi petrodollars in particular to play an important role in the success of the Carter Doctrine. The Near East and Southwest Asia "is the most rapidly changing area in the developing world," stated one discussion paper for a January Special Coordinating Committee Meeting. "Instability is inevitable. . . . The issue is how to direct change toward constructive goals—not how to prevent it." The document argued that appealing to Islamic and "independent" nationalist sentiments that ran counter to communism offered a significant advantage in promoting this goal. The paper went on to argue that the US government should encourage Saudi Arabia to cooperate with the United States in establishing and financing military and economic development in the area with the aim of increasing regional security. The paper also argued for the Carter administration to "continue working to draw Saudi Arabia and other Gulf states more closely into the Western economic system."[75] Petrodollar interdependence would continue to be a priority.

For their part, the domestic and foreign security fears of the Saudi royals had only increased. The Soviet invasion of Afghanistan compounded their belief in communist designs on Saudi Arabia. On January 9, 1980, the Saudis publicly beheaded Utaybi and sixty-two of his followers in eight different cities to communicate to the kingdom's residents the price of defying the monarchy.[76] Yet twenty-three days later the Shia community in Saudi Arabia's oil-rich eastern province launched strikes and demonstrations, celebrating the first anniversary of Khomeini's return to Iran and voicing their anger at being treated as second-class citizens, denied by the state an equal share of petrodollar revenues for the development of their community, access to higher-paying jobs in the local oil industry, or the right to publicly perform certain religious rituals. The National Guard violently suppressed the Shia demonstrations, killing several protesters. This prompted some Saudi Shia to organize in Iran, where they broadcasted propaganda attacking the Saudi monarchy over the radio into Saudi Arabia.[77] Within the span of three months the kingdom had been seriously challenged by two Islamist, anti-American inspired movements—one Sunni, one Shia.

Responding to these challenges, the Saudi monarchy, like the Carter administration, determined that a doubling down on petrodollar interdependence was the best chance of securing state interests, even if it had fueled some of the Islamist opposition to its rule. Riyadh considered superpower patronage, manifested through the provision of weapons, the surest way of thwarting domestic and foreign foes. In the words of Ambassador West, the Saudis continued to consider "their arms requests as the litmus test of the U.S.–[Saudi] relationship."[78] Riyadh increasingly emphasized a request for F-15 enhancements that had been barred in the 1978 sale and for AWACS.[79] Carter and Brzezinski concluded that such a sale would be particularly hard to pass in Congress during an election year, but, hoping to provide a somewhat positive answer, agreed to tell the Saudis that they would consult with Congress on the matter in 1981.[80] Frustrated with this response, the Saudi government emphasized to West their belief that F-15 enhancement "restrictions should be removed in view of the Soviet invasion of Afghanistan," and "repeatedly hinted that its patience with U.S. policies has its limits, and there are now strong indications that other options are indeed being actively considered." West feared that if the Saudis did not receive a more positive response, they might respond by reducing their oil production, reducing business with US firms, pursuing a nonaligned alliance of Islamic countries, improving relations with Moscow, and shifting to the French as their main arms supplier. "The adoption of such a strategy . . . would have a profound and injurious impact on U.S. vital interests," West argued. "Heretofore, the U.S.–Saudi special relationship has largely traded oil for security. For the Saudis to decide that their security is now best guaranteed elsewhere would deprive us of what is, in the final analysis, the only card the U.S. can play effectively."[81] In late June, Brown met with Prince Sultan, the Saudi defense minister and brother of Fahd, and promised to further study the Saudi arms requests but would not make a commitment at the present time. Sultan "agreed that Saudi Arabia would not push its request for these items at this time but insisted it was not withdrawing its request either."[82]

Saudi Arabia and the United States found it easier to collaborate on the arming of the mujahedin in Afghanistan. The day after the Soviet invasion, Brzezinski argued to Carter that the United States should lead an international coalition that would arm and train the Afghan resistance. A Soviet withdrawal was the "ultimate goal," Brzezinski would write a week later, but "even if this is not attainable, we should make Soviet involvement as costly as possible."[83] In late December 1979 Carter authorized the CIA to covertly provide arms to the mujahedin.[84] In July 1980 Saudi Arabia secretly agreed to match US funding for the mujahedin, making petrodollars an integral part of the Afghan resistance.[85] The Saudi royals had long feared Soviet encroachment, and aiding the mujahedin helped counter this perceived threat. Additionally, the Saudi monarchy had been working to prove its Islamic credentials and counter antimonarchical Islamist threats within the kingdom in the wake of the challenges to its Islamic legitimacy by the antimonarchical Islamist revolution in Iran and the Sacred Mosque seizure. By encouraging Saudis to donate to or join the mujahedin, the monarchy aimed to demonstrate its piety while channeling militant jihadist energy toward the Soviet Union rather than the US-allied House of Saud. With Riyadh's backing, Saudi religious authorities likewise spread promujahedin messages and the call for volunteers and donations for the Afghan struggle. Nongovernmental Saudi charities donated millions of dollars for the mujahedin, funds made possible by the rapid growth of the Saudi economy within the petrodollar order.[86]

A massive increase in the flow of petrodollars from Saudi Arabia and the other Arab monarchies to the United States in the wake of the second oil shock likewise reaffirmed and strengthened interdependence and US power. While US exports to Iran plummeted in 1979 and virtually ceased in 1980, in those years the consumption of US goods and services by Saudi Arabia continued to grow, totaling $10.6 billion. Furthermore, net OPEC investments once again flooded into the United States, reversing the decline of 1978. Most of this increase occurred due to Saudi purchases of Treasury securities, which jumped from $8 billion in June 1979 to $19.1 billion in December 1980, increasing the Saudi share of total foreign holdings of US Treasury securities from 7 to 15 percent. These loans assisted the Carter administration's military buildup against the Soviet Union and effort to improve the US economy. In the global banking system, the importance of petrodollars likewise returned, with new OPEC deposits constituting the equivalent of 30 percent of all international lending of BIS reporting banks in 1979 and 26 percent in 1980. Petrodollar recycling continued to be left primarily to the free market, with loans made primarily to a handful of oil-poor LDCs and OECs. In 1979 the US government worked to allow private finance to lend even more to sovereign borrowers by ending a rule that had limited commercial bank lending to a country to 10 percent of its capital.[87] International financial officials now largely considered high oil prices to be a permanent rather than temporary reality and believed they should be financed by normal (regular conditionality IMF loans or private lending) rather than emergency measures. No new IMF oil facility would be implemented to respond to the second oil shock.[88] The majority of LDCs largely denied private lending continued to rely on foreign aid and/or saw their economies stagnate.

For the Carter administration, improved cooperation with the Saudis constituted a rare silver lining to ever-darkening clouds. US military leaders discussed contingency plans for a feared Soviet invasion of Iran, debating "the wisdom of U.S. air attacks on invading Soviet forces . . . versus emplacing U.S. forces at some point where the Soviets had not yet arrived."[89] The Iranian hostage crisis dragged on for months without resolution. On April 7 the United States cut diplomatic relations with and instituted a total embargo against Iran.[90] Washington also secured a limited embargo against Iran from its European allies. Neither embargo, however, significantly harmed the Iranian economy, as US trade had already virtually ceased and the Europeans largely maintained the trade commitments they had made with Iran before the start of the crisis.[91] Seventeen days later, Carter launched a military rescue attempt of the hostages that quickly failed and left eight Delta force members dead due to a piloting error. Vance, who had opposed the plan, resigned before the operation commenced. At the June OPEC meeting, the official price rose to twenty-eight dollars per barrel for Saudi oil, thirty dollars for Gulf, and thirty-five dollars for Iranian; all but the Saudis added additional surcharges. On July 27, the shah, who earlier that year had left Panama for Egypt, succumbed to cancer. Nixon and Sadat attended his burial in Cairo. On September 12 Khomeini for the first time publicly listed his conditions for the release of the US hostages: the return of property stolen by the shah, the release of Iran's frozen assets, the cancellation of US sanctions and financial claims on Iran, and a US pledge of noninterference in Iran's affairs. While sticking points remained on the issues of releasing arms and the ability of the US government to locate and seize the shah's property, Carter viewed the outlining of conditions by Khomeini as encouraging and he authorized direct negotiations with Iran. Yet just as these talks got under way, Iraq invaded Iran on September 22.[92]

Saddam Hussein had formally ascended to president of Iraq in July 1979 after forcing al-Bakr from power. In the wake of the Iranian Revolution, Saddam's regime faced increased protests and antigovernment assaults by Shia Iraqis. Iranian state media and officials increasingly voiced their support for the overthrow of the secular Baathists and its replacement with an Islamic state. Saddam increasingly believed Iran was engaged in a concerted strategy to overthrow him. At the same time, Saddam believed that Khomeini had diplomatically isolated Iran and weakened its military through purges of suspected royalists. By some point in mid-1980, Saddam had calculated that a quick military victory over Iran was feasible, could restore territory to and boost the pan-Arab prestige of Iraq, and would either stop the Islamic Republic's meddling in Iraqi affairs or topple the government entirely.[93] Speaking to his Revolutionary Command Council about his war plans on September 16, 1980, Saddam evinced lasting anger and embarrassment over the ceding of Iraqi territorial claims of the Shatt al-Arab in the 1975 Algiers Agreement. Now, Saddam believed Iraq had its best opportunity to seize back Arab territory from Iran. "When we have the ability to return what is rightfully ours we will do it," Saddam declared. "No patriotic person would let go of what is rightfully his." But while Saddam believed international conditions were currently fortuitous and thus must be seized, he also believed Iraq needed a quick military victory to ensure its US, Zionist, and reactionary Arab enemies would not seize upon the war as a means to weaken Baghdad. "[We] must not accept [the] draining [of Iraqi] resources" through a protracted war, Saddam maintained. "We have to stick Iran's head in the mud and force them to say yes so we can get done quickly with this matter."[94]

At the start of the war, Iraqi forces held the initiative, seizing territory in the Iranian province of Khuzistan and laying siege to major cities there. The Iranian and Iraqi air forces, as well as the Iranian navy, mutually destroyed much of each other's oil production and distribution facilities, abruptly reducing the total of OPEC's oil output by 15 percent and raising Middle East oil prices to new record highs.[95] Petrodollar-purchased arms from the United States and the Soviet Union now set ablaze the oil they were meant to protect. Saddam announced his willingness to enter into negotiations with Iran a week into his invasion, but Khomeini refused his demands for the Shatt al-Arab. The war continued. Iraqi troops sustained their advance, capturing roughly ten thousand square miles of Iranian territory, including the major city of Khorramshahr, by November 10; but Saddam's invasion also generated a surge of Iranian patriotism that coalesced around Khomeini's regime, enabling it to pursue a strategy of long-term attrition that over time would disadvantage Iraq, a nation only one-third the size of Iran.[96]

The Carter administration sought to end the war as quickly as possible while pursuing a neutral stance between the belligerents. The White House feared the conflict might expand into Saudi Arabia or other Arab Gulf states and endanger oil supplies and the integrity of US allies, or that the war might create opportunities for the Soviets to either curry favor with Iran or seize parts of its territory. Either scenario risked a superpower confrontation that could lead to war. Washington had little influence in either Baghdad or Tehran to negotiate a cease-fire, however. The Carter administration continued to prohibit US arms sales to Iran or Iraq, policies implemented in the arms freeze in November 1979 for the former due to the hostage crisis and in the arms ban in December 1979 for the latter (along with Libya, South Yemen, and Syria) due to being designated by the State Department as state sponsors of terrorism. Washington also encouraged other nations to remain neutral in the war. The United States had limited success, however, in obtaining other countries' neutrality or preventing US arms from being sold by European, Israeli, Soviet, and Vietnamese dealers and governments to Iran.[97] The Arab world, meanwhile, became increasingly divided by the war, with Libya and Syria allying themselves with Iran and the Arab monarchies supporting Iraq.

While the Carter administration strove to be neutral in the Iran-Iraq War, the state media of both Baghdad and Tehran sought to cast the other as in league with the United States. Cartoons in al-Thawra regularly depicted Khomeini dressed in a US flag.[98] Al-Thawra also drew on its years of attacks on the shah's petrodollar purchases of US arms and transposed them on Khomeini. Cartoons depicted Khomeini impotently throwing missiles at Iraq while rid-ing on the back of Uncle Sam, and Iranian soldiers once again dropped guns labeled USA in fear of the Iraqi army. Asad and Qaddafi were also drawn along with Khomeini as students or lackeys of Uncle Sam.[99] In November the Iraqi government transported captured US arms like intact Chrysler M60 tanks and parts of downed F-4 jets to exhibits in different Iraqi cities, accompanied by posters that depicted a crazed Khomeini being manipulated by Uncle Sam, to physically drive home the point that the Iranians were armed by Washington and thus cast the Iraqi war effort as an anti-US one.[100] In the context of the ongoing hostage crisis, Khomeini's government argued that the United States was ultimately behind Iraq's assault. Iranian prime minister Mohammad Ali Rajai said on a Tehran radio program that he expected a long war "because it is the United States which continues the fighting."[101] In Tehran, banners went up depicting Carter and Saddam embracing, with captions such as "they are plotting to destroy us" attributed to Khomeini.[102]

During the Carter years, US popular media continued to regularly depict the petrodollar wealth of Arab sheikhs as a threat to Americans. The 1980 comedic film *Up the Academy* featured a teenage son of a sheikh sent to the United States who, despite having a million dollars in his bank account, compulsively

Figure 12. Iranian president Abol Hassan Bani-Sadr and an Iranian soldier flee Iraqi tank fire, dropping a rifle inscribed "USA" in the process. Published in *al-Thawra al-Usbu'ai* on November 1, 1980. Artist: Ali al-Karkhi.

steals trinkets like pool balls and candlestick holders, reinforcing the notion that Arabs unjustifiably took wealth away from Americans despite not needing it.[103] A 1978 episode of the television series *Alice* perpetuated the specter of Arabs using petrodollars to buy out the United States' property and values. A misogynistic oil baron who, as the titular character puts it, is "one of those Arabs who's coming over here to buy up the whole country" seeks to wed the sassy waitress Flo, but she throws his offered $100,000 ring into a soup bowl, demonstrating Americans' refusal to sell off their values for Arab petrodollars.[104] Other works sustained the narrative that Arab petrodollars subverted US sovereignty. In the song "Slow Train," on the 1979 album *Slow Train Coming*, Bob Dylan croons that "all that foreign oil controlling American soil . . . it's just bound to make you embarrassed" and "sheiks walkin' around like kings . . . [were] deciding America's future."[105] A 1978 episode of the television series *Police Woman* revolved around a white slavery ring targeting underage teenage girls for the service of wealthy Arab royals.[106] That same year another television police drama, *CHiPs*, ran an episode where law enforcement deals with an Arab prince who drives his Ferrari far in excess of the speed limit. The prince attempts to bribe two patrolmen, prompting officer Llewelyn Poncherello to state that such payoffs are illegal. The prince retorts, "I'm above your laws." Ponch remains uncorrupted, but the potential for and desire of Arabs to use their wealth to undermine US laws and governmental institutions has been established.[107]

Fictitious Arab bribes mixed with real US police work in the saga of Abscam. In February 1980 news broke that an FBI sting operation had caught several US congressmen accepting bribes from federal agents posing as wealthy Arabs and their representatives. Ironically, Senator Harrison Williams, who had earlier introduced legislation to place greater controls on foreign investment due to concerns about the potential of Arab wealth to influence US politics, was one of the individuals charged with corruption. The sting operation was the brainchild of Melvin Weinberg, a convicted fraudster turned FBI accomplice with a penchant for cons that involved current events. Weinberg and an FBI agent pretended to represent an imaginary Arab plutocrat, Kambir Abdul Rahman, head of Abdul Enterprises. The scam involved the two offering politicians millions in cash or investments in exchange for the passage of desired governmental action, including business permits and permanent residency for Abdul and his equally fictitious associate Yassir Habib, on the grounds that they feared revolutionary upheaval in their homeland, sometimes stated to be the UAE. On a few occasions, additional FBI agents posing as Abdul and Yassir participated in meetings with congressmen as well.[108]

When news of Abscam (short for Abdul Scam) broke in the press, it generated a flurry of US media attention. Abscam proved to be yet another irritant in US relations with the Arab world; the Arab League denounced the operation as a campaign to distort the Arab image, and Saudis privately expressed their aggravation to Ambassador West and US corporate leaders, asking why they should do business with a country that insulted Arabs. Outrage over the use of their ethnicity as part of the sting spurred Arab American activists, led by former Democratic senator from South Dakota James Abourezk, to found the American-Arab Anti-Discrimination Committee to combat the stereotyping of Arabs. Notably, the previous role of sensationalism about Arab wealth and anti-Arab stereotypes in the US media were a key part in making the scam believable, even self-fulfilling in the case of Williams.[109] Likewise, the sting further perpetuated popular US discourses about the undeserved wealth of Arabs, despite no actual Arab petrodollars being involved. Democratic New Jersey state senator Joseph Maressa, who was caught up in the sting for taking $10,000 in "legal fees" from the FBI agents (though ultimately not charged), defended his actions as a form of petrodollar recycling, telling the *New York Daily News* that "the Arabian Nights portrait these two agents painted was such that I felt like it would be patriotic to take some of this OPEC oil money and get it back to the United States."[110]

Abscam led to the political demise of Williams, one Republican and five Democratic US representatives, and the Democratic mayor of Camden, New Jersey, all of whom were convicted of bribery and imprisoned, along with twelve other men.[111] Americans' concern about petrodollar-linked corruption during the 1980 elections was not limited to these individuals, however. The failure of former Texas governor John Connally's bid for the Republican nomination for president in 1980, for example, stemmed in part from media attacks on his private ties to Arab investors (his law firm had represented Arab clients in the mid-1970s, including an Arab-owned private investment bank), which suggested Connally would betray the interests of Israel and/or Americans for petrodollars. When Jack Anderson raised the question in his *Washington Post* column as to "whether [Connally's] profitable links to the Arab oil moguls . . . will prove too bitter a pill to be swallowed by an American public outraged at the financial misery and national humiliation the United States has been suffering at the hands of the Middle Eastern petroleum potentates," he both observed an emerging line of attack on Connally and popularized it further.[112]

During his reelection campaign, Carter likewise came under attack for alleged petrodollar malfeasance. In the summer of 1980, the president endured a bought of bad press when it was revealed that his brother Billy Carter had received a $220,000 loan from the Libyan government, that the Carter administration had used Billy as a secret envoy to urge Tripoli to encourage Tehran to release the US hostages, and that Billy was required to belatedly register as a foreign agent of Libya (a term merely meaning he was a lobbyist for Libya but which could have the erroneous connotation of being a spy). While no evidence has been found that Billy attempted to influence the Carter administration's policies toward Libya, it is probable that the Libyans had hoped to gain leverage over Billy with the loan and through him a channel to the White House, though their efforts appear to have come to naught.[113] Regardless, the revelations of what some dubbed "Billygate" created an opening for opponents of the president. William Safire charged, with only circumstantial evidence, that Billy Carter "took advantage of his official hostage-crisis credentials to set up a multimillion-dollar oil deal" and made the misleading charge that "the President must have realized he had created a double agent."[114] While interviewing Billy Carter during a senate investigation in August, Republican senator from Indiana Richard Lugar suggested that Jimmy Carter had altered US foreign policy to support Billy, citing as evidence the fact that shortly after Billy met with Libyan officials about the US hostages, Qaddafi publicly claimed that he had received assurances that the United States would soon adopt a policy more favorable to the Arab world in the Arab-Israeli conflict. Lugar also made a point of raising Tripoli's support for terrorism, including a campaign of assassinations against Libyan dissidents in Europe starting that spring. While both Billy and Jimmy Carter denied making any policy assurances to Libya, such charges, however unsubstantiated, promoted the notion that the Carter administration was either too incompetent or corrupt or weak to deal with oil-rich foes.[115]

Petrodollars and arms purchased by them likewise featured in attacks on Carter in the final stretch of the general election. In October the campaign team for the Republican presidential nominee, Ronald Reagan, fearing a last-minute release of the hostages would give Carter a popularity boost, launched a preemptive media operation under the direction of future Reagan administration officials Richard Allen and William Casey presenting the Carter administration's negotiations with Iran as politically craven and undermining US national interests.[116] This narrative focused on the allegation that the White House was either considering an offer of or had released US arms, purchased by the shah but not yet transferred at the onset of the crisis, to Tehran in exchange for the hostages. William Safire argued in a New York Times editorial that the Iranians aimed "to extract an arms and money deal that only a desperate candidate would offer." Safire stated that "I suspect that an Iranian military official may be in the United States right now, going over a shopping list to choose which of the $550 million in rockets, bombs and other 'spare parts' will be airlifted to Tehran," which would endanger Americans by "involving ourselves in a Moslem war."[117] Two days later, the University of Chicago historian Daniel Pipes similarly alleged in a *New York Times* op-ed that the Carter administration was considering the release of $400 million worth of arms to Iran and argued this represented an abandonment of national security interests for the political interests of Carter's reelection. "With Election Day at hand, [Carter] appears prepared to do almost anything to bring the hostages home," Pipes concluded. "In the process, he might deal with extortionists, recklessly involve us in a remote war, and strengthen our enemies in Iran. The re-election of even a competent President would not be worth all this."[118]

On October 11 Carter had secretly approved a message to the Iranians listing $150 million worth of military equipment, including spare parts for aircraft, that would be delivered after the release of the hostages. The Iranians never responded to this message. There was thus an element of truth to Republican accusations that Carter had offered an arms-for-hostages deal, even if the nature of it was often exaggerated.[119] The release of such arms after the return of the hostages would have been legal, and US sanctions had been put in place for the purpose of securing the freedom of the Americans in Iran, a fact obscured in the Republican narrative. The strategic and political wisdom of such a decision was debatable. Carter judged the safety and freedom of the US hostages worth the concession to Iran. The Reagan campaign, seeking to move US popular opinion against Carter, argued that any military support to the hostile regime in Tehran was counter to US security, an unjustifiable rewarding of terrorism, and proof of the Carter's willingness to sacrifice US interests for his own political gain.

In the end, however, high rates of inflation and unemployment, spurred to a significant degree by the second oil shock, likely played the decisive role in dooming Carter's attempt at reelection. In the lead-up to election day, a majority of polled voters cited the "high cost of living" as the most important problem confronting the United States, a reaction to the fact that the inflation rate averaged 13.5 percent for the year.[120] The unemployment rate, meanwhile, hovered at 7.5 percent in October. At the end of the single presidential debate between Carter and Reagan, the latter asked the American people: "Are you better off than you were four years ago? Is it easier for you to go and buy things in the stores than it was four years ago?"[121] The message resonated. On November 4, Reagan defeated Carter with 50.1 percent of the popular vote and 489 electoral votes. Republicans likewise gained eleven seats in the Senate to seize the majority and thirty-three seats in the House, hamstringing a shrunken and divided

Democratic majority. The failure of the US-led petrodollar order in Iran and the corresponding second oil shock had severely damaged the US economy, in turn greatly diminishing the standing of the party in power in Washington at the time. Arguably, events in the MENA had never before played such an important role in a US election.

Events moved apace in the final months of the Carter administration. In December OPEC held its meeting in Indonesia and raised the price of Saudi oil to thirty-two dollars a barrel, other sources of Gulf oil to thirty-six dollars a barrel, and African oil to forty-one dollars a barrel.[122] Iran and the United States then finalized negotiations on the release of the hostages. Iran ultimately agreed to return the hostages, accept that claims on the shah's assets would have to be pursued in court, and accept that $5.1 billion of its frozen assets would be used to settle debts owed to US and foreign banks and an additional $1 billion placed in an escrow account for possible future arbitration payments. In return, the United States unfroze the roughly $5 billion in remaining Iranian assets, ended its sanctions against Iran, and pledged not to interfere in Iran's internal affairs.[123] Iran chose to decline obtaining the frozen US arms, apparently for the political reason of not wanting to restore any part of the arms-supply relationship with Washington established by the shah.[124] The Carter administration then stipulated that new licenses for any future arms transfers to Iran would have to be approved by the US government, including for arms already purchased but undelivered.[125] The hostages were released on January 20, 1981, as Reagan was sworn in as president. Carter's final achievement as president was the peaceful release of the captive Americans in Tehran. Now a fourth administration would confront the issues of the petrodollar economy.

Chapter 9

Recoveries and Crises

For nine months Najah Aboud, a twenty-nine-year-old Iraqi falafel cook turned tank driver, experienced a largely uneventful deployment in the Iraqi-occupied city of Khorramshahr. On occasion Najah followed orders to drive his Soviet-made armor into positions so that it could fire, but the targets were always beyond his range of vision, and the Iranians never fired back. Then, during a visit to his home city of Basra, his secret, unmarried love Alyaa privately revealed to him their newly born son, Amjad. Najah promised Alyaa they would be wed, and after taking a Polaroid of her and Amjad, he immediately returned to Khorramshahr and beseeched his captain for help in overcoming his and Alyaa's families' opposition to their marriage. The captain assured Najah he would have him wed to Alyaa within ten days. That night, however, Iranian forces launched a massive assault to retake Khorramshahr. In his tank Najah watched in horror as Iranians in US-made Bell Cobra helicopters launched wave after wave of missiles that turned Iraqi vehicles and posts into infernos. His armor out of ammunition and its radio connection to command lost, Najah exited the vehicle to better survey the situation. Within moments an explosion threw him in the air and then crashing back to earth. Bleeding from his forehead and chest, Najah heard surrendering Iraqi troops pleading for their lives and Iranian soldiers firing rifle rounds into them in response. Fighting intense pain, Najah crawled into an abandoned bunker and then collapsed next to the bodies of several dead Iraqis.

Zahed Haftlang was only thirteen when he joined the Basij, an Iranian volunteer militia, with a forged parental permission slip. A native of Masjed

Soleyman, not far from the front lines, Zahed was not a devout Muslim, but he had been angered by an Iraqi air strike that hit his school and killed some of his classmates, and he desired independence, respect, and adventure. Made a medic, Zahed assisted in the treating of wounded Iranian soldiers. Zahed lost any remaining romanticism of war, however, when his commander sent him and fellow child soldiers one by one into the night to run through a minefield to clear a path for the regular army to Khorramshahr. As Zahed sprinted in the darkness, he saw explosion after explosion, followed by a rain of children's torsos, limbs, and blood. Zahed survived, however, and then participated in the Iranian assault to retake Khorramshahr. With the battle still raging, Zahed was ordered to search bunkers, give aid to any wounded Iranians, and shoot any Iraqis. In the second bunker he entered, Zahed was startled by a moan from Najah. Zahed aimed his rifle at the Iraqi, and Najah held out his Quran. Zahed grabbed it and saw the photograph of Alyaa and Amjad. Moved by the image, Zahed not only spared Najah's life but hid him and secretly gave him medical care for days until the Iranian leadership declared Khorramshahr liberated and ordered that wounded Iraqis be treated in Iranian hospitals.

Both Najah and Zahed would survive the Iran-Iraq War, but the conflict would kill an estimated five hundred thousand Iranians and two hundred thousand Iraqis. Alyaa and Amjad were among the dead, victims of shelling during an Iranian assault on Basra. Zahed's betrothed, Mina Fadaei, would likewise be killed by an Iraqi bomb on the day they were to be wed.[1] Petrodollars had enabled the massive buildup of arms in Iran and Iraq, and they facilitated the resupply of weapons to the two states during their total war against each other. These arms contributed to some of the worst levels of death and destruction in the MENA in the modern era. The war constituted the most devastating outcome of the competing petrodollar orders instituted in the 1970s between the Soviet Union, the primary arms dealer to Iraq, and the United States, the primary arms dealer to Iran. Ironically, Iran now used US weapons to challenge US empire.

From 1981 to 1983, Iran gradually gained the initiative in its war against Iraq, dealing Iraqi forces a string of costly defeats and alarming the Arab monarchies. To secure US empire in the MENA, Reagan reaffirmed and expanded petrodollar ties with Riyadh. Saudi Arabia and the Arab monarchies in turn provided Iraq with billions of petrodollars, and the Reagan administration slowly improved relations with Baghdad in an effort to contain Iran. In its first three years, the Reagan administration succeeded in largely containing the Iran-Iraq War to the two belligerents and ensuring the flow of oil from the Gulf, facilitating a gradual moderation in the price of petroleum. This in turn assisted the Reagan administration's decision to apply economic sanctions against Libya owing to its resistance to US dominance in the MENA. Riyadh and Washington also coordinated increased petrodollar aid to antileftist forces around the world, most actively in Afghanistan. Finally, the first term of the Reagan administration witnessed an end of private petrodollar recycling to many LDCs, creating a financial crisis that enabled Washington to impose neo-liberal economic policies in those countries.

Ronald Reagan, a former Hollywood actor and governor of California, had won the devotion of movement conservatives through his simple, optimistic articulation of right-wing ideas and rhetoric of patriotic exceptionalism. Reagan had campaigned to restore US economic prosperity by freeing markets from government interference and reestablish US geopolitical hegemony by militantly challenging communism and terrorism.[2] From the start, Reagan's administration acutely understood the importance of MENA oil and petrodollars to US economic and geostrategic interests, as well as to Reagan's political popularity.

Saudi Arabia promptly pressed the new administration about its security concerns. On January 28, 1981, Sultan wrote to Caspar Weinberger, who had left his job as general counsel at Bechtel to serve as Reagan's defense secretary, about the F-15 enhancement package it had requested from the Carter administration in early 1980, which consisted of multiple bomb racks to improve the F-15s' air-to-ground bombing capabilities, Sidewinder missiles, additional fuel tanks and aerial refueling tanker aircraft to extend the F-15s' range, and AWACS to support the F-15s with better radar coverage. Sultan made it "clear that the Saudis are expecting a rapid and responsive answer" to this request.[3]

Like its predecessors, the Reagan administration believed Saudi Arabia constituted a key US ally and that arms sales were critical to maintaining the Saudi-US alliance. Secretary of State Alexander Haig, a former general, assistant to Kissinger, and chief of staff for Nixon and Ford, argued that "if we don't go through with a deal we will have a serious break with the Saudis."[4] The Reagan administration also valued Saudi Arabia for reasons shared by its predecessors. An NSC preparatory paper for Reagan on the Saudi request for F-15 enhancements argued that in return for a favorable decision, the United States "should be prepared to ask the Saudis to be more helpful in a number of areas in return for this favorable decision. Specifically, we should ask what they intend to do in the energy and security fields, including whether they will resume security assistance to moderate Arab states such as Egypt, Sudan, Morocco, and Tunisia."[5] In short, the Reagan administration sought to continue the existing system of petrodollar interdependence, linking US arms sales to Saudi assistance in bringing down oil prices, militarily defending the Persian Gulf from common adversaries, and financially supporting other US allies.

Many Reagan officials focused on the need for Saudi aid to Pakistan. An interagency study declared in late February there was "agreement that Pakistan is key to US efforts to resist Soviet aggression in Afghanistan and beyond and in constructing a viable security framework in Southwest Asia." US goals included strengthening Pakistan's political and military ability to withstand Soviet pressure and sustaining Pakistani support for the Afghan resistance against the Soviet army, so as to "make the costs to the Soviets of their Afghan adventure unacceptably high."[6] Pakistan's economy was teetering on the brink of collapse, however; it could not engage in a military buildup and covertly support the Afghan insurgency without considerable financial assistance. The Pakistani government demanded considerable US support in return for taking the risk of participation in a major covert operation against the Soviet army. Yet it was unclear to the Reagan administration how it would obtain such large funds for Pakistan, given limited US FMS credits and persisting reservations toward Pakistan in Congress. Haig strenuously argued that Pakistan was vital to US security and in legitimate need of perhaps $2 billion over the next five years to get its army "back in shape." He called for pressing the Saudis to contribute to a Pakistani aid package, thereby alleviating some of the demand on the United States.[7] Saudi assistance could hinge, however, on the ability of the Reagan administration to provide the arms Riyadh requested for itself.

In February Reagan expressed his inclination to approve the F-15 enhancement sale to Saudi Arabia but told his cabinet that "we don't want a domestic battle on this issue. We don't want pro-Israeli groups to start a campaign." He asked if Israel could "be encouraged to head off their supporters." Haig and Weinberger both expressed confidence that Israel could be persuaded not to press the issue with Congress, particularly if they sold more F-15s to Israel on credit.[8] Reagan then approved the Israeli and Saudi sales in principle, with final approval contingent on Israel accepting the US assistance package in exchange for muting opposition to the US arms sale to Saudi Arabia.[9]

Haig discussed the proposal with Israeli ambassador Ephraim Evron on February 23 and reported that Evron confirmed Israel "would project a low-key posture of opposition on the Saudi F-15 enhancement package."[10] On February 27 Reagan approved the sale of Sidewinder missiles, additional fuel tanks, and aerial refueling tanker aircraft to Saudi Arabia, as well as the assistance package for Israel. Reagan left for further study the sale to Saudi Arabia of the multiple bomb racks for the F-15s and the AWACS.[11] The Reagan administration had begun its first attempt at the Arab-Israeli arms balancing act, with the hope that its approach would mollify both sides and avoid the public wrangling with Congress that previous administrations had endured.

Public Israeli and congressional opposition to the F-15 enhancement package materialized even before the deal was formally approved or announced, however, due to press leaks.[12] Reagan's cabinet had agreed that the Israeli and Saudi sales would be announced separately so there would be no public linking of the two sales that might embarrass the two recipients, but the press accurately described the Israeli package as an offset to the Saudi sale.[13] On March 6, the White House publicly announced that it had approved the sale to Saudi Arabia of Sidewinder missiles, additional fuel tanks, and aerial refueling tanker aircraft, had decided against the sale of the multiple bomb racks, and would continue to study the possibility of selling AWACS. Noting congressional unhappiness that the sale would overturn the Carter administration's pledge against selling fuel tanks that would enable the F-15 to reach Israeli territory, State maintained that the increased danger of Soviet penetration of the region after events in Afghanistan and Iran made the reversal of the pledge necessary.[14] In mid-March twenty Democratic and Republican senators delivered floor speeches condemning the proposed sale, even though the administration had not yet formally submitted the package to Congress. The senators argued the sale would endanger Israel's security, heighten the ongoing arms race in the region, and reward the Saudis despite their opposition to Egypt and the Camp David peace accords.[15] US media also raised the specter that the United States was falling into the same trap it had with Iran, overarming a Middle East ally to the point of social upheaval. "There is a danger that [the Saudi and US] Governments will repeat the errors made in Iran and mistake defense for domestic security," the New York Times editorialized. "Americans . . . should never again encourage the delusion that modern weapons can ward off coups by colonels or revolutions in the mosques."[16]

On April 1, two days after Reagan was hospitalized after being shot by would-be assassin John Hinckley Jr., the NSC met without the president to discuss the possible sale of AWACS to Saudi Arabia. Weinberger championed the AWACS deal, claiming that from his talks with the Saudis, it was clear they would not accept a denial of the sale or tolerate much further delay. He also stated that he did not expect serious opposition from Congress. Others were warier. Vice President George H. W. Bush, who had much experience dealing with Congress, including serving as a representative of Texas, repeatedly stated that he was uncertain that Reagan had approved the AWACS sale or been sufficiently briefed on the matter. He insisted that "we have to realize that the

President is going to lose a lot of capital in getting this thing through even if he can." National Security Advisor Richard Allen agreed, arguing "that if the issue was not handled carefully it could result in the first-ever Congressional veto of a U.S. arms transfer agreement."[17]

At the end of the meeting, the NSC agreed that the AWACS sale would go forward. Despite the misgivings of many Reagan officials, they could not bring themselves to risk a further deterioration in Saudi-US relations. The next day the White House announced its tentative decision to sell Saudi Arabia five AWACS.[18] In response, around one hundred Democratic and Republican representatives protested the possible sale on the House floor.[19] Democratic senator from Delaware Joe Biden published an editorial in the *New York Times* arguing the sale threatened not only Israeli but also US interests, as it would "expose sensitive American technology, vital for the air defense of Europe, to the risks of espionage, defection, war, and overnight changes in government. We should have learned from the fall of the Shah that our sophisticated military equipment should not be entrusted to unstable regimes. . . . If the AWACS offered to him had actually been delivered, how secure would we be today?"[20] Undeterred, on April 21 the White House announced it was committed to selling the AWACS and other F-15 enhancements to Saudi Arabia, in part to reassure the Saudis in the face of mounting Israeli criticism of the package.[21] The White House would wait until October to formally propose the sale to Congress, but its determination to achieve passage had been set, and the political battle lines had been drawn. The AWACS sale would be the first major test for the Reagan administration to preserve petrodollar ties with Saudi Arabia in the face of Israeli opposition.

Prime Minister Begin sought to make this a difficult test. "We are going to see Reagan . . . and bring to him our case against the AWACS," Begin told reporters September 6 upon arriving in the United States for a ten-day visit. "This problem endangers very seriously the security of Israel."[22] Eleven days later, fifty senators cosponsored a resolution to block the proposed AWACS sale, with other senators claiming to be undecided but leaning against the transfer.[23] On September 20 Begin and a unanimous Israeli cabinet affirmed their "unreserved" opposition to the AWACS sale.[24]

The Saudi government lobbied hard, too, however. It hired a public relations consultant at $470,000 to head the AWACS campaign and had kept Frederick Dutton on a $200,000-a-year retainer to provide political news and strategy. Boeing and Westinghouse, which respectively built the planes and computers for the AWACS, lobbied Congress to approve the deal. John West also lobbied for the sale. While removed from his ambassadorship by the Reagan administration in March, West ended his tenure on good terms with the Saudis. Upon West's retirement Fahd had the Saudi government donate $500,000 to the nonprofit John C. West Foundation; West would use the money to fund professorships and seminars in Middle East studies at the South Carolina universities the Citadel and Winthrop College and programs at the Atlanta-based Southern Center for International Studies.[25]

On October 1 the Reagan administration formally notified Congress of its intention to sell Saudi Arabia an $8.5 billion F-15 enhancement package, including five AWACS, initiating the thirty-day period in which Congress could veto the deal.[26] It was the most expensive proposed arms transfer in US history. In campaigning for the sale, the White House focused on the Senate, which appeared less oppositional than the House.

But even in the Senate, success appeared uncertain. Democratic senator from Louisiana Russell Long, a supporter of the sale, privately warned the NSC that "the principal area of concern of those [senators] from states without large Jewish populations is the stability of the Saudi regime and the possibility of a repeat of the Iranian situation."[27] Believing Senate opposition was so large that "it is now necessary to 'pull a rabbit out of the hat,'" the NSC proposed obtaining a public Saudi pledge that the AWACS would operate under a joint Saudi-US military command.[28] The Saudi government refused any such public agreement, however, as an unacceptable embarrassment to Saudi sovereignty.[29] The specter of the Iranian Revolution thus loomed over the debates within the US government. Attempting to stave off critiques when formally notifying Congress, Reagan declared that "Saudi Arabia, we will not permit to be an Iran."[30] Later in the month Reagan expanded on this statement, saying that "I don't believe that the Shah's Government would have fallen if the United States had made it plain that we would stand by that Government." He then implied that standing by the Saudis meant selling them AWACS, and that failure to do so could lead to revolution there.[31] Senator Robert Byrd argued just the opposite, stating in a speech on the Senate floor that the sale would place "the mantle of a client state" on the House of Saud and thereby endanger it to the anger of Arab radicals.[32]

On October 14 the House disapproved of the AWACS sale in a bipartisan vote of 301 to 111, sending the issue to the Senate.[33] Reagan personally met with scores of senators, arguing the merits of the sale and that his credibility to foreign leaders was at stake. The Reagan administration was also rumored to offer promises of pork projects for the home states of senators who voted for the sale and threats of the termination of federal contracts in the states of senators who did not.[34] Bechtel, Mobil, and United Technologies, the latter being the producer of the AWACS engines, all lobbied the Senate as well.[35] On October 28, the day of the Senate vote, the Reagan administration remained unsure of the outcome, and the NSC staff drafted a paper with contingency plans if the sale was disapproved.[36] After a final day of debate, however, the Senate narrowly approved the sale fifty-two to forty-eight.[37]

Immediately after the vote Reagan messaged Khalid of his gratification that the sale had been approved, and reiterated his "personal desire to continue working with you and your government to strengthen the Kingdom's defenses, modernize its armed forces, and begin to build greater security cooperation between us." Reagan also thanked Khalid for Saudi Arabia's recent additional aid commitments to Pakistan and Sudan.[38] While it had cost a considerable amount of political capital, the Reagan administration had overcome Israeli lobbying and fears about possible Iran-style revolutions and passed the AWACS sale, preserving the US-Saudi system of petrodollar recycling.

The sale helped ensure that the Saudis would provide increasing amounts of aid to both Pakistan and the mujahedin, facilitating the growth of the resistance to the Soviet occupation of Afghanistan. By the end of 1981, the mujahedin moved freely in most of Afghanistan and had scored impressive losses on Soviet forces. By 1983, the CIA estimated that for every dollar of Saudi-US aid sent to the mujahedin, the Soviets lost four to five dollars in equipment and personnel. With their success in bloodying the Soviets, Washington was largely oblivious to, or at least ignored, the fiercely anti-US outlook of the major Afghan Islamist factions being funded by Saudi and US dollars.[39]

In the early 1980s the Saudis also continued their large purchases of Treasury securities. From December 1980 to December 1982, Saudi holdings of Treasury securities rose from $19.1 billion to $39.4 billion, totaling over 26 percent of all foreign holdings.[40] The over $20 billion in Saudi petrodollar deposits funded a significant portion of the $207 billion of federal deficit spending for FYs 1981 and 1982. Riyadh thus supported the US military buildup started under Carter in response to the Soviet invasion of Afghanistan and the Reagan tax cuts that aimed to stimulate US economic growth during a period of recession and rising unemployment. Despite the value that the Reagan administration held for Saudi petrodollars, however, US media continued to present Arab wealth as a threat to the interests of Americans. In the 1981 film *Earthbound* a sheikh threatens an American small business owner and the natural beauty of his wooded, mountain community with an effort to buy out his quaint local hotel and replace it with a "twenty-story monstrosity." A 1983 episode of the television series *Cagney and Lacey* featured an Arab driving his Rolls-Royce, with a license plate reading "OILBUX," over a Jewish American.[41]

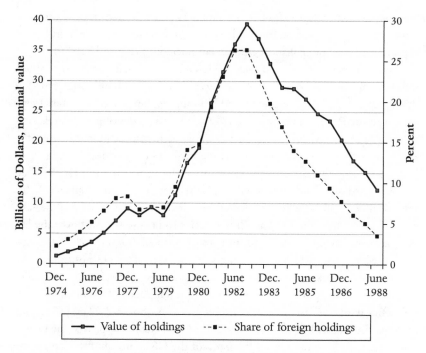

Figure 13. Saudi holdings of US Treasury securities, 1974–1988. Source: US Department of the Treasury.

When Reagan assumed office, the Iran-Iraq War was locked in a stalemate. Iraqi forces lacked the ability to advance farther into Iranian territory, while Iranian attempts to liberate their lands were repeatedly repulsed by entrenched Iraqi units.[42] Confronted with a drawn-out war for which it had not prepared, Baghdad looked for support from the new US administration. On February 6 Mazen Zahawi, Saddam's personal interpreter, had a private dinner with William Eagleton, head of the US Interests Section in Baghdad. While Zahawi insisted he only sought "the opportunity to exchange impressions" and did "not wish to be considered a formal channel" to Saddam, he proceeded to outline the desires of Iraq's leadership. Zahawi suggested that Baghdad was looking to restore relations with Washington as long as it coincided with an improvement in US policy toward the Palestinians, and thus not appear to be an act of weakness on Iraq's part. He stated that "the Iraqi leadership hoped that President Reagan's emphasis on U.S. national interests would lead him to develop good relations with the Arab world." Baghdad was unhappy with the Soviet Union due to its failure to fulfill Iraqi arms resupplies, Zahawi continued, and was looking to diversify Iraqi arms suppliers. Iraqi leaders were frustrated, however, by the United States' nearly yearlong refusal to grant an export license approving the sale of civilian Boeing aircraft (including 727s and 747s) to Iraq. A US export license was required since the United States listed Iraq as a state sponsor of terror. In veiled language, Zahawi was signaling that Iraq was interested in shifting away from Moscow and toward Washington, but it needed material support from the Reagan administration. While ultimately desiring arms, the Iraqis felt the sale of the civilian Boeing aircraft would be an important start in strengthening Iraqi-US relations. Eagleton duly reported this information to Haig.[43]

Haig favored the Boeing sale. He wrote to Reagan that King Hussein had argued, based on conversations with Saddam, that "the future course of U.S.-Iraqi relations will be strongly affected by our ultimate decision" on the sale. Furthermore, the failure of the United States to license the deal over the last year had contributed to decisions in Kuwait and Lebanon to turn to the European Airbus, and Saudi Arabia might follow suit. The US position in the global aircraft market, Haig argued, was at stake, as "U.S. aircraft companies may develop the reputation of being unreliable suppliers."[44] To further petrodollar ties with not only Iraq but also the larger Arab world, Haig pushed for granting the export license. Allen concurred, and Reagan approved the plan.[45] On April 1, Eagleton informed the Iraqis of the US approval of the sale, while indicating that "some improvement in the Iraqi position on [terrorism] had helped make it possible for us to move the license recommendation."[46]

Then, on June 7, Israel flew sixteen US-made warplanes over Saudi territory and into Iraq, bombing and destroying the Osiraq nuclear reactor. Israel then publicly justified the attack as necessary to prevent Iraq from acquiring a nuclear weapon. Iraqi foreign minister Sadun Hammadi insisted to Eagleton that "if the United States had wanted to restrain Israel . . . it could have done so. . . . Israel would not take such [an] action without consulting the United States."[47] The Reagan administration publicly and privately condemned the Israeli raid and maintained it had no foreknowledge of Israel's plan to attack Osiraq, but limited its response to suspending the transfer of four F-16s to Israel for two months.[48] Reagan privately assured Evron that "we did the minimum we could do under our law. . . . You should understand we are not reevaluating our relationship with Israel."[49]

Yet despite its anger at the Israeli raid and continued US assistance to Israel, Baghdad continued to seek better relations with the United States. Hammadi continued to reference to Eagleton "Iraq's willingness to improve relations."[50] Iraq's muted reaction to the Israeli raid indicated its rising fear of Iran. Iraqi forces were locked in a bloody stalemate, and time appeared to be on Iran's side as it mobilized its far larger population and economy for a war of attrition. The war had distinctly shifted Iraq's strategic calculus; rather than lead the charge against the US-led petrodollar order, Baghdad sought to integrate itself into the US system to shore up its capabilities against Iran.

Unlike Iraq, Iran did not reach out to improve relations with the incoming Reagan administration. Iran instead sought to achieve victory over Iraq without assistance from either of the superpowers. The Reagan administration's initial actions with Iran were similarly unfriendly. At the end of January, Haig affirmed that the United States would not grant export licenses for arms already purchased by Iran, thus denying the Iranians roughly $200 million of badly needed US arms and parts.[51] In April the Reagan administration launched an interagency group to study the future of US strategy toward Iran. US objectives focused on sustaining the uninterrupted flow of Persian Gulf oil to world markets, preventing Soviet dominance of Iran without reversing the Iraqi trend away from the USSR, maintaining a balance of power between the Arab states and Iran, and discouraging the export of the Iranian Revolution and terrorism to other countries. Like its predecessor, the Reagan administration particularly feared that the Islamic regime was leading Iran to the brink of civil war or total anarchy, creating conditions ripe for a Soviet-backed leftist takeover. The Reagan administration also held out hope, however, that the Islamic regime might stabilize and gradually become less hostile to the United States.[52]

In July, a senior interagency group had reached a broad consensus on Iran. It encouraged US support for a quick end to the Iran-Iraq War, both because it threatened Western access to Persian Gulf oil and because further Iranian setbacks could result in the collapse of the Iranian government and its replacement by leftists. To deter Soviet meddling in Iran, the United States should strictly warn the Soviets against such actions and increase the US military presence in the region. Iranian exile groups should not be supported unless they demonstrated credible support within Iran to challenge the current regime. To encourage the rise of moderates within the Iranian government, the United States should undertake an overt and covert propaganda campaign targeting the reputations of Iranian radicals while rewarding Iranian moderation with increased commercial ties. If there emerged a more stable Iranian government that sought a normalization of relations with the United States, the administration should pursue the proposal and offer a resumption of US arms sales to Iran pending the cessation of the Iran-Iraq War, thus incentivizing an end to the regional conflict and further blocking Soviet influence. Until the Iran-Iraq War ended, however, US arms should not be exported to Iran, either by the United States or by third parties. Left for further study was the issue of other nations' arms; State favored not opposing their export to Iran as the imbalance in arms was tilting in Iraq's favor and supplies by third countries could minimize Iran's reliance on direct Soviet arms sales, while the CIA and Defense argued that all arms transfers to Iran should be actively discouraged to induce Iran to accept mediation to end the war.[53]

At its outset, then, the Reagan administration viewed the Iran-Iraq War with trepidation, fearing it could cause another drop in the global oil supply and/or precipitate a leftist takeover of Iran. The Reagan administration thus sought an end to the conflict as early as possible. As part of this goal, and to more generally increase US influence in the region, the Reagan administration pursued better relations with Baghdad and aimed to cultivate moderates in Tehran. Much of the US strategy to curry Iranian and Iraqi favor relied on increasing their petrodollar ties with the United States. In the first few months of 1981, Iraq, concerned about its military position, also worked to increase these ties with the United States, while Iran, more confident about its long-term prospects, did not.

While the Reagan administration proceeded cautiously with Iran and tentatively improved relations with Iraq, it soon adopted an uncompromising posture toward Libya. A May NSC paper captured the Reagan administration's outlook on Libya, declaring the country "a major threat to U.S. interests throughout the Middle East/African region, and, in the broadest sense, to our concept of international order" due to Qaddafi's support for international terrorism, expansionist efforts in Chad, arrogation of the right to murder Libyan dissidents abroad, antagonism against Israel and Arab moderates, and suspected campaign to develop nuclear weapons.[54] With time, Qaddafi's confirmed and alleged actions took on immense personal significance for many in the Reagan administration, including Reagan himself. For these Reagan officials, the fact that Libya was a relatively weak state made it all the more necessary to demonstrate that the United States would not tolerate Qaddafi's challenges to US power, lest the Reagan administration appear lacking in resolve.

The Reagan administration's first overt action against Libya came on May 6 when it ordered the Libyan embassy in Washington closed, citing "a wide range of Libyan provocations and misconduct, including support for international terrorism."[55] Privately, Allen determined that "a policy is needed which will bring about a basic reorientation of those Libyan policies and attitudes which are harmful to our interests . . . [one which will] put Colonel Qadhafi on notice that the United States Government is now taking a new and more forceful approach."[56] On May 28 the NSC met to discuss further actions to take toward Libya. Allen set the tone with his opening statement that "it's fair to say that of all the many problems we face today none are more vexing than that posed by the unacceptable behavior of Libya's Qadhafi toward us and our allies." The meeting focused on Qaddafi's renewed efforts to claim international waters in the Gulf of Sidra as Libyan territory. To make good on his claim, Qaddafi had increasingly threatened or deployed force against foreign military ships and planes that entered the disputed waters. Haig and Weinberger proposed that a US fleet should enter the disputed zone in August as part of a training exercise to demonstrate that the United States would not accept Qaddafi's unilateral overturning of international law. "We should not be bluffed out of the Mediterranean by this madman," Haig declared.[57] Reagan approved the military exercise, as well as the launch of a media campaign to "focus world attention on Libyan misdeeds" a diplomatic campaign to persuade other countries to eliminate or cut back on their arms sales to Libya, an increase in assistance to countries threatened by Libya, and studies on how to prevent Libya from developing nuclear weapons.[58] On August 19 a squadron of Libyan fighters buzzed the US Sixth Fleet as it crossed the Gulf of Sidra; responding US fighters shot down two of the Libyan aircraft before the remainder withdrew.[59]

In the aftermath of the battle, the Reagan administration became increasingly convinced that Qaddafi was planning terrorist attacks against US citizens and interests. By September US intelligence believed there were credible reports that Qaddafi was even aiming to assassinate Reagan, leading the president to write in his diary that "it's a strange feeling to find there is a 'contract' out on yourself."[60] In October Haig sent a demarche to Libya claiming the United States had received reports that the Libyan government was planning to take actions against "U.S. persons, institutions and interests in Europe and elsewhere" and warned that Libya would be subjected to very serious consequences if it went through with these plans.[61] The Libyan government angrily denied the charges and challenged the United States to provide evidence for its claims.

Then, on October 6, Sadat was assassinated by four gunmen while reviewing a military parade celebrating the eighth anniversary of the Egyptian crossing of the Suez Canal during the 1973 war. Sadat's assassins belonged to a militant Islamist group called Islamic Jihad, which abhorred Sadat's secular dictatorship and its peace agreement with Israel. They had hoped to spark an Islamic revolution in Egypt with their act, but this failed to materialize, and Sadat was succeeded by Hosni Mubarak, who kept Egypt aligned with the United States and at peace with Israel. While no evidence has linked Qaddafi to the assassination, he did go on Libyan radio just hours after the attack to celebrate the demise of his adversary, declaring that "the sound of the bullets that resounded firmly and courageously in the face of as-Sadat this morning was in fact saying this is the punishment of those who betray the Arab nation." Reagan wrote in his diary that day that Qaddafi "is beneath contempt. He goes on radio (clandestine) and began broadcasting propaganda, calling for holy war etc. before Sadat's death was confirmed. This material had to have been already prepared. In other words, *he knew* it was going to happen." Whether Reagan persisted in his belief that Qaddafi was behind Sadat's murder is not clear, but his enduring animosity toward Qaddafi is apparent. In November additional US intelligence reports came in about alleged Libyan plots to assassinate Reagan or other top administration officials. Security was heightened, and Reagan even missed the funeral of Tex Thornton, founder of Litton Industries, due to concerns about a possible attack by a Libyan hit squad. On December 4 the *New York Times* broke a story about an alleged Libyan hit squad that had entered the United States to assassinate the president. On December 6 Qaddafi gave a live interview with ABC and forcefully denied the story. Later intelligence reports cast doubt whether Libya had ever actually targeted the president or other top officials, but many in the Reagan administration continued to reference the threat in the following months, and Reagan showed no evidence of discounting the original reports.[62]

On December 8 the NSC met to discuss Libya. Haig argued "business as usual was unacceptable no matter if Libya conducted a new terrorist incident or not" and pushed for economic sanctions. The NSC decided to further study this line of action and, as a preliminary step, have the US government call on US citizens and corporations in Libya to voluntarily leave the country and invalidated US passports for travel to Libya, thus minimizing the number of Americans Qaddafi could easily retaliate against. The Reagan administration also privately submitted a new demarche to Tripoli, making clear that it would consider a Libyan terrorist attack an act of war; Libya again responded with denials. The NSC also discussed the possibility of military strikes and seizing Libyan oil fields as US hostages if Libya took Americans hostage or launched a terrorist attack.[63]

By mid-January 1982, of the fifteen hundred Americans residing in Libya in December, only seven hundred remained, with three hundred expected to depart by the end of the month. Director of Central Intelligence William Casey, Haig, and Weinberger all continued to voice concern to Reagan about Qaddafi's capacity for terrorism.[64] There was interagency agreement that a unilateral US oil embargo against Libya would have little economic impact given the fungibility of oil but that it could serve as a powerful political signal to world leaders. State argued the administration should implement a US embargo on imports from and exports to Libya under the authority of the IEEPA to "remove the inconsistency between US political and economic policies toward Libya. Implementation of . . . [an] oil [import] embargo, an embargo of exports to Libya, and a ban on commercial transactions by U.S. firms within Libya will prevent continuation of the current cycle whereby U.S. oil income . . . translate[s] into Libyan income."[65]

Treasury, however, worried about the potential ramifications of a US embargo against Libya and the invocation of the IEEPA on Arab and other foreign investment in the United States. In December, Treasury secretary Donald Regan expressed concern that "the Saudis may get the wrong idea from U.S. economic action against Libya."[66] Regan argued that pursuing State's proposed course would likely provoke a Libyan reaction, including calling on standby letters of credit and expropriating US assets in Libya. In such a case, the United States' only recourse would be to block payments to Libya and freeze Libyan assets in the United States under the terms of the IEEPA. "The use of IEEPA will invoke the memory of the Iranian sanctions and asset freeze, and send a very troubling signal to world financial markets," Regan maintained. "We are still paying a heavy price for those measures—the growth of deposits in the United States by surplus countries has slowed considerably over the past two years. If we again interfere with financial flows for political purposes, we may experience a more permanent shift in financial resources away from U.S. institutions. The impact on Libya would be insignificant compared to the aggregate costs to U.S. interests that could result from such transfers by other countries, particularly the surplus OPEC countries." The perceived uncertainty of the US market would slow portfolio and direct investment in the United States and increase US borrowing costs via higher interests rates, which "would increase in particular the burden of U.S. debt. This is especially troubling in view of the crucial importance of increased investment to the success of our economic program." To avoid this danger, Regan proposed that the United States start with just an oil embargo against Libya, pursued under the Trade Expansion Act rather than the IEEPA. Additional economic measures could be employed later, Regan argued, but "for the present . . . because of the severe economic cost . . . I strongly recommend that we defer action on a unilateral embargo of U.S. exports to Libya."[67]

Reagan implemented a compromise between State's and Treasury's positions. On March 9 he signed National Security Directive Decision (NSDD) 27. The directive fulfilled State's desire for a ban on oil imports from Libya and implemented a general policy of denying licenses for export to Libya of goods and technology either related to oil and gas not readily available outside the United States or controlled for national security purposes. The directive acceded to Treasury, however, in not implementing a full embargo on US exports to Libya, and the administration invoked the Trade Expansion Act of 1962 rather than the IEEPA for its legal authority.[68] The limitations of NSDD 27 indicated that the US government remained concerned that its actions might scare off international, and particularly Saudi, investment in the United States—investment still viewed as critical to the US economy and government financing by Treasury. On the other hand, NSDD 27 further expanded the US government's efforts to diminish the oil revenues and restrict the petrodollar purchases of a MENA country, once again in large part pursued on the grounds of curbing state-sponsored terrorism.

Reagan reached the White House in large part due to Americans' frustration with rampant inflation, spikes in unemployment, and record-high oil prices. Yet his administration's initial policies on oil were similar to those of his predecessors. At the end of January 1981 Reagan decontrolled domestic oil prices and allocation by executive order, eight months ahead of the schedule implemented by the Carter administration but in keeping with its basic strategy.[69] Reagan also continued the general anti-inflation policies of the Carter administration, retaining Volcker and permitting him to tighten the money supply unhindered. Volcker pressed forward, bringing the targeted money supply to drop by 11 percent in May 1981, resulting in short-term interest rates jumping to an average of 16.3 percent that month.[70] Over the course of 1981 the tight money policy helped to bring the US inflation rate down from 11.8 percent to a still high 8.9 percent and strengthened the exchange rate value of the dollar, but it also caused an economic slowdown that contributed to a rise in the US unemployment rate from 7.5 to 8.5 percent.

The drop in inflation was assisted by a decline in the price of oil. In 1981 the average real price of benchmark crude oil fell by 12 percent from the record high of the previous year. At $35.93 a barrel, the average price of crude oil remained far more expensive than it was in the mid-1970s in both nominal and real terms. But the drop was evidence of important shifts in the global oil market. World demand for petroleum continued to decline due to significant improvements in energy efficiency, the rise of alternative energy sources, and a global economic contraction. The latter was spurred in part by high oil prices and in part by the strict anti-inflation efforts of the United States and other Western countries. At the same time, major new suppliers of non-OPEC oil were ramping up production in places such as Alaska, Mexico, and the North

Sea, and Saudi Arabia continued to produce oil at near-capacity. Iranian production also began to recover in spite of its ongoing war with Iraq. Analysts now spoke of an oil glut, and petroleum companies determined the risk of being cut off from adequate oil supplies was low while the cost of stockpiling had exceeded the likely profits of future sales. The combination of these factors precipitated the new downward trend in oil prices.[71]

For OPEC the problem of falling oil prices was compounded by a decline in market share as non-OPEC sources of oil developed in response to the 1973 shock came on line. In 1973 OPEC produced over half the world's oil, and as late as 1979 produced 46 percent of the world total. By 1981, however, OPEC production had declined to 37 percent and was surpassed in total output by the noncommunist, non-OPEC producers. In October 1981 Saudi Arabia and the other members of OPEC reached a compromise and reunified their pricing, with Saudi Arabia raising its price by two dollars and the other members lowering their price by two dollars to thirty-four dollars a barrel. As part of the deal, Saudi Arabia committed itself to a reduction in output, down to a maximum of 8.5 million barrels per day. Other producers continued to underbid OPEC, however, causing OPEC's decline in market share to continue. Worried about maintaining its pricing structure, OPEC decided to defend price at the expense of production. In March 1982 the members of OPEC agreed to limit their collective production to eighteen million barrels a day. Belatedly, OPEC recognized that high oil prices would not be maintained on their own volition.[72]

Iraq acutely felt even a slight decline in oil prices. This, coupled with Iranian bombings of Iraqi facilities, had caused Iraqi oil revenues to drop from $26 billion in 1980 to $10 billion in 1981. The Arab monarchies filled the gap; from September 1980 to the end of 1981, Iraq had received $10 billion in loans from Saudi Arabia, $6 billion from Kuwait, and $1 billion each from Qatar and the UAE.[73] Despite this assistance the Iraqi military suffered a series of setbacks starting in September 1981 with the Iranian liberation of Abadan and steadily abandoned additional Iranian territory.

In early 1982 Hammadi repeatedly pressed Eagleton on preventing US arms from being delivered to Iran, particularly from Israel. Eagleton assured Hammadi that Washington remained committed to barring US arms, including those from third parties, from being delivered to either Iran or Iraq.[74] On February 26 the Reagan administration removed Iraq from the list of countries formally regarded by the United States to be supporters of international terrorism under the 1979 Export Administration Act, lifting prohibitions on Iraq from receiving US government–financed export credits and restrictive controls on technology exports, some of which could have dual civilian-military uses. The administration maintained the decision had been made based on improvements in Iraqi behavior toward terrorism and a desire to encourage this behavior, but many observers believed it was intended to assist Iraq in the war against Iran.[75] Iraqi military setbacks continued, however. On May 23 Iran liberated Khorramshahr and captured over 12,000 Iraqi soldiers. From March to June the strength of the Iraqi military fell from 210,000 to 150,000 men and from 335 to about 100 combat planes.[76] In the days after the Iraqi defeat at Khorramshahr, Iraqi deputy prime minister Tariq Aziz took pains to communicate to Washington that Baghdad desired clear and regular consultation with the United States on the course of the war and any international peace initiatives.[77]

Israeli actions, meanwhile, were straining Saudi-US relations. In December 1981 the Israeli government formally annexed the Golan Heights territory it had militarily seized from Syria in 1967. Prince Fahd had planned to visit Washington in January 1982, but Yamani told Reagan that "after the Golan affair . . . [Fahd] feels that he has to remain in the Kingdom at this time. He is also afraid that if he comes [to the United States] without achieving anything, it would probably be better to have a delay." Yamani reaffirmed Saudi Arabia's desire for good relations with the United States but insisted that "Israel needs pressure from her friends."[78] When Weinberger visited Riyadh in February, Fahd told him "that US-Israel friendship need not compete with Arab states." Saudi Arabia, Fahd continued, "does not seek Israel's destruction, only its return to its 1967 boundaries . . . [something] even Arab confrontation states accept." Fahd warned, however, that "Israeli actions were driving more Arab states to look to USSR for help, even though none really liked communism."[79]

Saudi concerns were compounded on June 6 when Israel invaded Lebanon, still in the throes of civil war, in a campaign to remove the PLO from that country and facilitate the establishment of a friendly Lebanese government. The PLO fell back to West Beirut, and by mid-June the Israeli army had besieged the city and begun shelling PLO positions there. The Reagan administration initially supported Israel in its stated objective of clearing PLO missiles within forty kilometers of the Israeli border, but it balked at Israel's siege of an Arab capital, understanding its inflammatory impact on Arab popular opinion.[80] In the midst of the crisis, on June 12 King Khalid died and was succeeded by Fahd, who impressed on Washington the need for an end to the Israeli intervention in Lebanon.

On June 21 Reagan, reading directly from a pre-prepared speech, privately told Begin, who was visiting Washington, that "your actions in Lebanon have seriously undermined our relationships with those Arab governments whose cooperation is essential to protect the Middle East from external threats and to counter forces of Soviet-sponsored radicalism and Islamic fundamentalism now growing within the region. . . . I am determined to maintain our relationships with those Arab friends, particularly Saudi Arabia, Jordan, Oman, and, if possible, to improve them." Reagan stated that he sought to use the crisis as a launching point to revive the Arab-Israeli peace process and asked Begin to relax Israel's occupation policies in the West Bank to encourage Palestinian participation in negotiations. Reagan also insisted he would be providing military equipment to Saudi Arabia and Jordan, as he "believe[d] this strengthens Arab confidence in us, improves our strategic position, and encourages them to take risks for peace. I don't expect you to come out and approve this, but for heaven sakes, please don't oppose us. I want again to stress my commitment to maintain Israel's qualitative [military] edge. Our ultimate purpose is to create 'more Egypts' ready to make peace with Israel." Weinberger added that "the West would have a hard time surviving" if the Middle East oil fields were to fall into hostile hands and that the administration had been working to develop relationships with Arab countries to defend this vital resource, in part by supplying them with arms. Weinberger implied that Israeli resistance to such transfers had made the United States appear to be an unreliable arms supplier and thus weakened US ties with Arab allies. Reagan added that an Iranian victory in the Persian Gulf "could increase the threat to Israel ten times" due to the radicalism of Khomeini.[81]

Begin was unmoved by Reagan and Weinberger's arguments. He defended Israeli military actions as a defensive campaign against attacks conducted by an international PLO-Soviet terrorist network based in southern Lebanon. He argued that "Israel is surrounded by unprecedented stores of weapons" possessed by hostile states such as Iraq, Jordan, Libya, Saudi Arabia, and Syria. Jordan's increasingly close ties with Iraq were especially troublesome. Begin maintained that "the U.S. should not arm the Arabs. [Israel's] qualitative and quantitative edge is eroding. The Arabs have unprecedented wealth. Jews are not rich. Israel would go bankrupt trying to keep up with the Arab world." Perhaps as a means to counter the notion of Khomeini as a unique threat, Begin charged that "Saudi Arabia [is] one of the most fanatical, Islamic fundamentalist states in the world that is striving to destroy Israel . . . even though they talk of their anti-Soviet attitude, their money, nonetheless, goes to Moscow to pay for Arab arms."[82] Whereas the Reagan administration argued US arms sales to Arab countries would establish the trust needed to move the Arab-Israeli peace process forward, Begin cast Arab petrodollars and Arab arms, whether Soviet or US, as an existential threat to Israel.

As the Israeli army laid siege to Beirut, the Iraqi army withdrew from Iran. On June 9 Baghdad issued a statement that it was ready for a cease-fire and withdrawal to the international border, but Khomeini insisted on the overthrow of Saddam. Baghdad then ordered a unilateral Iraqi military withdrawal from Iran. Moscow and Washington, seeking to prevent an Iranian invasion of Iraq, secured a UN Security Council resolution on July 12 calling for a cease-fire. The next day Iran began an offensive into Iraqi territory, focusing on the populous city of Basra. In the marshes around Basra 130,000 soldiers engaged in the largest infantry battle since World War II. After two weeks of fighting, the Iraqis reversed the Iranian advance, but not all the way to the border.[83]

The Reagan administration watched the Iranian assault on Iraq with concern. The United States had continued to pursue a policy of neutrality in the Iran-Iraq War. Furthermore, it had pressured its Arab allies to refrain from joining the war on Iraq's behalf to avoid an expansion of the conflict that could endanger the Arab Peninsula kingdoms and the flow of oil from the Persian Gulf. The Reagan administration's stance of neutrality emanated from its desire to avoid increasing Soviet influence in either Iran or Iraq. The Arab kingdoms had placed a greater emphasis on balancing the power of both Iran and Iraq with the other to ensure neither could dominate them. With Iranian troops threatening Basra, the Arab kingdoms were increasingly concerned that Iran might succeed in installing an allied Khomeinist state in Iraq, leaving them vulnerable to the combined power of an Iran-Iraq alliance that would aim at overthrowing them. Sharing this concern, the Reagan administration initiated a senior interagency group to study whether the United States should begin to favor Iraq in the conflict by providing it with US arms, either directly or through third parties. The senior interagency group determined that the Iraqis were in fact "well-equipped with material" from other countries and did not need new arms supplies so much as better military training and leadership. The group concluded "that while an Iranian victory over Iraq was not in the U.S. interest, there was little that any outsider could do to offset the training and leadership weaknesses of the Iraqi forces. . . . The established U.S. posture of neutrality toward the conflict should be maintained." The Reagan administration appeared to have determined that if US arms sales to Iraq would have little effect on the military balance, the prospect for eventually establishing relations with Iranian moderates should not be risked. Washington recognized the Arab kingdoms would not be pleased with this position, but hoped it could convince them that the US military presence in the region would be sufficient to deter Iran from threatening them while an end to the Iran-Iraq War was pursued.[84]

In Lebanon the United States worked to negotiate a diplomatic solution to the war. George Shultz, who left Bechtel to replace Haig as secretary of state on July 16, endeavored to achieve the withdrawal of Israeli, PLO, and Syrian forces from Lebanon; the maintenance and strengthening of the government in Lebanon to the point that it could maintain order within its boundaries; and the resumption of the Arab-Israeli peace process with an aim of granting the Palestinians autonomy in the West Bank as part of Jordan. The United States successfully evacuated the PLO army in Beirut to Tunisia in late August. In September, however, the Lebanese president-elect Bashir Gemayel, a Christian militia leader backed by Israel, was assassinated. Israel, claiming a need to restore order, had its army occupy Beirut. Then, on September 16, the Israeli military facilitated a massacre of at least eight hundred Palestinian civilians in the refugee camps of Sabra and Shatila by Gemayel's militia; Israel's forces allowed the militia's soldiers to enter the camps, took no action to halt the killings, and launched illuminating flares in the night sky as the murders stretched out over two days.[85]

At Yasser Arafat's request, the Arab League held an emergency meeting a week later to address the tragedy. Placing ultimate responsibility for the carnage on Washington, the PLO called for the Arab states to cut oil production, withdraw their investments in the United States, and freeze all US economic agreements. Yet while the other Arab ministers declared that the United States bore "moral responsibility" for the massacre, they did not endorse any sanctions against it.[86] The lack of a united Arab response against the United States to the Israeli invasion of Lebanon and assaults on the Palestinians stood in marked contrast to the 1973 war and embargo. Petrodollar-linked transformations of US empire set the conditions for such a different Arab response in 1982 compared with 1973. As the Nixon administration had hoped, petrodollar ties had deeply enmeshed the economic and military well-being of Saudi Arabia with the US economy and political system, significantly raising the cost of an open break. Petrodollars had supported Egypt's separate peace with Israel and incorporation within US empire, undercutting both Egyptian and Soviet challenges to US policy toward Israel. Most importantly, the armies and ideology of the Islamic Republic of Iran, ironic outcomes of US petrodollar ties with the shah's regime, actively threatened the regimes of Iraq and the Arab monarchies, leaving them unwilling to seriously challenge Washington and risk losing desperately needed US assistance.

The Reagan administration persisted in its efforts to end the crisis in Lebanon, and in response to the Sabra and Shatila massacres it successfully pressured Israel to withdraw its army from Beirut and placed US Marines in the city as part of an international peacekeeping force. The deployment stabilized the immediate situation, but US diplomatic efforts to secure further Israeli or Syrian military withdrawals from Lebanon or achieve a resolution to the civil war there stalled.

The summer of 1982 also witnessed the onset of an economic crisis in much of the Third World, as the debt accumulated by many LDCs hit a breaking point. Most LDC loans were denominated in US dollars and set to floating interest rates either partially or entirely determined by US interest rates. The high interest rates pursued by Volcker dramatically increased the interest LDCs had to pay on their loans. At the same time, the worldwide drop in inflation assisted by the policies of Volcker and other Western countries meant the real inflation rate of LDC loans was even higher. The global recession depressed demand for LDC exports, decreasing the revenues and hard currency they needed to pay the interest on their debts. Western banks finally determined they could no longer risk extending additional loans to many LDCs. A debt crisis had already occurred in Poland the year prior. Then, in August 1982, Mexico, which had risen to the ninth-largest economy in the world the year prior, admitted to the US government that it could no longer service its loans. This set off a panic in the banking community, and new lending to LDCs was rapidly curtailed. By the end of the year, Argentina, Brazil, and Mexico were renegotiating their collective nearly $200 billion in private debts, which were owed primarily to US banks. The sums at risk of default posed a threat to the entire US banking system; Citibank's dollar exposure in Brazil alone by 1981 equaled 83 percent of its entire capital. From 1981 to 1985 over forty LDCs renegotiated their debt schedules. Most of the LDCs were in Africa and Latin America; they also included the Philippines and the communist nations of Poland, Romania, and Yugoslavia. Renegotiations also occurred with the OPEC members of Ecuador, Nigeria, and Venezuela. No oil-rich MENA countries renegotiated, but the oil-poor MENA countries of Mauritania, Morocco, Somalia, and Sudan did.[87]

Recognizing the threat large-scale defaults posed to the US and international banking systems, the Reagan administration, the IMF, and private banks collaborated to extend new loans and assistance to deeply indebted LDCs so that they could resume the repayments of their previous loans and restore economic growth and thus eventually repay the loans independently. The IMF conditioned new public and private loans to the deeply indebted LDCs on their implementation of austerity programs and the dismantling of protectionist trade laws. Desperate for capital, the deeply indebted LDCs reluctantly committed to these neoliberal policies.[88]

The members of OPEC were no longer a major source of aid or new deposits in Western banks to be recycled to LDCs. In 1982 net OPEC deposits in BIS reporting banks declined by $18.2 billion; the following year a net decrease of $13 billion occurred.[89] Saudi holdings of Treasury securities also declined (though the US government continued to finance its debt from other foreign sources attracted by high US interest rates, particularly Japan and West Germany in the 1980s and in later decades China; thus while petrodollars played an increasingly minor role in funding the US government, the model they provided persisted).[90] This was a result of the steady erosion of world oil prices, which fell by 14 percent in 1982 and then 13 percent in 1983, as well as a decline in OPEC's production and market share. Rising non–OPEC production and declining global consumption continued to undermine OPEC's strength. From 1980 to 1983 OPEC's revenues dropped from $275 billion to $154 billion. At the same time, the expenses of maintaining new industries, expanded bureaucracies, and general levels of consumption, and in some cases foreign loan repayments and wars as well, continued to grow. Algeria and Iraq took on increasing levels of debt to make up petrodollar shortfalls. Saudi Arabia began to draw down its capital reserves in order to cover expenses that had ballooned over the course of the previous decade. In March 1983 OPEC reluctantly lowered its official price from thirty-four to twenty-nine dollars a barrel. Saudi Arabia formally agreed to serve as a swing producer, raising or lowering its oil exports as required to maintain the OPEC price. Desperate for revenue, however, the other members of OPEC regularly sold their oil below the agreed price and beyond the volume of their allotted quotas.[91] As oil revenues dropped, the hopes for the NIEO further dimmed; even petrodollar recycling to LDCs through Western banks would remain relatively small for the remainder of the decade.

At the end of 1982 the state of the US and other OECD economies was mixed. Volcker's policies had hindered economic growth and shot the US unemployment rate to 10.8 percent, but they had also helped bring the US inflation rate down to 3.8 percent and reestablished a strong dollar. With inflation seemingly under control, the Reagan administration hoped to now shift toward addressing economic growth and unemployment. The NSC feared that an escalation of conflicts in the Middle East might still cause a significant drop in world oil supply and undercut Washington's anti-inflation and pro-growth efforts, however, and in March 1983 issued NSDD 87 to outline steps to prevent this outcome. They were in part a summation of the strategy of petrodollar interdependence pursued since the Nixon administration: "develop and maintain positive political, economic and security relations with key producing countries

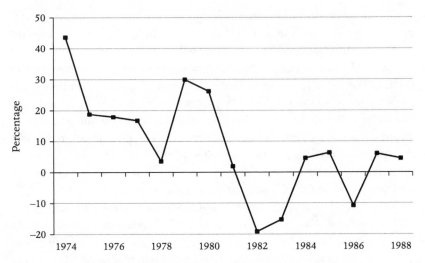

Figure 14. New OPEC deposits as percentage of new international loans by BIS reporting banks, 1974–1988. Source: Bank for International Settlements, *Annual Report*, various years.

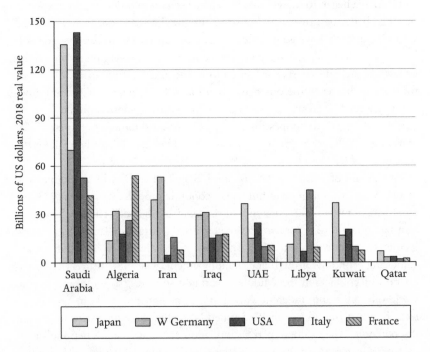

Figure 15. Exports to MENA members of OPEC, 1979–1988. Source: IMF, Direction of Trade Statistics.

to demonstrate that their interests are not served by oil supply disruptions, to develop economic relations that reinforce the production and exchange of oil, manufactured goods and financial assets." They were also an affirmation of Kissinger's peace process diplomacy and the Carter Doctrine, calling for the United States to "advance the peace process between Israel and the Arab states" and to "deter Soviet, Soviet proxy, or other radical interventions in the Persian Gulf."[92] The Reagan administration would attempt to do both as it confronted ongoing conflicts in Lebanon and at the Iran-Iraq border.

Over the course of 1983, as the Iraqi position continued to weaken, the Reagan administration began to move away from its position of neutrality in the war. During the second half of 1982 and throughout 1983, Iran launched a relentless series of ground invasions into Iraq. While the Iraqi military successfully kept the Iranian army on the fringes of Iraqi territory, the assaults drained Iraq of badly needed manpower and resources. Seeking to offset Iran's attacks on land and capitalize on Iraq's advantage in airpower, in August 1982 Saddam declared the northern end of the Persian Gulf a "maritime exclusion zone" and began subjecting Iranian ports and all merchant vessels to airstrikes. Saddam gained additional support after the death of Brezhnev on November 10. Brezhnev's successor, Yuri Andropov, abandoned the fruitless effort to gain influence in Iran and swung Soviet support firmly behind Iraq, ending Warsaw Pact arms deliveries to Iran and releasing large quantities of arms to Iraq, including one hundred-forty MiG-23 and Su-22 fighters and hundreds of T-72 tanks. Yet even with increased Soviet assistance, in 1983 the Iraqis only hit eight merchant ships bound for Iran and caused limited damage to Iranian ports, in part due to the success of Iranian F-14s in repelling Iraqi assaults.[93] Despite the limited efficacy of Iraqi attacks, the Reagan administration increasingly feared that they would lead Iran to retaliate by militarily closing off the Strait of Hormuz to international shipping and preventing Arab oil exports from leaving the Persian Gulf. Such an act would drastically cut into the world supply and drive oil prices back up after three years of steady decline, and could draw the United States into the Iran-Iraq War. On September 3, 1983, responding to Iraqi warnings that it would increase its attacks in the Persian Gulf, Shultz privately requested increased aid to Iraq from Kuwait, Qatar, Saudi Arabia, and the UAE as a means of assuaging Baghdad's fears and dissuading it from feeling forced to undertake such attacks. Shultz likewise impressed on Baghdad that it risked losing "international support if it provokes Iranian measures to close the Gulf."[94]

Later in the month, Shultz submitted a memo to Reagan. "Up to now, our dominant concern in the Iran-Iraq war has been to avoid pushing Iran toward the Soviet Union," Shultz wrote. The increasing desperation of the Iraqis, the threat of an expanded war cutting off the region's flow of oil, and the failure of the Soviets to make inroads with Iran, however, meant that "it may be time . . . to modify our posture of strict neutrality in that war." Without elaborating what they might be, Shultz suggested that "there may be additional steps we could take, political or economic, to help strengthen Iraq in its struggle with Iran."[95] As Iraq's military position weakened, support within the Reagan administration for a tilt toward Iraq strengthened.

Then, on October 23 at the US barracks in Beirut a suicide bomber detonated a truck laden with explosives, killing two hundred-forty-one Marines, the deadliest single day for the US military since the Vietnam War. The United States had failed to resolve the Lebanese conflict the year before, and due to its support for the Christian-dominated government in Beirut, many Lebanese militias, some backed by Iran and Syria, viewed the United States as favoring the Lebanese Christian right at their expense. Americans in Lebanon had increasingly come under attack by some of these militias, and the Reagan administration suspected Iran was responsible. Reagan and his cabinet presumed the barracks bombing was likewise planned by Iran, a belief bolstered by US intelligence reporting.[96] The Reagan administration did not opt for a direct strike against Iran, however, but instead implemented scattered military actions against Lebanese militias in the following months, acts that would lead to clashes with the Syrian air force resulting in two downed Navy jet fighters, before withdrawing all US forces from Lebanon in February 1984, and with them any serious hope that the United States would end the civil war there.[97] The larger aim of resolving the Arab-Israeli conflict to which the US intervention had been linked likewise fell to the wayside for the remainder of Reagan's presidency. Washington, as well as the Arab monarchies, determined that the most pressing issue in the MENA was the growing threat of Iran, and accepted an entrenched Israel and ongoing war in Lebanon as undesirable but permissible costs, despite the rising power in Lebanon of the Islamist Shia militia Hezbollah, a group that openly fought Israel and was accused of perpetrating attacks on Americans, displayed distinctly Khomeinist rhetoric, and had murky material ties with the Iranian state.[98] Anger over the Beirut barracks bombing would, however, contribute to the growing desire within the Reagan administration to support Iraq's war against Iran.

In its first three years the Reagan administration had reaffirmed Washington's petrodollar ties with Saudi Arabia and modestly improved its relations with Iraq. Meanwhile, shifts in the global economy, in part as a result of Reagan's decisions but largely emanating from policies predating his administration or emanating from other countries, led to a decline in the price of oil and key parts of the petrodollar economy, particularly the role of the OECs as major providers of deposits for international banking and the collapse of noncondi-tional private lending to LDCs. The Reagan administration also took new steps to diminish petrodollar ties between Libya and the United States and its allies. Yet the Iran-Iraq War continued to threaten the global oil market, and the Reagan administration's hostility toward Iran grew as it came to blame attacks on Americans in Lebanon as being Iranian inspired. In late 1983 the Reagan administration began taking greater direct action in supporting the Iraqi war against Iran.

Chapter 10

End of an Era

Abdelrahman Munif was born in 1933 in Amman to an Iraqi mother and a Saudi father. Munif spent part of his teenage years in Saudi Arabia, listening to the stories of Bedouins, oil traders, and emirs. Inspired by the ideals of Arab nationalism and outraged by the oppression of the Western powers and their local client regimes, in the early 1950s Munif joined the Iraqi Baath Party and in 1961 earned a doctorate degree in oil economics in Yugoslavia. Munif would be expelled from Iraq by the Hashemite monarchy in 1955 for opposing British influence over the country and stripped of his citizenship by the Saudi monarchy in 1963 for criticizing the regime in Riyadh. Munif hoped, however, that in the hands of republicans, petrodollars would improve Arab societies. He worked as an economist in the Syrian oil industry from 1961 to 1973 and then moved to Lebanon to begin a prolific career as a journalist on the oil industry and novelist on Arab society. As Lebanon descended into civil war, Munif returned to Iraq and served as editor in chief of *Oil and Development* magazine. Coming to understand the tyranny of Saddam Hussein, however, Munif resigned from the Baath Party and in 1981 left Iraq for France, where he wrote *The Wasteland (al-Tih)*, the first novel in an eventual quintet, *Cities of Salt*.[1]

Published in 1984, *The Wasteland* was immediately hailed as a classic in Arab literature, despite being banned in Saudi Arabia and several other Arab states. The events of the novel take place in a fictional Arab emirate and explore the wrenching transformations to the local preindustrial societies that occur when US oilmen first arrive and begin operations. The Eden-like Wadi al-Uyoun, "an outpouring of green amid the harsh, obdurate desert," is destroyed root and branch by never-before-seen machines as the Americans set up their oil drilling site, displacing the local Bedouins. The sleepy coastal village of Harran is likewise bulldozed to construct a modern port and pipeline for the oil industry, where Arab laborers find themselves increasingly controlled and abused by the Americans. The book explores at length how the Americans control the local population through the subordinate emir and other Arab functionaries, whom they buy off with a share of oil revenues and technological novelties like radios and automobiles. The emirate's rulers thereby become disconnected from the concerns of their people, and increasingly use force to uphold the new order. This trend climaxes when a local physician publicly denounces the emirate's leadership, warning the people of Harran that "money has corrupted many before you. It has corrupted nations and kingdoms. Money enslaves, it subjugates, but it never brings happiness." In response, the emirate's leaders arrest, torture, and kill the physician. At the book's conclusion, Munif reminds the reader through the words of another character, a religious leader, that the emirate's rulers are not the ultimate cause of the physician's death and all the other recent injustices: "I told you all before," the religious leader pronounces. "The Americans are the source of the illness and the root of the problem."[2]

While the events of the novel evoke the experience of the Arabian Peninsula in the 1930s and 1940s, Munif's attitude toward the effects of petrodollar wealth lay firmly rooted in the perspective of the 1980s. For secular Arab nationalists, Iranian Islamists, and Arab monarchists alike, the 1980s proved to be a decade of bitter disappointments, as petrodollar revenues were squandered in destructive wars and then became severely curtailed by a bottoming out of world oil prices. The optimism of the early 1970s within the Arab world and Iran had largely turned into anxiety or despair by the time the petrodollar era came to an end in the mid-1980s.

Conversely, for the United States the 1980s largely concluded as a decade of triumph, as many of the woes of the 1970s, including high oil prices, an Arab oil embargo, and the threat of revolutionary Iran, were largely contained, while US political and economic dominance over the Arab world rose to new levels and the Soviet empire endured global setbacks and then began to disintegrate. Yet in this moment of success, the US empire also sowed the seeds of resentments and future tragedies, including in Afghanistan, site of one of the clear Islamist victories of the decade, where some mujahedin began to strategize on how to roll back US imperialism in the Arab world. Ultimately, while the US-led petrodollar order stabilized aspects of US empire, it also enlarged realms of global instability that threatened the United States.

In late 1983 the Reagan administration began to increasingly tilt US support toward Iraq in the war against Iran. The Reagan administration's growing anger toward Iran in the aftermath of the Beirut barracks bombing was accompanied by rising fear that the Iraqis might in desperation escalate their attacks on Gulf shipping and thereby cause a cutoff of exports and another spike in world oil prices due to their mounting losses of troops and territory on the ground. In November 1983 the NSC prepared a report estimating that a complete closure of the Persian Gulf to oil tankers could decrease US GDP by 10 percent and raise unemployment by 4 percent, and have even more deleterious effects on the economies of US allies.[3] In December the White House sent Donald Rumsfeld, now CEO of the pharmaceutical company G. D. Searle, as a special envoy to Baghdad to discuss bilateral concerns. And on January 23, 1984, the US government added Iran to its list of nations that support international terrorism, subjecting it to US export sanctions on arms and dual-use materials.

In late February 1984 Iranian forces captured the southern Iraqi oil fields on the Majnoon Islands, site of one-sixth of Iraqi oil reserves. The Iraqis counterattacked, but by mid-March they conceded the loss, and a new stalemate began. As the battle raged, the NSC issued a paper determining that in order to "deter [an] escalation that could threaten U.S. interests in unimpeded access to Gulf oil and the security of the Gulf oil producer states," the United States would "take steps to help Iraq avoid defeat . . . [by] pursuing various means of helping Iraq redress the strategic balance." Such measures included the "export of non-military items to Iraq which may have military utility" and strengthening Iraq's economy with Export-Import Bank lending and support for new international pipelines to Iraq.[4] Washington proceeded to provide hundreds of millions of dollars of financing for Iraq and to sell easily militarized civilian aircraft, including six Lockheed L-100 Hercules transport planes, delivered in 1985, and eighty-six Hughes helicopters, deliveries beginning in 1986, though the Reagan administration declined to send Iraq substantial amounts of US arms due to opposition in Congress toward the fiercely anti-Israel regime in Baghdad. The United States also threatened economic retaliation against any country that sold arms to Iran, which proved significant in raising Iranian costs. Iraq could now rely on the USSR, France, and China to supply 85 percent of its military needs at regular prices and on the Arab monarchies to help finance its bills. Iran, however, reliably received open arms sales only from Syria, Libya, China, and North Korea, which provided only a third of Iranian military needs. Because of the threat of US sanctions, Iran had to obtain most of its arms on the black market, which increased the cost, a problem compounded by the fact that Iran lacked major foreign lenders.[5]

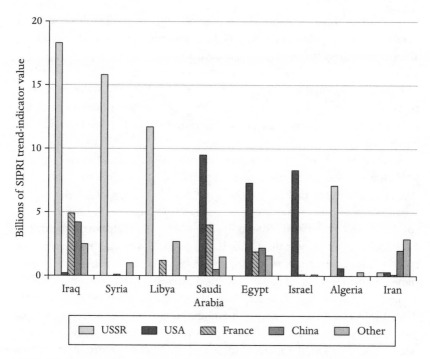

Figure 16. Arms transfers to largest MENA recipients, 1979–1988. Source: SIPRI, Arms Transfers Database.

The Reagan administration did not pursue major US arms sales to Iraq, because doing so could result in congressional opposition, undercut US international efforts to prevent arms from being sold to Iran, and complicate efforts to protect nonbelligerent shipping and normalizing ties with a post-Khomeini Iran.[6] In May the Reagan administration did, however, discreetly encourage Egypt and France to "enhance their training and operational advice" to the Iraqi military, the area the US government had determined Iraq most needed.[7] Even before this request, the French had sent a large number of military advisers and trainers to assist Iraqis in the use of advanced French arms, particularly Étendard jet fighters.[8] The Egyptians likewise already had around fifteen thousand "volunteers" serving in the Iraqi army by mid-1983, as well as additional military instructors training Iraqi soldiers. From 1981 to 1983 the Egyptians had also sold Iraq $2.7 billion worth of weapons.[9]

Meanwhile, stymied on the ground, Saddam continued to employ the strategy that the Reagan administration had hoped to prevent: using the Iraqi air force to attack vessels transporting Iranian oil in the Persian Gulf in an effort to cut off Iran's supply of petrodollars. In April Iraqi fighters hit three tankers, and six more in May. In early May the Iranians retaliated, not against Iraqi shipping, since that had ceased, but against Kuwaiti and Saudi tankers, with the intention of forcing the Arab monarchs to pressure Iraq to abandon its assaults on Iranian shipping. Riyadh instead declared a no-fly zone over much of the waters of the Gulf, raising the possibility of fighter clashes between Iran and Saudi Arabia.[10]

Back in March the Reagan administration had announced its intention to sell Raytheon Stinger shoulder-fired, anti-aircraft missiles to Jordan and Saudi Arabia but canceled this plan in the same month because of vocal congressional opposition over the risk of the weapons falling into the hands of terrorist groups, the latter a key talking point of the Israeli government. On May 23, eager to support the Saudis in the standoff with the Iranian air force and thereby protect the flow of Arab oil from the Gulf, the Reagan administration informed Congress of its renewed interest in selling twelve hundred Stinger missiles to Riyadh in response to an urgent request from King Fahd. The White House also raised the possibility that it might use a special legal provision that allowed the president to authorize an emergency transfer of arms deemed necessary to the national interest without the opportunity for Congress to vote on the sale. One week later the Reagan administration announced that it had sent four hundred Stingers to Saudi Arabia on such emergency authority, expressing in a statement its "grave concern with the growing escalation in the gulf . . . [that] could threaten Saudi Arabia and oil supplies on which much of the free world depends."[11]

Many congresspeople did not accept the Reagan administration's justifications for the emergency transfer, however, and expressed outrage. Republican senator from Wisconsin Bob Kasten argued the sale made a mockery of Congress' consultative role, and several Democratic and Republican senators again raised the possibility that the Stingers might come into the possession of terrorists.[12] Then, on June 5, two Saudi McDonnell Douglas F-15s intercepted two Iranian McDonnell Douglas F-4s on course to strike two Saudi tankers. Firing Raytheon Sparrow air-to-air missiles, the Saudi F-15s destroyed one Iranian F-4 and damaged the other, forcing it to retreat. In response, the Iranians launched twelve additional F-4s and six Grumman F-14s toward the Arabian Peninsula, which the Saudis met with twelve more F-15s and ten Northrop F-5s. In the course of an hour, the forty fighters, all made-in-the-USA, maneuvered against each other without firing, until the Iranian planes ran short of fuel and returned to base.[13] Rather than celebrate the Saudi victory, however, many US congresspeople attacked the arms-petrodollar complex. "Ex-clusively American weapons on both sides of the dogfight raise questions about fueling an arms race in the region," Democratic representative from Califor-nia Mel Levine said. "It's a constantly rising lake of arms," lamented Repub-lican senator from South Dakota Larry Pressler, who called for a freeze on all weapon supplies to the Middle East.[14]

The Saudis had demonstrated, however, that they could successfully counter Iranian air attacks with US-purchased fighters, validating supporters of US arms sales to the kingdom. The Saudi victory, coupled with Iran's limited sup-ply of fighters, forced the Iranian air force to take a cautious approach. As a result, a year after April 1984, Iran had hit only twenty-five ships, while Iraq had hit sixty-five.[15] Yet despite the merchant losses, oil prices continued to drop as tankers continued to trade in the Persian Gulf and oil markets remained confident that world oil supplies would continue to exceed demand.

On September 24, 1984, Tariq Aziz approached Shultz about resuming Iraqi-US relations. Shultz favored the proposal, arguing it would counter claims that US influence in the Middle East was threatened by new Soviet inroads, demonstrate that Israeli-US cooperation was not a barrier to improved US re-lations with hardline Arab states, demonstrate to Iran and Syria that violent opposition to US interests could stimulate US cooperation with their adver-saries, and improve the climate for possible Jordanian negotiations with Israel.[16] On October 3 Shultz informed Aziz that Reagan had accepted the proposal and would meet with him after the US presidential election. Aziz, pleased, stated that "Iraq greatly appreciated the 'highly constructive' U.S. efforts since last year to curb the flow of arms to Iran."[17] Reagan easily won reelection on November 6 against Walter Mondale, buoyed by a steady decline in the un-employment rate to 7.2 percent that month while keeping the inflation rate at the relatively low level of 4.1 percent, both achieved in part by declining oil prices. Twenty days later the resumption of Iraqi-US relations was announced.

In 1985 the bloody stalemate in southern Iraq continued. The Iraqi cam-paign of economic attrition persisted as well. Periodic Iraqi airstrikes against Iran's under-construction nuclear power plant at Bushehr delayed the already slow progress of the plant and by the end of the war caused over $4 billion in damages.[18] The Iraqis also continued their air attacks on Iran-bound tankers as well as the major Iranian oil terminal at Kharg, but achieved only a marginal impact on Iran's exports. Iran's attacks on tankers were even smaller in num-ber, and avoided Saudi fighters. The relatively low level of damage to oil ex-ports meant the war remained incidental to global oil prices, which continued to decline.

The year 1985 also witnessed a growing stalemate between the Reagan administration and Congress on arms sales. In 1983 the Supreme Court ruled as unconstitutional the legislation that enabled Congress to veto an arms sale with a simple majority of both houses; instead, Congress had to pass legislation to block a sale, which in turn could be overridden by the executive, and overturned only by a two-thirds vote in both houses of Congress, a significantly higher threshold. Yet despite this ruling, in January the Reagan administration was forced to delay a new sale of F-15s to Saudi Arabia, instead submitting the issue to a comprehensive review of the connection between arms transfers and regional peace, as it was not sure it had even one-third of Congress willing to back the sale, with congresspeople vocally raising their concern that the fighters might be used against Israel and their frustration that Saudi Arabia refused to recognize Israel before it returned to its pre-1967 boundaries.[19] With a US offer not forthcoming by that summer and not desiring a possibly bruising struggle with pro-Israeli lobbyists, Riyadh decided to purchase forty-eight British Tornado fighters instead, the first major Saudi purchase of non-US arms since the 1960s.[20] Saudi influence in Washington since 1981 had waned alongside its declining revenues.

As Congress' open hostility toward Riyadh grew, collaboration between the White House and the House of Saud increased in funding mutual allies. Over the course of the Iran-Iraq War, Saudi Arabia provided upward of $60 billion in loans to Baghdad, critical to Iraq's ability to hold off the Iranian military.[21] Saudi Arabia likewise continued to provide critical sums of aid and migrant jobs to North Yemen as a way of countering South Yemen and to Sudan as a counter to Ethiopia and Libya.[22] In addition to the aid of allied states, the Reagan administration looked to Riyadh for an unprecedented degree of covert support to military insurgencies in Nicaragua and Afghanistan.

In 1979 the leftist Sandinistas, fighting on a platform of democracy, national sovereignty, and assistance to the poor, overthrew the right-wing dictatorship of Anastasio Somoza in Nicaragua. Right-wing militants, dubbed the Contras, organized to resist the new Sandinista government and began to receive assistance from Washington under the Reagan administration. The Contras became a cause célèbre in the United States, with conservatives championing them as freedom fighters challenging Soviet influence in the Western Hemisphere and liberals becoming increasingly vocal in their condemnations of the Contras' widespread and systematic use of rape, torture, kidnapping, and thousands of summary executions against civilians as a means of terrorizing Nicaraguan supporters of the Sandinistas.[23] In December 1983 Congress forced a cap on funding to the Contras at $24 million, far less than the Reagan administration had wanted. To make up the difference, the White House secretly approached other countries for funds, starting with Israel. The Israelis declined, although they would later provide arms captured from the PLO. In May 1984, however, US national security advisor Robert McFarlane secured from Saudi ambassador Prince Bandar bin Sultan a pledge of $1 million a month from Riyadh for the Contras. Bandar told McFarlane "the donation signified King Fahd's gratitude for past Reagan administration support for the Saudi government."[24]

In October 1984, however, Reagan signed an omnibus budget appropriations resolution passed by Congress that included the second Boland Amendment, which stated that for FY 1985 (October 1984 to September 1985) no "agency or entity of the United States involved in intelligence activities" may expend funds in order to directly or indirectly support "military or paramilitary operations in Nicaragua by any nation, group, organization, movement, or individual." Despite the new law, NSC assistant Lieutenant Colonel Oliver North, with the direction of McFarlane, continued to arm the Contras. North secretly coordinated with a company controlled by former US Air Force general Richard Secord and Iranian-born businessman Albert Hakim, originally named Stanford Technology Trading Group International but later titled "the

Figure 17. Ronald Reagan and King Fahd at the White House, February 11, 1985. Courtesy of Ronald Reagan Presidential Library.

Enterprise," to sell arms to the Contras. The Enterprise disguised the sources and recipients of its funds by erecting numerous dummy corporations and bank accounts via a Swiss fiduciary. The funds for the arms sales overwhelmingly came from Saudi Arabia; of the $40 million that the Reagan administration fund-raised for the Contras during the period that the second Boland amendment was in effect, $32 million came from Riyadh. Indeed, while future developments would lead to a series of scandals popularly called Iran-Contra, in terms of illegal funding for the Nicaraguan rebels, the scandal could more accurately be called Saudi-Contra.[25]

Reagan was aware of the Saudi contributions to the Contras, and he made it clear to McFarlane that he wanted the Contras kept together "body and soul," regardless of US law.[26] By secretly overseeing arms sales to the Contras, McFarlane and North violated the express will of Congress and pursued foreign policy outside of the law, and Saudi petrodollars served as a primary funding source that made this circumvention possible. The result was the prolongation of a conflict that resulted in the deaths of thirty thousand Nicaraguan civilians, overwhelmingly caused by the Contras, until a negotiated settlement between Nicaraguan parties was achieved in the aftermath of the Cold War in 1990.[27]

In contrast to the Contras, Congress was widely supportive of funding the mujahedin in Afghanistan. By the end of 1983, the CIA estimated the Soviets had suffered 17,000 casualties and lost an estimated 350 to 400 aircraft and 2,750 tanks and armored carriers. Riyadh and Washington had each spent $200 million on the war to that point; the Soviets had spent $12 billion.[28] Yet despite increasingly brutal tactics, including escalated carpet bombings intentionally aimed at depopulating regions outside of their control and the laying of hundreds of thousands of land mines, the Soviets failed to hold the Afghan countryside, and certainly did not win Afghan support. Soviet efforts to improve the effectiveness of the Afghan government fared no better. The regime in Kabul remained massively unpopular, and by the mid-1980s its ineffective army had shrunk from ninety thousand to thirty thousand troops, mostly due to desertions.[29]

In part spurred by the lobbying of Democratic representative from Texas Charlie Wilson, in 1984 Congress raised US funding for the mujahedin for FY 1985 to $250 million, which was faithfully matched by Riyadh. In part due to the increase in funds, in part at the encouragement of Casey, on March 27, 1985, Reagan issued NSDD 166, which for the first time explicitly made it the policy of the US government to force the Soviets out of Afghanistan. Mikhail Gorbachev, who had assumed leadership of the Soviet Union eighteen days earlier, initially escalated the Soviet military campaign in Afghanistan but quickly determined he wanted Soviet forces out as well. That October Gorbachev told Babrak Karmal that the Soviet Union would soon withdraw its troops from Afghanistan and that he needed to broaden the base of his regime by including some mujahedin leaders if he hoped to see his government survive. Saudi Arabia and the United States kept up the pressure, raising aid to the mujahedin to $470 million each for FY 1986 and $630 million each for FY 1987. The United States also began to supply the mujahedin with Stinger missiles, which they began to use in September 1986 against Soviet helicopters to devastating effect. Unbeknownst to the US government, in November 1986 Gorbachev declared to the Politburo that Soviet troops should fully withdraw from Afghanistan within two years. That same month, Moscow replaced Karmal with another communist official, Muhammad Najibullah, as the leader of Afghanistan, hoping he could better achieve national stability. In December Gorbachev warned Najibullah to prepare for a withdrawal of Soviet forces within two years.[30]

Meanwhile, the Arab mujahedin in Afghanistan was expanding. In 1984 Osama bin Laden, a militant Saudi Islamist with considerable wealth from his family's construction business, which received large sums of petrodollars from Riyadh-hired projects, began collaborating with Abdullah Azzam, a Palestinian Islamist theologian and leading advocate for violent jihad against non-Muslim rule in Islamic lands. While Azzam considered liberating Palestine from Israeli-US domination as the Muslim world's most important goal, he considered the war against the Soviets as the most promising for near-term success and the development of jihadist forces that could later be deployed elsewhere. Bin Laden used his petrodollar wealth to recruit and pay the expenses of Arab volunteers to join the mujahedin and used his construction business to help build infrastructure for the Afghan resistance. The CIA considered bin Laden an effective and valuable ally in the Afghan war, though there is no clear evidence it had a working relationship or even direct contact with him. The war in Afghanistan provided bin Laden and other Arab mujahedin firsthand knowledge of asymmetrical warfare, radicalized the political outlook of its members toward favoring violence against foreigners and local collaborators who facilitated non-Muslim control or influence over the Islamic world, and created new points of contact and networks for organization. In 1986 Ayman al-Zawahiri, a militant Egyptian Islamist, settled in Pakistan to organize a global jihad with the hope of ending the Western-aligned dictatorship in Cairo. The next year Zawahiri and bin Laden would meet in Pakistan and begin collaborating.[31]

The high level of Saudi assistance around the world was all the more re-markable because Saudi oil revenues had declined from \$113.2 billion in 1981 to \$43.7 billion in 1984. The loss of Saudi revenues was partly due to the grad-ual decline in the price of oil but was primarily due to the steep decline in Saudi oil exports. By mid-1985 Saudi oil production was only a little more than a fifth of what it had been five years earlier. The drop in Saudi produc-tion was the key factor in bringing OPEC's market share of global oil pro-duction down to below 28 percent that year. The Saudis had steadily decreased oil production as part of the OPEC effort to shore up prices. Despite repeated warnings, however, the other members of OPEC continued to break their commitments, selling oil under the OPEC price and beyond the OPEC quo-tas to expand their own market shares. By unilaterally depressing its oil out-put, Saudi Arabia was propping up the value of the oil sold by the other members of OPEC, and of non–OPEC OECs, at its own expense. By the summer of 1985, the Saudi Kingdom determined it needed to reassert its authority within OPEC. Saudi Arabia abandoned its defense of the OPEC price and focused instead on increasing Saudi market share by ramping up production and selling exports at low prices aimed at undercutting competitors. Confronted by Saudi actions, other oil producers around the world quickly followed suit to defend their own market shares.[32]

The result was an oil shock in reverse; from late 1985 to early 1986 bench-mark oil prices fell by 70 percent, and some Gulf oil sold below \$7 a barrel. In 1986 the value of OPEC's petroleum exports dropped 42 percent from the previous year, falling below that of 1974 even before accounting for inflation, and would remain low for the remainder of the decade.[33] The decline in pet-rodollars meant new OPEC deposits to the international banking system remained marginal and oil-rich Arab trade with the United States and other countries dropped considerably. In 1982 the value of US exports to the oil-rich MENA countries peaked at \$13.6 billion; in 1986 they fell to \$6 billion and remained relatively low for the remainder of the decade.[34] The petrodol-lar era had come to an end.

While specific companies with deep ties to petrodollars or oil may have been harmed, the US economy as a whole benefited from the drop in petroleum prices, helping to bring the 1986 annual inflation rate down to 1.9 percent and leaving more money for other types of consumer spending. Combined with US policies of high interest rates, debt-fueled military spending, and tax cuts, the US economy also experienced high rates of GDP growth and a gradual reduction in unemployment during the mid-1980s. While many Americans voiced concern about deindustrialization, poverty-stricken communities, and stagnating wages, high petroleum prices no longer factored as a grievance. Most of the other OECD countries followed the US model of high interest rates and debt-fueled economic stimulus, with similar results. And while some in the MDCs raised concerns about rising government deficits or stagnating social services, few of its citizens would have traded the economic optimism of the mid-1980s for the malaise of the 1970s. The USSR, by contrast, suffered greatly from the drop in oil prices. The Soviet Union had increasingly relied on petroleum revenues to shore up its inefficient and technologically behind economy. The global oil price free fall caused Soviet hard currency earnings to be roughly halved, severely constraining Gorbachev's capacity to acquire foreign technology needed to modernize the Soviet economy or to fund the Soviet military and foreign aid programs.[35]

During the spring of 1985, Casey and McFarlane became increasingly preoccupied with restoring US influence in Iran. In early May McFarlane sent an NSC consultant, Michael Ledeen, to Israel to sound out Prime Minister Shimon Peres about the prospects of establishing contacts with moderate Iranian officials, with the hope of establishing working ties with these groups that could facilitate the ascension of a more pro-US leadership in the Iranian government after the death of Khomeini. That same month an intelligence estimate requested by Casey repeated warnings that the Soviets might increase their influence in Iran and suggested measures to counter this threat, including the lifting of US arms restrictions. Casey pushed for the adoption of these findings as an NSDD, which McFarlane had drafted in June, but Shultz and Weinberger opposed the draft NSDD. In July, however, Israeli officials informed Ledeen and McFarlane that they had a contact, Iranian businessman Manucher Ghorbanifar, with ties to moderates within the Iranian government seeking a renewed political dialogue between Iran and the United States. These Iranians proposed to use their influence with Lebanese groups that had abducted seven Americans, including CIA operative William Buckley, and obtain the hostages' release as an initial show of good faith. In return, these Iranians expected a reciprocal show of good faith in the US sale of Hughes TOW anti-tank missiles to Iran. The Israelis proposed to serve as an intermediary; Israel would sell some of their TOW missiles to Iran, and the United States would replenish the Israeli missile stocks.[36]

The proposal had appeal to factions in both the Israeli and US governments. Many Israeli strategists considered Iraq to be a more dangerous threat to Israel's security than Iran and thus sought to support the Iranian war effort to weaken the Iraqis. Supporting Iran likewise fit into a more general Israeli strategy of promoting an alliance among non-Arab states on the perimeter of the Arab world as a counterweight to Arab power. Casey and McFarlane were intrigued with the possibilities of restoring a friendlier government in Iran and securing the release of US hostages, notions strengthened by a July meeting between Ledeen and Ghorbanifar in which the latter claimed that moderates within the Iranian government were seeking an improvement in relations with the United States. Reagan's interest in the proposal focused on the release of the hostages. In contrast, Shultz and Weinberger were strongly opposed to the scheme. They discounted the claim that there were significant Iranian moderates residing within Iran's government, and they argued that the plan contradicted US efforts under Operation Staunch to weaken Iran's military offensive by denying it access to arms, could incentivize new hostage-taking efforts against Americans, and if revealed would harm US credibility around the world and particularly with Iraq. In August, however, Reagan authorized McFarlane to tell the Israeli government to proceed. On August 20 Israel delivered ninety-six TOW missiles to Iran. The Reagan administration did not report the transfer to Congress. In doing so, the Reagan administration violated the Arms Export Control Act twice over, as it forbade countries with US arms from transferring them to third parties if the United States could not legally transfer weapons to the third party itself (as was the case for Iran) and in all cases required notification of Congress.[37]

The NSC's program of transferring US arms to Iran grew in the following months and would continue when Admiral John Poindexter succeeded McFarlane as national security advisor in December 1985. From August 1985 to October 1986, the Reagan administration authorized eight transfers of US arms to Iran, both through Israeli intermediaries and directly through the CIA. The Reagan administration did not notify Congress about any of these transfers, thus repeatedly violating the Arms Export Control Act and the National Security Act. Reagan was directly involved in the arms sales to Iran; he authorized the sales, was briefed on the completion of transfers, signed a retroactive presidential finding for the initial arms transfers, wrote about activities in his diary, and explicitly told his administration not to report the arms transfers to Congress despite warnings from Shultz and Weinberger that this would violate US law. In total, from August 1985 to October 1986 the Reagan administration directly and indirectly transferred to Iran 2,004 TOW missiles, 18 Hawk missiles, and multiple pallets of Hawk missile spare parts.[38] TOW missiles proved to be particularly valuable in the Iranian conquest of the al-Faw peninsula in Southern Iraq in February 1986, a costly setback for Baghdad. Spare parts and missiles for Cobras enabled the Iranians to deploy thirty of the helicopters in July, which proved critical in recovering the Iranian city of Mehran from Iraqi forces.[39]

These actions marked the first resumption of the Iran-US petrodollars-arms complex since the 1979 Iranian hostage crisis. Despite being on a far smaller scale, US arms sales to the Islamic Republic shared a similar logic to those made to the shah's monarchy: improve relations with Iran and ensure a government friendly to US interests ruled there. Reagan and many of his staff hoped that the arms sales would secure the release of US hostages in Lebanon and a pledge from Iran that it and its allies abroad would foreswear the hostage taking of Americans in the future. Furthermore, some members of the CIA and NSC believed the arms sales could strengthen Iranian moderates within the government and military of the Islamic Republic, who at some point could seize power and restore relations and a working relationship with the United States. In short, some within the Reagan administration aimed to undo the effects of the Iranian Revolution with arms transfers to Iran.

Selling arms to Iran ultimately failed on both the issue of hostages and improved relations. Three US hostages were freed during the period of illegal arms sales, and during the same time pro-Iranian militias in Lebanon took two more Americans hostage and announced that William Buckley had died (the United States later determined Buckley had been tortured to death in June 1985). The Reagan administration repeatedly sent envoys to meet with alleged high-level Iranian moderates, including a secret mission to Tehran in May 1986 headed by McFarlane and North, but they were never received by top-level officials; even with lower-level officials, no framework for cooperation beyond the arms-for-hostages cycle was achieved. It is probable that the top level of Iran's leadership, including Khomeini, was aware of the secret US arms deals and managed them from a distance.[40] Yet with each setback, the Reagan administration recommitted itself to the arms transfer strategy, in part out of hope that the situation would improve with a new delivery, and in part out of fear that a cessation of shipments would lead the angered Iranians to order the murders of US hostages. The Reagan administration's effort had backfired; instead of establishing the basis for an Iran-US rapprochement and the end of hostage taking by Iran's proxies, the United States had strengthened Khomeini's military and demonstrated that taking Americans hostage under Reagan's watch paid off handsomely.

US arms sales to Iran would prove profitable to a separate campaign of the Reagan administration, however. When the CIA opted for direct arms transfers to Iran over the use of Israel as an intermediary, it chose the Enterprise, the corporate front it was already using to arm the Nicaraguan Contras, as the vehicle for the arms sales to Iran. By this point North now oversaw the operation details of the Contra aid program and the Iran arms sale program. Meeting with Ghorbanifar in January 1986, North learned the Iranians were willing to pay $10,000 for each TOW missile, whereas it cost North only $3,700 to purchase one from the US government. North realized the Enterprise could secretly sell the missiles to Iran at a profit and then apply the earnings to arming the Contras, and he proceeded to do just that. In the end, roughly $4 million generated from arms sales to Iran went to funding the Contras. When combined with Saudi Arabia's donations of $32 million, 90 percent of the roughly $40 million raised by the Reagan administration to illegally arm the Contras came from the two key petrodollar states of the MENA.[41]

While the Reagan administration continued its covert operations against the Sandinistas in 1986, it also launched new overt operations against Qaddafi. After imposing sanctions on Libya in March 1982, the Reagan administration's efforts at isolating Tripoli drifted. The failure of European allies to join in sanctions confounded the United States' effort to cause significant economic costs to Libya and created divisions within the administration on how to proceed. Defense, the NSC, and State sought additional unilateral US export controls on Libya as a signal of US displeasure with Qaddafi's policies. Commerce, the Trade Representative, and Treasury argued such a policy would have no impact on Libya's economy or policies and only harm US businesses at the expense of European rivals, and insisted that the United States instead focus on gaining European participation in sanctions, a development State felt was unlikely to occur.[42] With his cabinet at an impasse and European partners unwilling to restrict their trade with Libya, Reagan undertook no new sanctions against Libya for four years.

The Reagan administration, particularly Shultz, continued to have its eye on Libya, however. During a meeting on March 30, 1984, for example, Shultz told Reagan that they needed to get tough on governments that sponsored terrorists in order to reassure US allies like the Arab monarchies that Washington had the will to defend its interests after the US retreat from Lebanon. The administration "should almost seek an opportunity to do something against terrorism," Shultz argued. "We need to send a signal that we can do something about it. Need to look for an opportunity especially against Libya."[43]

Then, on December 27, 1985, seven members of the radical Palestinian splinter group Abu Nidal launched simultaneous terrorist attacks at El Al airline ticket counters at airports in Rome and Vienna, targeting anyone in the vicinity with machine gun fire and grenade explosions. Sixteen civilians were killed, including five Americans. The Reagan administration suspected the Libyan government had supported the attack, in part because Abu Nidal enjoyed safe haven in Libya. Qaddafi admitted no role in the assault, but he publicly praised Abu Nidal's actions and continued to allow the group to operate in Libya.[44] On January 8, 1986, Reagan, citing the airport attacks, declared that "the policies and actions in support of terrorism by the Government of Libya constitute an unusual and extraordinary threat to the national security and foreign policy of the United States" and ordered a total ban on US trade with Libya with the exception of humanitarian assistance, a stringent prohibition on Americans traveling to Libya, and a ban on new US loans to any Libyan national or entity. Reagan also redoubled his effort to persuade US allies to join in sanctions against Libya.[45] Once again, terrorism had led the US government to pursue a curtailment of petrodollar ties between the United States and a MENA petrodollar power. European allies only proved willing to ban the sale of arms to Libya, however, so the US sanctions continued to have minimal impact on the Libyan economy.

The Reagan administration further increased its pressure on Qaddafi by planning for another naval exercise in the contested Gulf of Sidra in March. US intelligence was fairly confident the Libyan military would take hostile action against US forces in response. Shultz argued that Libyan hostilities should trigger US attacks on military targets, terrorist camps, and industrial sites in Libya. "We should be ready to undertake action to hurt [Qaddafi], not just fire back," Shultz insisted. "Our forces should plaster him and military targets." Weinberger argued for greater restraint, contending that if they "end up leveling Tripoli, we will be accused of being non-proportional." Reagan opted for a middle route, ordering that "if hostile actions occur or appear imminent, we will attack the air bases where the planes or SAMs came from, whether they fire or not. If there are losses to the U.S., the Commander [of the US fleet] has the right to choose non-military targets." This was an escalation in the rules of engagement from the 1981 US naval exercise, in which US forces only attacked the Libyan forces engaged in hostile actions. On March 24 US naval forces entered the Gulf of Sidra and within two hours were unsuccessfully fired upon by a Libyan missile battery at Sirte. This initiated a series of skirmishes between US and Libyan forces. Two Libyan missile patrol boats were destroyed and the missile battery at Sirte was put out of action; the United States suffered no losses.[46]

Less than two weeks later, on April 5, a bomb exploded at a West Berlin discotheque frequented by US servicemen, killing two as well as a Turkish civilian. Within hours, Western intelligence agencies linked the terrorist attack to Libyan agents operating out of the Libyan embassy in East Berlin. In response, on April 15 the US Air Force and Navy launched aerial assaults targeting Libyan military and paramilitary targets, as well as Qaddafi himself, in and around Tripoli and Benghazi. Qaddafi survived the attack, though nearly one hundred Libyans did not; the United States lost one General Dynamics F-111 Aardvark fighter-bomber and its two crew members. The Reagan presidency would conclude without further overt Libyan-US hostilities; but Qaddafi would direct the December 1988 Lockerbie bombing that killed 270 people, including 180 Americans, though Libya's hand in the attack would initially be concealed.[47]

The escalating tensions between Libya and the United States unexpectedly intersected with a new Reagan initiative to sell arms to Saudi Arabia. In March 1986, the White House submitted the sale of $350 million worth of missiles, including Stingers, to Congress, arguing Iranian advances made the deal necessary to the kingdom's security. While Reagan had desired to offer a far larger arms package including F-15s and M1 tanks, he cut these items when more than two-thirds of the Senate informally expressed their opposition.[48] Even the greatly reduced proposal faced strong congressional resistance, however, led by Democratic senator from California Alan Cranston. In the aftermath of the Berlin bombing and US strikes on Libya, Cranston argued that with the United States engaged in "an undeclared war on terrorism," selling arms to Saudi Arabia would send the wrong message since the Saudis funded the PLO and Syria, both of which had supported groups that had participated in terrorism.[49]

On May 6 the Senate voted to block the sale, 73 to 22; the next day the House followed suit, 356 to 62. It was the first time Congress had ever voted down a foreign arms sale, and it was done with a veto-proof margin, a remarkable setback for Saudi influence in the United States. Many congresspeople cited Saudi Arabia's condemnation of the US strikes on Libya and its past financial support for Tripoli as a reason they voted against the sale.[50] Many lawmakers were also concerned that a vote appearing to hurt Israel would be unpopular with many American voters. But a final, petroleum-related reason also contributed to the lopsided vote tally. Congressional animosities toward Saudi Arabia may have been muted when the United States depended on the Arab world for oil, Democratic representative from Wisconsin Les Aspen told one reporter. But now, "the pressure is off. . . . There is less fear of the consequences of voting down the sale."[51]

Reagan vetoed the bill, but hoping to peel away some senators in order to avoid the veto being overturned, he removed the Stingers from the sale. As the measure returned to Congress, supporters of the deal emphasized the danger to US and Israeli interests if Iraqi or Saudi petrodollars fell into the hands of Khomeini's allies. "Iran is beginning to win its war-to-the-death with Iraq," warned one op-ed in the *New York Times*. "If the Ayatollah Ruhollah Khomeini's fanatical legions defeat Iraq, the road to Tel Aviv could run through Riyadh. . . . If a Khomeinitte regime came to power in Riyadh and focused Saudi Arabia's vast wealth on destroying Israel . . . the very survival of Israel would be in serious doubt."[52] Reagan warned Republican legislators that "this vote will have a profound effect upon our relations with the Arab world, not just Saudi Arabia."[53] On June 5 the Senate failed to override Reagan's veto by a single vote, sixty-six to thirty-four. The eight senators that switched their votes cited the removal of the Stingers and a desire to support Reagan's credibility as a mediator in the Middle East as their rationales. Despite the failure of the veto override, opponents of the sale could still claim a significant victory. "They got 10 percent of what they wanted," Cranston argued, noting the administration had had to cut not just the Stingers but F-15s and M1 tanks from the package as well. Conversely, Reagan's supporters, such as Senator Richard Lugar, maintained that the vote had preserved the prestige of the president in international affairs, a symbolic victory of even greater weight than the sale itself.[54] Four months later, the prestige of the president and his relationship with Congress would be thrown into even greater tumult due to revelations about two different arms deals involving Saudi and Iranian petrodollars.

On October 5, 1986, the Nicaraguan military shot down an Enterprise plane carrying arms for the Contras. One crew member, an American named Eugene Hasenfus, survived and was captured by the Sandinistas. Two days later, the Nicaraguans placed Hasenfus before the international media, where he stated that the Enterprise was working covertly for the CIA to arm the Contras. The Reagan administration publicly denied the claims. Later that month, however, Iranian officials fiercely opposed to cooperation with the United States began leaking details of the US arms-for-hostages deals with Iran and the secret visit of US officials to Tehran earlier that year. On November 3 the Lebanese magazine *al-Shiraa* published the disclosures, and the story was immediately headline news across the world. The next day Iranian officials publicly confirmed the general outlines of the news and revealed McFarlane's visit to Tehran.[55] At first, Reagan publicly denied that the United States had paid any ransom for the hostages, but the press continued to investigate, and the administration could not keep its story straight. Attorney General Edwin Meese launched an inquiry but failed to prevent North from illegally shredding thousands of documents related to the Contra and Iran operations. The Justice Department's investigators did discover at the NSC's offices an undestroyed file outlining the diversion of funds from Iran to the Contras, however. Meese informed Reagan of the finding, and on November 25 Reagan broke the news of the diversion, claimed to have just learned of it, and accepted Poindexter's resignation as national security advisor. The revelation increased public skepticism that Reagan was telling the truth, prompted Congress to begin its own investigations, and raised speculation that Reagan might be removed from office.[56] In the month after news of the scandal broke, a *New York Times* / CBS News poll found Americans' overall approval rating for Reagan plummeted from 67 percent to 46 percent.[57]

Many scholars have rightly argued that Reagan acted in an unconstitutional manner for multiple years during the Contra and Iran schemes. Reagan willfully contravened the laws passed by Congress, and in doing so violated the Constitution's fundamental system of checks and balances and instead attempted to secretly make the executive branch the sole entity conducting US foreign policy. Such a blatant and sustained effort to illegally flout Congress and the Constitution were strong grounds for impeachment and removal from office.[58] What has been understated, however, is that MENA petrodollars were critical in enabling the Reagan administration to conduct its unconstitutional foreign policies in the first place. Saudi oil wealth provided the overwhelming majority of the initial funds for the Contras secured after the Boland amendments, and the arms sales to Iran were both paid for by petrodollars and spurred by a war shaped by the two-decade-long petrodollars-arms complex. Soon, the Iranian funds were laundered to the Contras, intertwining two petrodollar schemes into one. Iran-Contra stands as one of the most significant examples of how the White House used MENA petrodollars to subvert US democracy.

Despite this, and the fact that Democrats controlled both the House and the Senate starting in January 1987, Reagan avoided impeachment. In December 1986, Reagan appointed the President's Special Review Board, composed of former Republican senator from Texas John Tower, former Democratic senator from Maine Edmund Muskie, and Brent Scowcroft, to investigate the Iran-Contra scandal with the hope of limiting the scope of investigations and produce a favorable report. When the board released its findings at the end of February, it concluded that Reagan appeared to have been negligent in his oversight of the NSC, but thereby not aware of its illegal activities. Reagan capitalized on popular assumptions about his hands-off management style, making it easier for him to disclaim responsibility for programs in which he had in fact been deeply involved. Congress held televised hearings of Reagan administration officials from May to August, which made public a wealth of new evidence demonstrating that Reagan had in fact directed the Contra and Iran schemes, if not the diversion between the two. The majority opinion of both congressional committees was that "it was the President's policy—not an isolated decision by North or Poindexter—to sell arms secretly to Iran and to maintain the Contras 'body and soul.'"[59] Despite such a determination, however, Congress did not initiate impeachment proceedings, largely due to perceived political self-interest. Democrats remained wary of directly attacking the still popular Reagan, who benefited from a strong economy and the fact that he would soon be leaving office at the end of his second term regardless. At the same time, many Republicans, including those in Congress, spun responsibility for Iran-Contra back onto Democrats due to their resistance to Reagan's foreign policy initiatives. North exemplified this tactic during his congressional testimony, where he successfully presented himself to television audiences as an honorable soldier following the higher values of national defense and presidential authority against the weak-willed and self-interested Democrats of Congress. Caught off guard by the popular outcry of support for North during his hearings, Democratic leaders calculated that attempting to remove Reagan was unlikely to succeed and may well rebound in Republicans' political favor. Democrats thus dropped the idea of impeachment and settled for publicly censuring Reagan, a decision that, while perhaps politically prudent, ceded considerable congressional authority to the executive branch.

On the international level, the revelations of the two White House schemes ended both the Enterprise operation and US negotiations with Tehran on American hostages and arms sales. The damage had already been done to US credibility in the Arab world, however. The revelation of US arms sales to Iran particularly incensed Saddam, as did Reagan's public explanations that they were part of an effort to improve Iranian-US relations. "Reagan said that we [Americans] are getting closer to Iran through weapons," Saddam opined during a meeting of the Iraqi Revolutionary Council in November 1986. "A nation like Iran needs weapons more when it is at war. So therefore, how many more years does Reagan need the war to continue so that he can get close to achieving the goals he has set and the influence he wants to get in Iran?" The United States and the Zionists, Saddam concluded, would seek to indefinitely prolong hostilities between Iran and Iraq, for in this way they could increase their influence over not only Iran but the other Arab Gulf states as well. US leaders "want to continue dealing with Iranians with some measure of flexibility, and they want Iraq to continue dealing with them with a measure of flexibility at the expense of our principles," Saddam groused. "They are scaring the Gulf countries so they can get privileges. . . . Their goal is to bring the danger [of Iran] closer to the Gulf states so they get even more from them."[60] For Saddam, the US arms sales to Iran strongly reaffirmed that he should not trust Washington and should consider the United States only as an opportunistic adversary. Despite this, Saddam continued to seek the Reagan administration's assistance, knowing that his regime could ill afford to reject any aid against the advancing Iranian army.

The revelations had a similar impact on the Arab monarchies; they were dismayed by the Reagan administration's actions, but reluctantly determined they had no alternative but to continue to press Washington for renewed support in the face of the enduring threat from Iran. At a national security meeting on February 12, 1987, Deputy Director of the CIA Robert Gates stated "the U.S. is in better shape than it might appear. . . . [Arab] moderates are closer together, due to fear [of Iran], and doing reasonably well. There are some doubts about the U.S. over arms sales to Iran but the moderate Arabs are still with us." Treasury Secretary James Baker said he "had been pleased with his [recent] trip to Saudi Arabia and his talks with Crown Prince Abdullah and others. They had accepted and appreciated [Reagan's] reassurances and said they, as friends, would stand behind the U.S. Basically, although scared about Iran and disappointed in us, they are still with us." For his part, Reagan sought to reassure and protect his Arab allies in the Gulf by intensifying US pressure against Iran. Reagan emphasized that the United States needed "to help Iraq in order to block Iranian and radical Shia expansionism." He rationalized the previous outreach to Iran as seeking "to bring victory to neither side" and "to end the war peacefully." But now, Reagan reiterated, "we need to help Iraq."[61] Ironically, the ultimate outcome of the illegal sale of arms to Iran, justified as part of a campaign to improve relations with Iranian leaders, would ultimately lead to the United States undertaking an increase in support for Iraq that would further poison Iranian-US relations for years to come.

By the end of 1986, both Iran and Iraq suffered from exhaustion due to the war. The attrition dealt by the numerically superior Iranian forces had increasingly taken its toll on Iraqi manpower, threatening a collapse of the Iraqi defensive lines. At the same time, Iraqi air assaults on Iranian oil exports and the drop in global oil prices had lowered Iran's GDP close to Iraq's, despite Iran having a population three times that of Iraq, putting the Islamic Republic in great economic danger.[62] Nor was an increase in petrodollars for Iran on the horizon. In December 1986 most of the members of OPEC, including Iran, accepted Saudi demands for adherence to smaller export quotas and prices pegged around eighteen dollars a barrel. Only Iraq refused to adhere to the quota system. Overall, however, in 1987 the members of OPEC demonstrated a new level of commitment to its pledges, for while the agreement meant relatively low profits, they feared even lower revenues if they continued their destructive undercutting of each other.[63]

Hoping a decisive victory would lead to an Iraqi Shia revolt and Saddam's overthrow, Iran launched a massive assault on Basra on December 24, 1986. In the next four months, forty thousand Iranians and ten thousand Iraqis perished. By mid-April, the Iranian assault succumbed to exhaustion. A Kurdish-Iranian offensive in Northern Iraq had likewise been halted.[64] Stalemated on the ground, both Iran and Iraq escalated attacks on rival tankers in the hopes of diminishing the other's finances. The Iraqi air assaults continued to effectively reduce Iranian oil exports, but on May 17, one Iraqi fighter attacked the US frigate *Stark* in an apparent case of mistaken identity. The attack killed thirty-seven crew members. Saddam immediately apologized for the incident and agreed to compensate the victims, but many in Congress seized on the incident as evidence that US support for Iraq in the Iran-Iraq War was ill advised, and some even suggested Saddam had intentionally struck the *Stark* as revenge for arming Iran.[65]

The attack on the *Stark* also contributed to congressional opposition to a new arms package for Saudi Arabia proposed by the Reagan administration in June, which included twelve F-15s, sixteen hundred Maverick missiles, and electronic upgrading equipment for F-15s and M60 tanks. Congress blanched at the proposal, as many believed Saudi F-15s had declined a US air controller's request to intercept the Iraqi fighter that attacked the *Stark*. The White House insisted the Saudis had followed protocol, but withdrew the package regardless. Reagan resubmitted the package in September, but Congress quickly obtained near-veto-proof signatures opposing the deal on the grounds that Saudi Arabia should not be rewarded for its continued support for the PLO and lack of cooperation with the United States on the Middle East and Gulf conflicts. The administration insisted the Saudis had cooperated closely with the United States on the mutual defense of the Gulf, but ultimately removed the Maverick missiles in order to secure the sale's passage that October.[66] Once again, the reduced supply of Saudi petrodollars mirrored the reduced clout of the Saudis on Capitol Hill.

Meanwhile, Iran focused its tanker attacks on Kuwait, increasingly through the mining of Kuwaiti sea lanes, hoping to induce Kuwaiti emir Jaber al-Ahmad al-Sabah to end his support for Saddam. Jaber instead turned to Washington for protection. The Reagan administration obliged, in May ordering the US

Navy to conduct minesweeping operations in the Gulf and in July commencing the reflagging of Kuwaiti tankers as American and providing them with US naval escorts. Reagan also increased the US naval presence in the region to fifty warships, including two aircraft carriers. An escalating cycle of confrontation resulted in numerous clashes between the US Navy and Iranian forces, with the Americans maintaining supremacy. These culminated in a major air and sea battle on April 18, 1988, in which the US Navy sank several Iranian ships and destroyed two Iranian offshore platforms while only losing one helicopter. That same day, Iraqi forces, benefiting from a larger flow of arms than its increasingly insolvent foe, successfully liberated the al-Faw peninsula in a lopsided victory over demoralized Iranian forces.

Tehran still refused a cease-fire, however. On April 27, Riyadh made the next move, severing relations with Iran in an effort to further isolate the ayatollahs and force them to the negotiating table. Two days later, Reagan increased the pressure on Iran even further, announcing the US Navy would now protect any neutral ship, not just US flagged ones, from Iranian attack. At the same time, the Iraqi military utilized its superior strength in fighters, tanks, and artillery, as well as chemical weapons, to continue its liberation of Iraqi territory. On June 28, Iraq liberated the Majnoon Islands. Then, on July 3, the US cruiser *Vincennes* accidently shot down a civilian Iranian passenger plane, killing all 290 people on board. While Reagan expressed remorse for the loss of life, some have claimed top Iranian officials believed the attack had been intentional, designed to convey the lengths the United States was willing to go to end the war. On July 12, Iraqi forces began an invasion into Iranian territory, seizing the city of Dehloran. With Iraqi forces advancing into Iran and the United States aggressively positioned off Iranian shores, Khomeini finally conceded that to safeguard his revolution he would have to postpone his goal of removing Saddam from power.

On July 20, Khomeini gave a speech before the international press. He began defiantly, contrasting his revolutionary Islam against the pseudo-Islam of his opponents. He condemned the Saudi rulers as "American stooges" who, in spreading Wahhabism around the world, promoted "the Islam of money and force . . . [of] the capitalists over the oppressed and the barefooted, and in a single word, 'American Islam.'" Iran, by contrast, was "in pursuit of desiccating the rotten roots of Zionism, capitalism and communism in the world." Khomeini then addressed the issue of accepting a cease-fire with Iraq. He asserted that if a cease-fire was necessary to defend the cause of true Islam, even honor should be sacrificed. "At the present moment, I consider acceptance of the [UN cease-fire] resolution as a move in the interest of the revolution,"

Khomeini pronounced. "Acceptance of this matter is more lethal for me than poison. Yet, I am pleased with the pleasure of God and for His pleasure I drank this beverage."[67] On August 20 the cease-fire between Iran and Iraq went into effect, their prewar borders restored. For this outcome, estimates show Iran and Iraq collectively lost an estimated 700,000 lives, suffered 1.8 million wounded, and forfeited $1.1 trillion.[68]

By 1988, the optimism of Arab secular leftists evidenced in 1973 that they could instate a new order in the MENA through petrodollar power had largely collapsed. In the MENA, Arab nationalism, socialism, and the NIEO had all suffered severe setbacks. War and related lower oil revenues had caused Iraq's GDP per capita to have dropped by 30 percent since 1980, and Baghdad owed a debilitating $40–$50 billion to Western and Soviet Bloc countries and $30–$40 billion to the Arab monarchies, undermining Iraq's claim to Arab leadership.[69] The drop in oil prices crippled Algeria's socialist economy, undercut its earlier leadership of the Third World, and contributed to wide-scale protests against the regime of Chadli Bendjedid (Boumediene's successor) by Islamists and leftists in 1988 that initiated several years of violent domestic discord.[70] The Soviet Union had proved increasingly unable to support leftists in the MENA, as the drop in oil prices and the war in Afghanistan placed incredible strain on its already teetering communist economy and undercut its geopolitical influence. The final withdrawal of Soviet troops from Afghanistan in February 1989 was just the latest in a string of global defeats for secular leftists. Saudi petrodollars had gone a long way in financing the CIA's program, the most expensive covert operation in history, to support the Afghan resistance.[71]

The drying up of petrodollar lending, aid, and remittances had contradictory effects for oil-poor LDCs around the world. Anger over the debt crises played a critical role in popular political mobilizations that led to the transition away from right-wing dictatorship in much of Latin America during the mid-1980s and the overthrow of communist regimes in Eastern Europe in 1989.[72] Yet even as these countries democratized, they also experienced widening wealth gaps and austerity. In other parts of the world, especially in the MENA, the result for oil-poor countries was not only growing poverty but a retrenchment of authoritarianism and corruption. In Sudan the economic downturn of the early 1980s was followed by a protracted civil war. Egypt had abandoned Arab nationalism and socialism in part for Sinai oil and petrodollar remittances, but in the mid-1980s these sharply declined in value, and in 1987 Egypt once again reluctantly signed on to a debt rescheduling program with the IMF conditioned on cuts to the welfare state. The Mubarak regime failed to fully meet its pledges, however, leading to a withholding of IMF funds, and ultimately would have to be bailed out by Washington, evidence of how dependent Egypt had become on the United States. Mubarak would implement economic "reforms" in the late 1980s and early 1990s, but these tended to further facilitate corruption and privileged rent positions that benefited the narrow elite connected to the Egyptian regime but that left upward of 95 percent of Egyptians even worse off in their standard of living.[73] For many Algerians, Egyptians, Sudanese, and others, the promise of Arab socialism or an NIEO seemed a distant memory.

Islamism had played a major role in the defeat of many secular leftists, had established itself as the governing ideology of Iran and Libya, and remained an ascendant ideology in the MENA during the 1980s. Yet the dreams of Islamists who desired an end to US empire in the MENA were largely unfulfilled. The United States and its regional proxies, both secular and Islamist, employed economic and military measures to undermine the Islamists who challenged them. Petrodollar flows proved critical to these struggles. Regimes from Egypt to Saudi Arabia either imprisoned local anti-US Islamists or redirected them to Afghanistan. Washington worked to weaken Libya through embargoes and limited military strikes, but the drop in oil prices likely did the most to undercut Qaddafi's geopolitical influence. The Islamic Republic of Iran proved to be the greatest challenger of US imperialism in the region, but while Khomeini managed to secure his regime at home and gain adherents abroad, the combined power of Arab petrodollars, Iraqi soldiers, and US (and others') arms halted the territorial spread of Khomeinism and took a terrible toll on Iran's people and economy.

The monarchies of the Arabian Peninsula had weathered the challenges of both Arab nationalism and Khomeinism. By the late 1980s they had rapidly developed their economies from just two decades earlier, now boasting some of the highest standards of living on earth for their citizens, and Saudi Arabia had emerged as a major regional power. To achieve these things, the Arab monarchies accepted the price of being part of the US empire. Yet the Arab monarchies suffered from the increased divisions of OPEC in the 1980s, as a failure to cooperate on price and production contributed to the collapse in petrodollar revenues. The loss of the shah as a partner and the ballooning, hostile militaries in Iran and Iraq also left the Arab monarchies far more dependent on the United States for their security. The Arab monarchies had far less ability to challenge Washington on issues like the Arab-Israeli conflict or arms sales during the 1980s than they had in the mid-1970s. Finally, kingdoms like Saudi Arabia found it increasingly difficult to balance the geostrategic demands of aligning with the

United States with the domestic demands of placating anti-US Islamists who might challenge the Saudi rulers' legitimacy.

In 1988 the United States was the biggest winner to come out of the petrodollar economy. Alliances with Western Europe and Japan, strained in the mid-1970s, had held. Washington had gained Egypt as a client and a more powerful and compliant Saudi Arabia. Israel enjoyed unprecedented security and remained closely tied to the United States. Petrodollars had been successfully utilized to expand global capitalism not only in the MENA and the West but also in the broader Third World and even the communist bloc. Low oil prices now contributed to booming US and Western economies and to declining Soviet and Iranian economies. At the end of 1988, the US unemployment rate had fallen to 5.3 percent while the inflation rate remained a manageable 4.4 percent. Yet even for the United States, the US-led petrodollar order produced undesired results, stoking anti-imperialist sentiment against the United States throughout the MENA. Khomeini's rule over Iran was the most obvious manifestation of this phenomenon at the time. Less recognized was the establishment of al-Qaeda by the petrodollar-funded Arab mujahedin in Afghanistan in 1988, an organization soon led by Osama bin Laden and increasingly focused on expelling the US empire from the MENA as Soviet forces withdrew from Afghanistan.[74]

Conclusion

On October 2, 2018, Jamal Khashoggi, a Saudi journalist and columnist for the *Washington Post*, entered the Saudi consulate in Istanbul to obtain legal documents for his upcoming wedding. Once inside he was assassinated by Saudi hitmen, who then dismembered his body with a bone saw and smuggled the pieces out of the building. Riyadh initially claimed to have no knowledge about Khashoggi's disappearance, but when Turkish intelligence provided evidence of his murder and caught the Saudi government in a lie, Riyadh reverted to the dubious claim that the journalist's death had been accidental and not condoned by Saudi leaders. US intelligence, however, determined that the Saudi crown prince, Mohammed bin Salman, the power behind the throne of his father King Salman, had ordered the killing to silence Khashoggi, who had publicly criticized his increasingly authoritarian rule and military intervention in Yemen.[1]

Despite the mounting evidence of the complicity of Prince Mohammed, on November 20 US president Donald Trump issued an exclamation-point-riddled statement defending the US alliance with Riyadh. "*America First!*" Trump began. "The world is a very dangerous place!" Iran was an example of such danger, he alleged, responsible for bloody wars in Syria and Yemen, the killing of "many Americans," and unparalleled sponsorship of terrorism. Conversely, Saudi Arabia, Trump claimed, "has agreed to spend billions of dollars in leading the fight against Radical Islamic Terrorism" and "to spend and invest $450 billion in the United States . . . a record amount of money. It will create hundreds of thousands of jobs, tremendous economic development, and much additional wealth for the United States. Of the $450 billion, $110 billion will be spent on the purchase of military equipment from Boeing, Lockheed Martin, Raytheon and many other great U.S. defense contractors." If these deals were canceled, China and Russia would acquire this business instead. Trump noted Prince Mohammed denied any knowledge of Khashoggi's murder, but argued his guilt or innocence ultimately did not matter: "Our relationship is with the Kingdom of Saudi Arabia. They have been a great ally in our very important fight against Iran . . . very responsive to my requests to keeping oil prices at reasonable levels." Trump concluded by arguing that this strategy was "called America First!," suggesting his policies toward Iran and Saudi Arabia were a break from his predecessors'.[2] In fact, Trump's defenses were firmly rooted in the logic of the US-led petrodollar order of the long 1970s: the Islamic Republic of Iran was a dangerous threat that must be countered, while petrodollar ties with oil-rich allies like Saudi Arabia provided the United States with support for its geopolitical and economic goals, absolving the Saudis of any criticisms.

Even before his official statement, some commentators had been challenging the factual and moral validity of Trump's oft-repeated claims on US arms exports to Saudi Arabia. Paul Krugman, for example, argued that the arms agreement figures were inflated and that there was no way hundreds of thousands of US jobs depended on Saudi purchases.[3] Independent senator from Vermont Bernie Sanders published an op-ed in the *New York Times* using Khashoggi's murder as a jumping-off point for his call to end US military assistance to the Saudis in waging their war in Yemen. Saudi Arabia militarily intervened in Yemen in March 2015 to stop the Iranian-supported Ansar Allah movement, popularly called the Houthis, from toppling the Saudi-backed dictatorship of Abdu Rabbu Mansour Hadi. Riyadh hoped to quickly bomb the Houthis into submission, but instead a bloody stalemate ensued. Saudi airstrikes in Yemen, supplied with US arms and intelligence, frequently hit civilians, killing thousands of noncombatant Yemenis. A Saudi blockade of the country, meanwhile, wrought widespread starvation and outbreaks of cholera, killing many more of Yemen's most vulnerable. In his op-ed, Sanders lamented that "American weapons have been used in a string of such deadly attacks on civilians since the war began" and insinuated that Saudi petrodollars were corrupting US policymaking by noting a report finding that "a former lobbyist for the arms manufacturer Raytheon, which stands to make billions of dollars from those sales, leads [US secretary of state Mike] Pompeo's legislative affairs staff."[4] Many Democratic and some Republican senators also spoke out against US support for the Saudi war in Yemen. "Our involvement in this terrible war is one thing that engenders more terrorism," Republican senator from Kentucky Rand Paul argued. "I think it's actually a risk to our national security to be involved with the Saudis."[5] US congressional and media opposition to Trump's arms deals with Saudi Arabia on economic, moral, and strategic grounds likewise echoed the debates over petrodollar ties during the 1970s. While the first petrodollar era had ended in the mid-1980s, its impacts would continue to shape international relations for years to come, and its structures would be further replicated during the second petrodollar boom that began in the mid-2000s.

The petrodollar boom of the long 1970s transformed the relationship between the MENA and US imperialism. Overcoming the challenges of the 1973 oil shock and Arab oil embargo, US and allied leaders, especially in Iran and Saudi Arabia, repurposed the system of US cooperative empire in the MENA away from one founded on cheap oil to one based on the interdependent utilization of petrodollars in investment, arms development, and aid projects. This US-led petrodollar order augmented the geopolitical power of the United States and its MENA allies and hastened the globalization of capitalism. Yet the economic disparities and authoritarian violence this system fostered also drove many Americans, Arabs, and Iranians to seek the reform or termination of MENA-US interdependence, spurring competing cultural narratives and political action. The greatest challenge to US-led petrodollar interdependence proved to be the Iranian Revolution and the establishment of the Islamic Republic, which turned Iran into one of the most powerful challengers of the US imperial order in the MENA. The Iranian Revolution further increased the importance of Saudi Arabia and the United States to each other. Both doubled down on petrodollar interdependence and pursued a more aggressive posture toward not only Iran but the Soviet Union, too. At the same time, Iraq, while not a US ally, served as a counterweight to Iran in its bloody eight-year war, a campaign propped up by both its and the Arab monarchies' petrodollars. During the mid-1980s the petrodollar economy largely collapsed when the price of oil plummeted, and the oil exporters' earnings correspondingly shrank.

Yet in many ways the structures and consequences of the petrodollar era of the long 1970s persisted and have shaped relationships up to the present. At the conclusion of the petrodollar-fueled Iran-Iraq War, the Islamic Republic stood weakened but unbowed. The horrific experience reaffirmed for many Iranians their opposition to US imperialism. After Khomeini died of natural causes on June 3, 1989, his publicized last testament lambasted the United States and Saudi Arabia and warned against interdependence with capitalism or communism. "I ask the youth . . . not to compromise their freedom, indepen-dence and human values for luxury, pleasure-seeking and other vices that are offered to them by the corrupt agents of the West or the East," Khomeini ex-horted. "Experience has taught us that these affiliated puppets think of noth-ing except degenerating the youth and making them feel indifferent towards their own destinies and that of their country. The agents are engaged in plun-dering our natural resources and expanding the level of consumerism among people. In short, they work to pave the way for colonization."[6] Khomeini was succeeded as supreme leader by his close partner Ali Khamenei. Relations be-tween Tehran and the new administration of US president George H. W. Bush remained mutually hostile, though the two did successfully negotiate an agreement wherein the last US hostages in Lebanon were released in 1991 after some of the shah's assets were returned to Iran.[7] The civil war in Lebanon had concluded the year prior, having killed an estimated 150,000 Lebanese, thou-sands of Palestinians and Syrians, and hundreds of Americans and Israelis.[8] The various Lebanese factions forged an uneasy truce under Syrian auspices, with Iranian-backed Hezbollah cementing its newfound influence in Beirut. The US independent counsel investigation of the Iran-Contra scandal was effec-tively ended in December 1992 by Bush's decision to pardon Weinberger (who was convicted of perjury), McFarlane, and four other officials. Prosecution of Reagan and Bush had been declined due to the developing Alzheimer's dis-ease of the former and statute of limitations issues with the latter; and while North and Poindexter were convicted of obstruction of justice in 1989 and 1990, they both successfully appealed on the grounds that their congressional testimony had tainted their trials.[9]

Petrodollar legacies likewise weighed heavily on Iraq. The Iran-Iraq War left Baghdad with a large military but an underdeveloped economy and deeply indebted to the Arab monarchies' billions in petrodollar loans. Saddam de-manded the Arab Gulf states forgive its loans in recognition of Iraqi sacrifices to defend the Arab world. Saudi Arabia showed a willingness to forgive the debt, but Kuwait, which had lent $15 billion to Iraq over the course of the war, resisted.[10] This contributed heavily to Saddam's decision to invade and annex Kuwait in 1990, allowing him to substantially increase Iraq's share of the oil market, seize Kuwaiti assets, and wipe away a good portion of his debts. Unwilling to allow Saddam to control such a large amount of oil or threaten Saudi Arabia, in 1991 Bush led an international coalition that drove Iraqi forces out of Kuwait and decimated Iraq's military and infrastructure. The US war effort relied heavily on the petrodollar structures of the Arab monarchies; arms and military bases that Saudi Arabia had purchased from the United States during the past two decades were used by US forces during and after the war, and the Arab monarchies directly reimbursed the United States, the United Kingdom, and France $84 billion for military expenses incurred during the conflict.[11]

In late 1991 the Soviet Union ceased to exist; in this era-defining event of international relations, the impact of petrodollar ties played a role too. The role of the mujahedin insurgency in Afghanistan, and the role of Saudi and US assistance to it, has sometimes been overstated as causing the Soviet collapse, bleeding the communist superpower to the breaking point. The Soviet Union spent roughly less than 2 percent of its state budget on the war in Afghanistan and lost over thirteen thousand soldiers—costs, to be sure, but not unbearable ones. The war had an incalculable role in destroying Soviet citizens' faith in the competency of their government and leadership's belief in the efficacy of communism, however.[12] And it left Afghanistan devastated, with hundreds of thousands killed and a civil society torn apart by fighting between mujahedin forces that only intensified after the Soviet withdrawal.

After the Gulf War, the Bush administration secured the maintenance of international sanctions that cut Iraq off from most trade with the rest of the world, which impoverished the country and led to the premature deaths of tens of thousands of Iraqis but failed to dislodge Saddam from power. In 1991 Washington also secured more limited international financial and trade restrictions on Libya after determining its role in the Lockerbie bombing. The administration of US president Bill Clinton implemented a series of policies that prohibited virtually all US trade with Iran and pressured other countries to follow suit on the grounds that Iran promoted terrorism and was seeking nuclear weapons. The US trend toward targeting hostile oil-rich MENA states' financial flows begun in 1979 thus accelerated in the 1990s.

Conversely, US efforts to militarily contain Iran, Iraq, and Libya in the 1990s relied in part on the expenditures of Arab allies. Saudi Arabia and the other Arab Gulf monarchies purchased billions of dollars' worth of US arms. At the start of the 1990s Egypt received a burst of renewed aid from the Arab monarchies, having fully repaired its ties with them by opposing Iraq's invasion of Kuwait, helping fund the Egyptian military.[13] Yet much of this spending by the oil-rich Arab states was funded on credit rather than by petrodollars. Oil prices continued on a downward trend in the 1990s, and the Arab monarchies found themselves deeply in debt to foreign creditors. Saudi Arabia even struggled to maintain its arms procurement payments to the United States.[14] Yet the narrative of the fabulously petrodollar-rich Arab remained strong in US culture, with Hollywood films of the decade like *Batman and Robin*, *Mars Attacks!*, and *Mouse Hunt* using cameos of sheikhs as symbols of extravagant wealth.[15]

The rise of al-Qaeda was likewise rooted in petrodollar histories. Osama bin Laden believed the Islamic world was being corrupted by Western-led globalization, and in the case of Saudi Arabia this was directly linked to Saudi petrodollar ties with the United States and capitalism. In 1994 bin Laden publicly declared that the Saudi Kingdom had "declared war on God" by legalizing within its realm "the practice of usury, which is now widespread in the country thanks to the usurious state institutions and banks, whose towers are competing with the minarets of the two Holy Sanctuaries." Two years later in a declaration of jihad against the United States, bin Laden declared the Saudi government illegitimate due to its allowing US troops to occupy Saudi Arabia since the Iraqi invasion of Kuwait, argued the economic woes of the kingdom had been perpetrated by the United States, and called on Muslims to liberate the country. Addressing the Saudi people, bin Laden claimed that it made no sense for Saudi Arabia to be "the biggest purchaser of weapons from America in the world and America's biggest trading partner in the region" while the United States occupied Saudi land and supported Israel. "Depriving these occupiers of the huge returns they receive from their trade with us [Saudis] is a very important way of supporting the jihad against them," bin Laden contended.[16] The social anomie resulting from the decline in the Saudi economy since the drop in oil prices in the mid-1980s likewise assisted bin Laden in recruiting Saudis to his cause.[17] The petrodollar-funded war against the communist government in Afghanistan ultimately led to its collapse in 1992, but also continued fighting between different mujahedin forces that spurred the rise of a new, violently puritanical Islamist group, the Taliban, which would seize control of most of the country in 1996 and allow al-Qaeda to operate there. Finally, their time as mujahedin fighters in the 1980s, funded in large part by Saudi petrodollars, provided top members of al-Qaeda with the experience needed to organize a sophisticated terrorist network, one capable of the unprecedented attacks of September 11, 2001, killing nearly three thousand people on US soil and bringing down the twin towers of the World Trade Center in New York, symbols of US-led globalization.

US president George W. Bush responded to the 9/11 terror attacks with a global war on terror. The second Bush administration first invaded Afghanistan to dislodge al-Qaeda and then Iraq in 2003 with the goal of triggering capitalistic, neoliberal reforms throughout the MENA, both by inspiring fear in the region's countries that US force would otherwise be deployed against them next and by offering the positive example of a thriving, reformed Iraq, reconstructed with Iraqi petrodollars.[18] The Baathist regime was easily toppled, and Saddam was captured and then executed in 2006 for crimes against the Iraqi people. But rebuilding Iraq proved to be a more herculean task than invading it, and the country descended into civil war and anti-US insurgencies, resulting in the deaths of thousands of Americans and hundreds of thousands of Iraqis. Meanwhile, the determination that Iran's nuclear program was not compliant with the Non-Proliferation Treaty and could soon be weaponized led Washington to escalate tensions with Tehran and negotiate international sanctions restricting arms and technology exports to and financial activities with Iran. In response to US sanctions, in 2008 Iran announced that it would no longer sell its oil in dollars and would instead trade in other currencies, like the euro, a minor but symbolic setback for the petrodollar.[19]

Fears about the conflicts in the Persian Gulf combined with rising global demand for energy to significantly increase the price of oil in the mid-2000s, with benchmark prices reaching record heights at over $145 a barrel in 2008, inaugurating a second petrodollar era for the MENA.[20] Comparing the first and second halves of the 2000s, the Arab monarchies saw the value of their petroleum exports rise from $700 billion to $1.5 trillion, and Iran's from $100 billion to $300 billion.[21] The new petrodollar boom revived the US-led petrodollar order with the Arab monarchies and Iranian spending to counter it. Yet while Saudi Arabia remained within the system of US empire, King Abdullah, who succeeded Fahd upon his death of natural causes in 2005, became increasingly frustrated with the Bush administration for unleashing anarchy in Iraq and unwittingly facilitating the rise to power of Iran-leaning Shia factions there.

The global Great Recession caused oil prices to briefly plummet, but by the end of 2010 they had rebounded back to near-record highs. Oil prices moderated somewhat after 2014, and in 2020 experienced an unprecedented collapse in the wake of the COVID-19 pandemic, but for the majority of the 2010s benchmark oil prices remained at or above the inflation-adjusted price of the 1973 oil shock. During the 2010s, the second petrodollar era continued; from 2010 to 2018, combined Emirati, Kuwaiti, Qatari, and Saudi oil exports exceeded $3.8 trillion; Iran's totaled $600 billion.[22] In this context US president Barack Obama expanded the strategy of using petrodollars for arming Arab allies to strengthen ties with them and counter Iranian power. In 2010 the Obama administration secured congressional approval for an unprecedented ten-year, $60 billion arms sale package to Saudi Arabia, which included eighty-four new Boeing F-15SA Strike Eagle jet fighters.[23]

Yet the revived US-led petrodollar order also encountered new challenges. Economically, the United States faced increasing competition from China; in 2014 the latter surpassed the former as Saudi Arabia's largest source of imports.[24] Politically, the Arab monarchies and Washington repeatedly clashed over responses to the 2011 Arab revolts and their aftermath. In allied countries the Obama administration offered modest support for pro-democracy movements, while the House of Saud pressed for violent support of authoritarianism. The Obama administration's acceptance of the overthrow of Mubarak in Egypt angered Saudi leaders as yet another unnecessary US abandonment of an ally. When the majority Shia Bahrainis protested against their Sunni monarchs, Obama pressed Abdullah not to militarily intervene and instead support negotiations between the Bahraini factions; Abdullah ignored these warnings and sent Saudi troops into Bahrain, violently suppressing the protests.[25] In Egypt the Muslim Brotherhood democratically rose to power, with its leader Mohamed Morsi becoming president—an outcome that further angered Saudi Arabia and the UAE, which had been in conflict with the Muslim Brotherhood since the 1990s. Abu Dhabi and Riyadh thus supported the July 2013 military coup in Egypt that deposed Morsi, as well as the Egyptian army's massacre of an estimated one thousand Morsi supporters in Cairo a month later. The Obama administration and the European Union publicly raised the possibility of cutting aid to Egypt to signal their disapproval, but the Saudi government declared that it and its Arab allies would make up the difference in any Western aid cuts to Egypt. The Western powers then dropped the issue.[26]

In the civil wars born of the 2011 uprisings as well, the Arab monarchies often found themselves at odds with the United States. During the Libyan uprising, both the Arab monarchies and Washington supported the overthrow of Qaddafi, despite a normalization of Libyan-US relations in the mid-2000s after Tripoli foreswore international terrorism and weapons of mass destruction programs. With crucial support from NATO air forces, Libyan rebels seized control of most of the country and then killed Qaddafi in October 2011. But in the civil war that followed the collapse of Qaddafi's regime, the Obama administration supported the UN-recognized government in Tripoli, which included Muslim Brotherhood politicians, while the UAE increasingly supported the warlord Khalifa Haftar.[27] In Syria, both the Arab monarchies and the United States called for the overthrow of Bashar al-Asad, but the Obama administration proved far more reluctant to risk arming Islamic militants or challenge Iranian and Russian support for Asad than the Arab Gulf monarchies.[28] In Yemen, Mohammed bin Salman led a coalition of the Arab states in militarily intervening against the Houthis in March 2015 after his father ascended to the throne upon the natural death of Abdullah earlier that year. The White House aided the Saudi war effort but became increasingly critical of the high rate of civilians killed by Saudi strikes. In its last year, the Obama administration blocked some arms deals to Saudi Arabia over the issue, further frustrating Riyadh.[29] Massive stockpiles of petrodollar-purchased arms in Libya,

Syria, and Yemen increased the destructive and stalemated nature of the civil wars there, each of which killed tens of thousands.

Perhaps the greatest dispute in Saudi–US relations emerged over the US-negotiated Iran nuclear deal. In response to the Iranian nuclear program, the Obama administration initially organized international sanctions on Iran that cut its oil exports in half by 2013, but in July 2015 Tehran and Washington reached an agreement providing oversight of Iran's nuclear program in exchange for the lifting of many international sanctions on Iran. Obama believed the deal essential to preventing a war in the region over fears of Iran developing a nuclear weapon; Saudi leaders focused on the threat that Iran's increased revenues posed in the two countries' proxy battles.[30]

Yet despite these disputes, indeed often because of them, the Obama administration continued to work to assuage Arab monarchs' fears and maintain petrodollar interdependence by selling arms. From FY 2009 to FY 2016 Washington approved $63.7 billion in FMS to Saudi Arabia, more than triple the amount to any other country and 24 percent of all US FMS for that period, as well as $17.8 billion for the UAE, $9.1 billion for Qatar, and $6.2 billion for Kuwait. Over half of all US FMS went to the MENA during these years, arms exports fueled by the petrodollar-funded conflicts of the region.[31]

The administration of Donald Trump would increasingly move to topple or at least weaken the government in Tehran by cutting off its oil revenues, withdrawing the United States from the Iran nuclear deal in May 2018, and thereafter working to reimpose international sanctions on Iran. These acts prompted countermeasures from Iran, including a September 2019 drone strike on Saudi oil facilities that temporarily took half of the country's entire production offline and an increase in Iranian support to anti-US Iraqi militias. When a US contractor was killed in a rocket strike by one such Iraqi militia in December 2019, Trump responded by assassinating Iranian general Qasem Soleimani at the Baghdad airport the following month, justifying the attack on the disputed claim that Soleimani was actively plotting imminent attacks on Americans. While a de-escalation of hostilities averted open war in the immediate aftermath of Soleimani's death, Tehran announced it was resuming unrestricted enrichment and production of uranium in response, heightening the long-term risks of conflict between Iran and the United States and its Middle East allies.

Trump also joined forces with Mohammed bin Salman to improve Saudi–US relations through petrodollar projects aimed at weakening Iran. Trump encouraged massive US sales of additional arms to Saudi Arabia, whose total military expenditures had risen to the third highest in the world in 2017, both to apply pressure on Iran and to wage war against the Iranian-backed Houthis in Yemen.[32] But bipartisan congressional displeasure with Saudi Arabia's authoritarianism and war in Yemen grew as well. In April 2019 Congress passed legislation to end US military support for Saudi forces fighting in Yemen and in July voted to block the sale of US arms worth eight billion dollars to Saudi Arabia. Trump vetoed these bills, however, and Congress did not have sufficient votes to overturn the vetoes. Still, cutting off arms to the Saudis remained popular with many Americans, a fact implicitly acknowledged by former US vice president Joe Biden on November 20, 2019, on the democratic presidential debate stage when he declared "I would end . . . the sale of material to the Saudis where they're going in and murdering children, and they're murdering innocent people."[33] In Yemen itself, narratives built around commemorations of the victims of Saudi airstrikes using US arms were widespread. One such airstrike in August 2018 involving a Saudi jet pilot and a US-made laser-guided bomb struck a school bus in the Yemeni town of Dahyan, killing forty-four children and ten adults. The tragedy sparked outrage across the country, and Yemenis built a shrine at the blast site, with large writing in Arabic and English on a nearby brick wall reading "America Kills Yemeni Children."[34]

Since the 1970s the US empire in the MENA has often been based on petrodollar interdependence. The durability of US international cooperative empire with oil-rich MENA countries since the 1970s has derived from its ability to accommodate the rising aspirations of US clients and provide them with greater economic and military power while simultaneously utilizing that greater power in the service of the United States. Yet while empire has been a cooperative endeavor between the United States and Arab (and until 1979, Iranian) elites, average Arabs and Iranians under US-aligned governments have largely been barred from having a voice in the nature of their countries' relations with the United States. As US-led globalization rapidly transformed these societies, bringing unprecedented wealth inequality, cultural changes, and state power, these ordinary people lacked democratic outlets to debate and negotiate how their countries should respond. Oil-rich US-allied regimes in the MENA instead utilized US arms and training to suppress dissent in their own countries and used their petrodollars and/or weapons to intervene in the affairs of other countries.

Oil-rich MENA countries that opposed US empire employed petrodollars in like ways to an inverse end, inflicting their own brands of violence and oppression in the region. Many of these countries would pay high costs for resisting the US-led petrodollar order. Qaddafi's Libya, Saddam's Iraq, and Khomeini's Iran all experienced US-backed sanctions and wars that significantly set back these countries' economic and social development.

While somewhat better insulated, Americans have not been immune to the undemocratic and violent currents of US empire and its petrodollar order, either. Iranian and Saudi petrodollars enabled the Reagan administration to flout the will of Congress and the rule of law to conduct war in Nicaragua. Saudi petrodollars helped arm, train, and radicalize the Arab mujahedin in Afghanistan who would later commit the 9/11 terror attacks.

Is it possible to transcend the illiberal and destructive tendencies of the petrodollar economy? Some in the MENA and the United States have argued that US-led sanctions, limited military strikes, or full-scale invasions aimed at toppling Middle Eastern dictatorships hostile to Washington can bring reform to the region. Where tried thus far, however, the results have been dismal. Sanctions have failed to dislodge a single MENA regime to date while often visiting hardship and even death on innocent people. Wars of liberation have unleashed bloody and regionally destabilizing civil wars in Iraq and Libya rather than model societies.

Others have pushed for an end to the mass consumption of oil as the solution: by diminishing the number of petrodollars, one would diminish their pernicious effects. The idea has merit, and there are additional good reasons for humanity to move away from the use of oil—the threat of global warming chief among them. But it is unclear how long it will take humankind to effect this fundamental energy shift. Furthermore, solely focusing on curbing petrodollars facilitates the erasure of the material, cultural, and political needs of the peoples of the MENA from consideration, needs that remain unfulfilled for far too many and could yet benefit from petrodollar investments.

Large-scale structures born of history and the ongoing quest for security have proved to be formidable obstacles to even well-intentioned reformers of the petrodollar economy. Still, the costs of the dictatorial US-led petrodollar order in the MENA are high, as are those of the authoritarian petrodollar systems in the region operating in opposition: growing economic inequality, the abuse of migrant workers, unaddressed cultural concerns, the circumscribing of civil and human rights, wasteful arms races, the torture and murder of dissidents, a lack of governmental accountability that spurs violent acts of resistance and potentially revolution, and wars that reap heartbreak and death. And while the structures of the petrodollar economy of the past several decades have proved powerful, they have also on occasion shown themselves to be malleable. Americans, Arabs, and Iranians may yet bring about another transformation of the petrodollar economy that achieves a more positive vision of interdependence between the MENA and the United States.

Notes

Introduction

1. Rumsfeld to Scowcroft, November 5, 1974, folder "'Cheney/Rumsfeldgrams' (1)," box 3, National Security Adviser (hereafter NSA), Kissinger-Scowcroft West Wing Office Files, 1969–1977 (hereafter KSWW), Gerald R. Ford Presidential Library (hereafter FL), Ann Arbor, MI.

2. Ibid.

3. Ibid.

4. Ian Skeet, *OPEC: Twenty-Five Years of Prices and Politics* (Cambridge: Cambridge University Press, 1988), 240–244.

5. Given the scope of this book, I have defined the MENA as the countries of the Arab League by 1977, Iran, and Israel.

6. For example, see Andre Simmons, *Arab Foreign Aid* (Rutherford, NJ: Fairleigh Dickinson University Press, 1981); Saad Eddin Ibrahim, *The New Arab Social Order: A Study of the Social Impact of Oil Wealth* (Boulder, CO: Westview Press, 1982); Benjamin J. Cohen, *In Whose Interest? International Banking and American Foreign Policy* (New Haven, CT: Yale University Press, 1986); Ethan B. Kapstein, *Governing the Global Economy: International Finance and the State* (Cambridge, MA: Harvard University Press, 1994); Diane B. Kunz, *Butter and Guns: America's Cold War Economic Diplomacy* (New York: Free Press, 1997); David E. Spiro, *The Hidden Hand of American Hegemony: Petrodollar Recycling and International Markets* (Ithaca, NY: Cornell University Press, 1999); and Gil Feiler, *Economic Relations between Egypt and the Gulf Oil States, 1967–2000* (Brighton: Sussex Academic Press, 2003).

7. These include Niall Ferguson et al., eds., *Shock of the Global: The 1970s in Perspective* (Cambridge, MA: Harvard University Press, 2010); Judith Stein, *Pivotal Decade: How the United States Traded Factories for Finance in the Seventies* (New Haven, CT: Yale University Press, 2010); Andrew Scott Cooper, *The Oil Kings: How the U.S., Iran, and Saudi Arabia Changed the Balance of Power in the Middle East* (New York: Simon & Schuster, 2011); Roham Alvandi, *Nixon, Kissinger, and the Shah: The United States and Iran in the Cold War* (Oxford: Oxford University Press, 2014); David S. Painter, "Oil and Geopolitics: The Oil Crises of the 1970s and the Cold War," *Historical Social Research* 39, no. 4 (2014): 186–208; Daniel J. Sargent, *A Superpower Transformed: The Remaking of American Foreign Relations in the 1970s* (Oxford: Oxford

University Press, 2015); Betsy A. Beasley, "At Your Service: Houston and the Preservation of U.S. Global Power, 1945–2008" (PhD diss., Yale University, 2016); Salim Yaqub, *Imperfect Strangers: Americans, Arabs, and U.S.-Middle East Relations in the 1970s* (Ithaca, NY: Cornell University Press, 2016); Fritz Bartel, "Fugitive Leverage: Commercial Banks, Sovereign Debt, and Cold War Crisis in Poland, 1980–1982," *Enterprise & Society* 18, no. 1 (March 2017): 72–107; Christopher R. W. Dietrich, *Oil Revolution: Anticolonial Elites, Sovereign Rights, and the Economic Culture of Decolonization* (Cambridge: Cambridge University Press, 2017); and Patrick Allan Sharma, *Robert McNamara's Other War: The World Bank and International Development* (Philadelphia: University of Pennsylvania Press, 2017).

8. Paul A. Kramer, "Power and Connection: Imperial Histories of the United States in the World," *American Historical Review* 116, no. 5 (2011): 1366.

9. Richard N. Cooper, *The Economics of Interdependence: Economic Policy in the Atlantic Community* (New York: McGraw-Hill, 1968), 4.

10. Edward W. Said, *Culture and Imperialism* (New York: Alfred A. Knopf, 1993).

11. I use Arabic and Farsi language sources that I have translated as well as ones that have been translated to English by others. On the need for an increase in scholarship on Middle East–US relations that seriously engages with the viewpoints, primary sources, or historiographies of Arabs and Iranians, see Ussama Makdisi, "The Privilege of Acting Upon Others: The Middle Eastern Exception to Anti-exceptionalist Histories of the US and the World," in *Explaining the History of American Foreign Relations*, 3rd ed., ed. Frank Costigliola and Michael J. Hogan (Cambridge: Cambridge University Press, 2016), 203–216.

1. Oil, US Empire, and the Middle East

1. Abdullah El Hammoud El Tariki, *Nationalization of Arab Petroleum Industry Is a National Necessity* (Cairo: Dar El-Hana Press, 1965), 1, 18–19.

2. Stephen J. Randall, *United States Foreign Oil Policy since World War I: For Profits and Security*, 2nd ed. (Montreal: McGill-Queen's University Press, 2005), 13–25, 33–40.

3. For an early example, see Emily S. Rosenberg, *Financial Missionaries to the World: The Politics and Culture of Dollar Diplomacy, 1900–1930* (Cambridge, MA: Harvard University Press, 1999).

4. David S. Painter, *Oil and the American Century: The Political Economy of U.S. Foreign Oil Policy, 1941–1954* (Baltimore: Johns Hopkins University Press, 1986), 34–37, 75–90.

5. Michael J. Hogan, *A Cross of Iron: Harry S. Truman and the Origins of the National Security State, 1945–1954* (Cambridge: Cambridge University Press, 1998); Melvyn P. Leffler, *A Preponderance of Power: National Security, the Truman Administration, and the Cold War* (Stanford, CA: Stanford University Press, 1992); Thomas W. Zeiler, *Free Trade, Free World: The Advent of GATT* (Chapel Hill: University of North Carolina, 1999).

6. Timothy Mitchell, *Carbon Democracy: Political Power in the Age of Oil* (London: Verso, 2011), 111.

7. Painter, *Oil and the American Century*, 96–110, 126.

8. Jeffrey A. Frieden, *Global Capitalism: Its Fall and Rise in the Twentieth Century* (New York: W.W. Norton, 2006), 281; Sargent, *Superpower Transformed*, 131–132.

9. Barry Eichengreen, *Exorbitant Privilege: The Rise and Fall of the Dollar* (Oxford: Oxford University Press, 2011), 2, 39–42; Mitchell, *Carbon Democracy*, 111.

10. William Stivers, *America's Confrontation with Revolutionary Change in the Middle East, 1948–83* (New York: St. Martin's Press, 1986), 10.

11. Ussama Makdisi, *Faith Misplaced: The Broken Promise of U.S.-Arab Relations: 1820–2001* (New York: PublicAffairs, 2010); James A. Bill, *The Eagle and the Lion: The Tragedy of American-Iranian Relations* (New Haven, CT: Yale University Press, 1988), 15–18.

12. Matthew F. Jacobs, *Imagining the Middle East: The Building of an American Foreign Policy, 1918–1967* (Chapel Hill: University of North Carolina Press, 2011), 145–146.

13. Odd Arne Westad, *The Global Cold War: Third World Interventions and the Making of Our Times* (Cambridge: Cambridge University Press, 2005), 154–155.

14. Dietrich, *Oil Revolution*, 26–60; Robert Vitalis, *America's Kingdom: Mythmaking on the Saudi Oil Frontier* (Stanford, CA: Stanford University Press, 2007), 71–74, 105–110.

15. Vitalis, *America's Kingdom*, 54–61, 92–95.

16. Mitchell, *Carbon Democracy*, 103–104.

17. Peter L. Hahn, *Caught in the Middle East: U.S. Policy toward the Arab-Israeli Conflict, 1945–1961* (Chapel Hill: University of North Carolina Press, 2004), 32–51; Painter, *Oil and the American Century*, 116–127.

18. Painter, *Oil and the American Century*, 165–171; Daniel Yergin, *The Prize: The Epic Quest for Oil, Money & Power*, 3rd ed. (New York: Free Press, 2009), 427–430; Peter L. Hahn, *Missions Accomplished? The United States and Iraq since World War I* (Oxford: Oxford University Press, 2012), 27.

19. US Agency for International Development, Country Summary, https://explorer.usaid.gov/data (accessed February 10, 2020).

20. Ibid.

21. Mary Ann Heiss, *Empire and Nationhood: The United States, Great Britain, and Iranian Oil, 1950–1954* (New York: Columbia University Press, 1997); Mark J. Gasiorowski and Malcolm Byrne, eds., *Mohammad Mosaddeq and the 1953 Coup in Iran* (Syracuse, NY: Syracuse University Press, 2004); Hugh Wilford, "'Essentially a Work of Fiction': Kermit 'Kim' Roosevelt, Imperial Romance, and the Iran Coup of 1953," *Diplomatic History* 40, no. 5 (November 2016): 922–947.

22. Bill, *Eagle and the Lion*, 94–130; Painter, *Oil and the American Century*, 172–198.

23. Kirk J. Beattie, *Egypt during the Nasser Years: Ideology, Politics, and Civil Society* (Boulder, CO: Westview Press, 1994); Matthew Connelly, *A Diplomatic Revolution: Algeria's Fight for Independence and the Origins of the Post-Cold War Era* (Oxford: Oxford University Press, 2002).

24. Charles Tripp, *A History of Iraq*, 3rd ed. (Cambridge: Cambridge University Press, 2007), 127–139.

25. Fred Halliday, *Arabia without Sultans* (London: Penguin Books, 1974), 66–67; Vitalis, *America's Kingdom*, 145–164.

26. Nathan Citino, *From Arab Nationalism to OPEC: Eisenhower, King Sa'ud, and the Making of U.S.-Saudi Relations* (Bloomington: Indiana University Press, 2002), 39–42; Galia Golan, *Soviet Policies in the Middle East: From World War II to Gorbachev* (Cambridge: Cambridge University Press, 1990), 44.

27. Golan, 140; Peter L. Hahn, *The United States, Great Britain, and Egypt, 1945–1956* (Chapel Hill: University of North Carolina Press, 1991), 180–193.

28. Hahn, *United State, Great Britain, and Egypt*, 193–225.

29. Golan, *Soviet Policies*, 47–54; Hahn, *United States, Great Britain, and Egypt*, 224–241.

30. Salim Yaqub, *Containing Arab Nationalism: The Eisenhower Doctrine and the Middle East* (Chapel Hill: University of North Carolina Press, 2004).

31. Citino, *Arab Nationalism to OPEC*, 145–160; Skeet, *OPEC*, 15–34.

32. Mitchell, *Carbon Democracy*, 144n1.

33. Robert B. Rakove, *Kennedy, Johnson, and the Nonaligned World* (Cambridge: Cambridge University Press, 2013), 62–66.

34. Quoted in Abdel Razzaq Takriti, *Monsoon Revolution: Republicans, Sultans, and Empires in Oman, 1965–1976* (Oxford: Oxford University Press, 2013), 53.

35. Asher Orkaby, *Beyond the Arab Cold War: The International History of the Yemen Civil War, 1962–68* (Oxford: Oxford University Press, 2017), 30–51; Madawi Al-Rasheed, *A History of Saudi Arabia*, 2nd ed. (Cambridge: Cambridge University Press, 2010), 113.

36. Rachel Bronson, *Thicker Than Oil: America's Uneasy Partnership with Saudi Arabia* (Oxford: Oxford University Press, 2006), 84–85.

37. Ibid., 86–92.

38. John P. Miglietta, *American Alliance Policy in the Middle East, 1945–1992: Iran, Israel, and Saudi Arabia* (Lanham, MD: Lexington Books, 2002), 207–210.

39. Takriti, *Monsoon Revolution*, 49–83.

40. Jesse Ferris, *Nasser's Gamble: How Intervention in Yemen Caused the Six-Day War and the Decline of Egyptian Power* (Princeton, NJ: Princeton University Press, 2012), 70–101, 142–214.

41. Halliday, *Arabia without Sultans*, 67.

42. Ronald Bruce St. John, *Libya and the United States: Two Centuries of Strife* (Philadelphia: University of Pennsylvania Press, 2002), 78–85; Dirk Vandewalle, *A History of Modern Libya*, 2nd ed. (Cambridge: Cambridge University Press, 2012), 68–71.

43. Jacobs, *Imagining the Middle East*, 180–184; Michael E. Latham, *The Right Kind of Revolution: Modernization, Development, and U.S. Foreign Policy from the Cold War to the Present* (Ithaca, NY: Cornell University Press, 2011), 147–150.

44. Ruhollah Khomeini, *Sahifeh-Ye Imam: An Anthology of Imam Khomeini's Speeches, Messages, Interviews, Decrees, Religious Permissions, and Letters*, trans. 'Abdul-Husayn Shirazi (Tehran: Institute for Compilation and Publication of Imam Khomeini's Works, 2008), 1:421.

45. Stephen McGlinchey, "Lyndon B. Johnson and Arms Credit Sales to Iran, 1964–1968," *Middle East Journal* 67, no. 2 (Spring 2013): 235–242.

46. US Department of State, *Foreign Relations of the United States* (hereafter FRUS, followed by dates and volume and document numbers), *1964–1968*, 34:191.

47. *FRUS, 1964–1968*, 34:198.

48. Skeet, *OPEC*, 35–44.

49. Abraham Ben-Zvi, *John F. Kennedy and the Politics of Arms Sales to Israel* (London: Frank Cass, 2002); Abraham Ben-Zvi, *Lyndon B. Johnson and the Politics of Arms Sales to Israel: In the Shadow of the Hawk* (London: Frank Cass, 2004).

50. *FRUS, 1964–1968*, 21:278.

51. On the causes and consequences of the 1967 war, see Guy Laron, *The Six-Day War: The Breaking of the Middle East* (New Haven, CT: Yale University Press, 2017); Wm. Roger Louis and Avi Shlaim, eds., *The 1967 Arab-Israeli War: Origins and Consequences* (Cambridge: Cambridge University Press, 2012).

52. Dietrich, *Oil Revolution*, 142–146; Yergin, *Prize*, 537–540.

2. The Road to the Oil Shock

1. Quoted in Allen J. Matusow, *Nixon's Economy: Booms, Busts, Dollars, & Votes* (Lawrence: University Press of Kansas, 1998), 240.

2. Bernard Gwertzman, "A Mideast Pledge," *New York Times* (hereafter *NYT*), September 6, 1973.

3. Ferris, *Nasser's Gamble*, 246–249.

4. Feiler, *Egypt and the Gulf*, 6–8.

5. Golan, *Soviet Policies*, 69.

6. Paul Thomas Chamberlin, *The Global Offensive: The United States, the Palestine Liberation Organization, and the Making of the Post-Cold War Order* (Oxford: Oxford University Press, 2012), 52; Christopher R. W. Dietrich, "Uncertainty Rising: Oil Money and International Terrorism in the 1970s,"

in Bevan Sewell and Maria Ryan, eds., *Foreign Policy at the Periphery: The Shifting Margins of US International Relations since World War II* (Lexington: University Press of Kentucky, 2017), 267–271.

7. W. Taylor Fain, *American Ascendance and British Retreat in the Persian Gulf Region* (New York: Palgrave Macmillan, 2008), 141–168; Simon C. Smith, *Ending Empire in the Middle East: Britain, the United States and Post-War Decolonization, 1945–1973* (New York: Routledge, 2012), 117–122.

8. Alvandi, *Nixon, Kissinger, and the Shah*, 29–37.

9. Robert Dallek, *Nixon and Kissinger: Partners in Power* (New York: HarperCollins Publishers, 2007), 60–64; Jeremi Suri, *Power and Protest: Global Revolution and the Rise of Détente* (Cambridge, MA: Harvard University Press, 2003).

10. On the foreign relations strategies of Nixon and Kissinger, see Dallek, *Nixon and Kissinger*; Raymond L. Garthoff, *Détente and Confrontation: American-Soviet Relations from Nixon to Reagan*, rev. ed. (Washington, DC: Brookings Institution, 1994); Jussi Hanhimäki, *The Flawed Architect: Henry Kissinger and American Foreign Policy* (New York: Oxford University Press, 2004); Fredrik Logevall and Andrew Preston, eds., *Nixon in the World: American Foreign Relations, 1969–1977* (Oxford: Oxford University Press, 2008); Keith Nelson, *The Making of Détente: Soviet-American Relations in the Shadow of Vietnam* (Baltimore: Johns Hopkins University Press, 1995); Sargent, *Superpower Transformed*; Barbara Zanchetta, *The Transformation of American International Power in the 1970s* (New York: Cambridge University Press, 2014).

11. National Security Study Memorandum 12, January 30, 1969, Richard M. Nixon Presidential Library (hereafter NL), Yorba Linda, CA.

12. Ben Offiler, *US Foreign Policy and the Modernization of Iran: Kennedy, Johnson, Nixon, and the Shah* (New York: Palgrave Macmillan, 2015), 128–129.

13. Suggestions on Approaching Iranians and Topics of Conversation, folder "Visit of the Shah of Iran, Oct. 21–23, 1969 [2 of 2]," box 920, National Security Council Files (hereafter NSC), NL.

14. Ibid.; Douglas MacArthur to William Rogers, October 9, 1969, folder "Visit of the Shah of Iran, Oct. 21–23, 1969 [1 of 2]," box 920, NSC, NL.

15. Alvandi, *Nixon, Kissinger, and the Shah*, 33–59.

16. Asadollah Alam, *The Shah and I: The Confidential Diary of Iran's Royal Court, 1969–1977*, trans. Alinaghi Alikhani and Nicholas Vincent (New York: St. Martin's Press, 1992), 38.

17. Background—Iran's Petroleum Industry, folder "Visit of the Shah of Iran, Oct. 21–23, 1969 [2 of 2]," box 920, NSC, NL, 6

18. Thomas Hughes to Rogers, March 13, 1969, folder "Iran Vol. I, Jan. 20, 1969–May 31, 1970 [2 of 3]," box 601, NSC, NL.

19. Alam, *Shah and I*, 49.

20. Herbert Brownell to Kissinger, March 10, 1969, folder "Iran Vol. I, Jan. 20, 1969–May 31, 1970 [2 of 3]," box 601, NSC, NL.

21. Matusow, *Nixon's Economy*, 243–244.

22. Brownell to Kissinger, March 10, 1969, folder "Iran Vol. I, Jan. 20, 1969–May 31, 1970 [2 of 3]," box 601, NSC, NL.

23. Dallek, *Nixon and Kissinger*, 99.

24. Matusow, *Nixon's Economy*, 245.

25. MacArthur to Rogers, November 24, 1969, folder "Iran Vol. I Jan. 20, 1969–May 31, 1970 [3 of 3]," box 601, NSC, NL.

26. Kissinger to Nixon, October 22, 1969, folder "Visit of the Shah of Iran Oct. 21–23, 1969 [1 of 2]," box 920, NSC, NL.

27. Flanigan to Kissinger, January 10, 1970, folder "Iran Vol. I Jan. 20, 1969–May 31, 1970 [1 of 3]," box 601, NSC, NL.

28. MacArthur to Rogers, November 27, 1969, folder "Iran Vol. I Jan. 20, 1969–May 31, 1970 [3 of 3]," box 601, NSC, NL.

29. Shah to Nixon, December 17, 1969, folder "Iran Pahlavi Shahanshah [1969–1974] [2 of 2]," box 755, NSC, NL.

30. Flanigan to Kissinger, January 10, 1970, folder "Iran Vol. I Jan. 20, 1969–May 31, 1970 [1 of 3]," box 601, NSC, NL; Flanigan to Kissinger, January 21, 1970, folder "Oil 1970 [2 of 2]," box 367, NSC, NL.

31. MacArthur to Rogers, February 17, 1970, folder "Iran Vol. I Jan. 20, 1969–May 31, 1970 [2 of 3]," box 601, NSC, NL; Kissinger and Flanigan to Nixon, February 25, 1970, folder "Oil 1970 [Dec 69–1970] [1 of 2]," box 367, NSC, NL.

32. Nixon to the shah, April 16, 1970, folder "Iran Pahlavi Shahanshah [1969–1974] [2 of 2]," box 755, NSC, NL; Nixon to the shah, July 30, 1970, folder "Iran Pahlavi Shahanshah [1969–1974] [2 of 2]," box 755, NSC, NL.

33. Kissinger to Nixon, October 13, 1969, folder "Prince Fahd Visit [Oct 1969] [1 of 1]," box 937, NSC, NL.

34. William Stoltzfus to Rogers, October 9, 1969, folder "Prince Fahd Visit [Oct 1969] [1 of 1]," box 937, NSC, NL; Rogers to Hermann Eilts, October 15, 1969, folder "Prince Fahd Visit [Oct 1969] [1 of 1]," box 937, NSC, NL.

35. Fred Halliday, *Revolution and Foreign Policy: The Case of South Yemen, 1967–1987* (Cambridge: Cambridge University Press, 1990), 21–24, 178–184; Takriti, *Monsoon Revolution*, 101–106.

36. *FRUS, 1969–1976*, 24:137.

37. St. John, *Libya and the United States*, 87–106.

38. *FRUS, 1969–1976*, 24:130.

39. Halliday, *Arabia without Sultans*, 68.

40. Rogers to Eilts, November 18, 1969, folder "Prince Fahd Visit [Oct 1969] [1 of 1]," box 937, NSC, NL.

41. *FRUS, 1969–1976*, 36:24; "NSC Meeting," December 10, 1969, folder "NSC Minutes Originals 1969 [5 of 5]," box H-109, NSC, NL.

42. Lee Dinsmore to Rogers, December 23, 1969, folder "Libya Jun 69–Jan 70 Vol I," box 738, NSC, NL.

43. "NSC Meeting," December 10, 1969, folder "NSC Minutes Originals 1969 [5 of 5]," box H-109, NSC, NL.

44. William B. Quandt, *Peace Process: American Diplomacy and the Arab-Israeli Conflict since 1967*, 3rd ed. (Washington, DC: Brookings Institution Press, 2005), 55–83; Yaqub, *Imperfect Strangers*, 28–42; Golan, *Soviet Policies*, 73.

45. Roger Owen and Şevket Pamuk, *A History of Middle East Economies in the Twentieth Century* (London: I.B. Tauris, 1998), 130–134.

46. Ibrahim, *New Arab*, 68–72.

47. Feiler, *Egypt and the Gulf*, 10–13.

48. Miglietta, *American Alliance*, 135–140, 169–170.

49. Golan, *Soviet Policies*, 76–78.

50. Craig Daigle, *The Limits of Détente: The United States, the Soviet Union, and the Arab-Israeli Conflict, 1969–1973* (New Haven, CT: Yale University Press, 2012), 155–191.

51. Golan, *Soviet Policies*, 78–81; Quandt, *Peace Process*, 86–97.

52. DeGolyer and MacNaughton, *Twentieth Century Petroleum Statistics* (2016).

53. Skeet, *OPEC*, 58–66.

54. *FRUS, 1969–1976*, 36:69, 72–78; Victor R. S. McFarland, "Living in Never-Never Land: The United States, Saudi Arabia, and Oil in the 1970s" (PhD diss., Yale University, 2014), 107–110.

55. C. Fred Bergsten to Kissinger, February 1, 1971, folder "Oil 1971 [1 of 2]," box 367, NSC, NL.

56. Skeet, *OPEC*, 67–69.

57. Edward R. F. Sheehan, "The Algerians Intend to Go It Alone," *NYT*, April 23, 1972; Yergin, *Prize*, 565–567.

58. Matusow, *Nixon's Economy*, 245–247.

59. Throughout the book, US unemployment rates are derived from the US Department of Labor, Bureau of Labor Statistics, "Labor Force Statistics including the National Unemployment Rate," https://www.bls.gov/data/ (accessed February 10, 2020).

60. Matusow, *Nixon's Economy*, chapters 3–7.

61. Barry Eichengreen, *Globalizing Capital: A History of the International Monetary System*, 2nd ed. (Princeton, NJ: Princeton University Press, 2008), chap. 4; Francis J. Gavin, *Gold, Dollars, and Power: The Politics of International Monetary Relations, 1958–1971* (Chapel Hill: University of North Carolina Press, 2004); Harold James, *International Monetary Cooperation since Bretton Woods* (Oxford: Oxford University Press, 1996), 209–238; Sargent, *Superpower Transformed*, 100–118.

62. Skeet, *OPEC*, 240–241.

63. Alam, *Shah and I*, 202.

64. Ibid., 82, 179.

65. NSDM 92, November 7, 1970, NL.

66. Ibid. (emphasis added).

67. Latham, *Right Kind of Revolution*, 157–173; Offiler, *US Foreign Policy*, 136–153.

68. NSDM 96, November 7, 1970, NL.

69. Memorandum of conversation (hereafter Memcon), Nixon, MacArthur, and Alexander Haig, April 8, 1971, folder "Iran Vol. III 1 Jan–31 Aug 71 [1 of 2]," box 602, NSC, NL.

70. Fain, *American Ascendance*, 180–191.

71. Alvandi, *Nixon, Kissinger, and the Shah*, 59–62.

72. Brandon Wolfe-Hunnicutt, "Oil Sovereignty, American Foreign Policy, and the 1968 Coups in Iraq," *Diplomacy & Statecraft* 28, no. 2 (2017): 235–253.

73. Golan, *Soviet Policies*, 167.

74. *FRUS, 1969–1976*, E-4:200, 201.

75. Alam, *Shah and I*, 225.

76. *FRUS, 1969–1976*, E-4:214.

77. James F. Goode, "Assisting Our Brothers, Defending Ourselves: The Iranian Intervention in Oman, 1972–75," *Iranian Studies* 47, no. 3 (May 2014): 448; Takriti, *Monsoon Revolution*, 293; *FRUS, 1969–1976*, 24:119.

78. Saunders to Kissinger, July 18, 1972, folder "Iran IV 1 Sep 71–Apr 73 [1 of 3]," box 602, NSC, NL.

79. Juan de Onis, "Roger Terms U.S. Arms Sales to Persian Gulf 'Stabilizing,'" *NYT*, June 12, 1973; Drew Middleton, "Shah of Iran Due in U.S. to Seek Weapons," *NYT*, July 22, 1973.

80. Miglietta, *American Alliance*, 212.

81. Nixon to Rogers, Presidential Determination No. 71-6, undated, folder "Presidential Determinations Thru 71-10 [Feb 1969–Mar 1971] [2 of 3]," box 370, NSC, NL.

82. NSDM 186, August 18, 1972, NL.

83. Kissinger to Nixon, May 26, 1971, folder "Saudi Arabia May 71 King Faisal Visit [1 of 2]," box 937, NSC, NL.

84. *FRUS, 1969–1976*, 24:151.

85. Matusow, *Nixon's Economy*, chap. 7.

86. Ibid., 220, 238.

87. DeGolyer and MacNaughton, *Twentieth Century Petroleum Statistics.*

88. Matusow, *Nixon's Economy,* 251–255; Yergin, *Prize,* 568–574.

89. Clyde H. Farnsworth, "Force on Monetary Scene: Oil Money from Mideast," *NYT,* March 16, 1973; Sargent, *Superpower Transformed,* 118–130.

90. Edwin L. Dale Jr., "That Arab Oil Wealth," *NYT,* June 10, 1973.

91. *FRUS, 1969–1976,* 36:180, 193; "Summary of Views on Longer-Term Economic Problems," September 18, 1973, folder "Departmental Correspondence: Council of Economic Advisors 1973 (2 of 2)," box 47, Executive Secretariat Files, 1966–1975, General Records of the Department of the Treasury, Record Group (hereafter RG) 56, National Archives and Records Administration (hereafter NARA), College Park, MD; Juan de Onis, "Mastery of World Oil Supply Shifts to Producing Countries," *NYT,* April 16, 1973.

92. Quoted in *FRUS, 1969–1976,* 36:193; William D. Smith, "Advice Is Offered," *NYT,* June 29, 1973.

93. Rogers to Nixon, November 4, 1972, folder "Saudi Arabia King Faisal ibn Abd al-Aziz Al Saud [1972]," box 761, NSC, NL.

94. *FRUS, 1969–1976,* 36:176.

95. Quandt, *Peace Process,* 98–105; Yaqub, *Imperfect Strangers,* 112–115.

96. Kirk J. Beattie, *Egypt during the Sadat Years* (New York: Palgrave, 2000), 127–133; Golan, *Soviet Policies,* 83, 147.

97. Quoted in Yaqub, *Imperfect Strangers,* 122–124; Yergin, *Prize,* 576–579; *FRUS, 1969–1976,* 36: 191.

98. Saunders to Kissinger, June 1, 1973, folder "Kuwait Vol. 1 Jan 20, 1969–Jun 30, 1974 [1 of 2]," box 620, NSC, NL.

99. Nixon to Faisal, August 31, 1973, folder "Saudi Arabia King Faisal ibn Abd al-Aziz Al Saud [1972]," box 761, NSC, NL.

100. Clyde H. Farnsworth, "Oil Nations Will Ask Rise in Prices at Oct. 8 Parley," *NYT,* September 17, 1973.

101. Quandt, *Peace Process,* 104–115.

102. Yergin, *Prize,* 581–584.

103. Quoted from *FRUS, 1969–1976,* 36:212, see also 214, 215, 219; Quant, *Peace Process,* 111–115.

104. Yergin, *Prize,* 587–588.

105. Yaqub, *Imperfect Strangers,* 133–135; Yergin, *Prize,* 588–591.

106. Dallek, *Nixon and Kissinger,* 525–533; Yaqub, *Imperfect Strangers,* 141–143.

107. *FRUS, 1969–1976,* 36:224, 229.

3. Pursuing Petrodollar Interdependence

1. *FRUS, 1969–1976,* 36:298; *FRUS, 1969–1976,* 36:300.

2. *FRUS, 1969–1976,* 36:303.

3. *FRUS, 1969–1976,* 36:228.

4. Throughout the book, US inflation rates are measured as the twelve-month percentage change in the consumer price index calculated by the US Department of Labor, Bureau of Labor Statistics.

5. Richard Halloran, "Cost Crisis in Oil Developing in Japan," *NYT,* January 23, 1974; Frank Costigliola, *France and the United States: The Cold Alliance since World War II* (New York: Twayne Publishers, 1992), 178.

6. Rüdiger Graf, "Making Use of the 'Oil Weapon': Western Industrialized Countries and Arab Petropolitics in 1973–74," *Diplomatic History* 36, no. 1 (2012): 202–204; Ethan B. Kapstein, *The Insecure Alliance: Energy Crises and Western Politics since 1944* (Oxford: Oxford University Press, 1990), 165–166; Sargent, *Superpower Transformed*, 155–157; Yaqub, *Imperfect Strangers*, 148.

7. *FRUS, 1969–1976*, 36:254.

8. *FRUS, 1969–1976*, 36:238, 248, 251, 254.

9. *FRUS, 1969–1976*, 36:238.

10. *FRUS, 1969–1976*, 36:239.

11. *FRUS, 1969–1976*, 36:241.

12. Johnson, "Trip Report to the Middle East," November 12, 1973, folder "Oil—Nov. & Dec. 1973 GLP," box 1, Records of Executive Assistant to the Deputy Secretary Gerald L. Parsky, 1973–1974, RG56, NARA.

13. *FRUS, 1969–1976*, 36:258.

14. Memcon, Yamani, Shultz et al., December 10, 1973, folder "Dec 73 Vol 1 Action-Briefing Memos & Memcons," box 1, Office of the Assistant Secretary for International Affairs AB Memos 1973–75 (hereafter OASIA), RG56, NARA.

15. Bernard Weinraub, "Oil Price Doubled by Big Producers on Persian Gulf," *NYT*, December 24, 1973.

16. Ibid.

17. *FRUS, 1969–1976*, 36:271.

18. *FRUS, 1969–1976*, 27:49.

19. *FRUS, 1969–1976*, 36:273.

20. *FRUS, 1969–1976*, 36:274.

21. *FRUS, 1969–1976*, 36:276.

22. *FRUS, 1969–1976*, 36:277.

23. OASIA Research, "Financial Consequences of OPEC Investment Funds," January 17, 1974, folder "Investment in the U.S. by Oil Producing Nations (3)," box 113, NSC Institutional Files (hereafter NSC IF), FL.

24. "Updating Fiscal Year 1974 Objectives," January 2, 1974, folder "Jan 74 Vol 1 Action-Briefing Memos & Memcons," box 1, OASIA, RG56, NARA.

25. Sidney Jones to Jack Bennett, "Technology Transfer Program," January 18, 1974, folder "Investment in the US by Oil Producing Nations (5)," box 113, NSC IF, FL.

26. Memcon, Hisham Nazir, Kissinger et al., December 15, 1973, folder "Memcons December 1973 HAK+Presidential [1 of 2]," box 1027, NSC, NL.

27. American Consul in Zurich to Department of State, February 7, 1974, folder "Investment in the US by Oil Producing Nations (5)," box 113, NSC IF, FL.

28. This fear periodically emerged in the press. One example is Clyde H. Farnsworth, "Arabs Cut Funds at Banks of U.S.," *NYT*, December 7, 1973.

29. *FRUS, 1969–1976*, 36:298.

30. *FRUS, 1969–1976*, 36:309.

31. Matusow, *Nixon's Economy*, 267; Sargent, *Superpower Transformed*, 155–160; Spiro, *Hidden Hand*, 80–88.

32. *FRUS, 1969–1976*, 36:327, 332.

33. Telephone conversation, Kissinger, Clements, March 7, 1974, 2:45 p.m., US Department of State Virtual Reading Room (hereafter DSVRR), http://foia.state.gov/Search/Search.aspx.

34. Telephone conversation, Nixon, Kissinger, March 11, 1974, 5:50 p.m., DSVRR.

35. Juan de Onis, "Most Arab Lands End Ban on Oil Shipments for U.S.," *NYT*, March 20, 1974.

36. Akins to Kissinger, March 21, 1974, DSVRR.

37. David Binder, "U.S. Will Supply Arms and Factories to Saudis," *NYT*, April 6, 1974.

38. Kissinger to Nixon, June 6, 1974, folder "Saudi Arabia June 6–7, 1974 Visit of Prince Fahd [1 of 3]," box 937, NSC, NL.

39. Bernard Gwertzman, "'Milestone' Pact Is Signed by U.S. and Saudi Arabia," *NYT*, June 9, 1974.

40. *FRUS, 1969–1976*, E-9 part 2: 109.

41. *FRUS, 1969–1976*, E-9 part 2: 113.

42. Quoted in Cooper, *Oil Kings*, 156.

43. Memcon, Harold Lever, the shah, December 3, 1974, Prime Minister's Office Files (hereafter PREM) 16–49, National Archives (hereafter NA), Kew, United Kingdom.

44. Skeet, *OPEC*, 111–112.

45. Memcon, Nixon, Simon, Scowcroft, July 9, 1974, folder "Memcons 1 June 1974–[Aug 8, 1974] HAK+Presidential [2 of 3]," box 1029, NSC, NL.

46. "Simon Quoted: Iran 'Shah's a Nut,'" *Los Angeles Times*, July 16, 1974.

47. Bank for International Settlements, *Forty-Fifth Annual Report* (Basel, 1975), 130–132.

48. Spiro, *Hidden Hand*, 32–37.

49. Edwin L. Dale Jr., "Prudence by Bankers Foreseen for Financings Related to Oil," *NYT*, June 19, 1974.

50. Memcon, Nixon, Simon, Scowcroft, July 9, 1974, folder "Memcons 1 June 1974–[Aug 8, 1974] HAK+Presidential [2 of 3]," box 1029, NSC, NL.

51. Ibid.

52. Spiro, *Hidden Hand*, 110.

53. "Simon's Tough Tour," *Time*, July 29, 1974.

54. Simon to Nixon, "Necessary Follow-Through on My Mid-East and European Discussions," undated, ca. July 30, 1974, folder "Memos for the White House 1974 (2 of 2)," box 61, Executive Secretary 1966–75 (hereafter ES), RG56, NARA.

55. "Saudi Arabia," date illegible, ca. July 1974, folder "Saudi Arabia 1974–1976 (2)," box 26, William E. Simon Papers (hereafter SP), Special Collections and College Archives, Lafayette College, Easton, PA.

56. *FRUS, 1969–1976*, 36:361.

57. Simon to Nixon, "Necessary Follow-Through on My Mid-East and European Discussions."

58. Ibid.

59. Ibid. (emphasis added).

60. Skeet, *OPEC*, 119–122.

61. *FRUS, 1969–1976*, 36:361.

62. Memcon, Kissinger, Simon et al., August 3, 1974, folder "Memcons 1 June 1974–[Aug 8, 1974] HAK+Presidential [1 of 3]," box 1029, NSC, NL.

63. *FRUS, 1969–1976*, 37:2.

64. Memcon, Kissinger, Simon et al., August 3, 1974, folder "Memcons 1 June 1974–[Aug 8, 1974] HAK+Presidential [1 of 3]," box 1029, NSC, NL.

65. For background on the Ford administration, see Yanek Mieczkowski, *Gerald Ford and the Challenges of the 1970s* (Lexington: University Press of Kentucky, 2005); Garthoff, *Détente and Confrontation*; Hanhimäki, *Flawed Architect*; and Sargent, *Superpower Transformed*.

66. *FRUS, 1969–1976*, 37:1.

67. *FRUS, 1969–1976*, 37:2.

68. *FRUS, 1969–1976*, 37:1.

69. Ibid.

70. Wreatham Gathright, "NSDM 278: Draft Report on Joint Commissions in the Near East and South Asia," January 28, 1975, folder "Joint Cooperation Commissions (3)," box 8, NSA, International Economic Affairs Staff: Files (hereafter IEASF), FL.

71. Skeet, *OPEC*, 112–116.

72. US Bureau of the Census, *Statistical Abstract of the United States* (Washington, D.C., various years).

73. Skeet, *OPEC*, 240–244.

74. Arthur Lowrie to Kissinger, August 2, 1974, folder "Iraq," box 603, NSC, NL.

75. Vandewalle, *Modern Libya*, 110.

76. Michael C. Jensen, "Petrodollar Outlook," *NYT*, February 13, 1975.

77. "Volcker's Successor Takes Tough Job," *NYT*, July 10, 1974; Clyde H. Farnsworth, "Middle East Lenders Bypassing Banks," *NYT*, March 3, 1975.

78. "Summary of Panel Discussion on Outlook for Current Account Financing via Private Capital Markets," William Hurst et al., 1975, folder "International Economic Policy 1975–1976," box 23, SP.

79. "Kissinger on Oil, Food, and Trade," January 13, 1975, *Business Week*.

80. James Akins to Kissinger, January 5, 1975, folder "Saudi Arabia - State Department Telegrams to SECSTATE-EXDIS (1)," box 29, NSA, Presidential Country Files for Middle East and South Asia (hereafter NSA PCF MESA), FL.

81. Akins to Kissinger, January 18, 1975, folder "Saudi Arabia - State Department Telegrams to SECSTATE-NODIS (3)," box 29, NSA PCF MESA, FL.

82. Kissinger to Akins, January 11, 1975, folder "Saudi Arabia - State Department Telegrams from SECSTATE-NODIS (2)," box 28, NSA PCF MESA, FL.

83. *FRUS, 1969–1976*, 37:32.

84. *FRUS, 1969–1976*, 37:39.

4. The Triangle to the Nile

1. Simon to Nixon, "Necessary Follow-Through on My Mid-East and European Discussions," undated.

2. Jeffry A. Frieden, *Banking on the World: The Politics of American International Finance* (New York: Harper & Row, 1987), 121–129.

3. Andrew Crockett, "Extended Fund Facility," March 6, 1974, folder "Chron. Jan–Mar 1974," box 1, Witteveen - Chronological Files (hereafter WCF), Office of the Managing Director Records (hereafter OMD), International Monetary Fund Archive (hereafter IMFA), Washington, DC.

4. Crockett, "Financing the Oil Facility," March 22, 1974, folder "Chron. Jan–Mar 1974," box 1, WCF, OMD, IMFA.

5. David Ekbladh, *The Great American Mission: Modernization and the Construction of an American World Order* (Princeton, NJ: Princeton University Press, 2011), 251–254; Sharma, *Robert McNamara's Other War*, 54–77.

6. "Meeting on Energy," January 22, 1974, Memoranda for the Record - Memoranda 08, folder "ID: 1771495 ISAD(G), Reference Code: WB IBRD/IDA 03 EXC-10-4543S," Series: Memoranda for the Record, Sub-Fonds: Records of President Robert S. McNamara (hereafter RPM), Fonds: Records of the Office of the President (hereafter ROP), World Bank Group Archives (hereafter WBGA), Washington, DC.

7. "U.S. Economic and Financial Assistance to Soften Impact of Recent Oil Price Increases," January 29, 1974, folder "Jan '74 Volume II Action-Briefing Memos & Memcons," box 1, OASIA, RG56, NARA.

8. Lever to Wilson, "The Oil Money Problem," December 13, 1974, PREM 16–49, NA.

9. Crockett, "New Oil Facility," February 14, 1974, folder "Chron. Jan–Mar 1974," box 1, WCF, OMD, IMFA.

10. Charles Cooper to Simon, "Guidance to McNamara on Borrowing from Oil Exporters and Related Issues," August 3, 1974, folder "Aug 74 Vol 1 Action-Briefing Memos & Memcons," box 2, OASIA, RG56, NARA.

11. Volcker to Shultz, "Letter from Witteveen re Oil Facility," March 26, 1974, folder "Mar 74 Vol 1 Action-Briefing Memos & Memcons," box 1, OASIA, RG56, NARA.

12. Cooper to Simon, "Guidance to McNamara on Borrowing from Oil Exporters and Related Issues," August 3, 1974.

13. Crockett, "New Oil Facility"; Witteveen to Shultz, March 21, 1974, folder "Chron. Jan–Mar 1974," box 1, WCF, OMD, IMFA.

14. Spiro, Hidden Hand, 99.

15. Crockett, "Saudi Arabia: Conversations with Authorities," April 19, 1974, folder "Chron Apr–Jun 1974," box 1, WCF, OMD, IMFA.

16. Crockett, "Kuwait: Conversation with Authorities," April 24, 1974, folder "Chron Apr–Jun 1974," box 1, WCF, OMD, IMFA.

17. Kunz, Butter and Guns, 263–264; Kapstein, Governing the Global Economy, 63.

18. Sharma, Robert McNamara's Other War, 81–91.

19. McNamara et al., January 28, 1976, Memoranda for the Record - Memoranda 12, folder "ID: 1771499, ISAD(G), Reference Code: WB IBRD/IDA 03 EXC-10-4543S," Series: Memoranda for the record, RPM, ROP, WBGA.

20. James Martin Center for Nonproliferation Studies, Middlebury Institute of International Studies at Monterey, Documents of the Fourth Conference of Heads of State or Government of Non-aligned Countries, 58–59, http://cns.miis.edu/nam/documents/Official_Document/4th_Summit_FD _Algiers_Declaration_1973_Whole.pdf (accessed February 10, 2020); Dietrich, Oil Revolution, 272–273; Robert Malley, The Call from Algeria: Third Worldism, Revolution, and the Turn to Islam (Berkeley: University of California Press, 1996), 141–145; Robert K. Olson, U.S. Foreign Policy and the New International Economic Order: Negotiating Global Problems, 1974–1981 (Boulder, CO: Westview Press, 1981), 13–14.

21. Kathleen Teltsch, "Poor Lands Urged to Control Goods," NYT, April 11, 1974.

22. Dietrich, Oil Revolution, 264–266; Olson, U.S. Foreign Policy, 14–19, FRUS, 1969–1976, 37:55. See also Paul Adler "'The Basis of a New Internationalism': The Institute for Policy Studies and North-South Politics from the NIEO to Neoliberalism," Diplomatic History 41, no. 4 (September 2017): 665–693.

23. Quote in FRUS, 1969–1976, 37: 41, see also 47, 65; Dietrich, Oil Revolution, 282–304; Daniel J. Sargent, "North/South: The United States Responds to the New International Economic Order," Humanity: An International Journal of Human Rights, Humanitarianism, and Development 6, no. 1 (Spring 2015): 207–211.

24. Daigle, Limits of Détente, 332–335; Yaqub, Imperfect Strangers, 147–152.

25. Simon to Nixon, "Necessary Follow-Through on My Mid-East and European Discussions," undated.

26. Beattie, Sadat Years, 134–146.

27. Ibid.

28. Marvin G. Weinbaum, Egypt and the Politics of U.S. Economic Aid (Boulder, CO: Westview Press, 1986), 32.

29. FRUS, 1969–1976, 36:332.

30. Eilts to Kissinger, April 1, 1974, folder "Arab Republic of Egypt Mar–Jun 30, 1974 [2 of 4]," box 639, NSC, NL.

31. Eilts to Kissinger, April 4, 1974, folder "Arab Republic of Egypt Mar–Jun 30, 1974 [2 of 4]," box 639, NSC, NL.

32. Eilts to Kissinger, April 20, 1974, folder "Arab Republic of Egypt Mar–Jun 30, 1974 [2 of 4]," box 639, NSC, NL.

33. Cooper to Kissinger, "Economic Assistance for the UAR," January 10, 1974, folder "Arab Republic of Egypt 1 Jan 1974–Feb 24 [1 of 2]," box 639, NSC, NL.

34. Quote from Eilts to Kissinger, January 29, 1974, folder "Arab Republic of Egypt 1 Jan 1974–Feb 24 [1 of 2]," box 639, NSC, NL; see also Eilts to Kissinger, February 6, 1974, folder "Arab Republic of Egypt 1 Jan 1974–Feb 24 [1 of 2]," box 639, NSC, NL; Eilts to Kissinger, February 7, 1974, folder "Arab Republic of Egypt 1 Jan 1974–Feb 24 [1 of 2]," box 639, NSC, NL.

35. Henry Tanner, "Bechtel Withdraws from Egypt Oil Role," NYT, April 13, 1974; Henry Tanner, "Egypt Counts on Canal and Oil to Bolster Self-Sufficiency," NYT, January 25, 1976.

36. Memcon, Kissinger, Sadat et al., May 1, 1974, folder "Memcons: Secretary-Sadat 1974," box 44, Records of Joseph Sisco, 1951–76, General Records of the Department of State, RG59, NARA.

37. Saunders to Kissinger, March 26, 1974, folder "Arab Republic of Egypt Mar–Jun 30, 1974 [1 of 4]," box 639, NSC, NL.

38. "Egypt," undated, ca. June 1974, folder "Egypt," box 21, SP.

39. Ibid.

40. Beattie, Sadat Years, 138–143.

41. Henry Tanner, "Egypt Will End Total Reliance on Soviet Arms," NYT, April 19, 1974.

42. "Egypt-U.S. Cooperation Group OKd," Los Angeles Times, June 1, 1974.

43. "Egypt Liberalizes Laws on Foreign Investment," Washington Post, June 11, 1974; Beattie, Sadat Years, 138–139.

44. Henry Tanner, "Nixon and Sadat Sign Sweeping Accord on Cooperation," NYT, June 15, 1974.

45. Eilts to Kissinger, July 16, 1974, folder "Arab Republic of Egypt July 1, 1974—," box 639, NSC, NL.

46. Gerald Parsky to Simon, "Additional Points to Be Raised with Hegazi," July 14, 1974, folder "Egypt—1974 File 1," box 2, Records of Assistant Secretary of International Affairs 1973–76 (hereafter RASIA), RG56, NARA.

47. "Simon's Tough Tour," Time, July 29, 1974.

48. Henry Tanner, "Egypt to Admit 4 Big U.S. Banks," NYT, July 17, 1974.

49. "Subject: Report of August 15, 1974 Meeting of the Joint U.S.-Egyptian Commission, Sub-Committee on Foreign Trade," undated, folder "Egypt: Visit to U.S. by Ismail Fahmy, Minister of Foreign Affairs August 1974," box 2, RASIA, RG56, NARA.

50. Memcon, Ford, Kissinger, Scowcroft, August 12, 1974, box 4, NSA Memoranda of Conversation (hereafter NSA MC), FL.

51. Memcon, Fahmy, Kissinger, Peter Rodman, August 12, 1974, folder "Memcon: Secretary-Fahmy, 1974," box 45, Records of Joseph Sisco, 1951–76, RG59, NARA.

52. Memcon, Ford, Kissinger, Scowcroft, August 13, 1974, box 4, NSA MC, FL.

53. "Bilateral Briefing Book: IBRD/IMF Annual Meeting—1974, Volume 1, Major Countries," September 24, 1974, folder "IBRD & IMF Annual Meeting—Egypt," box 31, SP.

54. Parsky to Kissinger, "Status of Economic Aspects of Joint U.S.-Egyptian Commission on Economic Cooperation," November 5, 1974, folder "Egypt–1974 File 1," box 2, RASIA, RG56, NARA.

55. Parsky to Shultz, "Your Visit to Egypt," November 5, 1974, folder "Egypt - Parsky Visit, Nov. 1974," box 2, RASIA, RG56, NARA.

56. "Issues/Talking Points: Emergency Assistance for Egypt," October 1975, folder "10/26–29 /75 - Egypt President Sadat (20)," box 15, NSA Presidential Briefing Material for VIP Visits (hereafter NSA PBM), FL.

57. Akins to Eilts, May 22, 1975, folder "Saudi Arabia - State Dept Telegrams to SECSTATE-EXDIS (2)," box 29, NSA PCF MESA, FL.

58. Richard Helms to Kissinger, May 29, 1975, folder "Iran - State Dept Telegrams to SECSTATE-NODIS (2)," box 14, NSA PCF MESA, FL.

59. Kissinger to Eilts, September 15, 1975, folder "Egypt - State Dept Telegrams from SECSTATE-EXDIS (2)," box 4, NSA PCF MESA, FL.

60. Owen, *Middle East Economies*, 181–184; "Arabs Agree on Vast Aid to Main Foes of Israel," *NYT*, October 30, 1974.

61. Memcon and Allon et al., August 1, 1974, folder "August '74 Volume I Action Briefing Memos & Memcons," box 2, OASIA, 1973–75, RG56, NARA.

62. Memcon, Dinitz, Kissinger et al., February 5, 1974, box 9, NSA MC, FL.

63. Quandt, *Peace Process*, 130–173.

64. Miglietta, *American Alliance*, 168–173.

65. Akins to Kissinger, December 18, 1974, folder "Saudi Arabia - State Dept Telegrams to SECSTATE-NODIS (2)," box 29, NSA PCF MESA, FL.

66. Ibid.

67. Kissinger to Aikens, December 27, 1974, folder "Saudi Arabia - State Dept Telegrams from SECSTATE-NODIS (1)," box 28, NSA PCF MESA, FL.

68. Houghton to Scowcroft, "CIA Analysis of Egyptian Military Intentions and Contingency Planning," March 14, 1975, folder "Outside the System Chronological File 3/11/75–3/20/75," box 2, NSA Outside the System Chronological Files, FL.

69. Quandt, *Peace Process*, 159–170.

70. Memcon, NSC Meeting, March 28, 1975, box 9, NSA MC, FL.

71. Ibid.

72. J. J. Goldberg, *Jewish Power: Inside the American Jewish Establishment* (New York: Perseus Books, 1996), 202–205.

73. Quandt, *Peace Process*, 165.

74. Ibid., 163–170.

5. The Petrodollar Economy

1. Andrus to Ford, March 2, 1976, folder "Andrus, Cecil D.," box 1, NSA Presidential Name File (hereafter NSA PNF), FL.

2. John Marsh to Andrus, March 26, 1976, folder "Andrus, Cecil D.," box 1, NSA PNF, FL.

3. Andrus to Ford, March 31, 1976, folder "Andrus, Cecil D.," box 1, NSA PNF, FL.

4. Scowcroft to Helms, April 20, 1976, folder "NSA Backchannel Messages Box 4 (6) Mideast-Africa," box 18, Remote Archives Capture (hereafter RAC), FL.

5. Helms to Scowcroft, April 24, 1976, folder "NSA Backchannel Messages Box 4 (6) Mideast-Africa," box 18, RAC, FL; Scowcroft to Helms, April 25, 1976, folder "NSA Backchannel Messages Box 4 (6) Mideast-Africa," box 18, RAC, FL.

6. Scowcroft to Helms, May 3, 1976, folder "NSA Backchannel Messages Box 4 (6) Mideast-Africa," box 18, RAC, FL.

7. Skeet, *OPEC*, 129–134.

8. Ibid., 240–244.

9. *FRUS, 1969–1976*, 37:55, 65, 80, 82.

10. Quote from, *FRUS, 1969–1976*, 37:106, see also 109, 111–113; Cooper, *Oil Kings*, 326–363; Giuliano Garavini, *The Rise and Fall of OPEC in the Twentieth Century* (Oxford: Oxford University Press, 2019), 261–266; Skeet, *OPEC*, 135.

11. United Nations, National Accounts Main Aggregates Database, https://unstats.un.org/unsd/snaama/Index (accessed February 10, 2020).

12. Kunz, *Butter and Guns*, 264.

13. James, *International Monetary Cooperation*, 277–285.

14. Frieden, *Global Capitalism*, 365–366.

15. Painter, "Oil and Geopolitics," 194–195.

16. Stephen Kotkin, "The Kiss of Debt: The East Bloc Goes Borrowing," in Ferguson et al., *Shock of the Global*, 80–86.

17. Cooper, *Oil Kings*, 205; Dietrich, *Oil Revolution*, 282–301; Frieden, *Banking on the World*, 123–142; Spiro, *Hidden Hand*, 60–79.

18. Given the difficulties of data collection, different agencies' estimates of OPEC assets differ by as much as 10 percent. Spiro, *Hidden Hand*, 57–58.

19. Bank for International Settlements, *Annual Report* (Basel, various years).

20. Cohen, *Whose Interest?*, 124–125; US Department of Treasury, "Securities (B): Portfolio Holdings of U.S. and Foreign Securities," https://www.treasury.gov/resource-center/data-chart-center/tic/Pages/ticsec2.aspx (accessed February 10, 2020).

21. Anthony Sampson, *The Money Lenders: Bankers and a World in Turmoil* (New York: Viking Press, 1981), 125–140; Phillip L. Zweig, *Wriston: Walter Wriston, Citibank and the Rise and Fall of American Financial Supremacy* (New York: Crown Publishers, 1995), 384–439.

22. For a general treatment of West's life, see Philip G. Grose, *Looking for Utopia: The Life and Times of John C. West* (Columbia: University of South Carolina Press, 2011).

23. "Investors, West, Tour Kiawah," unattributed newspaper article clipping, ca. April 1974, folder "West, Clippings, 1974 Apr–May," box 41, John Carl West Papers (hereafter JWP), South Carolina Political Collections, University of South Carolina, Columbia, SC.

24. Priscilla S. Meyer, "Kuwaitis' Resort Project off Coast of Carolina Proceeds amid Wild Rumors, Stiff Opposition," *Wall Street Journal*, February 26, 1975.

25. "Dear Governor West, I feel very sorry . . ." October 1974, folder "Kuwait, Kuwait Investment Company-Kiawah Island South Carolina (1 of 2)," box 8, JWP.

26. Henry Eason, "Kiawah Island Conflict Unfolds," June 2, 1974, *Greensville News*, folder "Clippings, 1974 June–Dec.," box 41, JWP.

27. Charleston Natural History Society to West, December 8, 1974, folder "Kuwait, Kuwait Investment Company-Kiawah Island South Carolina (2 of 2)," box 8, JWP; West to Sabah, December 10, 1974, folder "Kuwait, Kuwait Investment Company-Kiawah Island South Carolina (2 of 2)," box 8, JWP; West to the Charleston Natural History Society, December 10, 1974, folder "Kuwait, Kuwait Investment Company-Kiawah Island South Carolina (2 of 2)," box 8, JWP.

28. "Welcome to the State of Kuwait," ca. December 1974, folder "Kuwait, Kuwait Investment Company-Kiawah Island South Carolina (2 of 2)," box 8, JWP; West to Bader Al-Dawood, December 30, 1974, folder "Kuwait, Kuwait Investment Company-Kiawah Island South Carolina (2 of 2)," box 8, JWP.

29. Meyer, "Kuwaitis' Resort Project."

30. Jan Stucker, "West's Firm Seeks to Tie Economic Knot with Arabs," unattributed newspaper article clipping, May 17, 1976, folder "Clippings, 1976," box 41, JWP.

31. Ibid.

32. Helms to West, September 8, 1976, folder "Middle East, South Carolina State Development Board, South Carolina Trade Mission, General, 1976 Apr. and c. Apr.," box 27, JWP.

33. West to Cyrus Vance, January 20, 1977, folder "Ambassador to Saudi Arabia, 1977–1981, Appointment, 1977, General," box 11, JWP.

34. International Monetary Fund, Direction of Trade Statistics, https://data.imf.org/?sk=9D60 28D4-F14A-464C-A2F2-59B2CD424B85 (accessed February 10, 2020).

35. Dietrich, "Uncertainty Rising," 275–276; David Styan, France and Iraq: Oil, Arms and French Policy Making in the Middle East (London: I.B. Tauris, 2006), 109–128.

36. Alvandi, Nixon, Kissinger, and the Shah, chap. 3.

37. Takriti, Monsoon Revolution, 293–295, 304–307.

38. Ann Markusen et al., The Rise of the Gunbelt: The Military Remapping of Industrial America (Oxford: Oxford University Press, 1991), 10.

39. "Armaments: The Arms Dealers: Guns for All," Time, March 3, 1975.

40. Jonathan Nitzan and Shimshon Bichler, The Global Political Economy of Israel (London: Pluto Press, 2002), 206–219.

41. US Department of Defense, Defense Security Cooperation Agency, Fiscal Year Series: Foreign Military Sales, Foreign Military Construction Sales and Other Security Cooperation Historical Facts as of September 30, 2012 (Washington, D.C., 2012); Miglietta, American Alliance, 64–69, 209–217.

42. "The Executive Mercenaries," Time, February 24, 1975.

43. Eric Pace, "U.S. Influence on Iran: Gigantic and Diverse," NYT, August 30, 1976.

44. Miglietta, American Alliance, 64–69; "Armaments"; Brendan Jones, "'Made-in-U.S.A.' Label Helps Americans to Garner Large Share of Mideast Market," NYT, June 30, 1975; "Aladdin's Troubled Dream," Forbes, February 15, 1976, 28–40.

45. Jones, "'Made-in-U.S.A.'"; Walter McQuade, "The Arabian Building Boom Is Making Construction History," Fortune, September 1976, 112–115, 186–190; Steven Rattner, "Trade with U.S. Is Enormous; 28,000 Americans Work in Saudi Arabia," NYT, May 29, 1977; "Policy: Saudi Arabia's Growing Petropower," Time, July 11, 1977; "Jubail: The Biggest Is Getting Bigger," Construction Week, April 11, 2009.

46. Pascal Menoret, Joyriding in Riyadh: Oil, Urbanism, and Road Revolt (Cambridge: Cambridge University Press, 2014), 105–114.

47. Thomas C. Hayes, "Bechtel: A Reclusive Giant," NYT, July 8, 1982.

48. Alvandi, Nixon, Kissinger, and the Shah, 126–171; Jacob Darwin Hamblin, "The Nuclearization of Iran in the Seventies," Diplomatic History 38, no. 5 (November 2014): 1114–1135.

49. Shai Feldman, "The Bombing of Osiraq-Revisited," International Security 7, no. 2 (Fall 1982): 115–118.

50. Beasley, "At Your Service," 263–271.

51. Mieczkowski, Gerald Ford, 148–152.

52. Ibid.

53. Parsky to Simon, September 24, 1974, folder "Memos from Staff: Parsky 1974," box 54, ES, RG56, NARA.

54. Simon to Kent Frizzell, September 30, 1975, folder "Department Correspondence: Interior 1975," box 65, ES, RG56, NARA.

55. Waller to Ford, November 3, 1975, folder "Waller, William L.," box 2, NSA PNF, FL.

56. Bob Wyrick, "Nixon Aides Who Pushed Private Atomic Fuel Industry Now Have Top Jobs in It," Los Angeles Times, November 16, 1975; "Shultz Is Joining Bechtel; Bennett in Volcker Post," NYT, May 10, 1974; "Shultz Named Bechtel Corp. President," Washington Post, May 25, 1975.

57. Steven Rattner, "Trade with U.S. Is Enormous; 28,000 Americans Work in Saudi Arabia," *NYT*, May 29, 1977; "Policy: Saudi Arabia's Growing Petropower," *Time*, July 11, 1977; Pace, "U.S. Influence on Iran."

58. William P. Brown, "An Employee Orientation Program for Saudi Arabia Prepared for Fluor Corporation," August 28, 1975, folder 10, box 7, William E. Mulligan Papers, Special Collections, Georgetown University, Washington, DC.

59. Pace, "U.S. Influence on Iran."

60. Matthew K. Shannon, *Losing Hearts and Minds: American-Iranian Relations and International Education during the Cold War* (Ithaca, NY: Cornell University Press, 2017), 3, 15, chaps. 4–5; Yaqub, *Imperfect Strangers*, 285–289.

61. Simmons, *Arab Foreign Aid*, 25, 58–63, 174.

62. Richard P. Mattione, *OPEC's Investments and the International Financial System* (Washington, DC: Brookings Institution, 1985), 148; Golan, *Soviet Policies*, 148; Lars Hasvoll Bakke and Hilde Henriksen Waage, "Facing Assad: American Diplomacy toward Syria, 1973–1977," *International History Review* 40, no. 3 (June 2018): 565.

63. Ibrahim, *New Arab*, 32–37.

64. Ibid., 45.

65. Ibid., 71–73.

66. Owen and Pamuk, *Middle East Economies*, 100–101.

67. Ibrahim, *New Arab*, 25.

68. US Bureau of the Census, *Statistical Abstract of the United States*, various years.

69. Ibrahim, *New Arab*, 67–69, 113–115; F. Gregory Gause, III, *Oil Monarchies: Domestic and Security Challenges in the Arab Gulf States* (New York: Council on Foreign Relations Press, 1994), 70–75.

70. David M. Wight, "Kissinger's Levantine Dilemma: The Ford Administration and the Syrian Occupation of Lebanon," *Diplomatic History* 37, no. 1 (January 2013): 144–177.

71. Memcon, NSC Meeting, April 7, 1976, box 2, NSC Meetings File, FL.

72. Itamar Rabinovich, *The War for Lebanon, 1970–1985*, rev. ed. (Ithaca, NY: Cornell University Press, 1985), 55–56.

73. Eilts to Kissinger, April 19, 1975, folder "Egypt (6)," box 4, NSA PCF MESA, FL.

74. Kissinger to Ford, "Strategy for the Sadat Visit," October 24, 1975, folder "10/26–29/75 - Egypt - President Sadat (10)," box 15, NSA PBM, FL.

75. Bernard Gwertzman, "Administration Decision to End Arms Embargo on Egypt by Sale of C-130's," *NYT*, March 20, 1976; Bernard Gwertzman, "Kissinger and 3 Senators Meet on Egypt Arms Issue," *NYT*, March 26, 1976; "Congress Is Silent; Cairo Arms Deal On," *NYT*, April 15, 1976.

76. Henry Tanner, "Simon Commends Sadat on Economy," *NYT*, March 8, 1976.

77. "U.S. Businessmen's Study Tells Egypt Why Foreign Investment Lags," *NYT*, November 26, 1976.

78. Beattie, *Sadat Years*, 207; Owen, *Middle East Economies*, 135–137.

79. William J. Burns, *Economic Aid & American Foreign Policy toward Egypt, 1955–1981* (Albany: State University of New York Press, 1985), 220.

80. "Issues/Talking Points: Emergency Assistance for Egypt," October 1975, folder "10/26–29/75 - Egypt President Sadat (20)," box 15, NSA PBM, FL.

81. Adi Davar, "Egypt—Mr. McNamara's Meeting with Some Cabinet Ministers," April 10, 1974, folder "Contacts with member countries: Egypt - Correspondence 02," Series: Contacts—Member Country files, RPM, ROP, WBGA; John Gunter to Witteveen, March 7, 1974, folder "C-Egypt-810 Mission Gunter, John Feb. 1974," box 6, Country Files - Egypt (hereafter CFE), Central Files Collection (hereafter CFC), IMFA.

82. Gunter to Witteveen, November 25, 1975, folder "C-Egypt-810 Mission Gunter and Staff Oct.–Nov. 1975," box 6, CFE, CFC, IMFA.

83. Martijn Paijmans to McNamara, April 19, 1976, folder "Contacts with member countries; Egypt - Correspondence 03," Series: Contacts—Member Country files, RPM, ROP, WBGA.

84. Henry Tanner, "Cairo Reaps a Wind," *NYT*, January 21, 1977.

85. "Saudi Arabian Aid to Egypt," ca. August 1976, folder "Saudi Arabia (15)," box 28, NSA PCF MESA, FL.

86. Gunter to Witteveen, September 23, 1976, folder "C-Saudi Arabia-810 Mission Gunter, John W. Sept. 1976," box 3, Country Files - Saudi Arabia, CFC, IMFA.

87. Scowcroft to Ford, "Letter from President Sadat on Egyptian Economy—Proposed Reply," November 29, 1976, folder "Egypt - President Sadat (2)," box 1, NSA PCFL, FL.

88. Ford to Sadat, November 30, 1976, folder "Egypt - President Sadat (2)," box 1, NSA PCFL, FL.

89. Gunter to Witteveen, "Egypt—Discussions concerning Use of the Fund's Resources," December 23, 1976, folder "C-Egypt-810 Mission Gunter and Staff Dec. 1976," box 6, CFE, CFC, IMFA.

90. Tanner, "Cairo Reaps a Wind."

91. Beattie, *Sadat Years*, 207, 311n315.

92. Ibid., 206–212.

93. Feiler, *Egypt and the Gulf*, 24.

6. Visions of Petrodollar Promise and Peril

1. "Tacoma Due for Dubious Honor," *Tri-City Herald* (Kennewick, WA), November 15, 1974; "Arab Manure Buy Off," *Ellensburg* (WA) *Daily Record*, March 29, 1975; "No Pots of Gold in Piles of Muck," *Ottawa Citizen*, March 31, 1975; Herbert G. Lawson and Ray Vicker, "An Idea That Failed: Spreading Manure to Spread Wealth," *Wall Street Journal*, March 31, 1977.

2. Lawson and Vicker, "Idea That Failed."

3. Natasha Zaretsky, *No Direction Home: The American Family and the Fear of National Decline, 1968–1980* (Chapel Hill: University of North Carolina Press, 2007), 71–96; Meg Jacobs, *Panic at the Pump: The Energy Crisis and the Transformation of American Politics in the 1970s* (New York: Hill and Wang, 2016), chaps. 3 and 4.

4. Yaqub, *Imperfect Strangers*, 196–206, 285–289.

5. Benjamin Smith, *Market Orientalism: Cultural Economy and the Arab Gulf States* (Syracuse, NY: Syracuse University Press, 2015), 130–149.

6. L. Edward Shuck Jr., "10 Million vs. 600 Million," *NYT*, December 8, 1973.

7. Anthony Ripley, "Labor Chiefs Urge a Curb on Arab Oil; Support Rationing," *NYT*, January 24, 1975.

8. Miles Ignotus, "Seizing Arab Oil," *Harper's Magazine*, March 1, 1975, 62; Andrew Higgins, "Power and Peril: America's Supremacy and Its Limits," *Wall Street Journal*, February 4, 2004.

9. Jack G. Shaheen, *Reel Bad Arabs: How Hollywood Vilifies a People*, updated ed. (Northampton, MA: Olive Branch Press, 2015), 25–28.

10. *Ilsa: Harem Keeper of the Oil Sheiks*, directed by Don Edmonds (1976).

11. Ibid.

12. *The Happy Hooker Goes to Washington*, directed by William A. Levey (1977).

13. Ibid.

14. Melani McAlister, *Epic Encounters: Culture, Media, and U.S. Interests in the Middle East since 1945*, 2nd ed. (Berkeley: University of California Press, 2005), 136.

15. Spencer L. Davidson, "The U.S. Should Soak Up That Shower of Gold," *Time*, December 16, 1974.

16. "Faisal and Oil: Driving toward a New World Order," *Time*, January 6, 1975, 32.

17. Rattner, "Trade with U.S. Is Enormous."

18. "Policy: Saudi Arabia's Growing Petropower."

19. McQuade, "Arabian Building Boom," 112–115, 186–190.

20. Leonard Silk, "Odyssey: Redefining the Strength of Nations," *NYT*, November 20, 1977.

21. Jones, "'Made-in-U.S.A.'"

22. US Bureau of the Census, *Statistical Abstract of the United States*, 1978.

23. "Faisal and Oil," 8–9.

24. Jack G. Shaheen, *The TV Arab* (Bowling Green, OH: Bowling Green State University Popular Press, 1984), 57–58.

25. Bill Hinds and Jeff Millar, *Tank McNamara*, Washington Post, January 20–24, 1975.

26. Edward A. Pollitz Jr., *The Forty-First Thief* (New York: Delacorte Press, 1975), 54–58.

27. *Network*, directed by Sidney Lumet (1976).

28. Ibid.

29. Davidson, "U.S. Should Soak Up That Shower of Gold."

30. "Petrodollars Are Dollars," *National Review*, April 11, 1975, 384.

31. Thomas Borstelmann, *The 1970s: A New Global History from Civil Rights to Economic Inequality* (Princeton, NJ: Princeton University Press, 2011).

32. Peter Tanous and Paul Rubinstein, *The Petrodollar Takeover* (New York: G. P. Putnam's Sons, 1975), 58.

33. Quote from "A Local Arab Banker?," *Time*, February 3, 1975, 20; "Breaking a Bank Barrier," *Time*, February 17, 1975.

34. Jack Bennett to Simon, January 8, 1975, folder "Middle East 1975–1976," box 23, SP.

35. James Ganon, "US Ripe for Sheikhs," *Guardian*, January 28, 1974.

36. "Williams Sees Take-Over Threat," *NYT*, February 27, 1975.

37. Pranay Gupte, "Move to Study Foreign Investing in U.S. Reflects Concern on Rising Trend and Lack of Fresh Data," *NYT*, August 29, 1974; Brendan Jones, "Ford Aides Fight Senate Bill with Plan to Control Foreign Investment in U.S.," *NYT*, March 5, 1975.

38. Cohen, *Whose Interest?*, 128.

39. Jones, "Ford Aides Fight Senate Bill with Plan to Control Foreign Investment in U.S."; "Business Outlook Panel," April 23, 1975, folder "International Economic Policy 1975–1976," box 23, SP.

40. Kunz, *Butter and Guns*, 257.

41. Cohen, *Whose Interest?*, 125.

42. Edward Cowan, "List Is Extensive for Arab Boycott," *NYT*, February 26, 1975; see also Janice J. Terry, *U.S. Foreign Policy in the Middle East: The Role of Lobbies and Special Interest Groups* (London: Pluto Press, 2005), 93–109.

43. Seymour Topping, "Arab Oil Wealth Puts Pressure on Israel," *NYT*, January 4, 1975.

44. Juan de Onis, "Kuwait Quits 2 Deals Here with Boycotted Financiers," *NYT*, February 13, 1975.

45. Michael C. Jensen, "2 Senators Assail Arabs' Blacklist," *NYT*, February 15, 1975.

46. Edward Cowan, "Arabs' Blacklist Deplored by Ford," *NYT*, February 27, 1975; Brendan Jones, "Curb on Arab Investors Who Use Boycotts Urged," *NYT*, March 7, 1975.

47. Cowan, "Arabs' Blacklist."

48. Thomas P. Ronan, "Holtman Bill Designed to Defuse Arab Boycott," *NYT*, July 12, 1975.

49. Scowcroft and Ed Schmults to Ford, ca. November 20, 1975, folder "Country File - Saudi Arabia (1)," box 2, NSA IEASF, FL.

50. Philip Shabecoff, "Ford Takes Steps to Protect Jews in Arab Boycott," *NYT*, November 21, 1975.

51. "The Arab Boycott," *NYT*, September 14, 1976; "Ford Signs Tax Revision Measure; Calls It 'Positive and Long Overdue,'" *NYT*, October 5, 1976.

52. William Porter to Kissinger and Cyrus Vance, December 28, 1976, folder "Saudi Arabia - State Dept Telegrams to SECSTATE-NODIS (15)," box 30, NSA PCF MESA, FL.

53. "Armaments," 44.

54. "Mindless Arms Sales," *NYT*, August 11, 1976.

55. Joseph Kraft, "Letter from Riyadh," *New Yorker*, June 26, 1978.

56. Paul E. Erdman, *The Crash of '79* (New York: Simon & Schuster, 1976), 317.

57. Ibid.

58. James McCartney, "U.S. Does Booming Business Peddling Arms to All Comers," *Detroit Free Press*, September 22, 1974.

59. "U.S. Arms Sales in Persian Gulf Called 'Beyond Control,'" *Chicago Tribune*, January 3, 1976.

60. "Cutting Arms Sales," *NYT*, February 24, 1976.

61. Kenneth H. Bacon, "Foreign Military Sales Program Strains Pentagon Resources, Causes Problems," *Wall Street Journal*, February 17, 1976.

62. Mark Philip Bradley, *The World Reimagined: Americans and Human Rights in the Twentieth Century* (Cambridge: Cambridge University Press, 2016); Barbara J. Keys, *Reclaiming American Virtue: The Human Rights Revolution of the 1970s* (Cambridge, MA: Harvard University Press, 2014); Joe Renouard, *Human Rights in American Foreign Policy: From the 1960s to the Soviet Collapse* (Philadelphia: University of Pennsylvania Press, 2015).

63. "Iran Accused at Meeting Here of Torture and Repression," *NYT*, February 29, 1976.

64. "U.S. Is Warned by the Shah against Cutting Arms Flow," *NYT*, March 15, 1976.

65. Bernard Gwertzman, "President Vetoes Aid Bill, Charging It Restricts Him," *NYT*, May 8, 1976.

66. "Bowing to Critics, U.S. Cuts Request on Saudi Missiles," *NYT*, September 2, 1976.

67. John W. Finney, "Effort Collapses in Congress to Block Sale of Missiles to Saudi Arabia," *NYT*, September 29, 1976; Oberdorfer, "Saudi Missile Dispute."

68. Charles Mohr, "Carter Scores Ford on Missile Sale," *NYT*, October 1, 1976.

69. Edward Cowan, "U.S. Issues Reports about Arab Boycott," *NYT*, October 19, 1976.

70. Frank Lynn, "Ford, Campaigning in New York, Seeks Support of Jewish Voters," *NYT*, October 13, 1976.

71. Saddam Hussein, *On Oil Nationalisation in Iraq* (Baghdad: Ath-Thawra House, 1973), 30.

72. "Rafad al-Wisayya al-Amirkiyya 'ala Muqadarat al-'Alam wa Aqama 'Alaqat 'Adila wa Mutakalafi'a bayna al-Duwal al-Muntaja wa al-Mustahalaka," *al-Thawra* (Baghdad), January 27, 1974.

73. "Munhaj al-Istirad al-Jadid," *al-Thawra*, February 14, 1974; 'Ali al-Shaykh, Husayn al-Sa'adi, "al-Naft . . [sic] wa al-Tanmiyya al-Iqtisadiyya wa Tahsin Mustawa Ma'aisha al-Jamahir," *al-Thawra*, February 22, 1974.

74. Amer Rashad al-Jalili, untitled cartoon, *al-Thawra*, February 12, 1974; see also Amer Rashad al-Jalili, untitled cartoon, *al-Thawra*, February 24, 1974.

75. Untitled cartoon, *al-Riyadh*, October 21, 1973.

76. Ali al-Kharji, untitled cartoon, *al-Riyadh*, November 3, 1973.

77. "Amal Washintun Dhahala fi Mu'tamaraha hawl Izma al-Taqa," *al-Riyadh*, February 2, 1974.

78. Nasr al-Sihan al-'Amari, "Al-'Adl Athman min al-Naft," *al-Riyadh*, February 26, 1974.

79. Salah Jahin, untitled cartoon, *al-Ahram* (Cairo), March 14, 1974.

80. Salah Jahin, untitled cartoon, *al-Ahram*, March 16, 1974.

81. Samir 'Atallah, "'al-Thawra al-Naftiyya' Qalabat Nathra al-Gharb ila al-'Alam al-'Arabi," *al-Nahar* (Beirut), January 31, 1974; "Washintun wa Bun Taghriyan al-Amwal al-'Arabiyya," *al-Nahar al-Inma'i* (Beirut), February 3, 1974.

82. "Ghazu al-Sadarat al-Amirkiyya lil-Mintaqa al-'Arabiyya," *al-Thawra*, October 26, 1974.

83. Amer Rashad al-Jalili, "1 Adthar—'Eid al-Intisar," *al-Thawra*, March 1, 1977; see also "Bi-Taqa 'Eid," *al-Thawra*, December 9, 1975.

84. Saddam Hussein, *On Current Affairs in Iraq*, ed. Naji al-Hadithi, trans. Khalid Kishtainy (Baghdad: Translation & Foreign Languages House, 1981), 89–91, 95.

85. Ibid., 92–93.

86. Untitled cartoon, *al-Thawra*, December 20, 1974.

87. Mustafa Mahmoud, *Marxism and Islam*, 2nd ed., trans. M. M. Enani (Jeddah: Tihama Publication, 1985), 122–123.

88. Ahmad al-Najar, "al-Masarif al-Islamiyya," *al-Da'wa* (Cairo), July 1976; al-Hamza Da'abas, "Dhalik bi-Anhum Qalu Inama al-Bay' mithl al-Riba," *al-Da'wa*, October 1976; Mahmud Abu al-Sa'ud, "Fi Midan al-Iqtisad al-Islami," *al-Da'wa*, December 1976.

89. Charles Tripp, *Islam and the Moral Economy: The Challenge of Capitalism* (Cambridge: Cambridge University Press, 2006), 137–140.

90. Cohen, *Whose Interest?*, 133–140.

91. Saad Eddin Ibrahim, "Anatomy of Egypt's Militant Islamic Groups: Methodological Note and Preliminary Findings," *International Journal of Middle East Studies* 12, no. 4 (1980): 433.

92. "Tawsi'a wa Taqwiyya 'Awamal al-Ta'aawun bayna al-Mamlika wa Amrika," *al-Riyadh*, April 6, 1974.

93. "1,000 Miliyyun Riyyal li-Tatwir Shabka al-Swarikh fil-Mamlika," *al-Riyadh*, April 9, 1974.

94. Saddam Hussein, *Iraqi Revolution in the Service of Humanity: Saddam Hussein Speaks*, ed. Z. L. Kaul (New Delhi: New Wave Printing Press, 1978), 9, 13.

95. "Karmaykil: Istafdina Kathiran min Nidal al-Ba'ath dida al-Imbiryyaliyya," *al-Thawra*, February 24, 1974.

96. "Karmaykil: al-'Alam al-Taqdumi Yatab'a Tajraba al-'Iraq wa Intisaratihu al-Mustamira," *al-Thawra*, February 26, 1974.

97. See, for example, "Ma'auna Faniyya wa Qard Dun Fawa'id li-Afriqiyya min al-Duwal al-'Arabiyya al-Musadara lil-Bitrul fi Zil Ta'awanihuma," *al-Riyadh*, January 27, 1974.

98. Ali al-Kharji, untitled cartoon, *al-Riyadh*, April 7, 1974.

99. Feiler, *Egypt and the Gulf*, 163.

100. "1000 Milliyun Dular Hadiyya min al-Malik Faisal ila Sh'ab Misr al-Maqatil," *al-Ahram*, August 3, 1974.

101. "Ta'awan Iqtisadi wa Thaqafi Wasi'a m'a al-Sa'uddiyya," *al-Ahram*, August 7, 1974; "Faysil: Tadhhayat Misr Rafa'at Ras al-'Arab wa A'adat li-Hum Karamtihum," *al-Ahram*, August 9, 1974.

102. Salah Jahin, untitled cartoon, *al-Ahram*, January 15, 1975.

103. Feiler, *Egypt and the Gulf*, 163–167.

104. Mahmoud, *Marxism and Islam*, 48–49.

105. Ibid., 64.

106. Mohammad Reza Pahlavi, *Toward the Great Civilization: A Dream Revisited* (London: Satrap Publishing, 1994), 99, 121.

107. Ibid., 105–106.

108. Bill, *Eagle and the Lion*, 214.

109. Nikki L. Keddie, *Modern Iran: Roots and Results of Revolution*, 2nd ed. (New Haven, CT: Yale University Press, 2006), 200–208.

110. Ali Shari'ati, *What Is to Be Done: The Enlightened Thinkers and an Islamic Renaissance* (Houston: Institute for Research and Islamic Studies, 1986), 29–30.

111. Ibid., 100.

112. Khomeini, *Sahifeh-Ye Imam*, 3:6, 72–73.

113. Ibid., 3:114.

114. Ibid., 3:210–211.

7. Reform and Revolt

1. "Transcript of Foreign Affairs Debate between Ford and Carter," *NYT*, October 7, 1976.

2. On the foreign relations strategies of Carter and his administration, see Garthoff, *Détente and Confrontation*; Betty Glad, *An Outsider in the White House: Jimmy Carter, His Advisors, and the Making of American Foreign Policy* (Ithaca, NY: Cornell University Press, 2009); Sargent, *Superpower Transformed*; Justin Vaïsse, *Zbigniew Brzezinski: America's Grand Strategist*, trans. Catherine Porter (Cambridge, MA: Harvard University Press, 2018); Zanchetta, *Transformation of American International Power.*

3. Linda Charlton, "Mondale Scores Ford Arms Sales," *NYT*, August 31, 1976.

4. "Presidential Directive/NSC-18," August 24, 1977, folder "Presidential Directive 1–20," box 100, Vertical File, Jimmy Carter Presidential Library (hereafter CL), Atlanta, GA.

5. Jonathan Steele, "Carter's Invitation to a New Kind of Club," *Guardian*, January 27, 1977.

6. Lee Leseaze and George C. Wilson, "Arms Sales of $6 Billion Are Held Up," *Washington Post*, March 27, 1977; Bernard Gwertzman, "U.S. Reviews Missile Sales to Saudis," *NYT*, March 3, 1977; "Military Sales of $2 Billion Are Confirmed," *Washington Post*, March 30, 1977.

7. James Callaghan, Carter et al., March 11, 1977, PREM 16/1486, NA; Callaghan, Vance et al., March 31, 1977, PREM 16/1488, NA.

8. Peter Ramsbotham to United Kingdom Foreign & Commonwealth Office, January 26, 1977, PREM 16/1909, NA.

9. Callaghan, Giscard, Carter, Schmidt, May 9, 1977, PREM 16/1267, NA; "Quadripartite Summit, 9 May 1977: Arms Transfer Restraints," ca. May 1977, PREM 12/1267, NA.

10. Edward Walsh, "Arms Sales Curbs Set by Carter," *Washington Post*, May 20, 1977.

11. "Carter Sets Rules to Curb Sales of Arms Abroad," *Wall Street Journal*, May 20, 1977.

12. Walsh, "Arms Sales Curbs."

13. Alam, *Shah and I*, 543.

14. Bill, *Eagle and the Lion*, 227–231; Javier Gil Guerrero, *The Carter Administration and the Fall of Iran's Pahlavi Dynasty: US-Iran Relations on the Brink of the 1979 Revolution* (New York: Palgrave Macmillan, 2016), 28–38.

15. William Branigan, "Iran Said to Plan Cutbacks in Ambitious Radar Program," *Washington Post*, March 26, 1977; "Carter OKs Plane Sale to Iranians," *Los Angeles Times*, April 26, 1977; Norman Kempster, "U.S. to Sell 5 Radar Planes to Iran in Half-Billion-Dollar Deal," *Los Angeles Times*, April 27, 1977. See also Stephen McGlinchey and Robert W. Murray, "Jimmy Carter and the Sale of the AWACS to Iran in 1977," *Diplomacy & Statecraft* 28, no. 2 (2017): 254–276.

16. "Carter OKs Plane Sale to Iranians"; "Battle Expected on Radar Sale to Iran," *Washington Post*, June 23, 1977; "Clash Expected over Plan to Sell Iran Radar Planes," *NYT*, July 8, 1977.

17. Bernard Weinraub, "Controversy Grows over Carter's Move to Sell Iran Planes," *NYT*, July 12, 1977.

18. Bernard Weinraub, "Congressional Agency Denounces Plan to Sell Radar System to Iran," *NYT*, July 16, 1977.

19. Bernard Weinraub, "Two Senators Oppose Sale of Radar Planes to Iran," *NYT*, July 19, 1977.

20. Harold J. Logan, "Turner Stands by Warning on Radar-Jet Sale to Iran," *Washington Post*, July 22, 1977.

21. Harold J. Logan, "Senate Leader Would Delay Sale of Airborne Radar to Iran," *Washington Post*, July 24, 1977.

22. Executive Secretariat: Bureau of Intelligence and Research, "Current Reports," July 25, 1977, NLC-SAFE 17 B-3-14-1-5, RAC, CL (emphasis added).

23. "Administration Bars Delay Asked by Byrd in Radar-Plane Sale," *NYT*, July 26, 1977.

24. Harold J. Logan, "Carter Plans Radar Sale to Iran Despite Opposition," *Washington Post*, July 26, 1977.

25. NSC Middle East Staff to Zbigniew Brzezinski, "Evening Report," July 26, 1977, NLC-10-4-3-9-4, RAC, CL; Graham Hovey, "Carter Delays Iran Plane Sale after House Panel Opposes Deal," *NYT*, July 29, 1977.

26. "Iranians Are Canceling Purchase of U.S. Airborne Radar System," *NYT*, August 1, 1977.

27. Harold J. Logan, "Senators Introduce Resolution to Block Plane Sale to Iran," *Washington Post*, October 2, 1977.

28. Adam Clymer, "Senate Majority Leader Proposes Moratorium on Arms Sales to Iran," *NYT*, October 8, 1977.

29. Seymour M. Hersh, "Proposed Sale of Fighters to Iran Challenged within Administration," *NYT*, October 9, 1977.

30. Brzezinski to Carter, "Relations with the Shah," ca. November 1977, NLC-6-28-7-32-3, RAC, CL.

31. Stu Eizenstat and Kitty Schirmer to Carter, December 19, 1977, NLC-126-10-14-1-4, RAC, CL.

32. Alam, *Shah and I*, 535, 556; Cooper, *Oil Kings*, 366–387; Skeet, *OPEC*, 134–137.

33. *FRUS, 1969–1976*, 37:119; *FRUS, 1969–1976*, 37:126.

34. *FRUS, 1969–1976*, 37:130.

35. *FRUS, 1969–1976*, 37:132.

36. *FRUS, 1969–1976*, 37:134.

37. *FRUS, 1969–1976*, 37:139.

38. Skeet, *OPEC*, 137.

39. Terry, *U.S. Foreign Policy*, 106–108.

40. Cohen, *Whose Interest?*, 124–125; IMF, Direction of Trade Statistics; BIS, *Annual Report*, various years.

41. Sargent, "North/South," 211–213; Michael Franczak, "Human Rights and Basic Needs: Jimmy Carter's North-South Dialogue, 1977–81," *Cold War History* 18, no. 4 (2018): 447–464.

42. W. Carl Biven, *Jimmy Carter's Economy: Policy in an Age of Limits* (Chapel Hill: University of North Carolina Press, 2002), 85.

43. *FRUS, 1977–1980*, 18:161.

44. Biven, *Carter's Economy*, 120.

45. Bill, *Eagle and the Lion*, 233.

46. Keddie, *Modern Iran*, 164, 217, 223; Robert E. Looney, *Economic Origins of the Iranian Revolution* (New York: Pergamon Press, 1982), 262.

47. Ervand Abrahamian, *A History of Modern Iran* (Cambridge: Cambridge University Press, 2008), 158–162; Keddie, *Modern Iran*, 225–229; Mohammad Ayatollahi Tabaar, *Religious Statecraft: The Politics of Islam in Iran* (New York: Columbia University Press, 2018), 60–88.

48. Khomeini, *Sahifeh-Ye Imam*, 3:347–358.

49. Abrahamian, *History of Modern Iran*, 155–159; Keddie, *Modern Iran*, 226–227; Gil Guerrero, *Carter Administration and the Fall*, 72, 169.

50. Abrahamian, *History of Modern Iran*, 161; Bill, *Eagle and the Lion*, 235–236.

51. Christian Emery, *US Foreign Policy and the Iranian Revolution: The Cold War Dynamics of Engagement and Strategic Alliance* (New York: Palgrave Macmillan, 2013), 39–42.

52. *FRUS, 1977–1980*, 18:145; *FRUS, 1977–1980*, 38:147. See also Daniel Strieff, "Arms Wrestle: Capitol Hill Fight over Carter's 1978 Middle East 'Package' Airplane Sale," *Diplomatic History* 40, no. 3 (June 2016): 475–499.

53. *FRUS, 1977–1980*, 18:148.

54. *FRUS, 1977–1980*, 18:151.

55. *FRUS, 1977–1980*, 18:149.

56. *FRUS, 1977–1980*, 18:151.

57. Jason Brownlee, *Democracy Prevention: The Politics of the U.S.-Egyptian Alliance* (Cambridge: Cambridge University Press, 2012), 25–30.

58. Quandt, *Peace Process*, 183–196; "Egypt Cuts Relations with 5 Arab Nations Opposed to Peace Bid," *NYT*, December 6, 1977.

59. *FRUS, 1977–1980*, 18:237.

60. *FRUS, 1977–1980*, 18:161.

61. Vance to Carter, January 20, 1978, NLC-16-42-5-40-9, RAC, CL.

62. *FRUS, 1977–1980*, 18:167.

63. *FRUS, 1977–1980*, 18:162, 169.

64. Graham Hovey, "U.S. Plans First Jet Sale to Cairo, Reduces Israeli Order for Craft," *NYT*, February 15, 1978; Bernard Gwertzman, "Vance Asserts Arabs Must Get Warplanes Along with Israelis," *NYT*, February 25, 1978.

65. Gwertzman, "Vance Asserts Arabs Must Get Airplanes Along with Israelis."

66. Goldberg, *Jewish Power*, 202–205.

67. William Safire, "Word of Dishonor," *NYT*, May 1, 1978.

68. "No Eagles for Arabia," *New Republic*, March 4, 1978, 8–9.

69. "Vance Asserts Arabs Must Get Warplanes."

70. Bernard Weinraub, "'Package' Plane Sale to Mideast Opposed by House Committee," *NYT*, May 3, 1978.

71. *FRUS, 1977–1980*, 18:171.

72. Steven V. Roberts, "The Saudi Connection, Fred Dutton," *NYT*, April 2, 1978.

73. Richard Harwood and Ward Sinclair, "Lobbying for Warplane Brings Saudis out of Isolation," *Washington Post*, May 7, 1978.

74. Roberts, "Saudi Connection, Fred Dutton."

75. Steven V. Roberts, "Saudis Are Learning Public Relations Ways in U.S.," *NYT*, May 12, 1978.

76. Steven V. Roberts, "Arab Lobby's Specialty: Soft Sell, Tough Message," *NYT*, April 30, 1978.

77. "A Troubled Package for the Middle East," *NYT*, April 27, 1978.

78. Bernard Weinraub, "Vance Offering to Sell Israel 20 More F-15's," *NYT*, May 10, 1978; Bernard Weinraub, "Brown Says Saudis Will Accept Curbs on the Use of F-15's," *NYT*, May 11, 1978.

79. Bernard Weinraub, "Senate Panel in Tie on Vote to Thwart Mideast Jet Sales," *NYT*, May 12, 1978.

80. Bernard Weinraub, "Carter Letter to Senators Pleads for Plane Package," *NYT*, May 13, 1978.

81. Bernard Weinraub, "Debate Is Intense," *NYT*, May 16, 1978.

82. "Nation: F-15 Fight: Who Won What," *Time*, May 29, 1978.

83. Robert Shogan, "Carter's Mideast Policies Erode His Jewish Support," *Los Angeles Times*, July 23, 1978; Miglietta, *American Alliance*, 232–237.

84. Roberts, "Saudis Are Learning Public Relations Ways in U.S."

85. "Ta'rat Amirikiyya Hujumiyya lil-'Aduw wa Dafa'aiyya wa Mutakhalifa li-Misr wa al-Sa'udiyya!," *al-Thawra*, May 17, 1978.

86. "Kartir Yad'aw al-Sadat wa Beghin li-Isti'naf Mufawadat al-Taswiyya," *al-Thawra*, May 15, 1978.

87. "Muwdu'a al-Ghilaf fi Majala 'Taim' al-Amrikiyya Khas bil-Mamlika Dawla al-Sahra' al-'Izaami Tadkhul 'Asr al-Nafathat," *al-Medina*, May 25, 1978.

88. *FRUS, 1977–1980*, 18:173.

89. National Foreign Assessment Center, "Impact of US Arms Sales Restraint Policy," July 1978, NLC-28-6-5-4-6, RAC, CL.

90. George C. Wilson, "Carter's Arms Sales Policy Is Assailed," *Washington Post*, October 6, 1978.

91. US Department of Defense, *Fiscal Year Series*.

92. Brownlee, *Democracy Prevention*, 33; Jørgen Jensehaugen, *Arab-Israeli Diplomacy under Carter: The US, Israel and the Palestinians* (London: I.B. Tauris, 2018), 139–141.

93. *FRUS, 1977–1980*, 18:176.

94. Wilson, "Carter's Arms Sales Policy Is Assailed."

95. Biven, *Carter's Economy*, 113, 147, 162–169.

96. *FRUS, 1969–1976*, 37:160.

97. *FRUS, 1969–1976*, 37:161.

98. Biven, *Carter's Economy*, 169–171.

99. *FRUS, 1969–1976*, 37:168.

8. Revolution and Invasions

1. R. W. Apple Jr., "Khomeini Arrives in Iran, Urges Ouster of Foreigners," *NYT*, February 1, 1979.

2. Khomeini, *Sahifeh-Ye Imam*, 6:8–9.

3. James M. Markham, "Joy Explodes in Tehran Streets as Millions Welcome Ayatollah," *NYT*, February 2, 1979.

4. Keddie, *Modern Iran*, 230–233.

5. Glad, *Outsider*, 168–171.

6. *FRUS, 1977–1980*, 1:100.

7. Abrahamian, *Modern Iran*, 161; Keddie, *Modern Iran*, 234.

8. Skeet, *OPEC*, 158.

9. Keddie, *Modern Iran*, 234–238.

10. "Khomeini Arrives in Iran."

11. Glad, *Outsider*, 172.

12. Khomeini, *Sahifeh-Ye Imam*, 6:13–17; see also Ruhollah Khomeini, *Islam and Revolution: Writings and Declarations of Imam Khomeini*, ed. and trans. Hamid Algar (Berkeley, CA: Mizan Press, 1981), 259–262.

13. Keddie, *Modern Iran*, 238–239; Glad, *Outsider*, 172–173.

14. *FRUS, 1977–1980*, 18:255.

15. *FRUS, 1977–1980*, 18:176.

16. *FRUS, 1977–1980*, 18:177.

17. *FRUS, 1977–1980*, 18:179.

18. *FRUS, 1977–1980*, 18:181.

19. Untitled and unaddressed White House memorandum, February 6, 1979, NLC-1-9-5-10-5, RAC, CL.

20. Memcon, Presidential Review Committee Meeting (hereafter PRCM), January 23, 1979, NLC-15-3-6-8-8, RAC, CL.

21. Memcon, Policy Review Committee Meeting, February 1, 1979, NLC-15-32-4-7-9, RAC, CL.

22. Memcon, PRCM, January 23, 1979, NLC-15-3-6-8-8, RAC, CL.

23. Ibid.

24. Ibid.

25. Memcon, Policy Review Committee Meeting, February 1, 1979, NLC-15-32-4-7-9, RAC, CL.

26. *FRUS, 1977–1980*, 18:19.

27. *FRUS, 1977–1980*, 18:20.

28. *FRUS, 1977–1980*, 18:264, 266.

29. *FRUS, 1977–1980*, 18:269.

30. *FRUS, 1977–1980*, 18:20.

31. *FRUS, 1977–1980*, 18:271.

32. Paul Dresch, *A History of Modern Yemen* (Cambridge: Cambridge University Press, 2000), 150.

33. *FRUS, 1977–1980*, 9:59, 100.

34. Feiler, *Egypt and the Gulf*, 146.

35. *FRUS, 1977–1980*, 18:186.

36. *FRUS, 1977–1980*, 18:188.

37. West to Vance, March 19, 1979, NLC-128-11-22-11-1, RAC, CL.

38. Brownlee, *Democracy Prevention*, 35–36.

39. Marvine Howe, "Arabs, Deeply Split, Bar Stronger Steps against U.S., Egypt," *NYT*, March 29, 1979.

40. Marvine Howe, "Arabs Agree to Cut All Ties with Egypt Because of Treaty," *NYT*, April 1, 1979.

41. Christopher S. Wren, "Saudis Scuttle a Billion-Dollar Arms Consortium with Factories in Egypt," *NYT*, May 15, 1979.

42. Graham Hovey, "U.S. Puts Off Jet Sale to Egypt after Saudis Delay on Paying Costs," *NYT*, July 7, 1979.

43. Salah Jahin, untitled cartoon, *al-Ahram*, May 14, 1979.

44. Feiler, *Egypt and the Gulf*, 149.

45. Ibrahim, *New Arab*, 154–159.

46. Brownlee, *Democracy Prevention*, 36–37.

47. Skeet, *OPEC*, 158–167.

48. Biven, *Carter's Economy*, 177, 237–246.

49. In FY 1976 the United States authorized $7.11 billion in military sales agreements to Saudi Arabia, but due to the shift in defining the start of the fiscal year, FY 1976 was 1.25 years in length. US Department of Defense, *Fiscal Year Series*.

50. Ibid.

51. Bernard Gwertzman, "U.S. to Sell Saudis $1.2 Billion in Arms," *NYT*, July 14, 1979; "Pentagon Plans to Sell $1.23 Billion of Arms to Saudi Security Unit," *Wall Street Journal*, July 30, 1979.

52. Untitled cartoon, *al-Sharq al-Awsat*, June 20, 1979.

53. Ali al-Kharji, untitled cartoon, *al-Riyadh*, December 25, 1978.

54. Emery, *US Foreign Policy*, 46–89.

55. Keddie, *Modern Iran*, 245–246.

56. Khomeini, *Sahifeh-Ye Imam*, 6:401–402.

57. Bernard Gwertzman, "Iran Is Asking U.S. to Buy Back Its Jets," *NYT*, March 29, 1979; Philip Taubman, "Pentagon Is Called Lax on Arms Sales," *NYT*, July 29, 1979.

58. Emery, *US Foreign Policy*, 115–118.

59. Abrahamian, *Modern Iran*, 162–169.

60. Cohen, *Whose Interest?*, 147–159.

61. "Iran Tries to Prove Allegations about Shah," *NYT*, November 27, 1979; Ann Crittenden, "Shah's Assets Abroad Are Hard to Find," *NYT*, September 13, 1980.

62. Untitled cartoon, *Kayhan* (Tehran), November 15, 1979.

63. Sampson, *Money Lenders*, 236.

64. Quoted in James Buchan, "Secular and Religious Opposition in Saudi Arabia," in *State, Society and Economy in Saudi Arabia*, ed. Tim Niblock (New York: St. Martin's Press, 1982), 120–123; see also Al-Rasheed, *History of Saudi Arabia*, 138–143; Nazih Ayubi, *Political Islam: Religion and Politics in the Arab World* (London: Routledge, 1991), 100–103; Lawrence Wright, *The Looming Tower: Al-Qaeda and the Road to 9/11* (New York: Alfred A. Knopf, 2006), 88–92.

65. Graham Hovey, "Troops Rescue 100 in Islamabad; U.S. Offices Are Burned in 2 Cities," *NYT*, November 22, 1979; Michael T. Kaufman, "Body of 2d American Is Found in Islamabad Embassy," *NYT*, November 23, 1979.

66. "Embassy of the U.S. in Libya Is Stormed by a Crowd of 2,000," *NYT*, December 3, 1979.

67. Wright, *Looming Tower*, 94.

68. Skeet, *OPEC*, 168–169.

69. Steve Coll, *Ghost Wars: The Secret History of the CIA, Afghanistan, and bin Laden, from the Soviet Invasion to September 10, 2001* (New York: Penguin Press, 2004), 39–50; Melvyn P. Leffler, *For the Soul of Mankind: The United States, the Soviet Union, and the Cold War* (New York: Hill & Wang, 2007), 303–311, 328–337.

70. *FRUS, 1977–1980*, 6:248.

71. Jimmy Carter, *White House Diary* (New York: Farrar, Straus and Giroux, 2010), 382, 387–388.

72. *FRUS, 1977–1980*, 1:135.

73. *FRUS, 1977–1980*, 1:138.

74. On the long-term consequences of the Carter Doctrine and the militarization of US policy in the MENA, see Andrew J. Bacevich, *America's War for the Greater Middle East: A Military History* (New York: Random House, 2016).

75. "Elements of a U.S. Strategy for Security and Orderly Development in the Near East and Southwestern Asia," ca. January 14, 1980, NLC-17-18-28-4-0, RAC, CL.

76. Wright, *Looming Tower*, 94.

77. Al-Rasheed, *Saudi Arabia*, 141–142; Toby Craig Jones, *Desert Kingdom: How Oil and Water Forged Modern Saudi Arabia* (Cambridge, MA: Harvard University Press, 2011), 179–216.

78. *FRUS, 1977–1980*, 18:216.

79. *FRUS, 1977–1980*, 18:211.

80. *FRUS, 1977–1980*, 18:212.

81. *FRUS, 1977–1980*, 18:216.

82. *FRUS, 1977–1980*, 18:216.

83. Coll, *Ghost Wars*, 51.

84. Ibid., 58.

85. Ibid., 81–82.

86. Madawi Al-Rasheed, *Contesting the Saudi State: Islamic Voices from a New Generation* (Cambridge: Cambridge University Press, 2006), 104–106; Coll, *Ghost War*, 83.

87. Kapstein, *Governing the Global Economy*, 77.

88. Cohen, *Whose Interest?*, 124–125; Kunz, *Butter and Guns*, 264; IMF, Direction of Trade Statistics; BIS, *Annual Report*, various years.

89. Jasper Welch to Brzezinski, February 19, 1980, NLC-31-206-5-5-9, RAC, CL.

90. Cohen, *Whose Interest?*, 165.

91. Emery, *US Foreign Policy*, 167–169.

92. Skeet, *OPEC*, 169; Gary Sick, *All Fall Down: America's Tragic Encounter with Iran* (New York: Random House, 1985), 308–313.

93. Phebe Marr and Ibrahim al-Marashi, *The Modern History of Iraq*, 4th ed. (Boulder, CO: Westview Press, 2017), 142–145; Williamson Murray and Kevin M. Woods, *The Iran-Iraq War: A Military and Strategic History* (Cambridge: Cambridge University Press, 2014), 85–98; Chad E. Nelson, "Revolution and War: Saddam's Decision to Invade Iran," *Middle East Journal* 72, no. 2 (Spring 2018): 246–266.

94. Saddam et al., September 16, 1980, SH-SHTP-A-000-835, Saddam Hussein Regime Collection (hereafter SHRC), Conflict Records Research Center (hereafter CRRC), National Defense University, Washington, DC.

95. Yergin, *Prize*, 693.

96. Dilip Hiro, *The Longest War: The Iran-Iraq Military Conflict* (New York: Routledge, 1991), 40–49.

97. Special Coordination Committee Meeting, September 27, 1980, NLC-25-45-9-9-8, RAC, CL; Carter, *White House Diary*; Emery, *US Foreign Policy*, 184.

98. "Karikatir," *al-Thawra al-Usbu'ai*, September 20, 1980.

99. Ali al-Karkhi, "Karikatir," *al-Thawra al-Usbu'ai*, October 11, 1980; Ali al-Karkhi, "Karikatir," *al-Thawra al-Usbu'ai*, November 1, 1980.

100. "Captured American Arms Are Displayed in Iraq's Cities," *NYT*, November 10, 1980.

101. Quoted in Henry Tanner, "Iran Vows to Press War Despite Losses," *NYT*, September 30, 1980.

102. Pranay B. Gupte, "Iranians Rally Behind Bani-Sadr," *NYT*, October 8, 1980.

103. Shaheen, *Reel Bad Arabs*, 551–552.

104. Shaheen, *TV Arab*, 65–66.

105. "Slow Train," Bob Dylan Official Website, http://www.bobdylan.com/songs/slow-train/ (accessed February 10, 2020).

106. Shaheen, *TV Arab*, 51.

107. Yaqub, *Imperfect Strangers*, 283.

108. Ibid., 294–299.

109. Ibid.

110. Ward Morehouse III, "'Abscam' Fallout: Atlantic City Casinos," *Christian Science Monitor*, February 6, 1980.

111. Bruce Weber, "Angelo J. Errichetti, 84, Camden Mayor Convicted of Bribery, Dies," *NYT*, May 28, 2013.

112. Yaqub, *Imperfect Strangers*, 293.

113. Ibid., 315–321, 328.

114. William Safire, "The Hostage Profiteer," *NYT*, July 24, 1980.

115. David E. Rosenbaum, "Senators Assail Billy Carter," *NYT*, August 23, 1980.

116. Glad, *Outsider*, 272.

117. William Safire, "The Ayatollah Votes," *NYT*, October 27, 1980.

118. Daniel Pipes, "Beware, a Hostage Deal Might Hurt the U.S.," *NYT*, October 29, 1980.

119. Carter, *White House Diary*, 472; Sick, *All Fall Down*, 311–314.

120. Biven, *Carter's Economy*, 2–3.

121. "Transcript of the Presidential Debate Between Carter and Reagan in Cleveland," *NYT*, October 29, 1980.

122. Skeet, *OPEC*, 177.

123. Cohen, *Whose Interest?*, 166.

124. Warren Christopher et al., *American Hostages in Iran: The Conduct of a Crisis* (New Haven, CT: Yale University Press, 1985), 166–167.

125. Bernard Gwertzman, "How Hostage Pact Was Forged," *NYT*, January 28, 1981.

9. Recoveries and Crises

1. Zahed Haftlang, Najah Aboud, and Meredith May, *I, Who Did Not Die* (New York: Regan Arts, 2017).

2. For background on the Reagan administration, see Doug Rossinow, *The Reagan Era: A History of the 1980s* (New York: Columbia University Press, 2015); James M. Scott, *Deciding to Intervene: The Reagan Doctrine and American Foreign Policy* (Durham, NC: Duke University Press, 1996); and Sean Wilentz, *The Age of Reagan: A History, 1974–2008* (New York: HarperCollins, 2008).

3. "Background on Saudi Arabia's F-15 Request," undated, folder "NSC 0003 18 Feb 1981 [2/2]," box 91282, Executive Secretariat, NSC: Meeting Files (hereafter NSC MF), Ronald W. Reagan Presidential Library (hereafter RL), Simi Valley, CA.

4. "NSC Meeting," February 18, 1981, folder "NSC 3 18 Feb 1981 [1/2]," box 91282, NSC MF, RL.

5. "NSC Meeting," February 25, 1981, folder "NSC 4 27 Feb 1981 (Poland, Caribbean Basin, F-15, El Salvador) [2/4]," box 91282, NSC MF, RL.

6. "Pakistan IG," February 28, 1981, folder "16 on Pakistan March 2, 1981 (1 of 2)," box 91134, Near East and South Asia Affairs Directorate, NSC (hereafter NESA NSC), RL.

7. "NSC Meeting," March 19, 1981, folder "NSC 5 19 Mar 1981 (4/4)," box 91282, NSC MF, RL.

8. "NSC Meeting," February 18, 1981, folder "NSC 3 18 Feb 1981 (1/2)," box 91282, NSC MF, RL.

9. Ibid. On the F-15 enhancement sale to Saudi Arabia generally, see also Nicholas Laham, *Selling AWACS to Saudi Arabia: The Reagan Administration and the Balancing of America's Competing Interests in the Middle East* (Westport, CT: Praeger Publishers, 2002).

10. Haig to Reagan, February 23, 1981, folder "NSC 4 27 Feb 1981 (Poland, Caribbean Basin, F-15, El Salvador) (2/4)," box 91282, NSC MF, RL.

11. "NSC Meeting," February 27, 1981, folder "NSC 4 27 Feb 1981 (Poland, Caribbean Basin, F-15, El Salvador) (3/4)," box 91282, NSC MF, RL.

12. Judith Miller, "U.S. to Offer Israel Jets on Easy Terms," *NYT*, February 28, 1981.

13. Ibid.; "NSC Meeting," February 27, 1981, folder "NSC 4 27 Feb 1981 (Poland, Caribbean Basin, F-15, El Salvador) (3/4)," box 91282, NSC MF, RL.

14. Bernard Gwertzman, "U.S. Decides to Sell Equipment to Saudis to Bolster F-15 Jets," *NYT*, March 7, 1981.

15. "20 Senators Criticize Providing Equipment for F-15 to the Saudis," *NYT*, March 25, 1981.

16. "To Saudi Arabia, with Extended Arms," *NYT*, March 8, 1981.

17. "NSC Meeting," April 1, 1981, folder "NSC 7, 1 Apr 1981 (1/2)," box 91282, NSC MF, RL.

18. Ibid.; Bernard Gwertzman, "Israel Asks U.S. for Gift of Jets, Citing Saudi Sale," *NYT*, April 4, 1981.

19. "100 Members of the House Back Protest on Arms Sales to Saudis," *NYT*, April 8, 1981.

20. Joseph R. Biden Jr., "Stop Arms for Saudis," *NYT*, April 15, 1981.

21. Bernard Gwertzman, "U.S. Will Go Ahead on Deal with Saudis for 5 Radar Planes," *NYT*, April 22, 1981.

22. "Begin Arrives, Decries AWACS," *Washington Post*, September 7, 1981.

23. John M. Goshko, "50 Senators Back Resolution against AWACS Sale to Saudis," *Washington Post*, September 18, 1981.

24. William Claiborne, "Israel Reaffirms AWACS Opposition," *Washington Post*, September 21, 1981.

25. Phil Gailey, "The Great Divide, 1981," *NYT*, October 1, 1981; Ghazi Algosaibi to West, April 20, 1981, folder "West, Personal, Topical, Middle East Correspondence, Saudi Arabia Correspondence, 1981 Apr–Oct," box 28, JWP; West to Fahd, September 10, 1981, ibid.

26. John M. Goshko, "Reagan Sends AWACS Package to Congress," *Washington Post*, October 2, 1981.

27. Norman A. Bailey to Allen, "Meeting with Senator Russell Long," September 21, 1981, folder "AWACS (3)," box 1, Executive Secretariat, NSC: Subject File (hereafter NSC SF), RL.

28. "Revised AWACS Strategy #1," September 24, 1981, folder "AWACS (2)," box 1, NSC SF, RL.

29. Edward Cody, "Saudis Reject 'Sharing' on AWACS," *Washington Post*, October 4, 1981.

30. Goshko, "Reagan Sends AWACS Package to Congress."

31. Bernard Gwertzman, "President Says U.S. Should Not Waver in Backing Saudis," *NYT*, October 18, 1981.

32. Charles Mohr, "Democratic Chief in Senate Opposes Saudi AWACS Sale," *NYT*, October 22, 1981.

33. "Roll-Call Vote in House on Resolution against the Awacs Sale," *NYT*, October 15, 1981.

34. Steven V. Roberts, "Recipe for a White House Victory," *NYT*, October 29, 1981.

35. Jack Anderson, "Big Business Backing Saudis on AWACS Sale," *Washington Post*, October 26, 1981.

36. "AWACS Talking Points and Background Analysis," October 28, 1981, folder "AWACS (4)," box 1, NSC SF.

37. Charles Mohr, "Senate, 52-48, Supports Reagan on AWACS Jet Sale to Saudis," *NYT*, October 29, 1981.

38. Haig to Richard Murphey, October 29, 1981, folder "8106360," box 2, National Security Affairs, Assistant to the President for: Chronological File, RL.

39. Coll, *Ghost Wars*, 58–68.

40. US Department of Treasury, "Securities (B): Portfolio Holdings of U.S. and Foreign Securities."

41. Shaheen, *Reel Bad Arabs*, 198; Shaheen, *TV Arab*, 51.

42. Hiro, *Longest War*, 49–50.

43. Eagleton to Haig, February 7, 1981, folder "Iraq 1/20/81–12/31/83 (3 of 4)," box 37, Executive Secretariat NSC Country File (hereafter NSC CF), RL.

44. "Civil Aircraft Sales to Iraq," January 30, 1981, folder "Iraq 1/20/81–12/31/83 (4 of 4)," box 37, NSC CF, RL.

45. "Secretary Haig's Memo on Civil Aircraft Sales to Iraq," February 13, 1981, folder "Iraq 1/20/81–12/31/83 (4 of 4)," box 37, NSC CF, RL.

46. Eagleton to Haig, April 1, 1981, folder "Iraq 1/20/81–12/31/83 (3 of 4)," box 37, NSC CF, RL.

47. Eagleton to Haig, June 8, 1981, folder "Iraq 1/20/81–12/31/83 (2 of 4)," box 37, NSC CF, RL.

48. David Schoenbaum, *The United States and the State of Israel* (New York: Oxford University Press, 1993), 278.

49. Memcon, June 11, 1981, folder "President's Meeting with Israeli Ambassador Evron Re Israeli Raid, June 11, 1981," box 91141, NESA NSC, RL.

50. Eagleton to Haig, June 8, 1981, folder "Iraq 1/20/81–12/31/83 (2 of 4)," box 37, NSC CF, RL.

51. Bernard Gwertzman, "Haig Says Tehran Will Not Get Arms; Asks Trade Caution," *NYT*, January 29, 1981.

52. "Interagency Group Meeting on Iran," April 1, 1981, folder "IG (Interagency Group) on Iran 4/16/1981," box 91705, NESA NSC, RL.

53. "Senior Interdepartmental Group Memorandum—Iran," folder "SIF (Senior Interagency Group) on Iran 7/21/1981," box 91144, NESA NSC, RL.

54. "U.S. Policy toward Libya," folder "NSC Meeting on Libya/Caribbean May 15, 1981, Cancelled," box 91144, NESA NSC, RL.

55. Bernard Gwertzman, "U.S. Expels Libyans and Closes Mission, Charging Terrorism," *NYT*, May 7, 1981.

56. "NSC Meeting," folder "NSC Meeting on Libya/Caribbean, May 15, 1981, Cancelled," box 91144, NESA NSC, RL.

57. "US Policy toward Libya Minutes," folder "NSC Meeting on Libya, May 28, 1981," box 91144, NESA NSC, RL.

58. "U.S. Policy toward Libya," folder "NSPG Meeting on Libya, June 3, 1981," box 91144, NESA NSC, RL.

59. Douglas Little, "To the Shores of Tripoli: America, Qaddafi, and Libyan Revolution, 1969–89," *International History Review* 35, no. 1 (2013): 84–85.

60. Ronald Reagan, *The Reagan Diaries*, ed. Douglas Brinkley (New York: HarperCollins, 2007), 36.

61. Haig to American embassy in Brussels, October 2, 1981, folder "Terrorism (9/11/1981–10/2/1981)," box 11, NSC SF, RL.

62. Reagan, *Diaries*, 42, 50–52; Joseph T. Stanik, *El Dorado Canyon: Reagan's Undeclared War with Qaddafi* (Annapolis, MD: Naval Institute Press, 2003), 64–72.

63. Memcon, December 8, 1981, folder "NSC 29, 8 Dec. 1981 (3)," box 2, NSC MF, RL; National Security Decision Directive (hereafter NSDD) 16, December 10, 1981, RL; L. Paul Bremer III to James Nance, "Preliminary Libyan Response to Protest," December 11, 1981, folder "NSC Meeting—Libya, Monday, Dec. 7, 1981 (2/2)," box 91144, NESA NSC, RL; Steven R. Weisman, "Acts on Passports," *NYT*, December 11, 1981.

64. Memcon, January 21, 1982, folder "NSC 38, 21 Jan. 1982 (2)," box 3, NSC MF, RL.

65. "NSC Staff Summary of State Paper," February 3, 1982, folder "NSC 39, 4 Feb 1982 (Poland, Libya, Export Controls, Oil, Gas) (2/7)," box 91283, NSC MF, RL.

66. Memcon, December 8, 1981, folder "NSC 29, 8 Dec. 1981 (3)," box 2, NSC MF, RL; NSDD 16, December 10, 1981, RL; Bremer to Nance, "Preliminary Libyan Response to Protest."

67. Regan to William Clark Jr., "Economic Sanctions against Libya," February 3, 1982, folder "NSC 39, 4 Feb 1982 (Poland, Libya, Export Controls, Oil, Gas) (2/7)," box 91283, NSC MF, RL.

68. NSDD 27, March 9, 1982, RL.

69. Robert D. Hershey Jr., "President Abolishes Last Price Controls on U.S.-Produced Oil," *NYT*, January 29, 1981.

70. Rossinow, *Reagan Era*, 90.

71. British Petroleum, "Data Workbook—Statistical Review 2015," https://www.bp.com/en/global/corporate/energy-economics/statistical-review-of-world-energy/downloads.html (accessed February 10, 2020); Yergin, *Prize*, 693–701.

72. British Petroleum, "Data Workbook—Statistical Review 2015."

73. Hiro, *Longest War*, 76–77.

74. Eagleton to Haig, January 21, 1982, folder "Iraq 1/20/81–12/31/83 (1 of 4)," box 37, NSC CF, RL; Eagleton to Haig, February 23, 1982, folder "Iraq 1/20/81–12/31/83 (1 of 4)," box 37, NSC CF, RL.

75. Bruce W. Jentleson, *With Friends Like These: Reagan, Bush, and Saddam, 1982–1990* (New York: W. W. Norton, 1994) 33, 42.

76. Hiro, *Longest War*, 53–60.

77. Eagleton to Haig, May 27, 1982, folder "Iraq 1/20/81–12/31/83 (1 of 4)," box 37, NSC CF, RL; Eagleton to Haig, May 30, 1982, folder "Iraq 1/20/81–12/31/83 (1 of 4)," box 37, NSC CF, RL.

78. Memcon, December 18, 1981, folder "Memcons—President Reagan Dec. 1981 (2 of 2)," box 49, NSC SF, RL.

79. James Ealum to Haig, February 8, 1982, folder "Sec Def Trip to the M.E. (Middle East) Feb. 4–13, 1982," box 91987, NESA NSC, RL.

80. Rabinovich, *War for Lebanon*, 121–141.

81. Memcon, June 21, 1981, 11:05–11:50 a.m. and Memcon, June 21, 1981, 12:40–1:40 p.m., folder "Begin's Meeting with President, June 21, 1982 (1 of 4)," box 91987, NESA NSC, RL.

82. Memcon, June 21, 1981, 11:05–11:50 a.m. and Memcon, June 21, 1981, 12:40–1:40 p.m.

83. Hiro, *Longest War*, 63–64, 86–87.

84. Bremer, "Notification of OG Meeting," July 20, 1982, folder "IG Meeting 7/21/1982 Iran/Iraq," box 91147, NESA NSC, RL; Bremer, "SIG Meeting Summary of Conclusions," July 28, 1982, folder "SIG 7/26/1982," box 91146, NESA NSC, RL.

85. Seth Anziska, *Preventing Palestine: A Political History from Camp David to Oslo* (Princeton, NJ: Princeton University Press, 2018), 205–226.

86. "Arabs Blame U.S. in Beirut Deaths," *NYT*, September 22, 1982.

87. Jeffrey Sachs, "Managing the LDC Debt Crisis," *Brookings Papers on Economic Activity* 17, no. 2 (1986): 397n1; Zweig, *Wriston*, 742, 768.

88. Frieden, *Banking on the World*, 142–161; Kunz, *Butter and Guns*, 274–283; NSDD 96, June 9, 1983, RL.

89. BIS, *Annual Report*, various years.

90. Spiro, *Hidden Hand*, 156.

91. Yergin, *Prize*, 701–703; British Petroleum, "Data Workbook—Statistical Review 2015," bp .com/en/global/corporate/energy-economics/statistical-review-of-world-energy/downloads.html (accessed February 10, 2020).

92. NSDD 87, March 30, 1983, RL.

93. Pierre Razoux, *The Iran-Iraq War*, trans. Nicholas Elliott (Cambridge, MA: Harvard University Press, 2015), 227–241.

94. Shultz to multiple US embassies, "Iran-Iraq War: Next Steps with Gulf States on Deterring Escalation in the Gulf," September 3, 1983, folder "Iran-Iraq 1983 (1 of 2)," box 90583, NESA NSC, RL.

95. Shultz to Reagan, "Our Strategy in Lebanon and the Middle East," October 13, 1983, folder "NSDD 103 (Strategy for Lebanon) (1)," box 91291, Executive Secretariat, NSC: National Security Decision Directives (hereafter NSC NSDD), RL.

96. Reagan, *Diaries*, 190; NSDD 109, October 23, 1983, RL; David Crist, *The Twilight War: The Secret History of America's Thirty-Year Conflict with Iran* (New York: Penguin Press, 2012), 121–151.

97. Bacevich, *America's War*, 67–77.

98. Dominique Avon and Anaïs-Trissa Khatchadourian, *Hezbollah: A History of the "Party of God,"* trans. Jane Marie Todd (Cambridge, MA: Harvard University Press, 2012), 23–30.

10. End of an Era

1. Abdul-Hadi Jiad, "Abdul-Rahman Mounif," *Guardian*, February 4, 2004; Tariq Ali, "Abdelrahman Munif," *Independent*, January 29, 2004; Peter Theroux, "Abdelrahman Munif and the Uses of Oil," *Words without Borders*, October 2012, https://www.wordswithoutborders.org/article/abdelrahman-munif-and-the-uses-of-oil.

2. Abdelrahman Munif, *Cities of Salt*, trans. Peter Theroux (London: Vintage, 1994), 1, 553, 626.

3. William Martin to Robert McFarlane, "Energy Issues for Iran-Iraq Meeting," November 17, 1983, folder "Iran-Iraq 1983 (1 of 2)," box 90583, NESA NSC, RL.

4. Charles Hill to McFarlane, "Iran-Iraq: Crisis Pre-planning Guidance - Diplomatic Strategy," March 7, 1984, folder "NSDD 114 (U.S. Policy towards Iran-Iraq War) (3 of 3)," NSC NSDD, RL.

5. Hiro, *Longest War*, 159–161; Razoux, *Iran-Iraq War*, 280, 290–291, 549.

6. Hill to McFarlane, "Iran-Iraq: Crisis Pre-Planning Guidance - Diplomatic Strategy," March 7, 1984.

7. McFarlane, "Iraqi Military Needs," undated, folder "Iraq 1984 (5/2/1984–7/24/1984)," box 91689, NESA NSC, RL.

8. Styan, *France and Iraq*, 154–156.

9. Hiro, *Longest War*, 116.

10. Razoux, *Iran-Iraq War*, 304–307.

11. Bernard Gwertzman, "Reagan Formally Announces Sale of 400 Missiles to Saudis," *NYT*, May 30, 1984; see also NSDD 141, May 25, 1984, RL; Bernard Gwertzman, "Move Begins in Congress to Block Arms Sale to Jordan and Saudis," *NYT*, March 10, 1984; "Reagan to Revive Offer of Missiles to Saudi Arabians," *NYT*, May 24, 1984.

12. Bernard Gwertzman, "Senators Assail Arms Sale to Saudis," *NYT*, June 6, 1984.

13. Razoux, *Iran-Iraq War*, 307–308.

14. Wayne Biddle, "Use of U.S. Arms in Mideast Raises Concerns in Congress," *NYT*, June 7, 1984.

15. Hiro, *Longest War*, 143.

16. Geoffrey Kemp to McFarlane, "Iraqi Minister's Request to Call on the President to Announce Resumption of Relations," September 26, 1984, folder "Iraq 1984 (9/19/1984–11/20/1984)," box 91689, NESA NSC, RL.

17. "Secretary's Meeting with Iraqi FonMin: Bilateral Relations," October 3, 1984, folder "Iraq 1984 (9/19/1984–11/20/1984)," box 91689, NESA NSC, RL.

18. Razoux, *Iran-Iraq War*, 305.

19. Bernard Gwertzman, "New Arms Sales to Mideast Ended for a Few Months," *NYT*, January 31, 1985.

20. Bernard Gwertzman, "Saudis Say Reagan Cleared Purchase of British Planes," *NYT*, September 16, 1985.

21. Razoux, *Iran-Iraq War*, 562.

22. Bronson, *Thicker Than Oil*, 180–182.

23. Greg Grandin, *Empire's Workshop: Latin America, the United States, and the Rise of the New Imperialism* (New York: Henry Holt, 2010), 64–86, 110–134.

24. Lawrence E. Walsh, *Final Report of the Independent Counsel for Iran/Contra Matters*, vol. 1, (Washington, D.C.: U.S. Court of Appeals for the District of Columbia Circuit, 1993), part IV chapter 1.

25. Ibid., part I, part IV chapter 1, part V chapter 8, and part IX chapter 27.

26. Ibid. part IV chapter 1, part IX chapter 27.

27. Grandin, *Empire's Workshop*, 116; Stephen G. Rabe, *The Killing Zone: The United States Wages Cold War in Latin America*, 2nd ed. (Oxford: Oxford University Press, 2016), xxxix, 166–170.

28. Coll, *Ghost Wars*, 89.

29. Seth G. Jones, *In the Graveyard of Empires: America's War in Afghanistan* (New York: W. W. Norton, 2009), 25–29.

30. Coll, *Ghost Wars*, 158–160.

31. Thomas Hegghammer, *Jihad in Saudi Arabia: Violence and Pan-Islamism since 1979* (Cambridge: Cambridge University Press, 2010), 38–48; Coll, *Ghost Wars*, 154–164. On the connections between Saudi and US policies toward the Afghan War and the rise of international jihadist terrorism, see Mahmood Mandani, *Good Muslim, Bad Muslim: America, the Cold War, and the Roots of Terror* (New York: Pantheon Books, 2004), 119–77.

32. Skeet, *OPEC*, 241–244; Yergin, *Prize*, 727–732; British Petroleum, "Data Workbook."

33. Skeet, *OPEC*, 241–244; Yergin, *Prize*, 727–732; British Petroleum, "Data Workbook."

34. IMF, Direction of Trade Statistics; BIS, *Annual Report*.

35. Alfred E. Eckes Jr. and Thomas W. Zeiler, *Globalization and the American Century* (Cambridge: Cambridge University Press, 2003), 202.

36. Walsh, *Final Report*, part I, part IV chapter 1.

37. Ibid.; Malcolm Byrne, *Iran-Contra: Reagan's Scandal and the Unchecked Abuse of Presidential Power* (Lawrence: University Press of Kansas, 2017), 59–76, 106.

38. Walsh, *Final Report*, part IV chapter 1, part IX chapter 27; Reagan, *Diaries*, 350, 374–375, 381.

39. Razoux, *Iran-Iraq War*, 356, 366.

40. Walsh, *Final Report*, part I; Byrne, *Iran-Contra*, 186–207.

41. In addition to the Saudi donations and Iran arms sale profits, Taiwan contributed $2 million and private donations collected by the US nonprofit National Endowment for the Preservation of Liberty contributed $1.7 million for the Contras. Walsh, *Final Report*, part IX chapter 27.

42. Memcon, NSC Meeting Minutes, December 2, 1983, file "NSC 97, 12/2/1983 (Oil and Gas Export Controls, Libya, USSR)," box 5, NSC MF, RL.

43. Memcon, "NSPG Minutes," March 30, 1984, folder "NSPG 87, 30 Mar 1984," box 91307, Executive Secretariat, NSC: National Security Planning Group (hereafter NSC NSPG), RL.

44. Stanik, *El Dorado Canyon*, 104–107.

45. NSDD 205, January 8, 1986, RL.

46. Memcon, "NSPG on Libya," March 14, 1986, folder "NSPG 129, 14 Mar 1986 (Libya, Oil Strategy)," box 91308, NSC NSPG, RL; Stanik, *El Dorado Canyon*, 127–140.

47. Little, "To the Shores of Tripoli," 89–91.

48. Bernard Gwertzman, "Reagan Approves Arms for Saudis but Faces Hard Fight in Congress," *NYT*, March 1, 1986.

49. Bernard Gwertzman, "Big Missile Sale to Saudi Arabia Opposed by Key Congress Panel," *NYT*, April 24, 1986.

50. Steven V. Roberts, "House Turns Back Saudi Arms Sales," *NYT*, May 8, 1986.

51. Steven V. Roberts, "Blending a Chorus of No's to Saudis on Arms," *NYT*, May 19, 1986.

52. Mark N. Katz, "Yes—and Israel Gains," *NYT*, May 12, 1986.

53. Bernard Weinraub, "Reagan Asks Vote for Saudi Missiles," *NYT*, June 4, 1986.

54. Steven V. Roberts, "Senate Upholds Arms for Saudis," *NYT*, June 6, 1986.

55. Byrne, *Iran-Contra*, 1, 252.

56. Ibid., 256–279.

57. Richard J. Meislin, "46% Approve Reagan's Work," *NYT*, December 2, 1986.

58. Wilentz, *Age of Reagan*, chap. 8.

59. Byrne, *Iran-Contra*, 306.

60. "Meeting between Saddam and the Revolutionary," November 15, 1986, SH-SHTP-A-000-555, SHRC, CRRC.

61. Memcon, NSPG Meeting, February 12, 1987, folder "NSPG 144, 12 Feb 1987," box 91306, NSC NSPG, RL.

62. Razoux, *Iran-Iraq War*, 366–367, 377.

63. Yergin, *Prize*, 745.

64. Razoux, *Iran-Iraq War*, 400.

65. Ibid., 407.

66. David K. Shipler, "Saudi Arms Retreat," *NYT*, June 13, 1987; Elaine Sciolino, "64 Senators Urge Reagan to Drop $1 Billion Sale of Arms to Saudis," *NYT*, September 29, 1987; "House Acts to Oppose Sale of Arms to Saudis," *NYT*, October 1, 1987; "Saudi Deal Is Sent to Congress," *NYT*, October 30, 1987.

67. Khomeini, *Sahifeh-Ye Imam*, 21:75–78, 87–89.

68. Razoux, *Iran-Iraq War*, 569, 573–574.

69. Marr and al-Marashi, *Modern History of Iraq*, 160–161; Owen and Pamuk, *Middle East Economies*, 171.

70. John Ruedy, *Modern Algeria: The Origins and Development of a Nation*, 2nd ed. (Bloomington: Indiana University Press, 2005), 244–249.

71. Guinness World Records, "Most Expensive Covert Action," https://www.guinnessworldrecords.com/world-records/613906-most-expensive-covert-action (accessed February 10, 2020).

72. Bartel, "Fugitive Leverage"; Frieden, *Global Capitalism*, 374–378; Kotkin, "Kiss of Debt."

73. Galal Amin, *Egypt in the Age of Hosni Mubarak, 1981–2011* (Cairo: American University in Cairo Press, 2011); Timothy Mitchell, *Rule of Experts: Egypt, Techno-Politics, and Modernity* (Berkeley: University of California Press, 2002), 221–229.

74. Fawaz A. Gerges, *The Far Enemy: Why Jihad Went Global*, new ed. (Cambridge: Cambridge University Press, 2009), 119–150.

Conclusion

1. Julian E. Barnes and Eric Schmitt, "C.I.A., Citing Intercepts, Says Crown Prince Ordered Journalist's Killing," *NYT*, December 3, 2018.

2. US White House, "Statement from President Donald J. Trump on Standing with Saudi Arabia," November 20, 2018, https://www.whitehouse.gov/briefings-statements/statement-president-donald-j-trump-standing-saudi-arabia/ (accessed February 10, 2020).

3. Paul Krugman, "Arms and Very Bad Men," *NYT*, October 23, 2018.

4. Bernie Sanders, "We Must Stop Helping the Saudis in Yemen," *NYT*, October 25, 2018.

5. Natalie Andrews, "Senate to Vote on Withdrawing U.S. Support to Saudis in Yemen War," *Wall Street Journal*, December 9, 2018.

6. Khomeini, *Sahifeh-Ye Imam*, 21:421.

7. Razoux, *Iran-Iraq War*, 387.

8. Edgar O'Ballance, *Civil War in Lebanon, 1975–1992* (London: Palgrave Macmillan, 1998), x.

9. Byrne, *Iran-Contra*, 307–326.

10. Marr, *History of Modern Iraq*, 170–171; Razoux, *Iran-Iraq War*, 562.

11. Youssef M. Ibrahim, "Gulf War's Cost to Arabs Estimated at $620 Billion," *NYT*, September 8, 1992.

12. Westad, *Global Cold War*, 401–403; Artemy M. Kalinovsky, *A Long Goodbye: The Soviet Withdrawal from Afghanistan* (Cambridge, MA: Harvard University Press, 2011), 42–43.

13. Feiler, *Egypt and the Gulf*, 230–252.

14. Bronson, *Thicker Than Oil*, 207–209.

15. Shaheen, *Reel Bad Arabs*, 96, 349, 357.

16. Osama bin Laden, *Messages to the World: The Statements of Osama bin Laden*, ed. Bruce Lawrence, trans. James Howarth (London: Verso, 2005), 6–7, 29.

17. Mark LeVine, *Why They Don't Hate Us: Lifting the Veil on the Axis of Evil* (Oxford: Oneworld Publications, 2005), 143.

18. Bacevich, *America's War*, 239–250.

19. Mahmoud A. El-Gamal and Amy Myers Jaffe, *Oil, Dollars, Debt, and Crisis: The Global Curse of Black Gold* (Cambridge: Cambridge University Press, 2010), 124.

20. Yergin, *Prize*, 769.

21. Organization of the Petroleum Exporting Countries, *Annual Statistical Bulletin* (Vienna), various years.

22. Ibid.

23. Mark Landler and Steven Lee Myers, "Healing a Rift, U.S. Agrees to $30 Billion Fighter Jet Sale to Saudi Arabia," *NYT*, December 30, 2011.

24. World Bank, World Integrated Trade Solution, https://wits.worldbank.org/ (accessed February 10, 2020).

25. Helene Cooper and Mark Landler, "Interests of Saudi Arabia and Iran Collide, with the U.S. in the Middle," *NYT*, March 18, 2011.

26. Rod Nordland, "Saudi Arabia Promises to Aid Egypt's Regime," *NYT*, August 20, 2013.

27. Jon Lee Anderson, "The Unraveling," *New Yorker*, February 23, 2015.

28. Anne Gearan, "Kerry's Saudi Visit Underlines Differences on Syria," *Washington Post*, March 5, 2013.

29. Helene Cooper, "U.S., Concerned about Casualties in Yemen, Blocks Arms Sale to Saudi Arabia," *NYT*, December 14, 2016.

30. Joby Warrick, "Accord Follows 35 Years of Turbulent U.S.-Iran Relations," *Washington Post*, July 15, 2015; Loveday Morris and Hugh Naylor, "Arab States Fear a Bigger Regional Role for Iran," *Washington Post*, July 15, 2015.

31. US Department of Defense, Defense Security Cooperation Agency, *Foreign Military Sales, Foreign Military Construction Sales and Other Security Cooperation Historical Facts as of September 30, 2016* (Washington, D.C., 2016).

32. Stockholm International Peace Research Institute, Military Expenditure Database, https://www.sipri.org/databases/milex (accessed February 10, 2020).

33. "Transcript: The November Democratic Debate," *Washington Post* website, November 21, 2019, https://www.washingtonpost.com/politics/2019/11/21/transcript-november-democratic-debate/ (accessed February 10, 2020).

34. Robert F. Worth, "How the War in Yemen Became a Bloody Stalemate," *NYT*, October 31, 2018.

Bibliography

Official Archives

United Kingdom

The National Archives (NA), Kew.
   Prime Minister's Office Files (PREM).

United States

Gerald R. Ford Presidential Library (FL), Ann Arbor, MI.
   National Security Adviser, International Economic Affairs Staff: Files (NSA
      IEASF).
   National Security Adviser, Kissinger-Scowcroft West Wing Office Files (NSA
      KSWW).
   National Security Adviser, Memoranda of Conversation (NSA MC).
   National Security Adviser, Outside the System Chronological Files.
   National Security Adviser, Presidential Briefing Material for VIP Visits (NSA
      PBM).
   National Security Adviser, Presidential Correspondence with Foreign Leaders
      (PCFL).
   National Security Adviser, Presidential Country Files for Middle East and South
      Asia (NSA PCF MESA).
   National Security Adviser, Presidential Name File (NSA PNF).
   National Security Council Institutional Files (NSC IF).
   National Security Council Meetings File.
   Remote Archives Capture (RAC).

International Monetary Fund Archive (IMFA), Washington, DC.
    Central Files Collection (CFC).
    Office of the Managing Director Records (OMD).
Jimmy Carter Presidential Library (CL), Atlanta, GA.
    Remote Archives Capture (RAC).
    Vertical File.
National Archives and Records Administration (NARA), College Park, MD.
    General Records of the Department of State, Record Group (RG) 59.
    General Records of the Department of the Treasury, Record Group (RG) 56.
Richard M. Nixon Presidential Library (NL), Yorba Linda, CA.
    National Security Council Files (NSC).
Ronald W. Reagan Presidential Library (RL), Simi Valley, CA.
    Executive Secretariat, National Security Council: Country File (NSC CF).
    Executive Secretariat, National Security Council: Meeting Files (NSC MF).
    Executive Secretariat, National Security Council: National Security Decision
        Directives (NSC NSDD).
    Executive Secretariat, National Security Council: National Security Planning Group
        (NSC NSPG).
    Executive Secretariat, National Security Council: Subject File (NSC SF).
    National Security Affairs, Assistant to the President for: Chronological File.
    Near East and South Asia Affairs Directorate, NSC (NESA NSC).
World Bank Group Archives (WBGA), Washington, DC.
    Records of the Office of the President (ROP).

Personal and Organizational Collections

Mulligan, William E., Papers. Special Collections, Georgetown University, Washington, DC.
Saddam Hussein Regime Collection (SHRC). Conflict Records Research Center
    (CRRC), National Defense University, Washington, DC.
Simon, William E., Papers (SP). Special Collections and College Archives, Lafayette
    College, Easton, PA.
West, John Carl, Papers (JWP). South Carolina Political Collections, University of
    South Carolina, Columbia, SC.

Published Documents

Bank for International Settlements. *Annual Report*. Basel, various years.
Bin Laden, Osama. *Messages to the World: The Statements of Osama bin Laden*. Edited by
    Bruce Lawrence. Translated by James Howarth. London: Verso, 2005.
DeGolyer and MacNaughton. *Twentieth Century Petroleum Statistics*. 2016.
El Tariki, Abdullah El Hammoud. *Nationalization of Arab Petroleum Industry Is a National
    Necessity*. Cairo: Dar El-Hana Press, 1965.

Hussein, Saddam. *Iraqi Revolution in the Service of Humanity: Saddam Hussein Speaks*. Edited by Z. L. Kaul. New Delhi: New Wave Printing Press, 1978.

———. *On Current Affairs in Iraq*. Edited by Naji Al-Hadithi. Translated by Khalid Kishtainy. Baghdad: Translation & Foreign Languages House, 1981.

———. *On Oil Nationalisation in Iraq*. Baghdad: Ath-Thawra House, 1973.

Khomeini, Ruhollah. *Islam and Revolution: Writings and Declarations of Imam Khomeini*. Edited and translated by Hamid Algar. Berkeley, CA: Mizan Press, 1981.

———. *Sahifeh-Ye Imam: An Anthology of Imam Khomeini's Speeches, Messages, Interviews, Decrees, Religious Permissions, and Letters*. Vols. 1, 3, 6, 21. Translated by 'Abdul-Husayn Shirazi. Tehran: Institute for Compilation and Publication of Imam Khomeini's Works, 2008.

Organization of the Petroleum Exporting Countries. *Annual Statistical Bulletin*. Vienna, various years.

Shari'ati, Ali. *What Is to Be Done: The Enlightened Thinkers and an Islamic Renaissance*. Houston: Institute for Research and Islamic Studies, 1986.

US Bureau of the Census. *Statistical Abstract of the United States*. Washington, D.C., various years.

US Department of Defense, Defense Security Cooperation Agency. *Fiscal Year Series: Foreign Military Sales, Foreign Military Construction Sales and Other Security Cooperation Historical Facts as of September 30, 2012*. Washington, D.C., 2012.

———. *Historical Facts Book: Foreign Military Sales, Foreign Military Construction Sales and Other Security Cooperation Historical Facts as of September 30, 2016*. Washington, D.C., 2016.

US Department of State. *Foreign Relations of the United States [FRUS], 1964–1968*. Vols. 21, 34.

———. *Foreign Relations of the United States [FRUS], 1969–1976*. Vols. 24, 36, 37, E-4, E-9 part 2.

———. *Foreign Relations of the United States [FRUS], 1977–1980*. Vols. 1, 6, 9, 18, 38.

Walsh, Lawrence E. *Final Report of the Independent Counsel for Iran/Contra Matters*. Vol. 1. Washington, D.C.: U.S. Court of Appeals for the District of Columbia Circuit, 1993.

Online Data and Documents

Bob Dylan Official Website. http://bobdylan.com.

British Petroleum. "Data Workbook—Statistical Review 2015." https://www.bp.com/en /global/corporate/energy-economics/statistical-review-of-world-energy/down loads.html.

Guinness World Records. https://www.guinnessworldrecords.com.

International Monetary Fund, Direction of Trade Statistics. https://data.imf.org.

James Martin Center for Nonproliferation Studies, Middlebury Institute of International Studies at Monterey. http://cns.miis.edu.

Stockholm International Peace Research Institute (SIPRI). https://www.sipri.org.

Theroux, Peter. "Abdelrahman Munif and the Uses of Oil." *Words without Borders*, October 2012. https://wordswithoutborders.org/article/abdelrahman-munif-and-the -uses-of-oil.

United Nations, National Accounts Main Aggregates Database. https://unstats.un.org
    /unsd/snaama/Index.
US Agency for International Development, Country Summary. https://explorer.usaid.gov
    /data.
US Department of Labor, Bureau of Labor Statistics. https://www.bls.gov/data/.
US Department of State Virtual Reading Room (DSVRR). http://foia.state.gov/Search
    /Search.aspx.
US Department of the Treasury. "Securities (B): Portfolio Holdings of U.S. and Foreign
    Securities." https://www.treasury.gov/resource-center/data-chart-center/tic/Pages/tic
    sec2.aspx.
US White House. "Statement from President Donald J. Trump on Standing with Saudi
    Arabia." November 20, 2018. https://www.whitehouse.gov/briefings-statements/state
    ment-president-donald-j-trump-standing-saudi-arabia/. World Bank, World Integrated
    Trade Solution. https://wits.worldbank.org/.

Films

Ilsa: Harem Keeper of the Oil Sheiks, directed by Don Edmonds, 1976.
Network, directed by Sidney Lumet, 1976.
The Happy Hooker Goes to Washington, directed by William A. Levey, 1977.

Newspapers and Periodicals

al-Ahram (Cairo)
Business Week
Chicago Tribune
Christian Science Monitor
Construction Week
al-Da'wa (Cairo)
Detroit Free Press
Ellensburg (WA) *Daily Record*
Forbes
Fortune
Guardian
Harper's Magazine
Independent
Kayhan (Tehran)
Los Angeles Times
al-Medina (Medina)
al-Nahar (Beirut)
al-Nahar al-Inma'i (Beirut)
National Review
New Republic

New York Times (NYT)
New Yorker
Ottawa Citizen
al-Riyadh (Riyadh)
al-Sharq al-Awsat (London)
al-Thawra (Baghdad)
al-Thawra al-Usbu'ai (Baghdad)
Time
Tri-City Herald (Kennewick, WA)
Wall Street Journal
Washington Post

Books, Articles, and Dissertations

Abrahamian, Ervand. *A History of Modern Iran.* Cambridge: Cambridge University Press, 2008.

Adler, Paul. "'The Basis of a New Internationalism': The Institute for Policy Studies and North-South Politics from the NIEO to Neoliberalism." *Diplomatic History* 41, no. 4 (September 2017): 665–693.

Alam, Asadollah. *The Shah and I: The Confidential Diary of Iran's Royal Court, 1969–1977.* Translated by Alinaghi Alikhani and Nicholas Vincent. New York: St. Martin's Press, 1992.

Al-Rasheed, Madawi. *Contesting the Saudi State: Islamic Voices from a New Generation.* Cambridge: Cambridge University Press, 2006.

——. *A History of Saudi Arabia.* 2nd ed. Cambridge: Cambridge University Press, 2010.

Alvandi, Roham. *Nixon, Kissinger, and the Shah: The United States and Iran in the Cold War.* Oxford: Oxford University Press, 2014.

Amin, Galal. *Egypt in the Age of Hosni Mubarak, 1981–2011.* Cairo: American University in Cairo Press, 2011.

Anziska, Seth. *Preventing Palestine: A Political History from Camp David to Oslo.* Princeton, NJ: Princeton University Press, 2018.

Avon, Dominique, and Anaïs-Trissa Khatchadourian. *Hezbollah: A History of the "Party of God."* Translated by Jane Marie Todd. Cambridge, MA: Harvard University Press, 2012.

Ayubi, Nazih. *Political Islam: Religion and Politics in the Arab World.* London: Routledge, 1991.

Bacevich, Andrew J. *America's War for the Greater Middle East: A Military History.* New York: Random House, 2016.

Bakke, Lars Hasvoll, and Hilde Henriksen Waage. "Facing Assad: American Diplomacy toward Syria, 1973–1977." *International History Review* 40, no. 3 (June 2018): 546–572.

Bartel, Fritz. "Fugitive Leverage: Commercial Banks, Sovereign Debt, and Cold War Crisis in Poland, 1980–1982." *Enterprise & Society* 18, no. 1 (March 2017): 72–107.

Beasley, Betsy A. "At Your Service: Houston and the Preservation of U.S. Global Power, 1945-2008." PhD diss., Yale University, 2016.

Beattie, Kirk J. *Egypt during the Nasser Years: Ideology, Politics, and Civil Society*. Boulder, CO: Westview Press, 1994.

———. *Egypt during the Sadat Years*. New York: Palgrave, 2000.

Ben-Zvi, Abraham. *John F. Kennedy and the Politics of Arms Sales to Israel*. London: Frank Cass, 2002.

———. *Lyndon B. Johnson and the Politics of Arms Sales to Israel: In the Shadow of the Hawk*. London: Frank Cass, 2004.

Bill, James A. *The Eagle and the Lion: The Tragedy of American-Iranian Relations*. New Haven, CT: Yale University Press, 1988.

Biven, W. Carl. *Jimmy Carter's Economy: Policy in an Age of Limits*. Chapel Hill: University of North Carolina Press, 2002.

Borstelmann, Thomas. *The 1970s: A New Global History from Civil Rights to Economic Inequality*. Princeton, NJ: Princeton University Press, 2011.

Bradley, Mark Philip. *The World Reimagined: Americans and Human Rights in the Twentieth Century*. Cambridge: Cambridge University Press, 2016.

Bronson, Rachel. *Thicker Than Oil: America's Uneasy Partnership with Saudi Arabia*. Oxford: Oxford University Press, 2006.

Brownlee, Jason. *Democracy Prevention: The Politics of the U.S.-Egyptian Alliance*. Cambridge: Cambridge University Press, 2012.

Burns, William J. *Economic Aid & American Foreign Policy toward Egypt, 1955–1981*. Albany: State University of New York Press, 1985.

Byrne, Malcolm. *Iran-Contra: Reagan's Scandal and the Unchecked Abuse of Presidential Power*. Lawrence: University Press of Kansas, 2017.

Carter, Jimmy. *White House Diary*. New York: Farrar, Straus and Giroux, 2010.

Chamberlin, Paul Thomas. *The Global Offensive: The United States, the Palestine Liberation Organization, and the Making of the Post-Cold War Order*. Oxford: Oxford University Press, 2012.

Christopher, Warren, Oscar Schachter, Paul H. Kreisberg, and Abraham Alexander Ribicoff. *American Hostages in Iran: The Conduct of a Crisis*. New Haven, CT: Yale University Press, 1985.

Citino, Nathan. *From Arab Nationalism to OPEC: Eisenhower, King Sa'ud, and the Making of U.S.-Saudi Relations*. Bloomington: Indiana University Press, 2002.

Cohen, Benjamin J. *In Whose Interest? International Banking and American Foreign Policy*. New Haven, CT: Yale University Press, 1986.

Coll, Steve. *Ghost Wars: The Secret History of the CIA, Afghanistan, and bin Laden, from the Soviet Invasion to September 10, 2001*. New York: Penguin Press, 2004.

Connelly, Matthew. *A Diplomatic Revolution: Algeria's Fight for Independence and the Origins of the Post-Cold War Era*. Oxford: Oxford University Press, 2002.

Cooper, Andrew Scott. *The Oil Kings: How the U.S., Iran, and Saudi Arabia Changed the Balance of Power in the Middle East*. New York: Simon & Schuster, 2011.

Cooper, Richard N. *The Economics of Interdependence: Economic Policy in the Atlantic Community*. New York: McGraw-Hill, 1968.

Costigliola, Frank. *France and the United States: The Cold Alliance since World War II*. New York: Twayne Publishers, 1992.

Costigliola, Frank, and Michael J. Hogan, eds. *Explaining the History of American Foreign Relations*. 3rd ed. Cambridge: Cambridge University Press, 2016.

Crist, David. *The Twilight War: The Secret History of America's Thirty-Year Conflict with Iran*. New York: Penguin Press, 2012.

Daigle, Craig. *The Limits of Détente: The United States, the Soviet Union, and the Arab-Israeli Conflict, 1969–1973*. New Haven, CT: Yale University Press, 2012.

Dallek, Robert. *Nixon and Kissinger: Partners in Power*. New York: HarperCollins Publishers, 2007.

Dietrich, Christopher R. W. *Oil Revolution: Anticolonial Elites, Sovereign Rights, and the Economic Culture of Decolonization*. Cambridge: Cambridge University Press, 2017.

Dresch, Paul. *A History of Modern Yemen*. Cambridge: Cambridge University Press, 2000.

Eckes, Alfred E., Jr., and Thomas W. Zeiler. *Globalization and the American Century*. Cambridge: Cambridge University Press, 2003.

Eichengreen, Barry. *Exorbitant Privilege: The Rise and Fall of the Dollar*. Oxford: Oxford University Press, 2011.

——. *Globalizing Capital: A History of the International Monetary System*. 2nd ed. Princeton, NJ: Princeton University Press, 2008.

Ekbladh, David. *The Great American Mission: Modernization and the Construction of an American World Order*. Princeton, NJ: Princeton University Press, 2011.

El-Gamal, Mahmoud A., and Amy Myers Jaffe. *Oil, Dollars, Debt, and Crisis: The Global Curse of Black Gold*. Cambridge: Cambridge University Press, 2010.

Emery, Christian. *US Foreign Policy and the Iranian Revolution: The Cold War Dynamics of Engagement and Strategic Alliance*. New York: Palgrave Macmillan, 2013.

Erdman, Paul E. *The Crash of '79*. New York: Simon & Schuster, 1976.

Fain, W. Taylor. *American Ascendance and British Retreat in the Persian Gulf Region*. New York: Palgrave Macmillan, 2008.

Feiler, Gil. *Economic Relations between Egypt and the Gulf Oil States, 1967–2000*. Brighton: Sussex Academic Press, 2003.

Feldman, Shai. "The Bombing of Osiraq-Revisited." *International Security* 7, no. 2 (Fall 1982): 114–142.

Ferguson, Niall, Charles S. Maier, Erez Manela, and Daniel J. Sargent, eds. *Shock of the Global: The 1970s in Perspective*. Cambridge, MA: Harvard University Press, 2010.

Ferris, Jesse. *Nasser's Gamble: How Intervention in Yemen Caused the Six-Day War and the Decline of Egyptian Power*. Princeton, NJ: Princeton University Press, 2012.

Franczak, Michael. "Human Rights and Basic Needs: Jimmy Carter's North-South Dialogue, 1977–81." *Cold War History* 18, no. 4 (November 2018): 447–464.

Frieden, Jeffry A. *Banking on the World: The Politics of American International Finance*. New York: Harper & Row, 1987.

——. *Global Capitalism: Its Fall and Rise in the Twentieth Century*. New York: W.W. Norton, 2006.

Garavini, Giuliano. *The Rise and Fall of OPEC in the Twentieth Century*. Oxford: Oxford University Press, 2019.

Garthoff, Raymond L. *Détente and Confrontation: American-Soviet Relations from Nixon to Reagan*. Rev. ed. Washington, DC: Brookings Institution, 1994.

Gasiorowski, Mark J., and Malcolm Byrne, eds. *Mohammad Mosaddeq and the 1953 Coup in Iran*. Syracuse, NY: Syracuse University Press, 2004.

Gause, F. Gregory, III. *Oil Monarchies: Domestic and Security Challenges in the Arab Gulf States*. New York: Council on Foreign Relations Press, 1994.

Gavin, Francis J. *Gold, Dollars, and Power: The Politics of International Monetary Relations, 1958–1971*. Chapel Hill: University of North Carolina Press, 2004.

Gerges, Fawaz A. *The Far Enemy: Why Jihad Went Global*. New ed. Cambridge: Cambridge University Press, 2009.

Gil Guerrero, Javier. *The Carter Administration and the Fall of Iran's Pahlavi Dynasty: US-Iran Relations on the Brink of the 1979 Revolution*. New York: Palgrave Macmillan, 2016.

Glad, Betty. *An Outsider in the White House: Jimmy Carter, His Advisors, and the Making of American Foreign Policy*. Ithaca, NY: Cornell University Press, 2009.

Golan, Galia. *Soviet Policies in the Middle East: From World War II to Gorbachev*. Cambridge: Cambridge University Press, 1990.

Goldberg, J. J. *Jewish Power: Inside the American Jewish Establishment*. New York: Perseus Books, 1996.

Goode, James F. "Assisting Our Brothers, Defending Ourselves: The Iranian Intervention in Oman, 1972–75." *Iranian Studies* 47, no. 3 (May 2014): 441–462.

Graf, Rüdiger. "Making Use of the 'Oil Weapon': Western Industrialized Countries and Arab Petropolitics in 1973–74." *Diplomatic History* 36, no. 1 (January 2012): 185–208.

Grandin, Greg. *Empire's Workshop: Latin America, the United States, and the Rise of the New Imperialism*. New York: Henry Holt, 2010.

Grose, Philip G. *Looking for Utopia: The Life and Times of John C. West*. Columbia: University of South Carolina Press, 2011.

Haftlang, Zahed, Najah Aboud, and Meredith May. *I, Who Did Not Die*. New York: Regan Arts, 2017.

Hahn, Peter L. *Caught in the Middle East: U.S. Policy toward the Arab-Israeli Conflict, 1945–1961*. Chapel Hill: University of North Carolina Press, 2004.

——. *Missions Accomplished? The United States and Iraq since World War I*. Oxford: Oxford University Press, 2012.

——. *The United States, Great Britain, and Egypt, 1945–1956*. Chapel Hill: University of North Carolina Press, 1991.

Halliday, Fred. *Arabia without Sultans*. London: Penguin Books, 1974.

——. *Revolution and Foreign Policy: The Case of South Yemen, 1967–1987*. Cambridge: Cambridge University Press, 1990.

Hamblin, Jacob Darwin. "The Nuclearization of Iran in the Seventies." *Diplomatic History* 38, no. 5 (November 2014): 1114–1135.

Hanhimäki, Jussi. *The Flawed Architect: Henry Kissinger and American Foreign Policy*. New York: Oxford University Press, 2004.

Hegghammer, Thomas. *Jihad in Saudi Arabia: Violence and Pan-Islamism since 1979*. Cambridge: Cambridge University Press, 2010.

Heiss, Mary Ann. *Empire and Nationhood: The United States, Great Britain, and Iranian Oil, 1950–1954*. New York: Columbia University Press, 1997.

Hiro, Dilip. *The Longest War: The Iran-Iraq Military Conflict*. New York: Routledge, 1991.

Hogan, Michael J. *A Cross of Iron: Harry S. Truman and the Origins of the National Security State, 1945–1954.* Cambridge: Cambridge University Press, 1998.

Ibrahim, Saad Eddin. "Anatomy of Egypt's Militant Islamic Groups: Methodological Note and Preliminary Findings." *International Journal of Middle East Studies* 12, no. 4 (December 1980): 423–453.

——. *The New Arab Social Order: A Study of the Social Impact of Oil Wealth.* Boulder, CO: Westview Press, 1982.

Jacobs, Matthew F. *Imagining the Middle East: The Building of an American Foreign Policy, 1918–1967.* Chapel Hill: University of North Carolina Press, 2011.

Jacobs, Meg. *Panic at the Pump: The Energy Crisis and the Transformation of American Politics in the 1970s.* New York: Hill and Wang, 2016.

James, Harold. *International Monetary Cooperation since Bretton Woods.* Oxford: Oxford University Press, 1996.

Jensehaugen, Jørgen. *Arab-Israeli Diplomacy under Carter: The US, Israel and the Palestinians.* London: I.B. Tauris, 2018.

Jentleson, Bruce W. *With Friends Like These: Reagan, Bush, and Saddam, 1982–1990.* New York: W. W. Norton, 1994.

Jones, Seth G. *In the Graveyard of Empires: America's War in Afghanistan.* New York: W. W. Norton, 2009.

Jones, Toby Craig. *Desert Kingdom: How Oil and Water Forged Modern Saudi Arabia.* Cambridge, MA: Harvard University Press, 2011.

Kalinovsky, Artemy M. *A Long Goodbye: The Soviet Withdrawal from Afghanistan.* Cambridge, MA: Harvard University Press, 2011.

Kapstein, Ethan B. *Governing the Global Economy: International Finance and the State.* Cambridge, MA: Harvard University Press, 1994.

——. *The Insecure Alliance: Energy Crises and Western Politics since 1944.* Oxford: Oxford University Press, 1990.

Keddie, Nikki L. *Modern Iran: Roots and Results of Revolution.* 2nd ed. New Haven, CT: Yale University Press, 2006.

Keys, Barbara J. *Reclaiming American Virtue: The Human Rights Revolution of the 1970s.* Cambridge, MA: Harvard University Press, 2014.

Kramer, Paul A. "Power and Connection: Imperial Histories of the United States in the World." *American Historical Review* 116, no. 5 (December 2011): 1348–1391.

Kunz, Diane B. *Butter and Guns: America's Cold War Economic Diplomacy.* New York: Free Press, 1997.

Laham, Nicholas. *Selling AWACS to Saudi Arabia: The Reagan Administration and the Balancing of America's Competing Interests in the Middle East.* Westport, CT: Praeger Publishers, 2002.

Laron, Guy. *The Six-Day War: The Breaking of the Middle East.* New Haven, CT: Yale University Press, 2017.

Latham, Michael E. *The Right Kind of Revolution: Modernization, Development, and U.S. Foreign Policy from the Cold War to the Present.* Ithaca, NY: Cornell University Press, 2011.

Leffler, Melvyn P. *For the Soul of Mankind: The United States, the Soviet Union, and the Cold War.* New York: Hill & Wang, 2007.

———. *A Preponderance of Power: National Security, the Truman Administration, and the Cold War*. Stanford, CA: Stanford University Press, 1992.

LeVine, Mark. *Why They Don't Hate Us: Lifting the Veil on the Axis of Evil*. Oxford: Oneworld Publications, 2005.

Little, Douglas. "To the Shores of Tripoli: America, Qaddafi, and Libyan Revolution, 1969–89." *International History Review* 35, no. 1 (February 2013): 70–99.

Logevall, Fredrik, and Andrew Preston, eds. *Nixon in the World: American Foreign Relations, 1969–1977*. Oxford: Oxford University Press, 2008.

Looney, Robert E. *Economic Origins of the Iranian Revolution*. New York: Pergamon Press, 1982.

Louis, Wm. Roger, and Avi Shlaim, eds. *The 1967 Arab-Israeli War: Origins and Consequences*. Cambridge: Cambridge University Press, 2012.

Mahmoud, Mustafa. *Marxism and Islam*. 2nd ed. Translated by M. M. Enani. Jeddah: Tihama Publication, 1985.

Makdisi, Ussama. *Faith Misplaced: The Broken Promise of U.S.-Arab Relations: 1820–2001*. New York: PublicAffairs, 2010.

Mandani, Mahmood. *Good Muslim, Bad Muslim: America, the Cold War, and the Roots of Terror*. New York: Pantheon Books, 2004.

Malley, Robert. *The Call from Algeria: Third Worldism, Revolution, and the Turn to Islam*. Berkeley: University of California Press, 1996.

Markusen, Ann, Peter Hall, Scott Campbell, and Sabina Deitrick. *The Rise of the Gunbelt: The Military Remapping of Industrial America*. Oxford: Oxford University Press, 1991.

Marr, Phebe, and Ibrahim Al-Marashi. *The Modern History of Iraq*. 4th ed. Boulder, CO: Westview Press, 2017.

Mattione, Richard P. *OPEC's Investments and the International Financial System*. Washington, DC: Brookings Institution, 1985.

Matusow, Allen J. *Nixon's Economy: Booms, Busts, Dollars, & Votes*. Lawrence: University Press of Kansas, 1998.

McAlister, Melani. *Epic Encounters: Culture, Media, and U.S. Interests in the Middle East since 1945*. 2nd ed. Berkeley: University of California Press, 2005.

McFarland, Victor R. S. "Living in Never-Never Land: The United States, Saudi Arabia, and Oil in the 1970s." PhD diss., Yale University, 2014.

McGlinchey, Stephen. "Lyndon B. Johnson and Arms Credit Sales to Iran, 1964–1968." *Middle East Journal* 67, no. 2 (Spring 2013): 229–247.

McGlinchey, Stephen, and Robert W. Murray. "Jimmy Carter and the Sale of the AWACS to Iran in 1977." *Diplomacy & Statecraft* 28, no. 2 (June 2017): 254–276.

Menoret, Pascal. *Joyriding in Riyadh: Oil, Urbanism, and Road Revolt*. Cambridge: Cambridge University Press, 2014.

Mieczkowski, Yanek. *Gerald Ford and the Challenges of the 1970s*. Lexington: University Press of Kentucky, 2005.

Miglietta, John P. *American Alliance Policy in the Middle East, 1945–1992: Iran, Israel, and Saudi Arabia*. Lanham, MD: Lexington Books, 2002.

Mitchell, Timothy. *Carbon Democracy: Political Power in the Age of Oil*. London: Verso, 2011.

——. *Rule of Experts: Egypt, Techno-Politics, and Modernity*. Berkeley: University of California Press, 2002.

Munif, Abdelrahman. *Cities of Salt*. Translated by Peter Theroux. London: Vintage, 1994.

Murray, Williamson, and Kevin M. Woods. *The Iran-Iraq War: A Military and Strategic History*. Cambridge: Cambridge University Press, 2014.

Nelson, Chad E. "Revolution and War: Saddam's Decision to Invade Iran." *Middle East Journal* 72, no. 2 (Spring 2018): 246–266.

Nelson, Keith. *The Making of Détente: Soviet-American Relations in the Shadow of Vietnam*. Baltimore: Johns Hopkins University Press, 1995.

Niblock, Tim, ed. *State, Society and Economy in Saudi Arabia*. New York: St. Martin's Press, 1982.

Nitzan, Jonathan, and Shimshon Bichler. *The Global Political Economy of Israel*. London: Pluto Press, 2002.

O'Ballance, Edgar. *Civil War in Lebanon, 1975–1992*. London: Palgrave Macmillan, 1998.

Offiler, Ben. *US Foreign Policy and the Modernization of Iran: Kennedy, Johnson, Nixon, and the Shah*. New York: Palgrave Macmillan, 2015.

Olson, Robert K. *U.S. Foreign Policy and the New International Economic Order: Negotiating Global Problems, 1974–1981*. Boulder, CO: Westview Press, 1981.

Orkaby, Asher. *Beyond the Arab Cold War: The International History of the Yemen Civil War, 1962–68*. Oxford: Oxford University Press, 2017.

Owen, Roger, and Şevket Pamuk. *A History of Middle East Economies in the Twentieth Century*. London: I.B. Tauris, 1998.

Pahlavi, Mohammad Reza. *Toward the Great Civilization: A Dream Revisited*. London: Satrap Publishing, 1994.

Painter, David S. "Oil and Geopolitics: The Oil Crises of the 1970s and the Cold War." *Historical Social Research* 39, no. 4 (2014): 186–208.

——. *Oil and the American Century: The Political Economy of U.S. Foreign Oil Policy, 1941–1954*. Baltimore: Johns Hopkins University Press, 1986.

Pollitz, Edward A., Jr. *The Forty-First Thief*. New York: Delacorte Press, 1975.

Quandt, William B. *Peace Process: American Diplomacy and the Arab-Israeli Conflict since 1967*. 3rd ed. Washington, DC: Brookings Institution Press, 2005.

Rabe, Stephen G. *The Killing Zone: The United States Wages Cold War in Latin America*. 2nd ed. Oxford: Oxford University Press, 2016.

Rabinovich, Itamar. *The War for Lebanon, 1970–1985*. Rev. ed. Ithaca, NY: Cornell University Press, 1985.

Rakove, Robert B. *Kennedy, Johnson, and the Nonaligned World*. Cambridge: Cambridge University Press, 2013.

Randall, Stephen J. *United States Foreign Oil Policy since World War I: For Profits and Security*. 2nd ed. Montreal: McGill-Queen's University Press, 2005.

Razoux, Pierre. *The Iran-Iraq War*. Translated by Nicholas Elliott. Cambridge, MA: Harvard University Press, 2015.

Reagan, Ronald. *The Reagan Diaries*. Edited by Douglas Brinkley. New York: HarperCollins, 2007.

Renouard, Joe. *Human Rights in American Foreign Policy: From the 1960s to the Soviet Collapse.* Philadelphia: University of Pennsylvania Press, 2015.

Rosenberg, Emily S. *Financial Missionaries to the World: The Politics and Culture of Dollar Diplomacy, 1900–1930.* Cambridge, MA: Harvard University Press, 1999.

Rossinow, Doug. *The Reagan Era: A History of the 1980s.* New York: Columbia University Press, 2015.

Ruedy, John. *Modern Algeria: The Origins and Development of a Nation.* 2nd ed. Bloomington: Indiana University Press, 2005.

Sachs, Jeffrey. "Managing the LDC Debt Crisis." *Brookings Papers on Economic Activity* 17, no. 2 (Fall 1986): 397–431.

Said, Edward W. *Culture and Imperialism.* New York: Alfred A. Knopf, 1993.

Sampson, Anthony. *The Money Lenders: Bankers and a World in Turmoil.* New York: Viking Press, 1981.

Sargent, Daniel J. "North/South: The United States Responds to the New International Economic Order." *Humanity: An International Journal of Human Rights, Humanitarianism, and Development* 6, no. 1 (Spring 2015): 201–216.

———. *A Superpower Transformed: The Remaking of American Foreign Relations in the 1970s.* Oxford: Oxford University Press, 2015.

Schoenbaum, David. *The United States and the State of Israel.* New York: Oxford University Press, 1993.

Scott, James M. *Deciding to Intervene: The Reagan Doctrine and American Foreign Policy.* Durham, NC: Duke University Press, 1996.

Sewell, Bevan, and Maria Ryan, eds. *Foreign Policy at the Periphery: The Shifting Margins of US International Relations since World War II.* Lexington: University Press of Kentucky, 2017.

Shaheen, Jack G. *Reel Bad Arabs: How Hollywood Vilifies a People.* Updated ed. Northampton, MA: Olive Branch Press, 2015.

———. *The TV Arab.* Bowling Green, OH: Bowling Green State University Popular Press, 1984.

Shannon, Matthew K. *Losing Hearts and Minds: American-Iranian Relations and International Education during the Cold War.* Ithaca, NY: Cornell University Press, 2017.

Sharma, Patrick Allan. *Robert McNamara's Other War: The World Bank and International Development.* Philadelphia: University of Pennsylvania Press, 2017.

Shultz, George P. *Turmoil and Triumph: My Years as Secretary of State.* New York: Charles Scribner's Sons, 1993.

Sick, Gary. *All Fall Down: America's Tragic Encounter with Iran.* New York: Random House, 1985.

Simmons, Andre. *Arab Foreign Aid.* Rutherford, NJ: Fairleigh Dickinson University Press, 1981.

Skeet, Ian. *OPEC: Twenty-Five Years of Prices and Politics.* Cambridge: Cambridge University Press, 1988.

Smith, Benjamin. *Market Orientalism: Cultural Economy and the Arab Gulf States.* Syracuse, NY: Syracuse University Press, 2015.

Smith, Simon C. *Ending Empire in the Middle East: Britain, the United States and Post-War Decolonization, 1945–1973.* New York: Routledge, 2012.

Spiro, David E. *The Hidden Hand of American Hegemony: Petrodollar Recycling and International Markets*. Ithaca, NY: Cornell University Press, 1999.

St. John, Ronald Bruce. *Libya and the United States: Two Centuries of Strife*. Philadelphia: University of Pennsylvania Press, 2002.

Stanik, Joseph T. *El Dorado Canyon: Reagan's Undeclared War with Qaddafi*. Annapolis, MD: Naval Institute Press, 2003.

Stein, Judith. *Pivotal Decade: How the United States Traded Factories for Finance in the Seventies*. New Haven, CT: Yale University Press, 2010.

Stivers, William. *America's Confrontation with Revolutionary Change in the Middle East, 1948–83*. New York: St. Martin's Press, 1986.

Strieff, Daniel. "Arms Wrestle: Capitol Hill Fight over Carter's 1978 Middle East 'Package' Airplane Sale." *Diplomatic History* 40, no. 3 (June 2016): 475–499.

Styan, David. *France and Iraq: Oil, Arms and French Policy Making in the Middle East*. London: I.B. Tauris, 2006.

Suri, Jeremi. *Power and Protest: Global Revolution and the Rise of Détente*. Cambridge, MA: Harvard University Press, 2003.

Tabaar, Mohammad Ayatollahi. *Religious Statecraft: The Politics of Islam in Iran*. New York: Columbia University Press, 2018.

Takriti, Abdel Razzaq. *Monsoon Revolution: Republicans, Sultans, and Empires in Oman, 1965–1976*. Oxford: Oxford University Press, 2013.

Tanous, Peter, and Paul Rubinstein. *The Petrodollar Takeover*. New York: G. P. Putnam's Sons, 1975.

Terry, Janice J. *U.S. Foreign Policy in the Middle East: The Role of Lobbies and Special Interest Groups*. London: Pluto Press, 2005.

Tripp, Charles. *A History of Iraq*. 3rd ed. Cambridge: Cambridge University Press, 2007.

———. *Islam and the Moral Economy: The Challenge of Capitalism*. Cambridge: Cambridge University Press, 2006.

Vaïsse, Justin. *Zbigniew Brzezinski: America's Grand Strategist*. Translated by Catherine Porter. Cambridge, MA: Harvard University Press, 2018.

Vandewalle, Dirk. *A History of Modern Libya*. 2nd ed. Cambridge: Cambridge University Press, 2012.

Vitalis, Robert. *America's Kingdom: Mythmaking on the Saudi Oil Frontier*. Stanford, CA: Stanford University Press, 2007.

Weinbaum, Marvin G. *Egypt and the Politics of U.S. Economic Aid*. Boulder, CO: Westview Press, 1986.

Westad, Odd Arne. *The Global Cold War: Third World Interventions and the Making of Our Times*. Cambridge: Cambridge University Press, 2005.

Wight, David M. "Kissinger's Levantine Dilemma: The Ford Administration and the Syrian Occupation of Lebanon." *Diplomatic History* 37, no. 1 (January 2013): 144–177.

Wilentz, Sean. *The Age of Reagan: A History, 1974–2008*. New York: HarperCollins, 2008.

Wilford, Hugh. "'Essentially a Work of Fiction': Kermit 'Kim' Roosevelt, Imperial Romance, and the Iran Coup of 1953." *Diplomatic History* 40, no. 5 (November 2016): 922–947.

Wolfe-Hunnicutt, Brandon. "Oil Sovereignty, American Foreign Policy, and the 1968 Coups in Iraq." *Diplomacy & Statecraft* 28, no. 2 (June 2017): 235–253.

Wright, Lawrence. *The Looming Tower: Al-Qaeda and the Road to 9/11*. New York: Alfred A. Knopf, 2006.

Yaqub, Salim. *Containing Arab Nationalism: The Eisenhower Doctrine and the Middle East.* Chapel Hill: University of North Carolina Press, 2004.

——. *Imperfect Strangers: Americans, Arabs, and U.S.-Middle East Relations in the 1970s.* Ithaca, NY: Cornell University Press, 2016.

Yergin, Daniel. *The Prize: The Epic Quest for Oil, Money & Power*. 3rd ed. New York: Free Press, 2009.

Zanchetta, Barbara. *The Transformation of American International Power in the 1970s*. New York: Cambridge University Press, 2014.

Zaretsky, Natasha. *No Direction Home: The American Family and the Fear of National Decline, 1968–1980*. Chapel Hill: University of North Carolina Press, 2007.

Zeiler, Thomas W. *Free Trade, Free World: The Advent of GATT*. Chapel Hill: University of North Carolina, 1999.

Zweig, Phillip L. *Wriston: Walter Wriston, Citibank and the Rise and Fall of American Financial Supremacy*. New York: Crown Publishers, 1995.

Index

Page numbers followed by letter *f* refer to figures, letter *t* to tables.

Abdullah (king of Saudi Arabia), 73*f*, 272, 284–285
Aboud, Najah, 225–226
Abourezk, James, 221
Abu Ismail, Ahmed, 133
Abu Nidal, 266–267
Adham, Kamal, 65
Afghanistan, 200, 283. *See also* Soviet-Afghan War
Agency for Arab and International Cooperation, 98
Agnew, Spiro, 79, 139
Akins, James, 60–61, 68, 70, 83, 104
Alam, Asadollah, 36, 45, 109, 174, 178
Algeria, 20, 22, 24, 184; foreign debt of, 113, 247; imports of, 63, 82, 117–119, 122, 248*f*, 255*f*; NIEO and, 91–92; oil and, 43, 51, 67*t*, 275–276; in popular media, 186; United States and, 7, 29, 58, 64, 70, 82, 122
Ali, Anwar, 90
Alice, 220
All-African People's Revolutionary Party, 162
Allen, Richard, 222, 230, 234, 236–237
Allon, Yigal, 102–103
American Enterprise Institute, 53
American Express, 99

American Federation of Labor and Congress of Industrial Organizations, 139–140
American Israel Public Affairs Committee, 186
American Motors, 205–206
American Potato Company, 108
American-Arab Anti-Discrimination Committee, 221
Amin, Hafizullah, 212
Amuzegar, Jamshid, 180
Anderson, Jack, 221
Andropov, Yuri, 249
Andrus, Cecil, 108–109
Anglo-Iranian Oil Company (AIOC), 12, 14, 18–19, 31
Anti-Defamation League of B'nai B'rith, 151
Arab League, 10, 16, 32, 102, 150, 204–205, 221, 245
Arab Organization for Industrialization, 205–206
Arab-American Development Services, 116
Arabian Peninsula People's Union, 26
Arabian-American Oil Company (Aramco), 10–14, 17–21, 38, 40, 43, 55, 57, 122
Arab-Israeli War of 1948, 17–18
Arab-Israeli War of 1967, 28–29
Arab-Israeli War of 1973, 54–59
Arafat, Yasser, 33, 205, 245

Argentina, 113, 246
Asad, Bashar al-, 285
Asad, Hafez al-, 54, 126, 183, 219
Aspen, Les, 268
AT&T, 100, 146
Ateeqy, Abdul Rahman al-, 90–91
Australia, 15, 173, 191
Aziz, Tariq, 242, 257
Azzam, Abdullah, 261

Bahrain, 46, 58, 136–137, 285
Baker, James, 272
Baker, Virgil, 136
Bakhtiar, Shapour, 198–199
Bakr, Ahmad Hassan al-, 36, 156, 217
Bandar bin Sultan (prince of Saudi Arabia),
    259
Bangladesh, 161
Bani-Sadr, Abol Hassan, 210, 219f
Bank for International Settlements (BIS), 114,
    179, 216, 247–248
Bank of America, 83, 99
Baraheni, Reza, 155
Batman and Robin, 282
Bazargan, Mehdi, 199, 209–210
Bechtel: engineering projects of, 97, 122; in
    popular media, 152; US government and,
    101, 124, 149, 187, 227, 231–232, 245
Begin, Menachem, 184, 191–192, 205, 230,
    242–243
Belgium, 91
Bell Helicopter: Cobra and, 225, 265; 206
    JetRanger and, 48
Bendjedid, Chadli, 275
Benston, Lucy, 193
BFGoodrich, 150
Biden, Joe, 230, 287
bin Laden, Osama, 261, 277, 283
Blumenthal, Michael, 177–178, 193, 202
Boeing, 279; Airborne Warning and Control
    System (AWACS) and, 174–177, 184, 190,
    193, 209, 214, 227–232; F-15SA Strike
    Eagle and, 284; 727 and, 234; 747 and,
    234
Boumediene, Houari, 43, 92
Brazil, 113, 126, 246
Brezhnev, Leonid, 35, 58, 175, 249
Briggs, Richard, 136–137
British Petroleum, 12–15
Brown, Harold, 202–205, 215

Brownell, Herbert, 36–37
Brzezinski, Zbigniew, 177, 183, 185, 197,
    202–205, 213–215
Buckley, William, 263, 265
Burns, Arthur, 79–80
Bush, George H. W., 229, 281–282
Bush, George W., 283–284
Byrd, Robert, 175–176, 231

Cagney and Lacey, 232
Callaghan, James, 172–173
Canada, 71, 91, 114, 145
Carmichael, Stokely, 162–163
Carrier Corporation, 150
Carter, Billy, 221–222
Carter, Jimmy: Afghanistan and, 212–213, 215,
    232; arms and, 155–156, 170–178, 183–193,
    203–204, 214; economic policy of, 178–180,
    193–194, 207; Iranian Revolution and, 197,
    200, 203, 209–211, 216–217, 222–224;
    Ruhollah Khomeini and, 168–169, 182; in
    popular media, 170, 211, 219, 222–223; US
    elections and, 155–156, 170, 221–224; John
    West and, 116
Casey, William, 222, 238, 260, 263–264
Chad, 236
Charleston Natural History Society, 115–116
Chase Manhattan, 39, 75, 83, 97–99, 131,
    211
Chevron, 13–15
China, 116, 183, 247, 254–255, 279, 284
CHiPs, 220
Christopher, Warren, 203
Chrysler: M1 Abrams and, 203, 268–269;
    M60 and, 219, 273
Church, Frank, 151
Citadel, 231
Citibank, 75, 83, 99, 115, 131, 211, 246
Clark, Ramsey, 155
Clements, William, 64, 72, 84
Clinton, Bill, 282
Columbia University, 154
Compagnie Française Pétrole, 12, 15
Computer Sciences Corporation, 187
Connally, John, 221
Cooper, Richard, 6
Cranston, Alan, 268–269
Crash of '79, The, 152, 154
Cuba, 112, 184, 200, 203
Culver, John, 175–176

Dent, John, 150
Dhofar War, 26, 38, 48, 118
Dinitz, Simcha, 103
Du Pont, Pierre, IV, 154
Dutton, Fred, 187, 230
Dylan, Bob, 220

Eagleton, Thomas, 175
Eagleton, William, 233–234, 241
Earthbound, 232
East Germany, 113
Ebrahaim, Mohammed Kahlil, 136–137
Ecuador, 51, 246
Egypt: aid to, 32–33, 95–96, 101–104, 126,
    132–134, 204–207; Arab-Israeli conflict and,
    22–23, 28–29, 54–59, 70, 73, 105–107, 130,
    204–207; arms to, 74, 97, 100, 119*f*, 121*t*,
    130–131, 203–207, 255*f*; economy of, 41,
    85, 95–101, 275–276; foreign investment in,
    85–86, 94–95, 97–101, 131, 205–206;
    Iran-Iraq War and, 255; migrant labor from,
    41, 127–128, 206; militant Islamists and,
    161, 237, 261; North Yemen Civil War and,
    25–26, 32; in popular media, 164–165; shah
    and, 217; Soviet Union and, 41–42, 54–55,
    58, 95–96, 113; United Kingdom and,
    20–23; United States and, 8, 41–42, 81, 96,
    98, 245, 277
Eilts, Hermann, 96–97, 130–131
Eisenhower, Dwight, 19, 21–24
Enders, Thomas, 80
Erdman, Paul, 152, 154
Eshkol, Levi, 28
Ethiopia, 112, 183–184, 187, 200, 258
Euromarkets, 44–45, 70, 75, 114
Evron, Ephraim, 228, 234
Exxon, 12–15, 39, 146

Fahd (king of Saudi Arabia), 259*f*; Arab-Israeli
    conflict and, 39, 59, 105, 204, 242; death of,
    284; dollar and, 180; oil and, 38, 59; Saudi
    national security and, 73, 183–187, 200,
    256; John West and, 231
Fahmy, Ismail, 96–97, 100, 134
Faisal (king of Saudi Arabia): Arab-Israeli conflict
    and, 28, 50, 55–56, 104; death of, 105;
    North Yemen Civil War and, 25–26; oil and,
    60, 65–66, 70–72, 78; in popular media, 55,
    143, 157, 163–164; Saudi-US interdependence
    and, 71–74; US invasion fears of, 83–84

Faisal II (king of Iraq), 23
Fluor, 122
Ford, Gerald, 79–80, 114*f*; Egypt and, 99–100,
    104–107, 131–134; Israel and, 103–107; in
    popular media, 153*f*, 164, 170; Saudi Arabia
    and, 83–84, 104–105, 110; US Congress and,
    151, 155; US elections and, 155–156, 170–171
Forty-First Thief, The, 146
France: arms from, 41–42, 49, 119*f*, 172–174,
    188, 215, 254–256; empire of, 11–12, 15–16,
    20–24; exports from, 63, 112, 116–119, 122,
    186, 248*f*; Fifth Republic of, 209; oil and,
    12–15, 71; Persian Gulf War and, 282; Saudi
    Arabia and, 63–64, 105–106
Fulbright, J. William, 139

G. D. Searle, 254
Gates, Robert, 272
Gemayel, Bashir, 245
General Dynamics: F-16 Fighting Falcon and,
    120, 185, 189, 209, 234; F-111 Aardvark
    and, 268
General Electric, 36, 150
General Motors, 146, 148
General Telephone and Electronics, 122
Genesco, 100
Georgetown University, 139
Ghorbanifar, Manucher, 263–264, 266
Giscard d'Estaing, Valéry, 172–173
Gorbachev, Mikhail, 260–261, 263
Greenspan, Alan, 129
Group of 77, 86, 92–93
Grumman, 182; F-14 Tomcat and, 48–49, 79,
    120, 209, 249, 256
Guinea, 162–163
Gulf Oil, 12–15
Gunter, John, 133

Haberler, Gottfried, 53
Hadi, Abdu Rabbu Mansour, 279
Haftar, Khalifa, 285
Haftlang, Zahed, 225–226
Haig, Alexander, 73*f*, 227–228, 234–235,
    237–238, 245
Hakim, Albert, 259
Halliburton, 123
Hamadi, Fadoon, 124
Hammadi, Sadun, 234, 241
Happy Hooker Goes to Washington, The,
    141–142

Hasenfus, Eugene, 269

Hegazi, Abdel Aziz, 85, 99

Helms, Richard, 66–67, 108–109

Herblock, 153*f*

Hewlett-Packard, 150

Hezbollah, 250, 281

Hinckley, John, Jr., 229

Houthis, 279, 285–286

Hughes, 254; Phoenix and, 49; TOW and, 263–264, 266

Hussein (king of Jordan), 23, 50, 234

Hussein, Saddam: death of, 283; Iran and, 118, 217–219, 233–234, 249, 255–256, 271–274; Persian Gulf War and, 281–282; in popular media, 156, 159–160, 162; Soviet Union and, 47

Ibn Saud (king of Saudi Arabia), 13–14, 23

Idris (king of Libya), 24

Ilsa: Harem Keeper of the Oil Sheiks, 140–141

India, 47–48, 113, 115

Indonesia, 24, 224

Ingersoll, Robert, 80

International Monetary Fund (IMF), 86–93, 101, 112, 132–134, 216, 246, 275–276

Iran: arms to, 119*f*, 209, 255*f*; Baghdad Pact and, 21; coup of 1953 in, 19–20; dollar and, 193; economy of, 111; Egypt and, 101–102; IMF and, 91; imports of, 35–36, 81–82, 108–109, 116–125, 216, 248*f*; Iranian Revolution and, 181–183, 187, 195–203, 208–210, 214; oil exports from, 27–28, 35–38, 42–43, 110, 178–180, 197–198, 207; oil revenues of, 67*t*, 178–181, 284; Oman and, 48, 118; OPEC and, 24; Pakistan and, 47; in popular media, 148, 152, 158–160, 166–168, 269, 278–279; Syrian Civil War and, 285; US alliance with, 3–6, 14, 23, 45–49, 64, 78–81, 280; US arms and, 27, 35–36, 48–49, 117–121, 154–155, 173–176, 190–193, 209, 256–257, 263–266; US empire and, 7–8, 280; US sanctions against, 210–212, 216–217, 222–224, 282, 284, 286–287; Western imperialism and, 11–12, 14, 16. *See also* Anglo-Iranian Oil Company; Iran-Iraq War

Iran-Contra scandal, 259–260, 263–266, 269–272, 281

Iranian Oil Participants (IOP), 19, 36–38, 42–43

Iran-Iraq War, 217–219, 225–226, 233–236, 241–245, 249–251, 254–258, 263–266, 269–277, 280–281

Iraq: aid from, 125–126, 241; arms to, 117–119, 159–160, 219, 254–255; coup of 1958 in, 23; debt of, 247, 281; France and, 63, 254–255; imports of, 82, 116–119, 122–124, 159, 248*f*; Iraq War and, 283–284, 287–288; oil and, 29, 43, 52, 58, 67*t*, 70, 178; Persian Gulf War and, 280–281; in popular media, 156–160, 162–163, 269; Saudi Arabia and, 72–73, 183–187; Soviet Union and, 47–48, 113; terrorism and, 218, 234, 241; United Kingdom and, 12, 14–15, 20–21, 252; United States and, 7, 14, 18, 29, 58, 64, 70; Yemen and, 204. *See also* Iran-Iraq War

Iraq Petroleum Company (IPC), 12–14, 17, 23, 43, 47–48, 156, 159

Iraq War, 283–284, 287–288

Irwin, John, 43

Islamic Association of Students in America and Canada, 168–169

Islamic Jihad, 237

Ismail, Hafez, 54

Israel: Arab boycott against, 150–151, 155–156, 179; Arab-Israeli conflict and, 17–18, 22, 28–29, 54–59, 102, 128–131, 242–245; Arab-Israeli peace process and, 64, 71–72, 102–107, 132, 184, 191–192, 204–206; arms to, 28, 41, 119*f*, 121*t*, 170–173, 183–192, 255*f*; Iran-Iraq War and, 218, 259, 263–265; in popular media, 221–222, 269; United States and, 7, 17–18, 21, 41, 82*t*, 102–107, 277, 283

Italy, 49, 52, 63, 71, 110–112, 248*f*

Jaber al-Ahmad al-Sabah (emir of Kuwait), 273

Jamieson, Ken, 39

Japan: aid from, 102, 132; Arab boycott and, 179; economic growth of, 15, 34; exports of, 45, 65, 83, 112, 116–117, 145, 248*f*; foreign investment of, 75, 114–115, 149, 247; oil and, 56, 63, 71; United States and, 35, 45, 52

Javits, Jacob, 188–189

Johnson, Lyndon, 26–28, 32–35, 41, 47

Jones, David, 202

Jordan, 16; Arab-Israeli conflict and, 28–29, 40, 73, 129; petrodollar flows to, 102, 126–127; United States and, 23, 116, 243–245, 256–257

Karmal, Babrak, 212, 261
Kasten, Bob, 256
Kennedy, John, 24–28
Khalid (king of Saudi Arabia), 73f, 105, 200, 232, 242
Khamenei, Ali, 281
Khashoggi, Jamal, 278–279
Khomeini, Ruhollah: anti-US imperialism of, 27, 167–169, 181–182, 195, 198–199, 210, 219; Iranian Revolution and, 181–182, 195, 197–199, 209–211, 217; Iran-Iraq War and, 217–219, 243–244, 274–276; last testament of, 280–281; in popular media, 218–219, 269
Khuli, Lutfi, al-, 164
Kissinger, Henry, 34–35; Arab oil embargo and, 57–60, 62–72, 80, 83–84, 100; Arab-Israeli conflict and, 40–41, 54–59, 64–65, 70–73, 103–107; Egypt and, 94–97, 99–100; Iran and, 36–37, 67, 78–81, 110, 126; NIEO and, 93; in popular media, 139–140; Saudi Arabia and, 50, 53, 69, 71–74, 80–81, 95–97, 100, 155–157
Kramer, Paul, 4
Krugman, Paul, 279
Kurds, 47–48, 117–118, 159, 273
Kuwait, 24; aid from, 33, 97, 125–126, 134, 241, 249; foreign investment of, 76–78, 83, 115–116; Iran-Iraq War and, 256, 273–274; IMF and, 90–91; imports of, 117f, 124, 234, 248f; Lebanese Civil War and, 130; migrant labor in, 127; oil and, 13, 15, 52, 67–68, 77, 286; Persian Gulf War and, 281–283; in popular media, 165; United States and, 29, 50, 58, 64, 70
Kuwait International Investment Company, 151

Lazard Frères, 151
Lebanese Civil War, 126, 128–130, 242–246, 250, 252, 281
Lebanon, 16; imports of, 234; United States, 23, 149, 158, 263–265, 281. See also Lebanese Civil War
Ledeen, Michael, 263–264
Lever, Harold, 88
Levine, Mel, 257
Libya, 15–16; aid from, 33, 89, 125–126; anti-monarchism in, 27, 39; Arab-Israeli conflict and, 29, 58, 70–72, 184–186, 205,

243; imports of, 82, 113, 117–119, 183, 248f, 255f; Iran-Iraq War and, 218, 254; Libyan Civil War and, 285–288; migrant labor in, 126–127, 206; oil and, 24, 42–43, 52, 67t, 178, 276; in popular media, 152, 237; Saudi Arabia and, 187, 258, 266–268, 282; United States and, 7, 23, 40, 64, 84, 211, 222, 236–240
Libyan Civil War, 285–288
Litton Industries, 152, 238; DD-963 Spruance-class and, 120, 209
Lockheed: C-130 Hercules and, 48, 131; L-100 Hercules and, 254
Lockheed Martin, 279
Lockwood Greene Engineers, 116
Long, Clarence, 186
Long, Russell, 231
Lugar, Richard, 222, 269
Luttwak, Edward, 140–141

MacArthur, Douglas, II, 37, 46
Mahmoud, Mustafa, 160–161, 165–167
Maressa, Joseph, 221
Mars Attacks!, 282
Marwan, Ashraf, 104
Marxism and Islam, 160–161, 165–166
Masud, Muhammad, 104
Mauritania, 24, 29, 246
McClure, James, 108
McDonnell Douglas: F-4E Phantom and, 27, 35, 39, 41, 49, 55–56, 97, 118–120, 206, 209, 219, 256; F-15 Eagle and, 48, 103, 183–192, 214–215, 227–231, 256–258, 268–269, 273
McFarlane, Robert, 259–260, 263–265, 281
McGovern, George, 51
McNamara, Robert, 87–88, 91, 133
Meany, George, 139–140
Meese, Edwin, 269–270
Meir, Golda, 56
Mexico, 13, 113, 240, 246
Mobil, 12–15, 231–232
Mohammed bin Salman (prince of Saudi Arabia), 278–279, 285–286
Mohammed Reza Shah Pahlavi (shah of Iran), 14, 18–20; Cecil Andrus and, 108–109; cancer of, 209; death of, 217; foreign assets of, 210–211, 217, 224, 281; Iranian Revolution and, 181–183, 195–202, 205; Iranian students and, 125; nuclear energy

Mohammed Reza Shah Pahlavi (*continued*)
and, 122; oil and, 35–38, 42–45, 66–67,
78–81, 110, 178, 180; Pakistan and, 47;
Panama and, 212; in popular media,
152–155, 159–160, 166–168, 181–182,
210–211, 230; William Simon and, 74–75;
US arms and, 27, 35–36, 45–49, 118,
174–177, 193, 230
Mondale, Walter, 171–172, 257
Morocco, 22–23, 165, 227, 246
Morsi, Mohamed, 285
Mosaddeq, Mohammad, 18–20, 24, 31–32
Moss, John, 150
Mountain Viewing Farms, 136
Mouse Hunt, 282
Moynihan, Daniel Patrick, 189
Mubarak, Hosni, 237, 275–276, 285
Muhammad al-Badr (imam of North Yemen),
25
Munif, Abdelrahman, 252–253
Muskie, Edmund, 270
Muslim Brotherhood, 161, 285

Najibullah, Muhammad, 261
Nasser, Gamal Abdel, 20–29, 32, 37, 41, 85,
134
National Association of Manufacturers, 123
National Iranian Oil Company, 19
National Jewish Community Relations
Advisory Council, 106, 186
Netherlands, 71, 91
Network, 146–147
New Zealand, 15, 173–174, 191
Nicaragua, 258–260, 265, 269, 288
Nigeria, 51, 91, 246
Nixon, Richard: Arab-Israeli conflict and,
39–42, 57–58, 65, 68, 71–72, 103; Egypt and,
98; Iran and, 35–38, 45–49, 67, 199; oil prices
and, 31–32, 42–44, 51–52, 78; in popular
media, 156–157; Saudi Arabia and, 38–39, 50,
55–56, 71–74; shah's funeral and, 217; US
economy and, 45, 63, 76; Vietnam War and,
34–35; Watergate scandal and, 51, 54, 58, 79
Nkrumah, Kwame, 162
Non-Aligned Movement, 86, 91–92
North, Oliver, 259–260, 265–266, 269–271,
281
North Atlantic Treaty Organization (NATO),
63, 80, 112, 173, 191, 285
North Korea, 254

North Vietnam, 51
North Yemen, 25–26, 29, 32, 126–127,
200–204, 258
North Yemen Civil War, 25–26, 32
Northrop, 100; F-5E Tiger and, 183, 185, 189,
206, 256
Northwestern National Bank in Port Angeles,
137
Norway, 71

Obama, Barack, 284–286
Occidental Petroleum, 100
Oman, 50, 91, 184, 202, 205, 243. *See also*
Dhofar War
O'Neill, Thomas, Jr., 176
Organization of the Petroleum Exporting
Countries (OPEC), 24, 42–45, 51; dollar
and, 193–194; oil revenues of, 67t; oil
shocks and, 56–57, 66–67, 198, 207, 212,
217, 224; in popular media, 140, 143, 146,
166, 221; pricing debates within, 72, 78–81,
110, 178–180, 241, 262, 272–273

Pakistan: aid to, 126, 228, 232; Iran and,
47–48; militant Islamists and, 232, 261;
Soviet Union and, 197, 213; United States
and, 21, 74, 211
Palestine Liberation Organization (PLO): aid
to, 33, 102, 186, 268, 273; Egypt and, 184,
205; Israel and, 259; Lebanese Civil War
and, 128–130, 242–245; remittances and,
127
Palestinians: Iraq and, 233; Israel and, 17–18,
28–29, 33, 55, 126, 192; Kuwait and, 50;
Lebanese Civil War and, 281; migrant labor
and, 127
Panama, 179, 183, 212, 217
Parsky, Gerald, 100–101
Paul, Rand, 280
Peres, Shimon, 263
Persian Gulf War, 281–282
Petrodollar Takeover, The, 148
Philippines, 13, 246
Pipes, Daniel, 223
Planet Oil and Mineral, 36–37
Poindexter, John, 264, 270–271, 281
Poland, 113, 246
Police Woman, 220
Pollitz, Edward, Jr., 146
Pompeo, Mike, 279

Portugal, 63
Pressler, Larry-, 257
Proxmire, William, 154

Qaboos bin Said (sultan of Oman), 48, 118
Qaddafi, Muammar, 42, 82, 152, 219, 222,
    236–238, 266–268, 285
Qaeda, al-, 277, 283
Qatar, 46, 64, 206; aid from, 125, 241, 249;
    imports of, 117f, 248f, 286; oil and, 24, 58,
    67t, 70, 284, 286

R.J.B. Sales, 136
Rabin, Yitzhak, 105–106
Rajai, Mohammad Ali, 219
Randazzo, Michael, 136–137
Raytheon, 152, 279; Hawk and, 28, 264;
    Maverick and, 155, 273; Sidewinder and,
    155, 227–229; Sparrow and, 256; Stinger
    and, 256, 261, 268–269
Reagan, Ronald: Afghanistan and, 260;
    economic policy of, 240; Iran-Contra
    scandal and, 259–260, 264–265, 269–272,
    281; Iran-Iraq War and, 233–234, 257,
    272–274; Lebanese Civil War and, 242–243,
    250; Libya and, 236–240, 266–267; Saudi
    Arabia and, 227–233, 242–243, 268–269,
    273; US elections and, 222–223, 257
Regan, Donald, 239
Reza Shah Pahlavi (shah of Iran), 14, 18
Rockefeller, David, 39–41
Rockefeller, Nelson, 39, 105, 129
Rockwell International, 150
Rogers, William, 40–42, 54
Romania, 246
Rubinstein, Paul, 148
Rumsfeld, Donald, 1–3, 254
Russia, 279, 285
Ryan, Leo, 65

Sabah al-Salem al-Sabah (emir of Kuwait), 115
Sadat, Anwar: death of, 237–238; Egyptian
    economy and, 41, 85, 94–98, 132–134,
    205–206; Israel and, 54–58, 105–107,
    191–192, 204–206; shah and, 217; United
    States and, 41–42, 94–98, 130–131,
    183–184, 187, 205–206
Safire, William, 186, 222
Said, Nuri al-, 21, 23
Salman (king of Saudi Arabia), 278

Sanders, Bernie, 279
Saqqaf, Omar al-, 39, 60–61, 67–68, 71
Saud (king of Saudi Arabia), 23, 25–26
Saud bin Faisal (prince of Saudi Arabia),
    53–54, 201, 203–204
Saudi Arabia, 13–14; Abscam and, 221; aid
    from, 33, 95–97, 101–102, 113, 125–126,
    130–134, 185, 204–206, 241, 249, 258–262,
    275, 281–282, 285; Arab oil embargo and,
    29, 58–72; Arab-Israeli conflict and, 39, 50,
    54–59, 151, 179, 204–206; arms to, 50,
    119–121, 154–155, 183–192, 202–208,
    214–215, 227–232, 255–258, 268–274,
    278–280, 284–286; dollar and, 180, 193; fear
    of revolution in, 38–39, 252; foreign
    investment of, 83, 114, 149, 180, 205–206,
    216, 232–233, 239–240; IMF and, 90–91;
    imports of, 81–82, 116–117, 119–125,
    161–162, 216, 248f, 284; Lebanese Civil War
    and, 129–130; migrant labor in, 26, 122,
    127–128, 258; oil price and, 72, 78–81, 110,
    178–180, 202–203, 217, 224, 247–248,
    272–273; oil production of, 52, 178, 208,
    241, 247, 262; oil revenues of, 67t, 111, 262,
    284; Persian Gulf War and, 281–282; political
    instability of, 197, 201–205, 211–215; in
    popular media, 140, 143–148, 152, 161–165,
    188–190, 206, 208, 274, 279–281; South
    Yemen and, 200–201, 203–204; Soviet
    Union and, 200–201, 214–215; US
    interdependence with, 53–54, 61–62, 69,
    71–78, 80–81, 188–189; US invasion of, 59,
    68, 80, 83–84; US petrodollar partnerships
    with, 5–6, 45–46, 276–277, 280, 288. See also
    Arabian-American Oil Company; North
    Yemen Civil War; Yemen
Saunders, Harold, 49, 97
Schlesinger, James, 185
Schmidt, Helmut, 172–173
Scowcroft, Brent, 1, 79, 103–105, 108–110,
    270
Secord, Richard, 259
Shariati, Ali, 167
Shell, 12, 15
Shultz, George: Arab oil embargo and, 66;
    Bechtel and, 124; IMF and, 89–90;
    Iran-Iraq War and, 249–250, 257, 263–264;
    Lebanese Civil War and, 245; Libya and,
    266–267; petrodollar investments and,
    52–53, 101, 113, 149

Simon, William, 74–81, 85–86, 94, 97–99, 113–114, 123, 131, 165
60 Minutes, 74
Solarz, Stephen, 193
Soleimani, Qasem, 286
Somalia, 184, 187, 246
Somoza, Anastasio, 258
Sonny and Cher Comedy Hour, The, 146
South Africa, 165, 198
South Korea, 8, 113, 126
South Vietnam, 51, 138
South Yemen, 15, 26; aid to, 126; Egypt and, 184; migrant labor from, 127; Oman and, 118; Saudi Arabia and, 38–39, 72–73, 200–204, 258; Soviet Union and, 112, 183–184, 187, 200; terrorism and, 218
Southern Center for International Studies, 231
Soviet Union: aid from, 87, 112; arms control and, 172, 183, 191–192; Cold War and, 2, 14, 21, 34–35; Egypt and, 8, 22, 28, 33, 41–42, 55–59, 113; exports from, 24, 112, 116–119, 255*f*, 263, 277; Iran and, 27, 213, 216; Iran-Iraq War and, 218, 225–226, 233, 235–236, 244, 249–250, 254; Iraq and, 36, 38, 113; Libya and, 113; North Yemen and, 26; Saudi Arabia and, 71–73, 183–186; South Yemen and, 127, 184, 200–201; Syria, 28, 38, 113, 126–127. *See also* Soviet-Afghan War
Soviet-Afghan War, 212–215, 227–229, 232, 260–261, 275–277, 282–283
Sowayel, Ibrahim bin Abdullah al-, 71
Steele, Robert, 65
Sudan, 22, 29, 165, 205, 227, 232, 246, 258, 275–276
Sullivan, William, 197
Sultan (prince of Saudi Arabia), 73*f*, 183, 215, 227
Sweden, 91
Switzerland, 70, 91, 260
Syria, 16; aid to, 102, 126, 268; Arab-Israeli conflict and, 28–29, 54–60, 70–73, 184, 205, 242; arms to, 22, 55, 113, 119*f*, 126, 255*f*; Iran-Iraq War and, 218, 254, 257; migrant labor from, 127; oil and, 252; terrorism and, 218. *See also* Lebanese Civil War; Syrian Civil War
Syrian Civil War, 278, 285–286

Tank McNamara, 146–147
Tanous, Peter, 148

Tanzania, 113
Tariqi, Abdullah al-, 10–11, 24
Texaco (Texas Oil), 13–15
Texas Instruments, 152
Thornton, Tex, 238
Touré, Sékou, 162
Toward the Great Civilization, 166
Tower, John, 270
Truman, Harry, 14–19
Trump, Donald, 278–279, 286–287
Tunisia, 22–23, 227, 245
Turkey, 21, 278
Turki bin Faisal (prince of Saudi Arabia), 152
Turner, Stansfield, 175, 205

Union Carbide, 100
United Arab Emirates (UAE), 47; aid from, 91, 125–126, 241; foreign investment of, 83, 206; imports of, 117*f*, 122, 144, 248*f*; oil and, 24, 51, 67*t*, 110, 178, 284, 286; United States and, 58, 64, 70, 84, 136, 220, 249, 285
United Kingdom: economy of, 15, 37, 52, 110, 112, 129; empire of, 11–16, 19–22, 24, 26, 33–37, 46–50; exports from, 49, 113, 116–117, 119*f*, 172–174, 186; oil and, 12–15, 18–19, 71; Persian Gulf War and, 282
United Nations, 17–18, 92, 244, 274, 285
United Technologies, 231–232
University of Southern California, 139
Up the Academy, 219–220
US Council of the International Chamber of Commerce, 83
US Treasury securities, 76–78, 89, 114, 179, 216, 232–233, 247
Utaybi, Juhayman al-, 211–212, 214

Vance, Cyrus, 172, 177–178, 180, 183–185, 197–200, 217
Venezuela, 24, 91, 113, 246
Vietnam, 112. *See also* North Vietnam; South Vietnam; Vietnam War
Vietnam War, 34–35, 39, 45–46, 51, 83, 119, 123, 138, 142, 152
Vinnell, 120–121
Volcker, Paul, 89, 207, 240, 246–247

Waller, William, 124
Wasteland, The (al-Tih), 252–253
Weinberg, Melvin, 220

Weinberger, Caspar, 124, 227–229, 237–238, 242–243, 263–264, 267, 281
West, John, 115–116, 185–187, 190–192, 200–205, 214–215, 221, 230–231
West Germany: exports from, 112, 116–117, 122, 172–174, 248f; finance and, 52, 76, 247; foreign aid from, 91, 102, 132; oil and, 63, 71
Western Electric, 100
Westinghouse, 152, 230
Williams, Harrison, Jr., 150–151, 220
Wilson, Charlie, 260
Wilson, Harold, 88
Winthrop College, 231

Witteveen, Johannes, 87–90
World Bank, 86–89, 91, 93, 96, 101, 132–133
World Wide Marine, 136
Wriston, Walter, 114–115, 148

Yamani, Zaki, 54, 57, 65–66, 74, 83, 93, 242
Yemen, 278–279, 285–287. See also North Yemen; South Yemen
Yemeni Civil War, 278–279, 285–287
Yeo, Edwin, 150
Yugoslavia, 246, 252

Zahawi, Mazen, 233–234
Zawahiri, Ayman al-, 261